Windows
Vista

Windows
Vista

Jonathan Hassell and Tony Campbell

Apress®

Windows Vista: Beyond the Manual

Copyright © 2007 by Jonathan Hassell and Tony Campbell

ISBN-13 (pbk): 978-159059-771-2

ISBN-10 (pbk): 1-59059-771-0

Printed and bound in the United States of America 9 8 7 6 5 4 3 2 1

Lead Editor: Jim Sumser

Technical Reviewer: Judith Myerson

Editorial Board: Steve Anglin, Ewan Buckingham, Gary Cornell, Jason Gilmore, Jonathan Gennick, Jonathan Hassell, James Huddleston, Chris Mills, Matthew Moodie, Dominic Shakeshaft, Jim Sumser, Keir Thomas, Matt Wade

Project Manager: Sofia Marchant

Copy Edit Manager: Nicole Flores

Copy Editor: Kim Wimpsett

Assistant Production Director: Kari Brooks-Copony

Production Editor: Laura Cheu

Compositor: Susan Glinert

Proofreader: April Eddy

Indexer: Brenda Miller

Artist: April Milne

Cover Designer: Kurt Krames

Manufacturing Director: Tom Debolski

Distributed to the book trade worldwide by Springer-Verlag New York, Inc., 233 Spring Street, 6th Floor, New York, NY 10013. Phone 1-800-SPRINGER, fax 201-348-4505, e-mail orders-ny@springer-sbm.com, or visit http://www.springeronline.com.

For information on translations, please contact Apress directly at 2560 Ninth Street, Suite 219, Berkeley, CA 94710. Phone 510-549-5930, fax 510-549-5939, e-mail info@apress.com, or visit http://www.apress.com.

The source code for this book is available to readers at http://www.apress.com in the Source Code/ Download section. You will need to answer questions pertaining to this book in order to successfully download the code.

For Lara.
—Tony

For Lisa.
—Jon

Contents at a Glance

Contents

CHAPTER 5

Customizing Windows Vista 69

CHAPTER 6

Working with User Tools 89

CHAPTER 7

Administering Windows Vista 113

CHAPTER 19

Collaborating with Windows Meeting Space

CHAPTER 20

Using Windows Fax and Scan

CHAPTER 21

Working with Windows Media Player 11

CHAPTER 22

Working with Windows Movie Maker 299

About the Authors

JONATHAN HASSELL is an author, consultant, and speaker on a variety of IT topics. His published works include *RADIUS* (O'Reilly, 2002), *Hardening Windows, Second Edition* (Apress, 2005), *Using Microsoft Windows Small Business Server 2003* (Apress, 2006), and *Learning Windows Server 2003* (O'Reilly, 2006). His work appears regularly in such periodicals as *Windows IT Pro* magazine, *PC Pro*, and *TechNet Magazine*. He also speaks worldwide on topics ranging from networking and security to Windows administration. He is currently an editor at Apress.

TONY CAMPBELL is an experienced Microsoft consultant specializing in the architecture and design of secure, Microsoft-centric business solutions. He also has vast experience in many other industry niches such as networking, collaboration, security, business logic, and disaster recovery and resilience. Tony has been involved with all sizes of businesses, from the very small to the very large, and has successfully delivered secure, reliable, robust solutions to more than 150,000 clients in his 18 years in the business. Tony started his career back in the 80s as a "green-screen" mainframe programmer for the British Meteorological Office, finally arriving after a long journey in his current role as a self-employed IT consultant and author.

Tony is a regular contributor to a variety of journals distributed across the globe and has been involved in the production of software manuals, user guides, white papers, hardware manuals, and training courses for many of his clients in the past decade. His love of writing has led to the publication of his fiction in a variety of small presses and magazines.

About the Technical Reviewer

JUDITH M. MYERSON is a systems architect and engineer. Her areas of interest include middleware technologies, application development, web development, software engineering, network management, servers, security management, information assurance, standards, RFID technologies, and project management. Judith holds a Master of Science degree in engineering, and is a member of the IEEE organization. She has reviewed/edited a number of books, including *Hardening Linux*, *Creating Client Extranets with SharePoint 2003*, and *Microsoft SharePoint: Building Office 2003 Solutions*.

CHAPTER 1

Introducing
Windows Vista

Microsoft Windows Vista is by far the most exciting operating system to hit the market since Windows 95 replaced Windows 3.11 back in the summer of 1995.

Vista is the long-awaited and much-anticipated operating system replacement for Windows XP; with more than five years in the making, it demonstrates well that Microsoft has indeed listened to its customers during coding, because the result is a revolutionary new way of converging work and play on the PC of the 21st century.

Microsoft has focused a massive development effort on improving our confidence in this operating system, and its integrated suite of applications, with a much improved Windows interface known as Aero and a new focus on connectivity and security (integrated firewall and antispyware applications are just two of the more obvious security enhancements), results in a radical shift away from the Windows XP modus operandi.

Fundamentally, tasks that used to be complicated, confusing, or just plain difficult to achieve with previous versions of Windows are now much simpler and cleaner, and in many cases, your system's configuration will be optimized for you by default. This shift to offer IT as a simple end-user service is an important development in Microsoft's approach, and it offers better out-of-the-box experiences akin with the next-generation Web 2.0 service-oriented approach being adopted by Microsoft's main competitors.

Whether you are an IT professional or a home user, you'll find that the new, simpler, plain-English interfaces for configuring Vista allow you to get much more done in far less time, and the configuration wizards are so far abstracted from the underlying registry and policy settings needed to make things happen that you'll never be more than a few clicks away from making your PC do exactly what you want it to do.

Through the five available variations on the core operating system, Vista offers a solution fit for practically any audience: from the needs of the basic home user who needs secure and seamless access to the Internet for web and email to the most exploitative power user who has equally high demands for both professional and leisure activities. The rest of this chapter takes you on a whistle-stop tour of the editions of Vista, covering the fundamental differences between each and who the target audience of each is. Then we'll go on to appraise the new and improved features of Vista over

Windows XP and look at some of the features that make Vista such an appealing investment for home and business users.

Vista Editions

Stock keeping units, or SKUs (phonetically: *skews*) as they are commonly known, are unique product codes assigned to retail products as a way to track the inventory of commercial companies.

For Microsoft, the use of SKUs is no different; however, in the context of Vista, SKUs are being used outside the bean counters' offices to identify the five versions of the product, of which there is a discrete code assigned to each.

The five versions of Vista are as follows:

- Windows Vista Home Basic
- Windows Vista Home Premium
- Windows Vista Business
- Windows Vista Enterprise
- Windows Vista Ultimate

The five Vista SKUs comprise a common code base across all versions of the product. The uniqueness attributed to each version is attained from the last remaining components (only about 5 or 6 percent of the total build) that make each SKU different. For example, Home Basic does not ship with the Media Center component installed, while Home Premium and Ultimate both have it installed.

The differentiation between SKU product codes is largely irrelevant to you as a user; the simple fact that you'll see five different editions of the operating system *is* what's important. What's paramount for you is what each edition does, why each is different, and, most important, which one is appropriate in your case.

In addition, in Vista, deploying applications and functionality such as language packs takes place through a much more componentized approach than previous versions, allowing IT professionals to create Vista deployments that best match their users' needs. This approach mirrors what Microsoft has been doing with Windows CE for years, where modular builds allow you to install the components you need and pay for only the functionality you require.

It might seem, at first glance, like offering five editions of the operating system is somewhat overkill. Why would you possibly need five different versions of what basically is the same code base? However, there is justification, unlike with Windows XP, which offered at least six versions (Home Edition, Professional Edition, Media Center Edition, Tablet PC Edition, Professional x64 Edition, and Starter Edition), with each version being targeted at a different market audience. With Vista, for technology consumers, there are the two Home editions: Home Basic and Home Premium. Home

Basic is the entry-level version (the cheaper of the two), while Home Premium is more feature rich and targeted at power users who require more from their system than simply word processing and Internet connectivity.

| **NOTE** All versions of Vista are available for both 32-bit and 64-bit PC platforms.

Small-business and enterprise customers also have two choices, the Business and Enterprise editions, where Business applies to practically all small- and medium-sized business needs, and Enterprise is really necessary only when the size and complexity of the organization becomes global. Then there is the Vista Ultimate edition. This edition of Vista contains all the functionality available across all four previously discussed versions of the operating system, including features such as the enterprise security capability called BitLocker Drive Encryption (covered in Chapter 11). In this way, home and small-business users can benefit from the increased tool set and capabilities in Vista Ultimate and be as flexible as required in how they use their PC technology.

NOTE A sixth Vista SKU is available that doesn't form part of the core five detailed previously. This is known as the Vista Starter edition. There is good reason to differentiate between this SKU and the other five since this edition is aimed at developing countries and other emerging markets. This SKU won't be available to the general public; its distribution is targeted at where the need is greatest. Emerging markets will benefit immensely from this SKU through low-cost licensing (with only a 32-bit option available for low-cost PCs), allowing these markets to receive the educational benefits of getting connected without having to break the bank.

Home Basic

As the name might suggest, Home Basic is the entry-level version of Vista (still containing 95 percent of the code base); it's aimed at the home user who wants the benefits of the enhanced Vista solution (security, search, better interface, and so on) but does not require some of the Home Premium upgrades, such as Media Center and DVD Maker.

Home Premium

Home Premium builds on the Home Basic version with a number of enhancements, such as the introduction of the Windows Aero user interface; compatibility with Tablet PCs; enhanced mobility features, such as multiple PC synchronization; and a variety of new digital media applications, such as Media Center and DVD Maker. Home Premium is really aimed at power users who use their PCs as lifestyle commodities as well as productivity devices; it should be considered by anyone who wants to process and consume a lot of digital media content through this interface.

Business

Vista Business is the entry-level business SKU and is more powerful than the entry-level home solution, Home Basic, since it has to meet the rigorous demands of business operations. Vista Business can join a Windows domain to attain central control using Group Policy, and it also benefits from enhanced security not available to home users in the shape of a much improved Encrypting File System (EFS). Vista Business is perfect for all business customers who require the improved security, productivity, and collaborative capabilities delivered by Vista.

Enterprise

Vista Enterprise builds on the Vista Business edition with a number of compatibility enhancements, such as Subsystem for UNIX Applications (SUA) for running a complete UNIX environment that allows UNIX applications to interoperate with Vista (this was originally a Windows 2003 server add-on that has now been ported to Vista). Vista Enterprise also appeals to customers with high security requirements where capabilities such as full disk encryption are essential. The integration of Virtual PC Express also permits you to run multiple operating system environments on a single PC, which is extremely useful for developers and IT professionals who exploit the services of a powerful laptop when on the road.

Ultimate

Vista Ultimate is the all-singing, all-dancing Big Kahuna of the Vista operating system, containing all the features of all four previously discussed SKUs. In this way, businesses and home users have the choice of installing a single PC operating system that works best for the advanced home user and also integrates well into the business space. Specifically, business customers who have a high demand for consuming digital content (for example, media-oriented companies such as newspapers or television stations) can immediately see the benefit of having DVD authoring and Media Center on the desktop, even though this desktop is integrated into a policy-controlled infra-structure that maintains enterprise management and security control over its workstations.

Upgrading Vista Versions

The biggest benefit for the consumer of Microsoft's modular approach to the delivery of Vista is that you can upgrade at any time to a higher, more functionally rich version, using Windows Anytime Upgrade. The software supplied on the source disk that was installed on your system when it came will contain the SKUs for all the versions of Vista. If you are running Home Basic, for example, and decide you'd rather have the multimedia capabilities of Home Premium, the software you need is right there on your disk. All you need to do is purchase the upgrade license online and install the top-up modules that turn Home Basic into Home Premium.

Table 1-1 shows all the available upgrade paths.

Table 1-1 Upgrade Paths Available for Vista SKUs

Current Version	Available Upgrades
Home Basic	Home Premium, Ultimate
Home Premium	Ultimate
Business	Enterprise, Ultimate
Enterprise	Ultimate
Ultimate	

> **TIP** To quickly find out which of the SKUs you currently have installed on your PC, open the Welcome Center (Start ➤ Control Panel ➤ System and Maintenance ➤ Welcome Center), and check the top of the screen.

You can start an upgrade whenever you like from the Start menu by clicking Windows Anytime Upgrade and following the on-screen instructions.

> **NOTE** You can find the application for running Windows Anytime Upgrade in the Vista `%SystemRoot%\System32` folder. The file is `WindowsAnytimeUpgrade.exe`.

New and Improved in Vista

Vista undoubtedly offers a wide variety of new and improved features over its predecessor, Windows XP. However, it would be impossible to cover every feature delivered with Vista in this chapter (that would take a complete book in itself), so instead, the rest of this chapter explains what constitutes the Vista headlines—those features and components of this new operating system that make it stand out from previous versions.

When you've digested this list of new and improved features, you'll see for yourself why Vista is such a paradigm shift for Microsoft.

The Interface

The first feature you'll notice that's different in Vista (although not markedly so) is the Start menu, as shown in Figure 1-1. It has not had a complete overhaul; instead, it's more akin to a makeover, adding only one key change to the Windows XP Start menu—integrated search. Your recently accessed applications still appear on the left side of the menu, immediately beneath the Internet and E-mail items, and launch Internet Explorer and Windows Mail (the new version of Outlook Express), respectively. Also note that the word *Start* is no longer emblazoned on the Start button; instead, the button is simply a shaded circle with a Windows logo emblazoned upon it. You'll immediately see the interface changes the moment you log in.

Figure 1-1 *The Vista interface is a graphically rich and easy-to-use improvement on XP.*

The look and feel of the desktop has also changed, with the Aero interface available in all but the Vista Home Basic edition (video card permitting). Aero delivers an increased level of graphical interaction with the Windows desktop (a level that, quite frankly, should have been available in Windows XP) whereby Vista makes better use of modern graphics cards to leverage the same technology game designers are using. In this way, the Aero Glass effect allows better screen drawing and window rendering and provides much improved direct draw capabilities to Windows applications. The Glass effect provides an element of translucency to Window borders that, for no other reason than it looks good, is a must.

On the right side of the desktop is a new active area (akin to the old Active Desktop technology) called the Sidebar. Here, you can implant small applications known as *gadgets*, which run directly on the desktop. Gadgets can uplink to live, dynamic web content, such as RSS feeds, or can provide simple desktop extensions, such as a clock or a picture slide show.

Further improvements in the interface are apparent when you start using Windows Explorer (right-click the Start menu, and select Explore). You'll see the icons displayed in a folder are somewhat bigger and more meaningful than their predecessors, and many appear as thumbnails of the content inside the file rather than simply as fixed images.

NOTE It was always the case that photographs were displayed as thumbnails in Folder view, but thumbnails are now available in many other file formats, showing some of the content from the file itself.

Taskbar thumbnails are also a great help to you when you are looking for a particular application that has been minimized to the taskbar. If you hover your mouse pointer over an application minimized on the taskbar, a thumbnail of the application's interface pops up on the desktop and shows you what's happening.

Another great (although gimmicky) feature of the Aero interface is the new application tabbing capability known as Flip and its graphically enhanced older brother, Flip 3D. To cycle through applications you are currently running, you can still press Alt+Tab. This is known as Flip, which displays thumbnails of the application in the same format as they appear as taskbar thumbnails. Flip 3D, on the other hand, displays a radically different 3D stacking effect, as shown in Figure 1-2. We discuss activating and using Flip 3D in Chapter 3.

Windows Explorer has also had a makeover. The interface contains as many as ten discrete areas you can control, including menu bars, the preview pane, a links area, a folders list, file metadata, and the pervasive search box, common throughout all the Vista applications.

Commonly accessed configuration utilities, such as the Control Panel, have also changed, with these changes reflecting the abundance of new and improved functionality you have to control through Windows Vista's interface. For this reason, the Vista Control Panel expands on the old Windows XP category view to offer 10 categories that can allow access to 42 different configuration applets.

Figure 1-2 *Flip 3D is a radical new approach to tabbing through applications.*

Instant Search

Search is one of the most important improvements in the Vista interface; it's much more pervasive and powerful than in Windows XP. The Windows Search service is started as a local system service when Vista starts (allowing it to search and index everything on the computer), automatically creating indexes of all sorts of content stored on your hard drive.

Search is embedded into practically every Vista application (take a look at Media Player or Photo Gallery to see what we mean) and has been designed to be immediately accessible from every screen without you needing to hunt through countless menus to locate it.

> **NOTE** Search is context based, meaning that the search you perform will return content based on the application from which you searched. In this way, if you search from the Start menu, you will receive hits based on items available through the Start menu; however, if you search on the same term in Photo Gallery, hits will be based on the metadata associated with items in your gallery.

Another big improvement with Search is that it starts working as soon as you start typing. In this way, you can immediately see (through hits on partially defined search criteria) whether you are on the right track. You can also perform more advanced searches using plain-English operands on a wide variety metadata types, which results in a powerful and extremely versatile approach to locating content on your system.

Pervasive Metadata

A piece of metadata (known in Vista as a *tag*) is some additional snippet of information about a file that describes something about that file. Examples of metadata are a document's date of creation and the name of the camera used to take a digital photograph.

The Windows Search service indexes content on your PC based on these tags and allows the results to be displayed in a variety of ways. Windows Explorer also uses these tags to group items into related stacks whereby, for example, you can group albums from a particular artist, irrespective of where those files actually reside on your physical disk configuration. In this way, folder views can contain content from a number of physical sources, based on the metadata used to describe the files.

Communications

The communications stack in Vista (known as the *next-generation* TCP/IP stack) has been reengineered from the ground up to cater to advancements in both wired and wireless networking technologies and to improve network performance while cutting down on data transfer times. Vista also provides support for both TCP/IPv4 and the next-generation 128-bit addressing model, TCP/IPv6.

From a user's perspective, faster network access, a more reliable network service, and proactive network monitoring provide an all-round better networked experience, and for nontechnical users, setting up the network has never been easier using the Network and Sharing Center and the Network Map.

User-facing applications, such as Internet Explorer 7 and Windows Mail (formerly Outlook Express), have had a dutiful overhaul from the Windows XP versions, and new collaborative features such as Windows Calendar (see Figure 1-3) allow you to share free/busy information with whomever you choose.

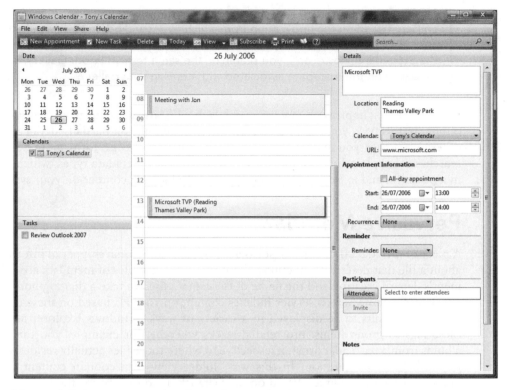

Figure 1-3 *Stay organized with Windows Calendar.*

Digital Media and Gaming

The ability to manipulate and consume digital content has greatly improved in Vista with a new version of Media Center (available in the Home Premium and Ultimate editions), a new application called Photo Gallery, and the ability to author your own DVDs using DVD Maker.

Since its introduction to the general public at the Consumer Electronics Show (CES) in January 2002, Media Center (known then as FreeStyle) has gone from strength to strength. With the advent of Windows XP Media Center Edition 2005, the product became more stable, became functionally rich, and really popped up on the radar of mainstream hardware manufacturers. So much was the success of Media Center that it comes now as an integral part of two of the Vista SKUs and will undoubtedly change the way we look at the role of PCs in the home. The Vista version of Media Center sports a much improved interface that really best uses the size of a large television (see Figure 1-4) and contains support for high-definition (HD) TV and a variety of online resources that start to blur the edges between local content and content sources from the Internet.

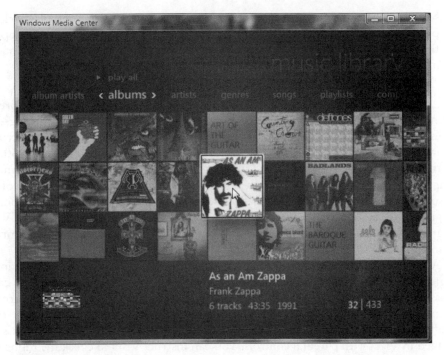

Figure 1-4 *Media Center's new interface is a vast improvement on previous versions.*

Vista Media Center also integrates well with the Xbox 360, utilizing this consumer gaming machine as a Media Center extender whereby content can be streamed over a network from the Media Center PC to the Xbox where it can be output. Vista's Sleep mode also allows you to start your system (and Media Center) in only a few seconds, aligning your Media Center experience better with that of consumer DVD players.

The Windows DVD Maker is a new application included in Windows Vista Home Premium that allows you to author your own multifaceted DVDs, complete with menu controls, chapters, and so on. DVD Maker can create DVDs of movies you produce using Windows Movie Maker or can create a rolling slide show from your Photo Gallery with overlaid music tracks to create the perfect slide show.

Windows Media Player 11 is the latest version of Media Player and, although developed to be compatible with previous versions of Windows, can release its full potential only when running on Vista, because of its reliance on facilities such as Windows Search.

Another much improved application is the latest Vista version of Movie Maker, with many enhanced transitions and fades as well as support for burning DVDs and creating HD-encoded content.

Photo Gallery is yet another new application in all the Vista SKUs that helps organize your collection of digital photographs, wherever they are stored on your network. Metadata search capabilities built into Photo Gallery allow you to stack and group images, edit photographs in the gallery, and create extremely customizable slide shows based on tags.

> **NOTE** A great enhancement (although just a minor touch) to sound playback is per-application volume. This allows you to adjust the volume for individual applications on your system instead of with previous Windows systems where you had much less granularity over this control.

And finally, we'll say a few words about gaming. DirectX 10 is the latest DirectX graphics platform and has been completely redesigned to deliver the most cutting-edge graphics available anywhere on the planet. It might seem a little odd that Microsoft enhanced the PC beyond even the capabilities of its gaming console, the Xbox 360, but the thing is, PCs (with the latest and greatest video cards) are as capable of running complex, graphically rich games as their counterparts in the dedicated world of the console. In fact, with the ability of these new video interfaces to render great-looking 3D graphics at a much higher resolution than what's available on a plain old TV set, we are looking at an imminent revolution—and more than likely an upset—for the console manufacturers in the near future.

Also, concerned parents will be happy to note that Microsoft has paid a lot of attention to the pleas from adults who share their PCs with kids, where the kids could access content that adults want to keep from them. Parental controls have been around in Internet Explorer for a few years, but nothing was in place to stop kids from installing games with adult content and playing them on the PC. However, this has changed in Vista with parental controls. You can instruct Vista to check the rating of a game against your local certification authority (the Entertainment Software Rating board in North America) and allow only specific categories, such as Early Childhood or Teen to play, thereby barring games with Intense Violence or Blood and Gore ratings.

It is also possible to turn off game play altogether. In this way, you can control gaming time, allowing access to installed games only when homework has been finished.

Mobility

To make Vista a compelling upgrade for Windows XP users, Microsoft has addressed the problems previously endemic with mobility computing, such as the problems keeping files in sync between PCs and mobile devices, problems seamlessly synchronizing files with network servers for offline working, and problems third-party application developers have when creating applications capable of synchronizing across devices.

Sync Center (a new Control Panel applet) is designed to address these synchronization problems, offering a single-user interface for all mobile device synchronization needs.

Windows SideShow is a new technology that allows hardware manufacturers to install an auxiliary display on your computer system (on the screen, keyboard, Bluetooth connected to your cell phone, and so on) and pump content from Vista to this screen. This is possible even when Vista is switched off or sleeping. You can opt to have SideShow display content from Windows Mail whereby any new emails that come into your system are shown without you having to periodically open your laptop and run the application.

One of the biggest problems facing Windows XP Media Center Edition 2005 was that it didn't have a decent hot-start capability. Media Center is an excellent piece of technology and can really improve your ability to consume and manage digital content; however, penetration into the living room of a Media Center device is possible only when you can access this media content as easily as you can when you use a discrete device such as a DVD player. On a DVD player, you press the On button, insert the movie, and away you go. Simple! Windows XP required a lot more messing around to get to the point where you were ready to watch your content, and people who didn't appreciate the complexity of what was going on under the hood saw this delay only as a failing. Addressing this, Windows HotStart is a new technology that provides a fast system start-up, resuming Vista directly into Media Center or other such applications virtually instantly.

Vista's much improved support for Table PCs, including revisions to touch-screen technology, digital inking, and handwriting recognition, aggregates into a much better, integrated capability that not only works with today's mobility technologies but also remains cognizant of future industry developments.

Finally (although not specifically related to mobility, but you'll see why it's included here), Vista comes with a built-in viewer for Microsoft's new file format, known as the XML Paper Specification (XPS). XPS is Microsoft's answer to the universally accepted Portable Document Format (PDF) and will undoubtedly cause a stirring in the pit of Adobe executives' stomachs. In the same way that PDF files are easily transportable across platforms, XPS is based on an Extensible Markup Language (XML) schema that defines the way documents must be displayed, allowing the components of the document to be rendered on the end-user device, so documents originating in one place will look the same in another. For example, an XPS document viewed in the Vista XPS viewer will look the same, containing the same components in the same places, as when viewed on a Windows Mobile–enabled cell phone (and there it is: the mobility link).

Security

Across the entire Microsoft spectrum of server and workstation products, IT security has never been so critical to the future of businesses—and Microsoft knows it! This is exactly why initiatives such as Trustworthy Computing (http://www.microsoft.com/mscorp/twc) are championing wholly new approaches to code developing and security testing, with security no longer an afterthought to development—instead it's sitting right at the top of the requirements list.

Vista is the first operating system release from Microsoft to benefit from this security-centered pitch shift, meaning, right there under the hood, Vista is doing everything possible to keep out the bad guys, protect your privacy, and make sure you stay up and running even when the most formidable of new viruses are circulating the globe.

One of the most obvious, in-your-face security enhancements in Vista is User Account Control (UAC). At first glance, you'll probably want to switch it off because you are constantly bombarded with pop-up windows, halting your progress until you authorize Vista to proceed. Even the simplest of processes, such as adding new users, pops up the UAC dialog box, saying "Windows needs your permission to continue." The thing is, this is probably the single most effective way of stopping covert processes from performing tasks in the background that you don't know are running. Having you, the user, authorize actions such as account changes means you will always see when something is being modified. If the dialog box suddenly pops up asking you to confirm you want to add a new user but you never started that task yourself, you can be sure that some piece of malware on your system started to do it for its own subversive needs.

Another new feature included in Vista is Windows Defender (previously known as Windows AntiSpyware). This is an extremely effective anti-malware product, residing in memory and scanning for unusual system behavior that might be a result of spyware, adware, or other kinds of privacy-infringing services. In the same way an antivirus product scans your file system on a regular interval, Windows Defender runs full or partial system scans, either looking deep into the registry and file system or performing a more simple scan of your installed services that might reveal potentially malicious code. Windows Defender connects to Microsoft on a regular schedule to check for malware definition updates or engine upgrades, so it keeps up-to-date with the latest exploits.

> **NOTE** You should think of Windows Defender as a complementary product to your overall PC defense system. You'll still need to have an antivirus product installed, such as McAfee's VirusScan (http://www.mcafee.com) or Trend Micro's Internet Security 2007 (http://www.trendmicro.com).

Windows Firewall has also been revamped for Vista, no longer being constrained to monitoring only inbound connections (probably the biggest drawback of previous versions and the main reason why Windows XP users installed products such as ZoneAlarm); it is now as capable as many of its rivals in protecting against unauthorized outbound connections from your system that might come from worms, Trojans, or other such malware.

Internet Explorer has a whole bunch of new security features and improvements. Switching on Internet Explorer Protected Mode when surfing the Web prohibits web pages from writing to anywhere on your system but the Temporary Internet Files folder. In this way, malicious executable code cannot be dumped into the Windows Startup folder to run the next time you reboot (a typical exploit instigated from adware- or malware-containing sites). ActiveX Opt In allows you to completely control the use of ActiveX code on your system, offering you a toolbar that allows you to authorize its use when you need it rather than having it enabled all the time. The Phishing Filter will check against an online database of registered web sites where phishing attacks have come from in the past and will warn you that the site is dangerous.

Windows Mail (the replacement for Outlook Express) incorporates a new Junk Mail Filter akin to the one installed in Office Outlook. This provides you with complete control over what does and does not make it into your inbox, with safe sender and blocked sender filters and an email phishing filter that protects your inbox from emails trying to lure you to a site.

Windows Service Hardening is a new paradigm determining how service accounts are utilized by the system. Accounts attributed to services are derived on a least-privilege basis rather than, as with Windows XP, service accounts running in an administrative context that can be more dangerous if compromised. In this way, a hacker could still compromise a service, but the hacker would no longer be able to take administrative control of your system as a result of this.

Vista also incorporates one of the most-asked-for requirements that security-oriented customers wanted: full disk encryption. Unlike the EFS, BitLocker Drive Encryption encrypts and protects your entire system partition, including the operating system files that you could not protect with EFS. BitLocker can use a Trusted Platform Module (TPM) to increase security further since this TPM is a physically separate hardware module for recording security keys that might be easier compromised in the operating system.

Network Access Protection (NAP) is another new service used to keep an eye on the patch state and security settings of Vista, warning you when you are falling behind with your patching or when your antivirus signatures are out-of-date.

Enhancements to the file system in the form of the new Transactional NTFS (TxF) allow Vista to roll back files where problems have been encountered during a file system operation.

Finally, as mentioned, parental controls have been enhanced to allow concerned parents to place restrictions on kids' accounts, block access to inappropriate web sites, stop the installation and playing of inappropriate games, and much, much more.

Deployment

Vista is far ahead of its predecessors, with some new modularization and imaging technologies built right in that allow administrators to better deploy and patch PCs under their control. The old problem with multilingual infrastructures where a separate build was required for each language you shipped (and each patch had to be engineered individually for each version) is no longer an issue; Vista's modular approach means you can add the language pack onto the core build, installing whatever bits are necessary for your audience.

For home and small-business users, upgrading to Vista—or specifically, transferring users to a newly built Vista workstation—is easy using Windows Easy Transfer. This technology replaces the Windows XP Files and Settings Transfer Wizard and is compatible with transferring in files and settings from Windows XP or Windows 2000 workstations. It has been improved significantly from previous versions of this facility; it now supports a broader range of media devices (USB drives, DVD, and so on), and it can export your entire system (including all user account and associated files and settings) and re-create it exactly on the target device.

The Windows Preinstallation Environment (PE) is a new feature of Vista that helps you with installation, troubleshooting, and system recovery. Windows PE is a bootable shell of the operating system that collects information about the installation you are intending to do; it can also analyze your Vista installation and report and fix problems with the operating system files already installed. Windows PE is a direct replacement for the MS-DOS environment that was always used in previous versions of Windows and, unlike these previous versions, can access NTFS partitions as well as FAT partitions. Windows PE comes with a collection of useful system administration tools for managing partitions, administering devices, and tweaking network connectivity, as well as the old favorite net command with all its powerful abilities to manage users, groups, permissions, services, and shares.

Deploying the base operating system and additional modules (language packs and version top-ups) is much easier and cleaner than in previous versions of Windows. This is because of a new component of the Vista deployment suite known as Windows Imaging (WIM). WIM allows you to modify operating system images offline (you can even modify the content in a folder format if required), individualizing them to suit your target audience and adding patches and applications where required. When you've finished testing your new image, you can ship either the entire image or simply what has changed.

XML answer files are a significant improvement in deployment technology over the previously obscure answer files that were such a fundamental part of Windows XP unattended installations. With this format of answer file, only a single file is necessary (rather than the multiple files required with Windows XP), and you can easily create an answer file from scratch using the Windows System Image Manager (SIM) tool.

Performance and Stability

There is no denying that Vista is faster at starting than Windows XP. This, put simply, is because Vista is better engineered. You still have to wait for applications to become available, but these applications' initialization routines do not effect Vista since it partitions its own start-up routines asynchronously from that of other applications and scripts, having them execute in their own time as system background tasks. So, they do not have any impact on the start-up and login process. Coupled with the new Sleep state shutdown option (taking the best parts of Standby and Hibernate), Vista can easily start from a seemingly off state (disk has stopped spinning, and so on) to fully operational in less than five seconds. Quite impressive really!

The entire Windows Update experience has been significantly improved using Restart Manager, which is a lot more intelligent than previous operating system–patching technologies. The Restart Manager significantly cuts down on the number of reboots required when you install a patch and makes patch integration seamless and immediate (great news from a security standpoint).

One of the best performance enhancements in Vista is the Superfetch service (resident and operating by default as a Windows service) that preempts users' working practices by learning how a user works and then keeping one step ahead in preloading files before they are requested.

Improved input/ouput (I/O) cancellation support allows developers to better capture and deal with an application service error; where previously I/O issues might have frozen the operating system, I/O cancellation cannot eliminate the need for a reboot to release the blockage.

Vista also includes a whole arsenal of tools for administrators and users for diagnosing disk, memory, and application problems, as well as the reliability monitoring services that send application problems to Microsoft to be analyzed and fixed in collaboration with the application developer. Figure 1-5 shows the new Reliability and Performance monitoring interface, with a much cleaner view of exactly what's going on under the hood.

Lastly (but by no means least), the Startup Repair Tool (SRT) can automatically fix many common Windows start-up problems without rebooting; however, if it cannot remedy the problem automatically, it starts Windows and runs the SRT in an enhanced mode, allowing comprehensive diagnostic utilities to scan the Windows event logs for the source of the problems before offering a fix.

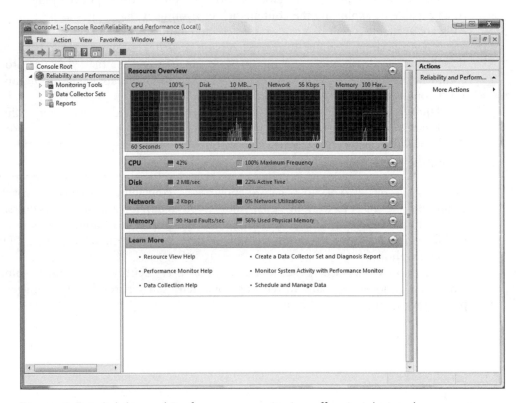

Figure 1-5 *Reliability and Performance monitoring offers insight into how a system is running.*

For Developers

Vista comes with an all-new development set of application programming interfaces (APIs) known collectively as the Windows .NET Framework version 3.0 (code-named WinFX in Vista beta versions).

A number of essential components form the basis of the Windows .NET 3.0 Framework, namely:

- Windows Presentation Foundation (WPF)
- Extensible Application Markup Language (XAML)
- Windows Communications Foundation (WCF)
- Windows Workflow Foundation (WF)
- Mobile PC
- Windows CardSpace

The WPF APIs provide developers with the foundation for developing applications capable of exploiting the content-rich environment that comes as part of Vista. APIs are available for all of Vista's interfaces and applications.

XAML is simply a more abstracted version of WPF, allowing simple .NET functionality to be developed using this markup language rather than delving into the complicated depths of .NET. You can use XAML to create application plug-ins for Vista components, such as for Media Center.

The WCF is the .NET Framework component that provides networking APIs for developers. Its paradigm is more centered on web services than previous versions of .NET, and it provides great functionality for developers grasping Web 2.0 development principles.

The Windows Workflow Foundation has been developed to provide developers with the tools for creating workflow-enabled applications, containing an in-process workflow engine and the ability to work in Visual Studio 2005 to develop graphical workflows.

Mobile PC APIs are included to allow the development of applications that are mobile enabled to run on Windows Mobile devices, personal digital assistants (PDAs), and smart phones.

Windows CardSpace is the next-generation user identity management solution whereby developers are able to develop consistent and secure identity management paradigms within their applications.

CHAPTER 2

Meeting the Hardware Requirements

There is no denying that Vista will not be installable on every PC platform that once supported a Windows operating system. Most of us are used to upgrading our PCs in one way or another, adding a chunk of memory here or a mass of disk space there to make sure new games or business applications work as required. Vista is no different. Many PCs will, quite simply, not be up to the task. Nevertheless, a lot of computer systems will be upgradeable; some of them might just need a new processor, graphics card, and motherboard BIOS upgrade. However, some older machines (systems that might have also suffered under the weight of Windows ME, for example) might be coming to the end of their natural lives, and in these cases, you'll need to buy a new system if you want Vista.

Simple guidelines, such as the minimum memory requirement of 512MB, offer a good place from which to start. If you have less than this, you will need to upgrade. If your motherboard does not support this much memory, it's time for a new machine. Similarly, your processor should be at least an 800MHz Pentium or equivalent (not too much to ask by today's standards); however, to really get good performance from Vista, especially if you are planning on doing anything with large applications or games, you'll be looking at Intel's Pentium 4 or Celeron chipsets running at speeds in excess of 3GHz.

Thankfully, Microsoft has addressed the issue of PC assessment quite well for Vista by introducing the Vista Upgrade Advisor. This tool will analyze your PC against minimum Vista requirements and offer some advice about how you should proceed. This chapter covers the advisor as well as other hardware requirements for running Windows Vista.

Using the Windows Vista Upgrade Advisor

The Windows Vista Upgrade Advisor is an extremely useful guide, illustrating how your system will fare when you try to upgrade to Vista. It quizzes you on the features you require from Vista, assesses the most appropriate edition to meet your needs, and then provides a report that offers guidelines on upgrading your system if required.

Download and install the Windows Vista Upgrade Advisor from Microsoft's web site at `http://www.microsoft.com/windowsvista/getready/upgradeadvisor`.

After you've installed the Windows Vista Upgrade Advisor, click Start System Scan to begin the assessment process.

You are then asked to select the features you expect to use in Vista, such as Elegant User Experience with Windows Aero and Watch and Record TV. These questions allow the Windows Upgrade Advisor to assess which edition of Vista will be most appropriate to your needs. As you answer the questions, you'll see, at the bottom of the screen, that the edition of Vista changes to suggest which is right for you. In the example shown in Figure 2-1, the selections of Elegant User Experience with Windows Aero, Watch and Record TV, and Connect to Corporate or Campus Networks create a need for Vista Ultimate.

Figure 2-1 *The Windows Vista Upgrade Advisor suggests the most appropriate edition of Vista.*

When you've selected the features you want Vista to provide, click the Next button at the bottom of the screen. This will take you to the hardware assessment screen, as shown in Figure 2-2.

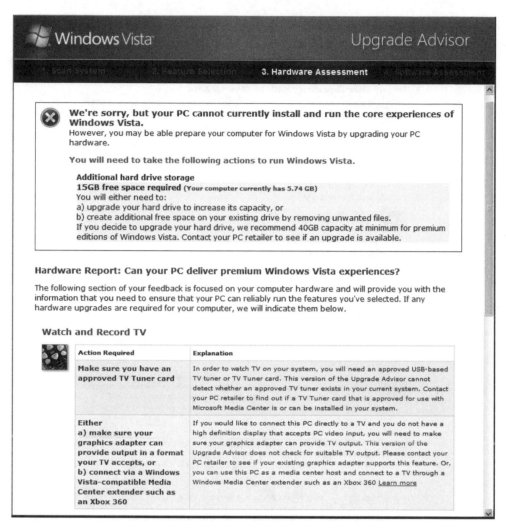

Figure 2-2 *In this case, the assessment has shown this PC's hard drive to be lacking in space.*

The report will first offer an assessment of any critical deficiencies your system is showing, such as not enough memory or hard drive capacity. In the example shown in Figure 2-2, you can see that the hard drive in this system has only 5.74GB of space left, while the Vista Ultimate edition minimum requirement is that at least 15GB is free.

The report then assesses each of the features you selected previously, determining whether your current system hardware can meet the requirements.

Notice that the feature Watch and Record TV has been flagged in red as a problem. This is because no TV tuner card is installed in this system.

The report also offers assistance about how to rectify any problems (it's straightforward in this case to install a TV tuner), as well as gives you information about looking into other possible usage scenarios, such as how you might stream TV from this PC over a network to a Media Center extender, such as an Xbox 360.

> **NOTE** You should print the hardware and software assessments to help you when you go shopping for new system components.

When you've finished with the hardware assessment, click Next at the bottom of the screen. The Windows Vista Upgrade Advisor now will perform a software assessment of your system's device drivers to see which hardware devices require support directly from the manufacturer rather than through the default installation of Vista.

> **NOTE** Although Vista will support a wide variety of device types, these devices are standard items on modern PC equipment, such as network interface cards, screen drivers, and sound cards. You'll still have to get drivers for printers, scanners, TV tuner cards, and other such additional items from the manufacturer.

You'll see a list of device drivers that Vista will not provide by default, and in each case you'll have to contact the hardware manufacturer for an updated driver, as shown in Figure 2-3.

When you've finished with the software assessment, scroll to the bottom of the screen, and click Next. The final page of the Window Vista Upgrade Advisor will offer you a short summary report of its findings and the option to save or print the report for later use.

Figure 2-3 *The report suggests you get driver updates directly from the manufacturer.*

Buying the Right PC

If you have the luxury of buying a new computer, then you should try to get one that has the edition of Vista you need already preinstalled. That way, you can ensure that the manufacturer's choice of Vista editions is as close to being right for your own needs as possible. Nevertheless, always check the machine specifications, especially for extras, before handing over your credit card.

> **CAUTION**   Although Vista Home Premium and Vista Ultimate come with the Media Center application built in, you should be extremely careful when buying your PC that all the hardware requirements to make a Media Center system usable have been included. If you primarily want to use your system as a Media Center PC in the living room, you'll need to make sure it has been designed with a low-noise cooling system, a TV tuner card, heaps of disk space, and wireless keyboard and remote control features. If you have not been offered all this extra capability with a Home Premium solution, you should question the wisdom of using that particular SKU with that hardware platform.

Upgrading from Windows XP

If you bought a commercial PC in the months before Vista's launch, you have a 90 percent chance of having one flavor or another of Windows XP, and if that system is labeled as either Windows Vista Capable or Premium Ready PC, then you'll be able to follow the Vista upgrade path to at least one of the Vista SKUs with no problem at all. At that point, it's a matter of selecting whether to upgrade through the SKUs and, in doing so, which extra hardware add-ons you might require.

What Is a Windows Vista Capable PC?

Any PC carrying the Windows Vista Capable PC logo has already been approved as able to run Vista. Remember that all editions of Vista deliver the core capabilities discussed in Chapter 1; only the extensions obtained through the upgrades to Business, Enterprise, or Home Premium/Ultimate require additional hardware capabilities.

You can guarantee that a Windows Vista Capable PC will run the basic Vista user interface; however, it won't necessarily be able to handle the high-end graphics requirements of Windows Aero Glass.

Table 2-1 lists the requirements for running a Windows Vista Capable PC.

Table 2-1 Basic System Requirements for a Windows Vista Capable PC

Hardware Feature	Minimum Vista Capable PC Requirement
Processor	A processor of at least 800MHz is required to run the most basic editions of Vista.
RAM	512MB.
Video card	Must support DirectX 9.0 or later with 32MB graphics memory.

What Is a Windows Vista Premium Ready PC?

The distinction between a Windows Vista Capable PC and a Windows Vista Premium Ready PC is that the latter system will support the enhanced features you get with the more feature-rich premium SKUs (Enterprise, Home Premium, and Ultimate).

You'll see in Table 2-2 that the Windows Vista Premium Ready PC requirements are a lot higher than the Widows Vista Capable PC requirements. This distinction identifies the difference between a basic, usable Vista computer and one that really shows off the capabilities of this next-generation operating system.

Table 2-2 Hardware Requirements for Running Enhanced Vista Features

Hardware Feature	Vista Premium PC Requirement
Processor	1GHz 32-bit x86 or x64 processor
RAM	1GB
Video card	Must support DirectX 9.0 (or later), Pixel Shader 2.0, 32-bits per pixel, WDDM driver
Graphics memory	64MB for resolution of 1,310,720 pixels and up to 256MB for resolution of 2,304,000 (figures are aimed at single-monitor usage—adjust higher for additional monitors)
Disk space	15GB for Vista on a minimum drive size of 40GB
Optical drive	DVD-ROM drive
Audio	Basic sound card
Network	Basic Internet access (modem or broadband)

Other hardware features, such as TV tuner cards (DVB-T or analog), FM receiver cards, DVD writers, and webcams will all enhance the Vista experience but are not required by default for the Windows Vista Premium Ready PC badge.

Buying a New System

If you are going to buy a new PC with Vista already installed on it, you can use the benchmarks of the Windows Vista Capable PC and Windows Vista Premium Ready PC badges to assess what you are buying. Nevertheless, these guidelines will offer you only an assessment as to whether your system meets the minimum requirement, not necessarily *your* requirement. At this stage, you'll need to look long and hard at the applications (games and business applications, specifically) that you want to run on your PC and then add hardware, such as memory, to cope with the requirements.

For this example, we'll stick with the Media Center example, since it illustrates well the additional requirements you'll place upon your system if you want to use it as a Media Center PC in your living room, potentially streaming media content over a network to a Media Center extender, such as an Xbox 360.

Table 2-3 shows a typical specification for a Media Center PC, including the extra hardware features required to capture video, write DVDs, interface with a wireless keyboard and remote control, and store enough video, digital pictures, and music to make it worthwhile.

Table 2-3 Recommended Specs for a PC Running Windows Vista Ultimate Edition

Hardware Feature	Highly Specified Media Center PC
Processor	Intel Pentium 4 3.0GHz and 1MB cache.
RAM	Aim for 2GB, although 1GB will suffice.
Video card	Must support DirectX 9.0 (or later), Pixel Shader 2.0, 32-bits per pixel, WDDM driver.
Graphics memory	64MB for resolution of 1,310,720 pixels and up to 256MB for resolution of 2,304,000 (figures are aimed at single-monitor usage—adjust higher for additional monitors or if you intend to run a monitor and TV together).
Disk space	400GB should ensure you can store plenty of AV content.
Optical drive	DVD±RW.
Backup device	USB-connected external hard drive for backing up your precious content.
Audio	7.1channel surround sound.
Network	100Mbps Ethernet + 802.11g wireless (802.11a+g is even better for Media Center).
TV tuner	A combination of digital or analog tuner cards to maximize your viewing/recording capabilities. Look for high-definition TV (HDTV)–compatible hardware.
FM tuner	Analog FM tuner for standard radio reception.
Chassis	Hi-fi style casing with LCD status display.
Media interface	Front-mounted memory card reader for CompactFlash, MicroDrive, Memory Stick Pro, Smart Media, and SDRAM.
FireWire	IEEE 1394 interface for high-speed AV content transfer from digital camcorder.
Wireless keyboard	Essential for sofa surfing.
Remote control	Turns your PC into a fully integrated hi-fi component.

Understanding the Windows Experience Index

Vista provides you with a quick and easy assessment of how your PC is coping with the operating system; it uses a scoring mechanism known as the Windows Experience Index. This is a numerical value, calculated by a useful Vista application known as the Windows System Assessment Tool (WinSAT) that collects information from five key hardware areas and scores each one for its capabilities. The five key areas being assessed are as follows:

- Processor
- Memory (RAM)
- Primary hard disk
- Graphics
- Gaming graphics

To see what the Windows Experience Index is on your computer, click the Start menu, right-click Computer, and then select Properties. At the top of the screen Vista reports on performance issues it has detected with your system. Immediately beneath this, you'll see the Windows Experience Index, with a breakdown of the five key areas being assessed, as shown in Figure 2-4.

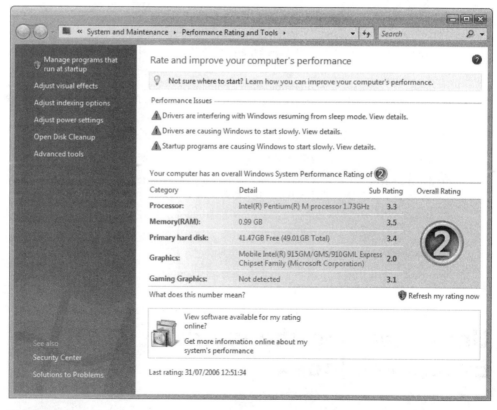

Figure 2-4 *Use the index rating to determine whether your PC is capable of running new applications.*

The overall rating (on the right side of the screen) equates to the lowest score from the five subratings. The higher the overall rating, the better your system.

Software vendors can benefit from using WinSAT by interrogating the standard XML report it produces and using it to tailor how applications exploit your edition of Vista. In this way, applications can dynamically add or remove capabilities as your system's hardware changes.

NOTE The WinSAT utility creates output as an XML-formatted file stored in your system directory, %SystemRoot%\Performance\WinSAT\DataStore. Each time you run WinSAT, you will generate a new XML file in this folder with the date of the assessment appended to the beginning of the filename, as in 2007-01-01 12.00.00.000 Assessment (Formal).WinSAT.xml.

You'll also see a file in this directory with the word Initial inside the bracketed part of the filename. This is the system performance assessment carried out when Vista was first installed on your computer.

CHAPTER 3

Installing and Setting Up Vista

Microsoft has strived to make Vista the easiest operating system in the Windows family to install. As with most of the changes and enhancements to usability in Vista, Microsoft has placed an emphasis on making it easy for both home users and enterprise administrators to install, with new and improved installation mechanisms that simplify the process for single installations and with much improved deployment tools that help administrators get their builds ready to ship to thousands of PC systems across the globe.

This chapter first looks at the Vista licensing model, installing single copies of the operating system from scratch using the Vista installation media as well as some of the new techniques open to administrators for packaging and rolling out automated builds across an enterprise or installing the operating system in its entirety on a removable device.

> **NOTE** Whatever your requirement, be it a stand-alone or a multiple-system installation, you must first make sure your target hardware is capable of running the Vista operating system. Refer to Chapter 2, where we discussed hardware compatibility, before you attempt to install Vista on the target computer system.

Obtaining the Software License

You can obtain a copy of the Vista software license and media in a variety of ways depending on the route you have taken, either as an individual or as a business, for acquiring your software.

Licensing Vista in the Home

Home users have it easy; you have only three approaches for obtaining any of the three available SKUs for home use:

- Buy a PC with Vista already installed.
- Buy the Vista upgrade to move from an earlier version of Windows.
- Buy the full operating system media installation kit.

Since January 2006, OEM hardware manufacturers will be shipping new PCs with some flavor or another of Vista preinstalled (Home, Home Premium, or Ultimate). In this case, you will automatically receive a license for running a single instance of the operating system SKU, and you may or may not (it depends on the OEM) get the installation media to reinstall the operating system if you need to rebuild your system.

> **NOTE** Most OEMs ship an image recovery solution for the complete system with their PC packages rather than simply for the base operating system. If you plan to upgrade to one of the more feature-rich SKUs from the low-end SKU that came with your system, you can buy the license from Windows Anytime Upgrade.

If you are upgrading from a previous version of Windows (Windows XP or Windows 2000, for example) to Vista, the license is somewhat cheaper than a completely new license purchase. This is the preferred option for most home users who already have a Vista-capable computer running a previous version of Windows or for someone planning to upgrade the specific hardware components they need to make them Vista compatible (such as adding a WDDM graphics card and extra memory).

The final option available to home users is to buy a new Vista software license that allows it to be installed on a blank hard drive without upgrading from a previous version of Windows. This is the most expensive option by far but is the only one available for a user who is thinking of building a PC and doesn't have a current, validated, pre–Vista Windows license.

Licensing Vista in Business

A plethora of licensing options are available to business users who are looking to upgrade to or roll out Vista. It's a matter of determining which overall licensing model best suits your enterprise and then obtaining the software media through that channel agreement.

Five licensing models are available to businesses:

- Microsoft Open License
- Microsoft Open Value
- Microsoft Select License
- Microsoft Enterprise Agreement
- Microsoft Enterprise Subscription Agreement

In addition to these licensing models, the Software Assurance maintenance program supplies businesses with planning assistance, training benefits, and much more. You can find more information about the business licensing models and Software Assurance on Microsoft's licensing web site at `http://www.microsoft.com/licensing`.

Installing Vista on a Single Computer

Installing Vista from the installation CD is really straightforward whether you are performing an upgrade or a fresh installation.

If you are doing an upgrade, you should boot up your PC and log into the older operating system with an account that has administrative privileges and then insert the Vista upgrade media into your optical drive. The setup screen should automatically run, and the Vista Setup program will launch.

> **TIP** If your system has autorun disabled, you can still start the installation from the CD by navigating to the CD in Windows Explorer and double-clicking `setup.exe`.

If you are installing a fresh copy of Vista and don't want to go down the upgrade path, you should power on your PC and then insert the installation media into your optical drive. If your system requires you to press a certain key sequence to boot from the optical drive, do so and wait for the installation splash screen to start.

Once the setup routine has started, the following steps should get you up and running in no time:

1. Click the Install Now button to start installing Vista.

2. If you are performing a fresh installation of Vista, you will not be able to go to the Internet for updates; however, if you are performing an upgrade, you should allow the Setup program to access the Internet to download any critical patches or hotfixes during the installation phase. This will save you from having to do this later.

> **NOTE** If you want to speed up the installation time, then select the option for not connecting to the Internet for patches. You can always use Windows Update when your system is fully installed and running.

3. Business users can skip this step; however, home users who have a product key for their software will be required to enter the key exactly as it is stated on the license agreement. When you're done, click Next.

> **TIP** You can authorize Vista to automatically activate itself when you connect to the Internet by leaving the Automatically Activate Windows When I'm Online box checked. If you'd rather do this manually when you're happy you are up and running, you should uncheck it and then activate it manually using the System applet in the Control Panel.

4. Scroll through the license agreement (reading it, of course), then click I Accept the License Terms (Required to Use Windows), and finally click Next.

5. If you're upgrading from a previous version of Windows, you now have the choice of performing an upgrade or a custom (Advanced) installation. An upgrade will leave all your previously configured files and folders in situ; however, if you ask Vista to install using the Custom (Advanced) option, the upgrade will move the previous version of Windows to one side with all your files and folders now residing under a new folder called Windows.old.

> **TIP** Although, on the face of it, an upgrade might seem like the best way of ensuring your system remains intact, upgrades can retain problems as well as files and folders. A far better way of making sure your system feels "fresh and clean" when you move to Vista is to back up your old data onto removable media and then import it into Vista later. This way, you can remove the old operating system and start with a pristine installation. If you are moving from Windows XP, consider using the File and Settings Transfer Wizard available by clicking Start ➤ All Programs ➤ Accessories ➤ System Tools ➤ File and Settings Transfer Wizard. Once you get Vista up and running, you can import these files and settings using Vista's new version of this feature called Windows Easy Transfer (Start ➤ All Programs ➤ Accessories ➤ System Tools ➤ Windows Easy Transfer).

6. You are now asked where you would like Vista to be installed on the hard drives in your system. Select the partition you would like Vista installed on, and then click Next. You can use various commands here for working with existing partitions, such as formatting, deleting, and extending. If you have an existing partition on your system that you want to completely overwrite, you can delete it and create a new one using the maximum available disk space.

> **TIP** If you are installing Vista on a hard drive that requires a specific driver to be installed that Vista does not have by default—for example, you're installing it on an external RAID system—you should click the Load Driver button and insert the manufacturer's media for that system.

7. This is the slow part: go make yourself a cup of tea, or maybe open a beer. Vista runs through the entire installation process without any more help, copying files to your system and rebooting a whole array of times until finally, you'll see a prompt asking you to specify your country or region and your preferred keyboard layout. Make sure you select the right options for your locale before clicking the Next button.

8. Next you are asked to create your first user account—typically this account will be the one you use for administrative tasks in the future, not the one you use for day-to-day activities, although this is completely up to you. Type the username and optional password; it is advisable you give this account a password since it will be used for administrative tasks. You are also required to select a picture that represents this account from the list of eight available at the bottom of the screen. When you're done, click Next.

9. Now you are required to enter a meaningful computer name (this is how your system will appear on your network, should you have one) and select your desktop background. When you've done this, click Next.

10. When you see the Help Protect Windows Automatically screen, it is best from a security perspective to allow Vista to automatically install updates for you when they become available. However, if you do not want to allow Vista this amount of freedom, you can opt to have Vista ask you later. When you're ready, click Next.

11. Next, review, and change if necessary, the time zone settings to suit your locale (the default is always GMT-08:00). If you want to have your system adjust for daylight saving time, leave the checkbox Automatically Adjust Clock for Daylight Savings Changes selected, and then click Next.

12. Finally, you are ready to start your nice, fresh installation of Vista for the first time. When you see the message saying "You're Ready To Start," click Start.

Deploying Vista

A major design factor for Vista was to make the operating system much easier than its predecessors to perform unattended installations and mass deployments. These two important characteristics of Vista will undoubtedly help both large and small organizations alike deploy Vista across different user communities and different countries (using the componentized language packs) and, indeed, help cut down the cost of deployments since a lot less can go wrong. This section covers the following:

- Component modularization
- Unattended answer files using Windows System Image Manager (SIM)
- Windows Preinstallation Environment (Windows PE, or WinPE)
- System Preparation Tool (sysprep.exe)
- Imaging using ImageX
- Hardware independence

Two further facilities are available in Vista to help upgrade from previous Windows operating systems:

- Windows Easy Transfer
- User State Migration Tool

> **NOTE** The unattended installation and deployment of Vista is a large topic with all the options available within the various components, such as the unattended answer file, being wide and varied in capability. This book offers an introduction to these methodologies and technologies, but there's nothing like experimentation to really see what's happening.

You'll need to obtain a number of items before you can embark on creating useful deployment images using these technologies:

- The source Vista product DVD
- The Windows Automated Installation Kit (Windows AIK)
- At least two computers: one computer, known as the *technician* computer, for creating your deployable image, and a second system, known as the *master* computer, for testing your image
- A removable media device, such as a USB memory stick
- A writable CD

> **NOTE** The Windows AIK is available for download from Microsoft's web site. Search Microsoft.com for *WAIK*. Make sure to follow the installation instructions to install it on your technician computer when you download it. It is essential for the following walk-throughs. You should also download the Windows AIK documentation files, including the WAIK.chm and unattend.chm help files. The unattend.chm file is especially useful because it contains a complete description of all the component settings available for use with the Windows SIM.

> **TIP** You will also need to acquire some good CD- or DVD-authoring software to burn the final ISO image you generate onto the optical media, or if you prefer, you can use the facilities built into Vista.

A Brief Word on Modularization

It helps to think of the components available for the modularization of Vista as building blocks. Some of these building blocks are essential in creating the base platform (known as MinWin) for all of the operating system functionality, not forming part of this opt-in/opt-out paradigm, whilst other components modify or add value to this base operating system and come as part of the associated SKU license agreement (at an extra cost). Other modules, such as the deployable language packs and device drivers, personalize Vista to make it applicable to each independent hardware platform and locality.

The beauty of this modular approach to the operating system is that 95 percent of the image will remain the same even if you are deploying different SKUs with different language packs.

System image files, known as Windows Imaging (WIM) files (with the extension .wim), are compressed files containing all the installation files necessary to install the customized version of Vista you have created using this technology.

Creating Unattended Answer Files

The first step in creating any customized installation of Vista is to generate the answer file that defines what's in and what's out of your installation using Windows SIM.

> **TIP** You can run Windows SIM on a computer running Windows XP, Windows Server 2003, or Vista. All you need is the source Vista DVD.

The following procedure will create your initial answer file for completing the rest of the process:

1. Create a new folder somewhere on your technician computer to store the images and answer files, for example, c:\vista_images. From now on, this folder will be referred to as the <image> folder.

2. Insert the Vista DVD into the optical drive on your technician computer, and then navigate to the \Sources folder using Windows Explorer.

3. Copy the install.wim image file to your <image> folder.

> **CAUTION** The install.wim file is practically 2.5GB in size, so it will take a few minutes to copy to your <image> folder.

4. Start the Windows SIM by clicking Start ➤ All Programs ➤ Microsoft Windows AIK, and then click Image Manager.

5. Select File ➤ Select Windows Image; then, in the dialog box that opens, locate the <image> folder, and select install.wim.

6. Select the appropriate version of Vista you are planning to deploy, and then click OK.

7. Select File ➤ New Answer File. If you do not already have a catalog created on your technician computer, click OK to create one. You must create a new catalog for each version of Vista you're deploying.

8. Next, you need to add the components you want to include in your installation. Click the Windows Image pane, and expand the Component node. This will display all the available components and associated settings available for each one. To add components to your installation, right-click the component, and select the appropriate configuration pass containing the settings in which you are interested. To get more information about what each of the components and associated settings can do for you, access the Unattended Windows Setup Reference help file included in the Windows AIK documentation download (unattend.chm), as shown in Figure 3-1.

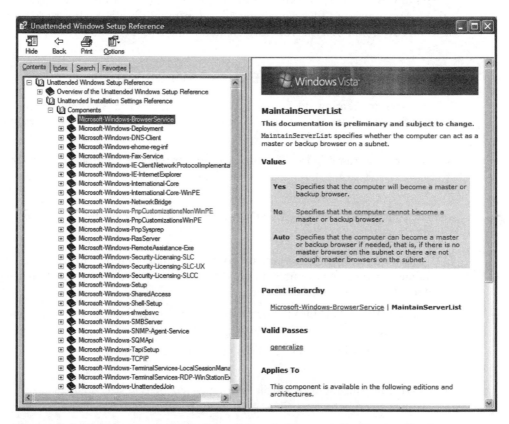

Figure 3-1 *The Unattended Windows Setup Reference help file details all component settings.*

When you are installing Vista, a number of *configuration passes* take place, whereby the operating system performs certain actions at certain stages of the installation. Many of these actions occur during prescriptive phases and cannot occur during a later or an earlier configuration phase. A good example is disk configuration. You can configure the disk configuration option of allowing the user selection of the installation partition through the user interface (UI) using the following configuration component setting: `Microsoft-Windows-Setup\DiskConfiguration\WillShowUI`. The value of the `WillShowUI` setting will determine the actions, as shown in Table 3-1.

Table 3-1 Component Settings for UI Control During Vista Installation

Component	Value	Outcome
WillShowUI	Always	The UI is always displayed.
	OnError	The UI is displayed if an error occurs during setup.
	Never	The UI is never displayed, even if there is a catastrophic, unrecoverable error.

You will need to add five components to create a basic Vista installation, as shown in Table 3-2.

Table 3-2 Components Required for a Basic Vista Installation

Component	Associated Configuration Pass
Microsoft-Windows-Setup\DiskConfiguration\Disk\CreatePartitions\CreatePartition	1 Windows PE
Microsoft-Windows-Setup\DiskConfiguration\Disk\ModifyPartitions\ModifyPartition	1 Windows PE
Microsoft-Windows-Setup\ImageInstall\OSImage\InstallTo	1 Windows PE
Microsoft-Windows-Setup\UserData	1 Windows PE
Microsoft-Windows-Shell-Setup\OOBE	7 oobeSystem

> **NOTE** The oobeSystem pass refers to the *out-of-box-experience* pass when the system performs the first boot after installation. This is commonly referred to as the Windows *welcome pass,* and it's where the user first interacts with the Vista operating system after the initial WinPE pass.

You will now see the unattended script in XML format in the Answer File pane. Go through the complete list of component settings, and set them as shown in Table 3-3.

Table 3-3 Additional Component Settings to Finish Creating the Answer File

Component	Value
`Microsoft-Windows-Setup\DiskConfiguration`	WillShowUI = `OnError`
`Microsoft-Windows-Setup\DiskConfiguration\Disk`	DiskID = `0`
	WillWipeDisk = `true`
`Microsoft-Windows-Setup\DiskConfiguration\CreatePartitions\CreatePartition`	Extend = `false`
	Order = `1`
	Size = <specify the hard disk size in MB>
	Type = `Primary`
`Microsoft-Windows-Setup\DiskConfiguration\Disk\ModifyPartitions\ModifyPartition`	Active = `true`
	Extend = `false`
	Format = `NTFS`
	Label = `Vista` (or whatever volume label you'd prefer)
	Letter = `C`
	Order = `1`
	PartitionID = `1`
`Microsoft-Windows-Setup\ImageInstall\OSImage`	WillShowUI = `OnError`
`Microsoft-Windows-Setup\ImageInstall\OSImage\InstallTo`	DiskID = `0`
	PartitionID = `1`
`Microsoft-Windows-Setup\UserData`	AcceptEula = `true`
`Microsoft-Windows-Setup\UserData\ProductKey`	Key = <type your product key as it appears on the media>
	WillShowUI = `OnError`
`Microsoft-Windows-Shell-Setup\OOBE`	HideEULAPage = `true`
	ProtectYourPC = `3`
	SkipMachineOOBE = `true`
	SkipUserOOBE = `true`

This unattended answer file will ensure that there is no user input required during the installation unless there is an error with the hardware or with accessing the media.

> **TIP** You can check that the settings you have configured in the answer files are correct using the Windows SIM. Select Tools ➤ Validate Answer File. If you receive any errors, you can correct these by double-clicking the error message, changing the value, and then revalidating.

When you have completed generating the answer file, select File ➤ Save Answer File, and save the file as AutoUnattend.xml. Finally, you should copy the AutoUnattend.xml file to a removable device, such as a memory stick or floppy disk, to be used in conjunction with Vista Setup.

Setting Up Your Master Computer

The next stage is to install a fresh copy of Vista on your master PC using the AutoUnattend.xml answer file you just created. The process is as follows:

1. Insert your Vista product DVD and your AutoUnattend.xml file (on the removable media) into your master PC, and power it up. When the Vista setup.exe program runs, it searches all available removable media devices for an unattended answer file named AutoUnattend.xml.

2. Setup will proceed using the settings defined in the previous stage, installing Vista based on the answers supplied in AutoUnattend.xml.

3. When Vista installs, configure any specific settings within the operating system you deem important, such as security settings, firewall settings, policy settings, and so on.

> **NOTE** You should also install any applications at this stage that form part of your system's core baseline; for example, you might want your users to have Adobe Acrobat Reader, Sophos antivirus software, and a specific virtual private network (VPN) client for business connectivity on each of your machines. If you install them now, they'll be included, configured correctly for use in your business, in the image.

You now have a perfectly valid way of building a system from scratch with little to no user interaction. All you need to do at this stage is supply the Vista build software and a unique product ID (or an enterprise key if you have a license agreement), and the system will install completely automatically. However, if you continue with the following sections, you'll be able to easily deploy the image to many systems at once, facilitating mass rollouts at an enterprise level.

So, after you have finished configuring the installation, you need to do what is called a *generalization* of the system using sysprep.exe, whereby you remove all specific information from the image so you can deploy it over and over again.

Generalizing Your Master Computer Using Sysprep

On your master computer installation, you will need to run the `sysprep.exe` command from the command prompt to remove all specific installation characteristics from this system before it can be imaged. To do this, do the following:

1. Start the command prompt by pressing the Windows Logo+R, then typing **cmd.exe**, and finally pressing Enter.

2. Type **C:\Windows\System32\Sysprep.exe /oobe /generalize /shutdown**, and then press Enter.

3. Sysprep removes all machine-specific information and then shuts Vista down, ready for the imaging process.

Using WinPE and ImageX to Create the Image

To create an image for use in any deployment scenario, you will need to use the WinPE and ImageX utilities to start the preinstallation environment and then snapshot the image off the master computer. This is a two-stage process: first you create the WinPE boot environment on a CD, and then you create the system image on a network share.

> **TIP** Before you start, it is a good idea to have already created a network share available for streaming the image to as well as a blank, writable CD for copying the WinPE software.

Start on the technician computer, creating the WinPE media, by doing the following:

1. Open a command prompt (press Windows Logo+R, type **cmd.exe**, and press Enter).

2. Type **cd Program Files\Windows AIK\Tools\PETools**, and then press Enter to change into the tools folder.

3. Type **copype.cmd <architecture> <destination folder>**, and then press Enter where <architecture> is either x86, amd64, or ia64 and the <destination folder> is the folder in which you want to create the build environment.

4. Copy ImageX into your <destination folder> by typing **copy C:\Program files\ Windows AIK\Tools\x86\imagex.exe <destination folder>** and then pressing Enter.

5. Using `notepad.exe` (type **Notepad** at the command prompt, and press Enter), create an exclusion file called `wimscript.ini` with the following content:

```
[ExclusionList]
ntfs.log
hiberfil.sys
pagefile.sys
"System Volume Information"
RECYCLER
Windows\CSC
[CompressionExclusionList]
*.mp3
*.zip
*.cab
\WINDOWS\inf\*.pnf
```

6. This exclusion file will ensure that these sorts of files are not included in the image, thus saving space and deployment time for the generated image. Save the exclusion file to the <destination> folder.

> **TIP** ImageX automatically looks in the folder it is installed in for the `wimscript.ini` exclusion file. These files must coexist in the same physical folder on your technician computer for this exclusion to work.

7. Now you can create the image from your master computer by typing **oscdimg -n -bc:\<destination folder>\etfsboot.com c:\ <destination folder>\ISO c:\ <destination folder>\vista_winpe.iso** and then pressing Enter.

8. Finally, you will need to burn the resultant ISO image (in this case `vista_winpe.iso`) onto a blank optical disk using whatever burning software you usually use.

Now you must insert the WinPE media disk you just created into your powered-down master computer and press the power button. Make sure when the system starts that you instruct your system to boot from the CD or DVD drive. This is essential for the next step of capturing the image to work properly. You will now be using the WinPE media disk with the ImageX software embedded in it to grab the Vista installation image from your master computer. To complete this process, do the following:

1. The master computer will boot up and start the WinPE software, launching a command prompt for you to run WinPE commands such as ImageX.

2. At the command prompt, change the folder to the folder where ImageX is stored.

3. To capture the image from your master computer system, type **Imagex.exe / compress fast /capture C: C:\myvista.wim "Customized Vista Installation" / verify**, and then press Enter.

4. You can now copy this image file onto a network share since WinPE inherently provides network support for installing images remotely from a distribution server.

> **NOTE** The ImageX command has a variety of switches and capabilities associated with it. For a full list of its capabilities, type `ImageX /?`. Then press Enter.

And that's it. Your master image is now ready for deployment.

Using WinPE and ImageX to Deploy the Image

Once you have created the WinPE start-up disk and taken your image snapshot of your master computer, you are ready to deploy it to a target system.

To complete this stage of the process, you'll need the WinPE disk, the image you stored on the network share and a target computer on which to test your installation.

> **TIP** It's common for IT professionals to use the master computer to test the image. If your image is not quite right, you can always tweak it, reconfigure it in whatever way you need, and then return to the generalization stage. If you are sending the image to a system with an already installed operating system, you'll have to remember to override the CD/DVD-ROM boot order by pressing the appropriate function key.

Here is the process for deploying your image:

1. Insert your WinPE disk into your target computer, and then reboot it, remembering to override the boot order if necessary.

2. When WinPE starts up and you see the command prompt, type **diskpart**, and then press Enter.

3. Now, from the diskpart environment, type the following commands, pressing Enter after each, inserting the appropriate disk size in megabytes where it says <xx>:

```
Select disk ()
Clean
Create partition primary size=<xx>
Select partition 1
Active
Format
Exit
```

4. You now need to mount the network share as a locally mapped drive on this target computer. Type **net use X: \\<computer_name\<share_name>**, and then press Enter.

5. Copy the Vista image you created earlier from the network share to the new partition on this computer by typing **copy X:\myvista.wim c:** and then pressing Enter.

6. Finally, you have to apply the image to the system using ImageX. To do this, use the following command: **D:\<imageXfolder>\Imagex.exe /apply C:\myvista.wim c:**, and then press Enter.

And that's it. You've now successfully deployed an image to your target computer. You can deploy this image to as many systems as you want.

More on ImageX

ImageX is an extremely powerful command for capturing, manipulating, and deploying .wim files. The options and switches used in the previous example deployment only scratch the surface of what's possible using ImageX.

The following is a list of ImageX capabilities:

- You can use it to split images across multiple disks.
- You can use it to stitch split images back together again.
- You can use it to mount images as Windows folders so that you can edit image elements using Windows Explorer.

> **NOTE** A limitation when mounting images is that ImageX will happily mount a .wim file with both read and write on an NTFS file system, whereas images mounted on FAT, ISO, and UDF file systems will be read-only. By inference, you cannot alter a read-only image mounting.

For a full list of command-line options and switches available for ImageX and other associated deployment tools, see the Windows Automated Installation Kit User's Guide (part of the Windows AIK download).

More on WinPE

WinPE, which was introduced in Vista, gets around many of the limitations previous operating systems had with the DOS shell that traditionally started from the Windows installation floppy disks or CD.

WinPE facilitates access to and installs drivers for a much wider range of hardware devices and is much better at handling error exceptions during setup—you can pick up where you left off if the system stops for some reason.

From the WinPE shell, you also have the option of running many of the Vista applications that might be necessary for enterprise customers to create the necessary build environment. Most significantly, WinPE is network enabled for both IPv4 and IPv6 networks.

So, coupled with the ability to access NTFS folders as seamlessly as FAT folders, theoretically you can connect across your LAN (or WAN) to any NTFS network folder and access some scripts or configuration files during this early stage of the installation phase. This is extremely powerful for system administrators who, in the past, had to perform much of the configuration of the system post-installation.

> **NOTE** The whole matter of deployment and what best suits your needs in your environment comes from trying the endless possibilities of these tools. Deploying Vista can be as easy or as complicated as you need it to be, and with the introduction of network connectivity at the installation and file-copying stages, you can even augment images on the fly using these tools. The possibilities are now endless.

The net command (used for manipulating and creating users, groups, and network shares; acquiring network statistics; sending Messenger service messages; and much, much more) is inherent in the WinPE environment, as is diskpart for managing disks, partitions, and volumes.

You can use Drvload to tactically add device drivers to the system during the installation phase; these are drivers that are necessary to access hardware required for the file copy and image application to start. For example, a RAID-based disk subsystem might require specialized drivers to mount the installation point of where you are targeting the Vista image. Drvload allows you to install this driver before commencing with the Vista file copy and the subsequent oobe phase of the installation.

As you saw earlier, WinPE is highly customizable insomuch as that you can add capabilities to the environment that don't exist by default. In the same way that we introduced ImageX into WinPE earlier (during the WinPE media creation phase of the deployment), you can add any other tools you might need to bolster its capabilities—it's a simple matter of re-creating that WinPE ISO image.

Finally, WinPE does, for good reasons, have its limitations. If it were as extensible as Vista, cunning users would soon see the possibilities of bolstering WinPE (since it's based on Vista components) to the extent that Vista is not required, therefore bypassing the need to acquire a license. Table 3-4 shows some of these limitations, highlighting why you still need Vista.

Table 3-4 Limitations of WinPE

Characteristic	Description
Memory	The computer you are running WinPE on must have a minimum of 256MB of RAM.
Image size	WinPE is too big to fit on floppy disks but fits comfortably on a writable CD.
Video	A Video Electronics Standards Association (VESA)–compatible display is mandatory.
Server service	No Windows Server service runs in WinPE; consequently, you cannot access WinPE across the network, although you can instigate connections yourself.
Network	IPv4 and IPv6 are the only supported networking protocols.
Drive mappings	WinPE is a nonpersistent environment, so drive mappings are lost after a reboot.
Applications	Although you can bolster WinPE with useful applications when necessary, it will not support advanced runtime libraries such as the .NET Framework or Windows on Windows (WOW) for running 16-bit DOS applications.
Timeout	WinPE will automatically restart after 24 hours in an attempt to prevent it from being used instead of Vista.

Ultimately, WinPE is an integral part of Vista deployment, and its extensibility offers administrators a new way of tackling old problems with renewed vigor. To learn more about WinPE, refer to http://www.microsoft.com/technet/windowsvista/deploy.

Using Microsoft Solution Accelerator for Business Desktop Deployment

For the true enterprise-scale business, Microsoft has developed the Microsoft Solution Accelerator for Business Desktop Deployment (BDD), which came about as a result of the increasing complexity of rolling out large-scale operating system deployments with their associated applications. The BDD complements Windows AIK by providing a further multitude of tools and guidelines for creating a truly lite-touch deployment.

> **NOTE** *Lite touch* is as close as Microsoft has gotten with the technology to the holy grail of system deployment known as *zero touch*. Lite touch is effectively a complete installation of the operating system and business applications with the absolute minimum of user or administrator input. This is achieved through scripting, XML answer files, and the new .wim Vista imaging system.

BDD delivers an integrated deployment tool that helps you work with all the associated deployment facilities, such as ImageX, Windows SIM, and WinPE. This deployment tool is known simply as the BDDWorkbench, downloadable from http://www.microsoft.com/downloads, and as a prerequisite, you'll need to install the Windows AIK before BDDWorkbench will run.

Using Windows Easy Transfer

Deploying an image to a new PC is only half the migration story. What about users coming from a previous operating system environment, such as Windows XP, who have personalized their system in such a way that best facilitates their way of working? They certainly will not want to lose their configuration: just imagine losing your settings, files, email, contacts, and Internet Explorer favorites as a result of moving to Vista—you'd want to go straight back to Windows XP the way it was before.

To mitigate this problem, Microsoft has improved on the old Files and Settings Transfer Wizard in Windows XP with the all-new Windows Easy Transfer.

For all intents and purposes, Windows Easy Transfer follows the same paradigm as its predecessor for copying files and folders, email, contacts, and Internet Explorer settings and favorites, but it has been enhanced to also cover multiple user accounts and a wide array of targeted program settings that the Files and Settings Transfer Wizard didn't do. Table 3-5 shows exactly what's transferred using Windows Easy Transfer.

Table 3-5 File and Program Settings Transferred Using Windows Easy Transfer

Settings	Description
Files and folders	Everything contained within the My Documents folder on Windows 2000 and Windows XP or the Documents folder on Vista, as well as the Shared Documents folder.
Email and contacts	Email messages, account settings, and address books from Outlook Express, Outlook, or Windows Mail.
Program settings	These are settings that ensure Vista is configured as your old computer was; however, before you copy the settings to the new computer, you must install those applications on the new system.
User accounts	User-specific configuration such as personalization of desktop color schemes, mapped network drives, Start menu commands, and taskbar configuration (most of the stuff covered in Chapter 2).
Internet Explorer settings and favorites	Favorites and cookies are transferred from Internet Explorer.

NOTE Windows Easy Transfer will facilitate transferring users from Windows 2000, Windows XP, or indeed another computer running Vista. Note, however, that upgrading the operating system to Vista, rather than starting from scratch with a new installation, will automatically transfer your files and settings to Vista.

You can facilitate the transfer of your files and settings in several ways:

- By CD or DVD ROM
- By USB-connected external hard disk or flash drive
- Over the network
- Via a USB Easy Transfer cable

If you are transferring a lot of files and settings, you'll need to make sure the method you select from the aforementioned list is capable of containing all your data. A few megabytes of files and email will easily fit on a USB flash drive; however, if you have 20GB of files, settings, email, and shortcuts, you'll need to consider using a direct network connection, a USB-connected external hard drive with the appropriate capacity, or a USB Easy Transfer cable.

NOTE A USB Easy Transfer cable is specifically designed to work with Windows Easy Transfer, transferring data at speeds of up to 1GB per minute (a lot faster than your average LAN). If you didn't get a USB Easy Transfer cable with your PC when you bought it, you can order it from any good electronics outlet, such as Belkin (http://www.belkin.com).

The first stage in transferring files and settings from an old computer is to install the Windows Easy Transfer software on that system. You can do this by copying Windows Easy Transfer onto your removable hard disk or USB flash drive if necessary or using the media that comes with your USB Easy Transfer cable if you are using one.

> **TIP** You can find the Windows Easy Transfer application in %SystemRoot%\System32\ migwiz; the file is called migwiz.exe. It might save you a few minutes doing it this way than doing it the official way. You just start Windows Easy Transfer, starting the process of copying your files to your new computer. Then you are prompted to install Windows Easy Transfer on the old computer using a variety of available methods, whereby you come out of Windows Easy Transfer and complete the process.

Once you have copied Windows Easy Transfer to your old computer, start it, and you'll see the screen shown in Figure 3-2.

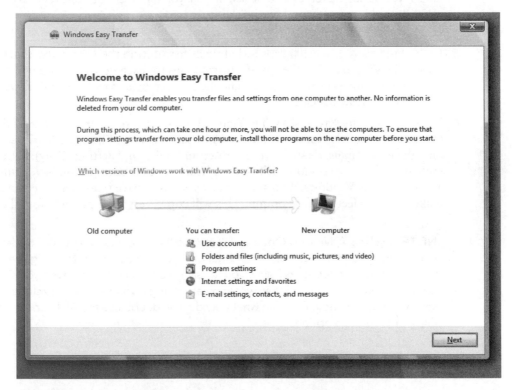

Figure 3-2 *Starting Windows Easy Transfer*

The following procedure shows you how to copy files and settings to the intermediary device prior to loading them on your new system:

1. Click Next on the screen shown in Figure 3-2.

2. Click Start a New Transfer.

3. Select My Old Computer as the system from which you are transferring files and settings.

4. Select the transfer media option applicable to you, such as USB East Transfer cable, network, or removable storage device.

> **NOTE** If you are using a USB Easy Transfer cable, you should follow the instructions that came with the cable to insert the CD in the old computer and run through the device installation routine. When it's installed, you plug the USB Easy Transfer cable into the Vista computer, where it will be automatically recognized and activated. If you opt to use a network connection, you have the option of directly streaming the settings to the new computer or, if you prefer, to store them in a staging area of a mutually accessible network share. The network share has the benefit of being able to be backed up independently in case something happens to your source PC. If you select the removable device option, you get to choose between CD/DVD, USB flash drive, or external hard disk.

5. Each of the transfer mechanisms is slightly different from the others, depending on the media type, so follow the specific instructions for each depending on which you are using. Figure 3-3 shows the screen when you transfer to a USB flash drive. When you're ready, click Next.

6. When you see the screen shown in Figure 3-4, you can select from either of the topmost two options for a quick copy (All User Accounts, Files, and Settings) or only the logged in user's stuff (My User Account, Files, and Settings Only). Selecting the latter of the two options will copy only one user account. If you have multiple accounts (many Windows 2000 and Windows XP users have more than one account), make sure to select the first option. This will copy everything possible for all users.

> **NOTE** Clicking Advanced Options will instruct Windows Easy Transfer to determine exactly what can be copied and will give you the option of tailoring the copy to better suit your needs and allow you to tailor the selections. However, you should be absolutely positive you know what you are doing if you decide to exclude some settings or files without knowing what they do. If in doubt, use the All User Accounts, Files, and Settings option.

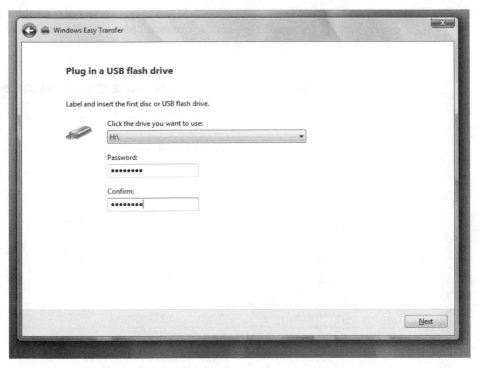

Figure 3-3 *Select the target device from the list, and then click Next.*

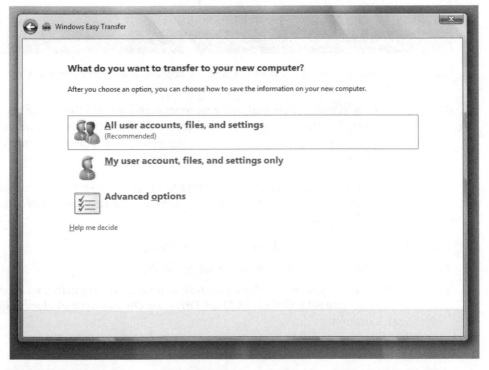

Figure 3-4 *Select from one of three options to decide what to transfer.*

7. When you see the screen shown in Figure 3-5, you can click any of the folder nodes to see exactly what's going to be copied to your new computer. When you are ready to start the process, click the Transfer button.

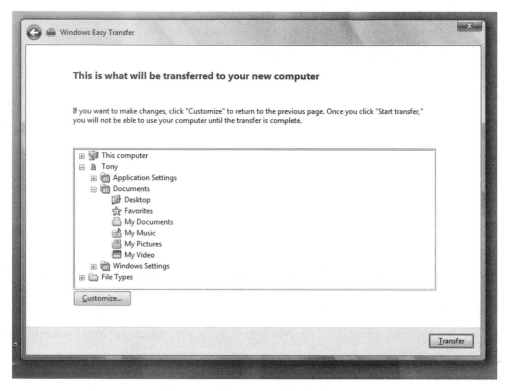

Figure 3-5 *Explore the files and settings to be copied, and then click Transfer.*

8. Windows Easy Transfer then analyzes your system to estimate the size of the data being transferred to the new system, and then it collect the files and settings on the designated transfer media. This can take a long time (many hours) to complete if you have a lot of data, so you'll have to be patient.

When the process is complete and you have your files and settings on the staging media, start Windows Easy Transfer again, this time on the new computer, and then complete the following procedure:

1. On the first screen (refer to Figure 3-2), click Next.

2. On the next screen, click Continue a Transfer in Progress.

3. Choose the media type (network or removable device) you are using, and then select On a CD or DVD, On a USB Flash Drive, or On an External Hard Disk or Network Location.

4. Select the location of the files and settings on the media, and then click Next.

5. Windows Easy Transfer now copies all files and setting from the intermediary to the new system. This can take quite some time to complete if you have a lot of data, so go make a cup of tea, or if there is a lot of data, watch a movie.

Using the User State Migration Tool

Although Windows Easy Transfer is a giant leap forward in functionality from its predecessor for home and small-business users, it cannot satisfy the high demand for data migration in an enterprise environment where you are looking to migrate potentially hundreds, if not thousands, of users from old systems to new ones, all within a Windows domain environment. To address this problem, Microsoft created the User State Migration Tool (USMT). It's worth remembering that if you are upgrading from a previous version of Windows, rather than starting afresh, you don't need USMT.

The latest version of USMT (version 3.0) allows you to migrate users from Windows 2000 with SP4 or Windows XP with SP2 to Vista.

> **NOTE** You can also use USMT 3.0 to migrate from Windows 2000 with SP4 to Windows XP.

USMT 3.0 includes two independent tools for scanning and loading user settings from one system to another: ScanState and LoadState. *ScanState* will gather all user- and application-specific settings from the old computer and save them to a target folder, either on a network share or on a removable hard disk, creating a single image file called usmt3.mig. *LoadState* will take the usmt3.mig file from the shared folder and apply it to the new PC. This process is similar to that of the Windows Easy Transfer process; however, the main differences between the two facilities are as follows:

• USMT is XML driven and highly scriptable.

• You can automate bulk scans and loads using USMT.

• USMT works within a Windows domain.

For more information about USMT, see the Microsoft TechNet web site at http://www.microsoft.com/technet/WindowsVista/library/usmt.

You can download USMT from http://www.microsoft.com/downloads.

CHAPTER 4

Finding Your Way Around the Desktop

There's no denying it—Windows has had a makeover. The Vista interface is arguably the most graphically appealing and user-friendly PC interface available on
the market; in addition, the graphics have been enhanced in such a way that they best
expose the information on the screen, rather than simply look pretty.

You'll see that application windows now glide smoothly across the screen in a way
never before possible with previous versions of Windows, with transparency properties
that allow you to quickly assess the information the windows contain more quickly and
effectively.

This chapter is essentially a whistle-stop tour of the Vista user interface, exposing
some of the new features and capabilities the desktop has to offer.

Logging In to Vista

Logging in to Vista is somewhat different depending on whether you are part of a
Windows domain or whether you are a member of a Windows workgroup (effectively
a stand-alone edition).

If you are operating in a Windows domain, when the operating system first starts,
you will see a blank screen. You are required to press the Ctrl+Alt+Del key sequence
(known as the *secure attention sequence*) to reveal the Vista Log On screen. This secure
attention sequence instructs the Vista kernel that you are ready to log in, and the operating system then starts the process, prompting you for your username, password, and
domain information.

NOTE The interface you see when logging in to Vista is provided by a system .dll known as the graphical identification and network authentication (GINA) file. The Winlogon process loads the GINA, and then when you have successfully authenticated using the right username and password, Winlogon proceeds to load your profile and apply any system or group policies to the account. If you have installed a secondary authentication system, such as a biometric fingerprint reader, the original GINA file (msgina.dll) will be replaced with a proprietary one that manages authentication.

If you are operating Vista stand-alone or as part of a workgroup, then authentication is handled locally on the PC, and the interface is somewhat different. You will see a set of icons on the screen that represent each user configured on the system. If you click the icon representing you as a user, you will be asked for the password for that account (if you have set one up), and then the Winlogon process will take over and set the user environment up for that user as usual.

Once you have logged in to Vista, you can quickly switch to another user account (assuming such activity is allowed by the system's owner or administrator) by pressing the secure attention sequence (Ctrl+Alt+Del) again and selecting Switch User from the menu. In a workgroup configuration, you will again see the login screen you saw when the system first started. In a Windows domain environment, you'll have to press the secure attention sequence a second time (part of the security solution in the domain is to have the system verify the command you selected was intended) before you proceed.

Exploring the Vista Desktop

As with most new things, once you familiarize yourself with them, they become second nature. Vista is no different; the first time you log in (especially if you are used to the desktop in any of the predecessors in the Windows family), you will be amazed at how different it looks. However, it won't take you long to learn the interface (it's very intuitive), and once you pick up the jargon and understand the new paradigm of how information is arranged, you'll be whizzing around like an expert.

The first feature you'll see when you log in to Vista is the desktop, shown in Figure 4-1. It is automatically dressed in one of Vista's striking scenic photographs (the *vistas*), and you'll immediately see the graphical improvements previously discussed—these graphics are extremely high quality. To the right of the desktop is a new feature known as the Windows Sidebar. This is a semitransparent application interface, not unlike the old Active Desktop, where you can "bolt in" Windows gadgets (more on those later) to provide instant access to information on your computer, such as the clock, or information pulled from the Internet, such as share prices or news feeds.

Figure 4-1 *The revised Vista desktop*

Personalizing the Desktop

Consider the desktop simply the canvas on which your user interface is painted. This canvas is highly configurable; you can set it to suit any number of requirements. Personalizing the desktop in most cases is for aesthetic purposes, but there are some important reasons why you'd change settings such as icon size and font size, such as if a user is visually impaired.

You can personalize the desktop through a Control Panel applet called Personalization. To start this applet, select Start ➤ Control Panel ➤ Personalization.

> **TIP** As with most tasks in Vista, you can get to the same configuration dialog box in a multitude of ways. In the case of Personalization, you can right-click any blank space on the desktop and select Personalize.

Figure 4-2 shows the list of options available for customizing your desktop.

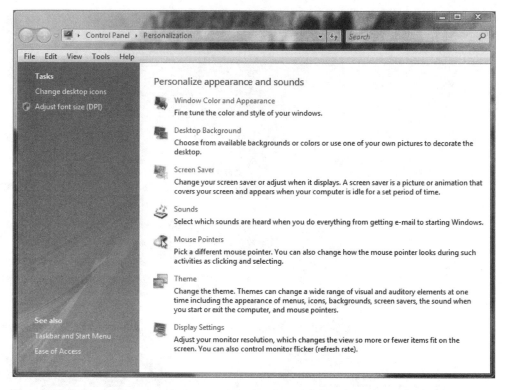

Figure 4-2 *Customize the desktop using the Control Panel applet called Personalization.*

> **NOTE** Desktop settings are specific for each user account and are stored in the system registry under HKEY_USERS. When you log in to Vista, your profile is copied from HKEY_USERS to HKEY_CURRENT_USER. You can find the specific registry keys associated with your user account's desktop settings in the registry under HKEY_CURRENT_USER/Control Panel/Desktop. In Vista, you access the registry using the regedit.exe command: just press Windows Logo+R, type **regedit.exe**, and press Enter.

In the task pane, you'll see two items listed:

- Change Desktop Icons
- Adjust Font Size (DPI)

Selecting Change Desktop Icons will allow you to select which icons are painted onto the desktop (Vista tries to be as minimalist as possible to begin with, displaying only the Recycle Bin by default). You'll notice in Figure 4-3 that you can also change the icons used to represent these capabilities. Click Change Icon to select from hundreds of icons stored in %SystemRoot%\System32\imageres.dll. If you want to change the location where Vista looks for icons, you can click the Browse button and select a new folder.

Figure 4-3 *Add or remove desktop icons depending on whether you like a tidy or busy interface.*

If you click Adjust Font Size (DPI), you can adjust the dots per inch (dpi) used for text on the screen. A higher dpi will increase the size of the characters; conversely, a lower dpi will allow you to fit more information on the screen. And you can choose from two presets: the default of 96 dpi or a larger font size of 120 dpi.

> **NOTE** Changing the dpi does not affect the resolution of the screen display. However, if you increase the resolution of the screen, the size of the characters displayed will naturally get smaller along with everything else. To counter this, after increasing your screen resolution, you can increase the dpi.

Back in the Personalization applet, if you select Window Color and Appearance, you'll see the screen shown in Figure 4-4. Here you'll find eight color schemes already defined for you. Alternatively, if none of these suit you, you can click Show Color Mixer and create your own using the color mixer controls for hue, saturation, and brightness. If you click the link Open Classic Appearance Properties for More Color Options, you'll be taken to an Appearance dialog box like the one you're probably used to working with in Windows XP.

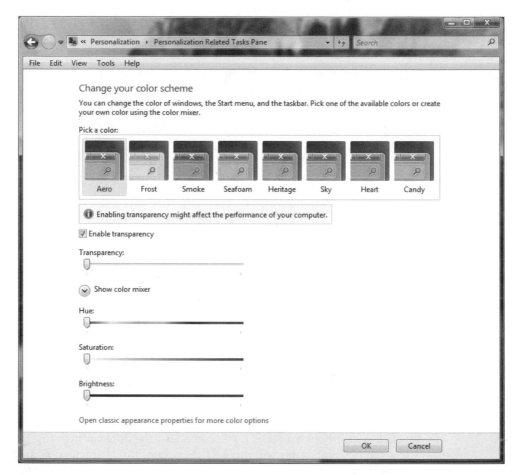

Figure 4-4 *Create your own custom color scheme using the color mixer controls.*

Clicking Desktop Background allows you to select the canvas that covers your desktop. You'll find a whole range of vistas, textures, paintings, pictures, and solid colors that you can apply to your desktop. Alternatively, if you have some pictures of your own that you'd like to try as your desktop, click the Browse button, and locate the picture in the appropriate folder.

> **TIP** If you find a picture you'd like to use as your desktop background, you can right-click the image file in Windows Explorer, and select Set As Desktop Background on the context menu.

Next on the list of configurable items is the system screen saver. A screen saver will switch on when your system is idle, preventing what's known as *screen burn*—when an image permanently displayed on a monitor can "burn" a residual image into the fabric of the monitor coating and cause damage.

> **TIP** A better option than relying on a screen saver (and more environmentally friendly) is to forget about a screen saver and instead use the Power Options applet in the Control Panel to change your power plan to switch power off to the screen altogether after your preferred timeout. This way, you don't save only your screen, but you also save the planet. Usefully, from the Screen Saver Settings dialog box, you can click a direct link that opens the Power Options applet in the Control Panel.

Screen savers really have a dual purpose, with the screen-saving capability no longer as important as the security feature of opening the login screen when the session resumes. Many users (especially in a business domain environment) rely on this feature to lock a user's workstation when the user goes to make coffee—which is particularly useful if you work in the Department of Defense, for example.

Using the Personalization screen, you can also change the default sounds used to notify the user of certain events, such as the New Mail Notification, and you can change how the cursor looks using the mouse properties (by clicking Mouse Pointers).

You can also apply themes in Vista, whereby you apply an entire package of configuration controls in one go, changing the background, sounds, icons, cursors, and various other low-level controls to change your system's look and feel. Vista has a few built-in themes, and you can download others from the Internet, either from Microsoft's web site or from another theme supplier.

> **TIP** If you really hate the new Windows look offered by Vista, you can always switch to the Windows Classic theme, forcing your system to look like Windows XP.

We'll cover display settings and monitor configuration in detail in Chapter 5, so for now that's it for desktop personalization.

Using the Windows Sidebar

On the right side of the desktop sits the Windows Sidebar. This highly configurable interface is essentially a framework for developers to create gadget applications that provide useful information or functionality that a user might want immediately accessible on the desktop. Since the Windows Sidebar is only the container for the gadgets operating inside it, you can't really configure an awful lot about it. Try right-clicking a blank piece of the Sidebar (where there is no gadget application footprint), and you'll get a context menu comprising the following five items:

- Bring Gadgets to the Front
- Add Gadgets
- Properties
- Help
- Close Sidebar

Of all of these options, the most important for configuring the look and feel of the Windows Sidebar are Properties and Close Sidebar. You'll find a detailed guide to using the Windows Sidebar in Chapter 6, but for now, we'll show how you switch it on and off and change its position on the desktop.

If you select Properties from the Windows Sidebar context menu, you'll see the screen shown in Figure 4-5.

Figure 4-5 *Use the Windows Sidebar's Properties screen to change its position on the desktop.*

If you select the checkbox Start Sidebar When Windows Starts, the Windows Sidebar will always start when you log in. It will automatically align itself to the right of the desktop; however, if you prefer it on the left (and you'll have to move any icons you currently have on the left side, or it will cover them), then you can select the Right radio button and click OK.

If you have more than one monitor (using multiple desktops or an extended desktop), you can decide which monitor should host the Windows Sidebar. Simply open the monitor number selector list, choose the number that corresponds to the monitor (from your Display Properties), and click OK.

From the Windows Sidebar context menu, selecting Close Sidebar will close the Windows Sidebar application, leaving you with an icon to start it in the Quick Launch toolbar. All you need to do to start it again is click the icon.

Customizing the Start Menu and Taskbar

Situated at the bottom of the screen is the Windows taskbar. This taskbar is like its Windows XP predecessor, acting as a dashboard to which you bolt on controls for quick access; however, you'll notice a few subtle differences between Vista and Windows XP.

Pinned to the left of the taskbar is the Vista Start button, replacing the old Windows XP Start button with this new Vista symbol.

To the immediate right of the Start button you'll see the Quick Launch toolbar. By default, three small icons represent Internet Explorer, Show Desktop, and Switch Between Windows. Clicking any of these icons will launch the associated application.

> **TIP** Selecting Switch Between Windows launches Flip 3D, usually accessed by pressing Windows Logo+Tab; however, the difference is that it will not return to the desktop until either you select a window with the mouse or the Enter key or you hit the Escape key.

If you want to add a new application icon to the Quick Launch toolbar, simply create a desktop shortcut for that application or folder (right-click the application or folder icon, and select Create Shortcut), and then drag the shortcut to the Quick Launch toolbar. You can reorder the icons on the Quick Launch toolbar by dragging them to the location you want them. The double arrow to the right side of the Quick Launch toolbar will expand the menu to include items not shown automatically in the limited space available. This way, you can have as many applications and folders as you need available through this toolbar.

To delete an icon from the Quick Launch toolbar, right-click it, and select Delete.

If you prefer (or plan to create some elaborate menu hierarchies), you can also manage the Quick Launch toolbar directly from the file system by clicking the double arrow symbol to the immediate right of the Quick Launch toolbar and then selecting Open Folder. This opens the folder shown in Figure 4-6.

Remember to add shortcuts here rather than files since the Quick Launch toolbar works on shortcuts only. Deleting shortcuts will immediately remove them from the Quick Launch toolbar.

Next, the taskbar (this part is usually blank when there are no minimized applications) has become a little more interactive than before. Any applications minimized to the taskbar now have the ability to display a thumbnail of the running application, known as a *taskbar thumbnail*.

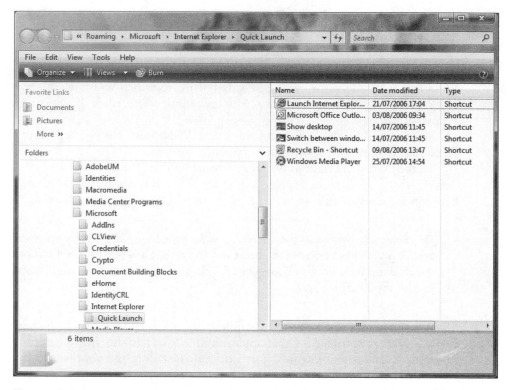

Figure 4-6 *You can customize the Quick Launch toolbar using shortcut icons stored in a folder.*

To modify the size and shape of the taskbar—for example, if you want more space for the Quick Launch toolbar or to make it double height for more minimized applications—right-click any piece of blank space, and uncheck Lock the Taskbar. You can now resize it vertically by dragging the top edge of the taskbar up, or you can resize it horizontally by using any of the dividers that separate each of the integrated toolbars.

> **TIP** Remember to lock the taskbar again when you have finished configuring it. This way you will not inadvertently change your taskbar without actively unlocking it again.

On the far right of the taskbar you'll see the *notification area*. This is composed of two different icon types: system icons and notification icons. You can configure which of the four available system icons appear here by right-clicking the taskbar, selecting Properties, and then switching to the Notification Area tab, as shown in Figure 4-7.

Figure 4-7 *Configure the notification area to display the system icons of your choice.*

You can switch on or off the clock, volume, network, and power system icons using the appropriate checkboxes, and if you want to modify how the rest of your icons are handled by the notification area, such as hiding them when they have not been used for a while, you can click Customize and then go through each one in turn, deciding from the drop-down list how each will be handled.

If you right-click the taskbar, select Properties, and then switch to the Taskbar tab, you have the following options available:

- Lock the Taskbar
- Auto-Hide the Taskbar
- Keep the Taskbar on Top of Other Windows
- Group Similar Taskbar Buttons
- Show Quick Launch
- Show Windows Previews (Thumbnails)

We've already discussed locking the toolbar, so we won't cover that again. Auto-hiding the taskbar drops the taskbar off the bottom of the screen, allowing the entire background image to be displayed. To access the taskbar, if you select Auto-Hide the Taskbar, you should point your cursor at the bottom of the screen. The taskbar will pop up and be usable whilst the cursor is hovering over it. If you decide you don't want the taskbar to be on top of other applications, you can uncheck Keep the Taskbar on Top of Other Windows. This means when you maximize a window, that windows will cover the taskbar. This can be somewhat annoying if you rely on the taskbar to navigate your system. Grouping taskbar buttons allows the taskbar to keep windows generated from the same application together as a group. In this way, for example, you can group all your Internet Explorer windows and subsequently close them together if you choose to do so. The taskbar icon for a group tells you how many windows of that type are open in that group. You can also switch off the Quick Launch toolbar if you don't use it by selecting Show Quick Launch, and if you really hate those new taskbar thumbnail images that keep popping up, you can switch those off, too.

Switching to the Toolbars tab, you can actually add more toolbars to your taskbar than are displayed by default. The toolbars available are as follows:

- Address
- Windows Media Player
- Links
- Tablet PC Input Panel
- Desktop
- Quick Launch

The Address toolbar docks a URL address entry textbox on the taskbar, allowing you to type in a URL. Internet Explorer will then open and go to that site.

If you select the Media Player MiniPlayer toolbar, Media Player turns into a miniature media control pad when you minimize the application. This is really useful!

The Links toolbar is an Internet Explorer function, and it allows you to drag a web page's icon from the Internet Explorer address bar to the Links toolbar to give you a desktop-based Internet favorites capability.

The Tablet PC Input Panel toolbar is useful when you are using a Tablet PC since it reveals the toolbar that allows quick access to the writing pad; however, you'll certainly need a digital inking device to see the benefit of this toolbar.

The Desktop toolbar is extremely useful in providing you with a collection of file- and system-related links, such as access to your profile folders, access to the network, or complete access all the Control Panel applets.

Finally, you yet again have the ability to control whether you see the Quick Launch toolbar.

Switching Through Windows

Everyone knows how to switch between windows using Alt+Tab, right? Every version of Windows since Windows 3.0 has had this ability built in, with Vista being no different. However, Microsoft has recognized that previous versions of Alt+Tab were somewhat less helpful than they could have been, and therefore Microsoft has improved the presentation of this function.

So, as with most features in Vista, an updated version of Alt+Tab, known as Flip, is now available in the high-end Vista systems that use the Windows Aero desktop. Flip comes in two forms, Flip and Flip 3D.

Using Flip

Flip is essentially a graphically enhanced version of the old Alt+Tab capability, whereby you are presented with a horizontal bar containing icons, with some informative text about each one displayed at the top as you cycle through them, as shown in Figure 4-8.

Figure 4-8 *Superficially, Flip appears similar to the old Alt+Tab functionality.*

The major improvement when using Flip is that you are no longer looking at meaningless static icons where you must rely on the text to help you make your decision; instead, you are now presented with the same horizontal list as before, but this time it comprises dynamic icons that present exactly what the running application is displaying. In this way, you can easily switch between one application window and another based on the window contents and not just a cryptic text reference.

Using Flip 3D

You'll find the improvement Flip brings to windows switching to be good, but taking the interface one stage further (and again showing off the wonderful new graphical capabilities Vista has to offer), you can use the enhanced window-switching capability known as Flip 3D, as shown in Figure 4-9.

Figure 4-9 *Flip 3D shows off Vista's graphical superiority with live dynamic content.*

To use Flip 3D functionality, press the Windows Logo key on your keyboard and simultaneously press the Tab key.

TIP You can lock both Flip and Flip 3D on the screen until you either select a window or press Escape to return to the desktop. For both key sequences, simply add the Ctrl button to lock the Flip or Flip 3D screen on your display (Alt+Ctrl+Tab or Windows Logo+Ctrl+Tab). If you lock Flip on the screen, you should use the arrow keys or mouse to select the window you are interested in and then press Enter or just click to activate it. If you lock Flip 3D on your screen, either use the arrow keys or the wheel on your mouse to select the desired window, and then press Enter or click to select it.

CHAPTER 5

Customizing Windows Vista

Getting the very best from the Vista interface depends largely on how your hardware and software drivers interact with each other. As long as you have compatible drivers and are using a Windows Display Driver Model (WDDM)–compliant graphics card, Vista will do the hard part for you. Nevertheless, you should be aware of a few options as a user for customizing your system, and this chapter will reveal those options to you.

Configuring the Windows Sidebar and Windows SideShow will allow you to further enhance the Vista experience; Windows SideShow works even when the system is shut down.

Finally, we'll take you on a tour around the local computer policy to show how you can configure exactly how your interface looks (this is a lot more granular than what is available from the standard interface settings dialog box), concentrating on your desktop configuration, the Start menu, and the taskbar.

Customizing Display Settings

Vista selects the best screen resolution, colors, and refresh rate available for your display when it's installed. However, sometimes these settings are not the best for use in your environment; for example, the highest screen resolution might make the text in your windows too small to read.

It's worth really getting to know the control you have over your display settings and knowing which options are available to help you better interact with the interface.

You can configure your display using the Display Settings dialog box, available by right-clicking the desktop, selecting Personalize from the context menu, and then selecting Display Settings (see Figure 5-1).

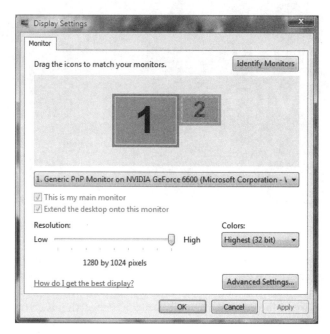

Figure 5-1 *Use Display Settings to change your screen resolutiom, colors, and refresh rate.*

You can control three main areas of functionality through this dialog box:

- Multiple monitor configurations
- Screen resolution and color
- Advanced settings related to drivers and troubleshooting

If you have two monitors connected to your system (common in docked laptop scenarios), you can perform two tasks: either you can extend your desktop to span both displays, effectively extending your desktop to cover both monitors, or alternatively, you can have both monitors show the same image. Having the image replicated on both screens can be useful if you are presenting to an audience and need one screen pointing outward and another pointing toward yourself.

To configure multiple monitors, you first need both your monitors and graphics cards connected, with the appropriate drivers installed to support them. Laptops tend to have a hardware interface on the connection panel to allow you to add an external screen alongside the laptop screen. If you have a desktop PC, you will more than likely (unless your current graphics card supports two monitors inherently) install a second graphics card to connect the additional monitor.

When you have both monitors up and running, to find out which monitor is which with regard to how Vista will be addressing them, click Identify Monitors at the top of the Display Settings dialog box. A large number will briefly appear on the screen showing you which monitor is which (see Figure 5-2).

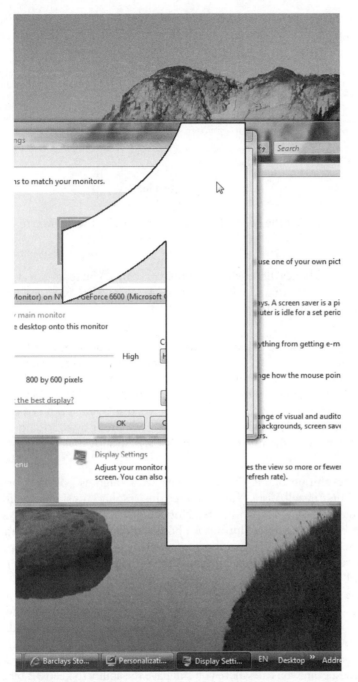

Figure 5-2 *Click the Identify Monitors button to help you recognize which monitor is which.*

Once you have both monitors installed, you can switch the displays by simply dragging the icon for monitor 2 to the left of monitor 1. If you do this when monitor 2 is disabled, you have the option of enabling it as a result of trying to reconfigure it. You will see the dialog box shown in Figure 5-3, which asks whether you want to enable monitor 2.

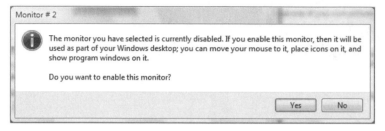

Figure 5-3 *Vista warns you that the second monitor is not enabled and offers to enable it for you.*

Using the two checkboxes beneath the monitor icons, you can select which monitor will be the main monitor and whether you'd like to have an extended desktop rather than two independent desktops.

> **NOTE** Extending the desktop effectively bolts the second display onto the right side of the first display. In this way, the Start menu and primary desktop icons remain on the left side of your main desktop, but you can now drag windows and applications off to the right and place them on the secondary display. Maximizing a window will expand the window to fill the monitor it is displayed in but not expand it to cover both desktops. You can switch the monitors' order by dragging the second monitor in front of the first one in the Display Settings dialog box.

By default, the resolution of the display will be set as high as possible for your hardware when you first install Vista. You can alter this resolution using the slider in the middle of the dialog box if you so desire. Notice, if you start moving the slider along the axis, Vista can set screen resolutions for both standard and widescreen aspect ratios. You should select settings that are most appropriate for the monitor type you are using—a widescreen setting will look squashed on a standard monitor, and a standard aspect ratio will look stretched on a widescreen monitor.

There is a subtle difference between the settings required for a CRT monitor and those required for an LCD monitor. LCD monitors have much better color-rendering capabilities and can display the highest color depth; however, both LCD and CRT monitors will require the color capability to be set to at least 32 bits to make sure you get all the effects Vista has to offer. To do this on a CRT monitor, adjust the screen resolution to the highest point you can where you still have the ability to keep 32-bit color.

Table 5-1 shows Microsoft's recommended screen resolution settings for a CRT monitor.

Table 5-1 Optimum Screen Resolution Based on the Screen Size of a CRT Monitor

Monitor Screen Size	Resolution
15-inch screen	1024×786 (or widescreen equivalent if necessary)
17- to 19-inch monitor	1280×1024 (or widescreen equivalent if necessary)
20-inch and bigger	1600×1200 (or widescreen equivalent if necessary)

Another consideration when adjusting your display settings is the refresh rate. The refresh rate is the frequency at which the image is redrawn on your monitor by the hardware. Some monitors may flicker as a result of the refresh rate being set too low. Modern monitors should be set to have a refresh rate of at least 75 Hertz (Hz) to make sure you eliminate flicker. If you are experiencing monitor flicker, check the refresh rate by right-clicking the monitor icon in the Display Settings dialog box and then selecting Properties. Next, click the Monitor tab to reveal the dialog box shown in Figure 5-4.

NOTE Because of the nature of how LCD monitors work, refresh rates are not an issue and should not come into the equation for optimizing your display settings.

Figure 5-4 *If you are experiencing monitor flicker, check the refresh rate.*

> **TIP** To see all the modes of operation available to you for your display, click Advanced Settings, and then on the General tab click List All Modes. This lists all the possible combinations of resolutions, colors, and refresh rates available for your hardware.

Further options for configuring your display are available when you click the Advanced Settings button at the bottom of the Display Settings dialog box, shown in Figure 5-5.

Figure 5-5 *Advanced Settings for configuring graphics adapter and troubleshooting problems*

On the Adapter tab, clicking the Properties button will open the graphics card properties dialog box. This is where you can examine or update the current driver; look for specific driver properties, such as hardware IDs and the hardware bus number; and find the resources the device uses in memory.

As we mentioned, clicking the Monitor tab will reveal the current screen refresh rate and allow you to change this from a drop-down list. Clicking Properties on this tab will open the monitor driver properties dialog box where you can examine or update the current driver and view its properties.

If you click Troubleshoot, you have the opportunity to run through some helpful diagnostics that try to determine why your setup is not performing as you would expect.

Finally, clicking the Color Management tab offers a single button called Color Management, which in turn opens the Color Management dialog box shown in Figure 5-6.

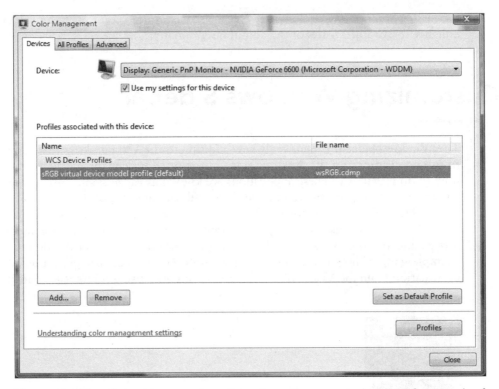

Figure 5-6 *The Color Management dialog box allows you to best configure color for each device.*

You can use color management to ensure that color is as best represented on an output device as it can be, irrespective of whether that device is a monitor or a printer. The characteristics of the color as shown on the monitor are different from those on a printer, fundamentally because of the different process used to generate the color. The bottom line is, the resultant color we expect to see has to be identical. However, without ensuring that color is managed and adapted for each device to maintain consistency, the same image composed of the same digital information would appear differently on each device to which it's sent.

To help, you can use *color profiles* in Vista to map color characteristics of a particular device to the color expected to be generated from the digital image information. Mapping these color profiles allows each device to adjust itself in such a way as to ensure consistency across hardware platforms. When a new device is installed on your system, a color profile is usually included with the installation.

Most of the time you won't have any reason to mess around with color profiles since they are specific to devices and are added by the manufacturer to ensure the best color rendition by its device. If a color profile is badly conceived, then no one will buy the product—or you'll be pretty quick to get your money back.

The only time you might need to modify color profiles is in an environment where you are working with specialized equipment, such as commercial photographic processing and printing equipment; you can use customized color profiles to change or enhance the characteristics of the output intentionally.

Customizing Windows Sidebar

The Windows Sidebar is that lovely new addition to the Vista desktop that allows you to run applications on the desktop, much in the same way as the old Active Desktop used to do previously. These applications are known as *gadgets*, and Vista comes with a whole bunch of them for you to configure and use right out of the box.

Gadgets, like the one shown in Figure 5-7, are small, functionally specific applications that you can use to bring some application integration into the immediate foreground of your working environment by presenting them on the desktop. The example gadget shown in Figure 5-7 is an RSS feed gadget that picks up RSS feed information from the Vista RSS Feed Store (configured using Internet Explorer).

Figure 5-7 *You can easily bolt gadgets, such as this one displayng RSS feeds, onto the Sidebar.*

> **NOTE** Really Simple Syndication (RSS) feeds are subscription news feeds that push information to interested parties. RSS has really taken off on the Internet, and many, many web sites provide feeds. Vista has embraced this new technology and integrated it into its heart.

To see the full list of gadgets available to you in Vista, right-click anywhere on the Sidebar (even on another gadget if you want to), and select Add Gadgets from the menu. You are then presented with a complete list of all available gadgets, as shown in Figure 5-8.

Table 5-2 shows a brief description of these default gadgets.

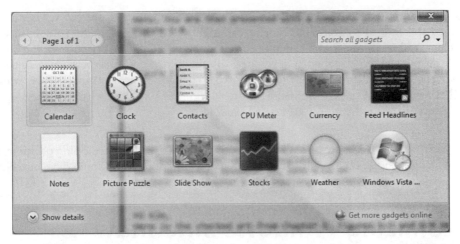

Figure 5-8 *Add any of the default gadgets that come with Vista to the Sidebar.*

Table 5-2 Default Gadgets That Come with Vista

Gadget Name	Description	Requires an Internet Connection?
Calendar	Offers a simple view of the date on an easy-to-read calendar	No
Clock	Displays the time on a traditional clock face	No
Contacts	Displays contact information sources from Windows Mail	No
CPU Meter	Tells you how hard your processor is working	No
Currency	Converts one currency into another	Yes
Feed Headlines	Displays data from the RSS Feed Store in Internet Explorer	Not directly but relies on feeds from Internet Explorer
Notes	Displays sticky notes for the desktop	No
Picture Puzzle	Provides a desktop game where you rearrange a jumbled picture	No
Recycle Bin	Provides a desktop control for emptying the Recycle Bin	No
Slide Show	Displays a slide show of pictures in your gallery	No
Stocks	Reports on your favorite stocks	Yes
Weather	Shows the latest weather based on your postal code	Yes
Windows Vista Countdown	Shows the number of days until retail launch	No

Adding gadgets to the Sidebar is as easy as dragging it from the Gadget Gallery onto the Sidebar. Alternatively, you can right-click the gadget of your choice, and select Add from the context menu.

New gadgets are being developed all the time, and the best ones appear on Microsoft's Windows Live Galley web site. To get a look at what gadgets are available, click Get More Gadgets Online. This opens Internet Explorer with the Windows Live Gallery web site: http://gallery.microsoft.com.

> **TIP** If you are a software developer and are interested in developing gadgets, start by looking at http://microsoftgadgets.com for a primer and some development tips.

Customizing Windows SideShow

Another new technology to ship with Vista is something called Windows SideShow. This enables laptop OEMs to include an auxiliary display on the outside of a device and allow data to be pumped from the operating system to that display without the user having to search for the data. In this way, users can be alerted about new email, for example, and then examine them without having to open the laptop and power on the screen. This technology saves portable device battery time (you don't have to power cycle the device to check your email—it's telling *you* when you should be looking).

So, where does the SideShow display get its information from? This is the clever part. Gadgets developed for the Windows Sidebar can be exploited by these auxiliary displays, and in the same way that a gadget delivers information to the Vista desktop, information can be directed to a SideShow display. This means as long as you have an appropriate gadget to do the job, all those share prices, RSS feeds, and contacts that you usually have to open the laptop to check are right there on the outside casing of the system. Neat, huh?

> **CAUTION** Gadgets developed specifically for the Windows Sidebar will not work with SideShow, although the concept of gadgets in both cases is the same. You need to obtain SideShow-enabled gadgets that provide the services you require.

Vista comes with two default SideShow gadgets, and we envisage that OEMs will develop many more over time depending on the PC package they are offering. The two SideShow gadgets that come with Vista are as follows:

- Windows Mail gadget for reading messages in your inbox
- Windows Media Player gadget for listening to media files

If you happen to install a Sidebar gadget that you can also use on a SideShow auxiliary display, you need to switch on the gadget using the Control Panel as follows:

1. Click the Start button, and then select Control Panel.
2. Select Windows Sideshow from the list of items.
3. Enable the appropriate gadget for the device.

> **NOTE** If you have enabled a Sidebar gadget to display information about a Side-Show-enabled device, you must keep the gadget active in the Sidebar. Removing the gadget from the Sidebar will remove the capability from the SideShow device, and you will have to set it up again through the Windows SideShow Control Panel interface.

So, the big question is, how does it keep information current when the computer is sleeping? Simple! It doesn't. Instead, Vista will periodically wake up and update itself, push any updates to the SideShow device, and then pop back off to sleep. This is a lot less power hungry than you switching on the monitor, opening your applications, and searching for the information yourself.

> **CAUTION** SideShow can wake your system up and obtain up-to-date information only if Vista is asleep. You need to leave the system logged in and hibernated for this to work. If you have logged out or completed a full system shutdown, SideShow will not function.

Customizing with the Local Computer Policy

The foundation of all configuration in Vista is the same as that of its predecessor, Windows XP, where real customizing was possible only when you lifted the hood and got down into the engine.

To start you in the right direction, the following sections give you a brief overview of what the local computer policy is all about.

How the Local Computer Policy Relates to the Registry

On every Windows computer since Windows NT, there has been a configuration database known as the *registry*. The registry came about as a direct result of the difficulty network administrators had in controlling the disparate set of configuration files they needed to tamper with in the old days of Windows 3.11.

In this legacy environment, every application and operating system had a specific initialization and configuration file that contained all the information about its function in the environment.

As the Windows operating system became more complex and the number of these configuration files grew exponentially, specific system files, such as `system.ini` and `win.ini`, outgrew the maximum size limit of 64KB. It became extremely difficult to keep control over what was going on with every application and system service, and administrators ended up with a virtually impossible task.

So, to make things easier, Microsoft introduced a new way of centralizing the control of both applications and the operating system when Windows NT came along, collapsing all the stand-alone configuration into a central store known as the *registry*.

This meant administrators had to look in only one place when they needed to configure any aspect of their system's functionality.

Vista is no different from any of its predecessors with the registry still sitting right at the heart of configuration and control. Take a look at Figure 5-9 for an example of what the registry looks like.

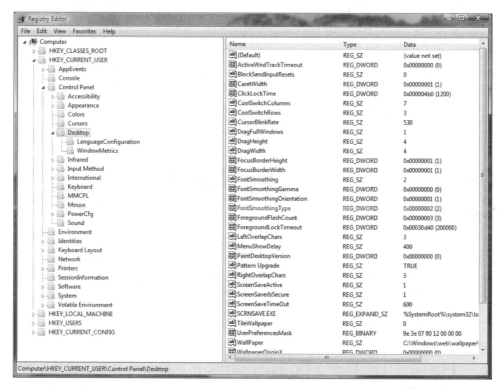

Figure 5-9 *The registry is much easier to navigate than separate configuration files.*

To look inside the registry, you can use a tool known as the Registry Editor, available if you use the Run (Windows Logo+R) dialog box, type **regedit.exe,** and press Enter.

So the registry was the first step (and believe it or not, it was a giant leap forward) toward a better way of operating and controlling your Windows system, but there were still one or two drawbacks:

- It was still devilishly complicated to understand with many megabytes of configuration data ending up under one roof.

- Keys and values (the configuration items contained within the registry) did not obviously correlate to the associated resultant change to the system when altered—it was fairly obscure terminology.

- Much of the data in the registry was composed of numerical switches, and the range of available values was not immediately available without either experimenting or contacting the software designers who wrote it.

- In some cases, you could alter the default functionality in an application, but the only way to do this was through the introduction of new registry keys that were not installed with the application by default.

From these four problems evolved the concept of a computer policy. A *computer policy* in Windows terms is a plain-English version of the registry (not the whole thing, just the bits we as users or administrators are interested in), and a policy is used to adapt the contents of the registry. If you first refer to Figure 5-9 and then look next at Figure 5-10, you'll see the difference between looking directly into the registry database and using a computer policy.

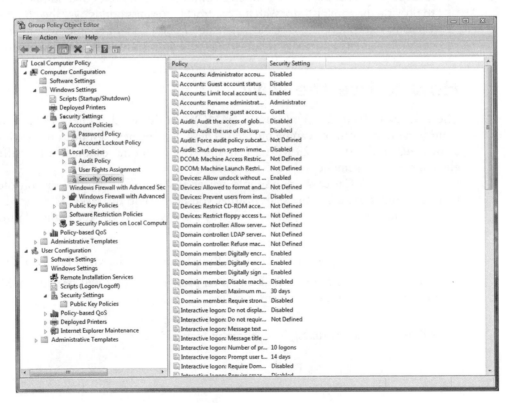

Figure 5-10 *A computer policy is a plain-English mapping of the registry database.*

So now, configuring Windows is much easier. Users and administrators alike have a plain-English route into the registry database that allows them to make decisions and configuration changes to Vista without having to navigate the database.

Local Policy vs. Domain Policy

Policy is policy, wherever it's applied from, but the difference between a policy applied locally compared to that of a policy applied from a Windows domain is that a local policy is controlled, modified, and responsible only for touching the registry on the computer upon which it is configured. A domain policy, on the other hand, is dished out by *domain controllers* (the big server systems that sit at the heart of a Windows server–based network) and is used to centrally apply a policy to groups of computers under its control. However, the settings (except for a few specific to the system operating in this domain environment) are largely the same, and in the few examples you'll look at here, they are identical.

> **NOTE** If you start looking further into policies and how they work, it's worth bearing in mind that domain policies always, and we mean *always*, take precedence over local policies. A domain policy, when a computer is a member of a domain, is there to provide the administrator with the control his business needs over the computers. The only exception to this rule is when a computer cannot contact a domain controller and a local policy differs from a previously enforced domain setting.

How to Use the MMC

The Microsoft Management Console (MMC) is a universal framework into which management applications can be plugged. These management applications are known as *snap-ins*, and Vista has 28 MMC snap-ins, with each one responsible for different elements of management and configuration.

Using the MMC is easy; it's a simple matter of starting the framework console and then selecting, from a list, the snap-ins that you need to do the tasks.

This short guide shows you how to create a custom MMC for manipulating the local computer policy:

1. Press Windows Logo+R to expose the Run dialog box, shown in Figure 5-11.

2. Type **mmc** in the text entry field, and then press Enter. This will start the MMC framework without any snap-ins installed.

3. Click the File menu, and then select Add/Remove Snap-in. This will open the Add or Remove Snap-ins dialog box shown in Figure 5-12.

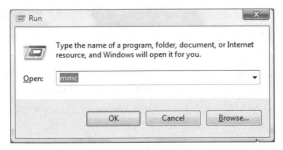

Figure 5-11 *Start the MMC framework application from the Run dialog box.*

Figure 5-12 *When the MMC first starts, it has no snap-ins installed.*

4. The MMC framework is blank (see Figure 5-13) and needs the appropriate snap-in to be installed for managing the local computer policy.

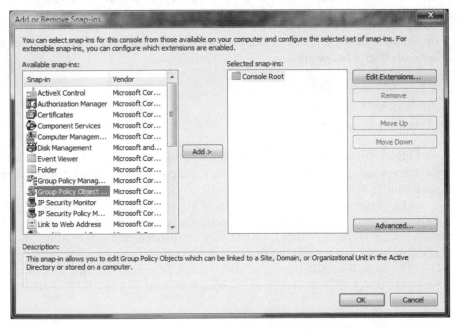

Figure 5-13 *Select the snap-in you need from the list, and then click Add.*

5. From the left column, select the Group Policy Object snap-in, and then click Add.

6. When you see the Select Group Policy Object Wizard stating that the Group Policy Object is Local Computer, click the Finish button.

7. You are now returned to the Add or Remove Snap-in dialog box where you should now see Local Computer Policy added to the right column. Click OK.

8. You are now returned to the MMC, and the Local Computer Policy snap-in is now available in the left column under Console Root (see Figure 5-14).

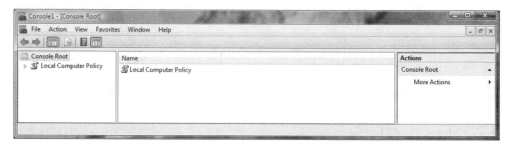

Figure 5-14 *The snap-in is now added to the MMC and is ready for use.*

If you want to save your newly created console, you can click the File menu and save the console with the Local Computer Policy snap-in already added. This is a custom MMC and will have the file extension of `.msc`.

How to Use the Local Computer Policy

Using the MMC, expand Local Computer Policy, and then expand the User Configuration node on the left side of the console. You'll notice that there are three subnodes beneath User Configuration:

- Software Settings
- Windows Settings
- Administrative Templates

The Software Settings subnode contains information specific to applications that have been installed on your system. There is a good chance that none of these appears on a vanilla Vista installation.

The Windows Settings node contains Microsoft-specific information for controlling Vista, such as scripting information for login and logout, security settings for policy such as the approach to public key certificates, and information about printers and Internet Explorer settings.

Although interesting and certainly worth browsing (try not to change anything that you don't fully understand) is Administrative Templates, which you'll look at here. You might be wondering why we've veered away from covering desktop settings and customizing the interface, but really, we haven't. All this buildup with the MMC is to show you the most powerful set of tools available for the fine-grained configuration of your system that you have available: the local computer policy's administrative templates.

Right, this is it. Expand Administrative Templates; expand Control Panel, as shown in Figure 5-15; and then highlight Display. Now, in the right column, you can set the screen-saver timeout. This new policy value will override whatever was previously set in the interface.

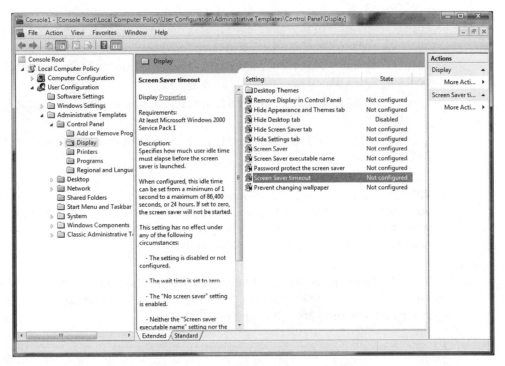

Figure 5-15 *Configuring your screen-saver timeout using the local computer policy*

Double-click the Screen Saver Timeout setting to reveal the properties box for that particular policy setting. In the resulting dialog box, you'll see that this policy setting is currently set to Not Configured. The other two options are Enabled and Disabled.

If a policy setting is set to Not Configured, this does not mean it doesn't do anything; instead, it means that the local computer policy overlay will not do anything to the corresponding registry setting when it is applied the next time you log in. If you enable or disable the policy setting, these actions are explicitly taken when you log in, and this is set in the policy.

CAUTION You should be sure to read the description of the policy setting in full and be especially attentive to the context of positive or negative action being taken as a result of the policy being applied. For example, if the policy says "Hide Desktop tab" and you enable it, this will actively remove the Desktop tab when you next log in.

Settings that really affect the look and feel and availability of desktop items are under the following policy paths:

- `Local Computer Policy/User Configuration/Administrative Templates/ Control Panel`

- `Local Computer Policy/User Configuration/Administrative Templates/ Control Panel/Add Remove Programs`

- `Local Computer Policy/User Configuration/Administrative Templates/ Control Panel/Display`

- `Local Computer Policy/User Configuration/Administrative Templates/ Desktop`

- `Local Computer Policy/User Configuration/Administrative Templates/ Start Menu and Taskbar`

TIP For local computer policy changes, remember that for a change to take effect, you must log out and back in again. When you log in, the policy is applied to create your session, so to make sure your session is affected in the right way by your change, you need to log out and then log back in.

The local computer policy is specific for each user who logs into the system. When you look in the registry, `HKEY_CURRENT_USER` contains the keys and values that the local computer policy settings are modifying (see Figure 5-16).

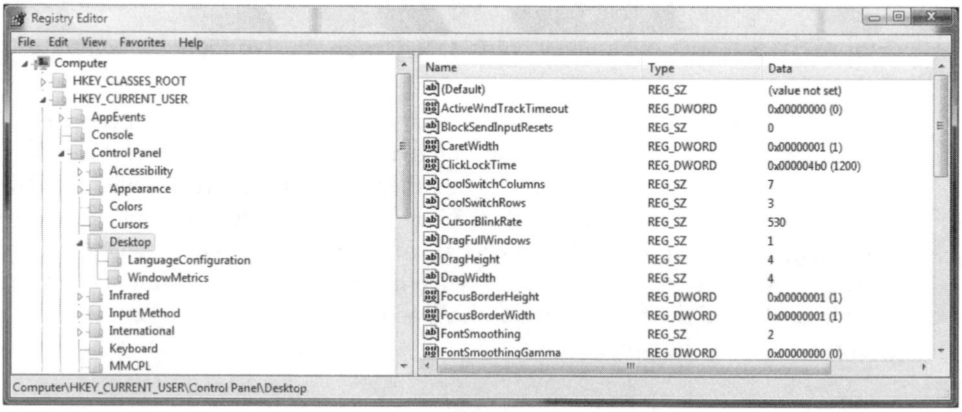

Figure 5-16 *The registry contains the superset of all configuration items set by policy.*

When users log in to Vista, their specific registry settings are loaded from a different set of keys and values unique to them from beneath HKEY_USERS; then when the user logs off, part of the logoff process is to copy the HKEY_CURRENT_USER settings back into the store under HKEY_USERS. When another user logs in, their own unique settings are copied to HKEY_CURRENT_USER, and this set of keys and values is then used to create that user's environment. In this way, each user remains unique, and the policy is applied correctly and in some cases differently, depending on which user it is that logs in.

We hope this short tour around the local computer policy wasn't too grueling for you, but no matter—most of the time you won't have to do any of this, because usually everything you need for customizing Vista is available right there in the interface.

CHAPTER 6

Working with User Tools

When you first log in to Vista, you'll see a bare desktop aside from a couple of familiar icons, such as the Recycle Bin, and you'll also see the Windows Sidebar on the right side of the screen.

By way of introducing itself, Vista opens what's called the *Welcome Center* to offer new Vista users quick and easy access to the most commonly used and exploited features and tasks within the operating system.

This chapter covers the features and tasks available through the Welcome Center and then goes into more depth on the new and improved features of the Start menu and Windows Explorer.

Exploring the Welcome Center

The Welcome Center, shown in Figure 6-1, is a useful portal to the most commonly used features of Vista that are not immediately accessible through the Start menu (although it soon becomes apparent that they are not hard to find even without the Welcome Center).

When you first see the Welcome Center, take note of the opt-out checkbox in the bottom-left corner. Once you become more familiar with Vista and no longer need the Welcome Center to appear every time you log in, uncheck this box.

> **NOTE** If you stop the Welcome Center from opening automatically on login, you can always access it again at any time in the future through the Start menu (Start ➤ All Programs ➤ Accessories ➤ Welcome Center).

Figure 6-1 *The Welcome Center appears each time you log in to Vista.*

If you click Show All 14 Items, you'll see eight more tasks and utilities made available through the Welcome Center interface. Table 6-1 discusses the features.

Table 6-1 Features and Tasks Accessible Through the Welcome Center

Feature	Description
View Computer Details	This opens the Control Panel ➤ System applet where you can view basic information about your PC, including the Windows Experience Index, covered in Chapter 2.
Transfer Files and Settings	Use this feature to import files and settings from another computer, covered in detail in Chapter 3.
Add New Users	This runs the User Account Control Panel ➤ Manage Accounts feature where you can add accounts to your local system and modify them. This feature is not available if Vista is a member of a Windows domain.
Connect to the Internet	This runs a wizard that will help you get your PC connected to the Internet.
Windows Ultimate Extras	This is a fast link to the Windows Ultimate Extras online web site where Microsoft publishes new software and services especially for Ultimate SKU users.

Table 6-1 Features and Tasks Accessible Through the Welcome Center *(Continued)*

Feature	Description
What's New in Windows Vista	This starts Windows Help and Support in the What's New section.
Personalize Windows	From here you can modify settings such as appearance, sounds, and mouse pointers. We cover this personalization in Chapter 4 and Chapter 5.
Register Windows Online	This connects online to Microsoft to allow you to register your copy of Vista.
Windows Media Center	This is a shortcut to start the Windows Media Center entertainment software.
Windows Basics	This starts Windows Help and Support, focused on an introductory page to all the basic Vista functionality.
Ease of Access Center	This starts the Control Panel applet called Ease of Access Center where you can adjust an accessibility option for the hearing or visually impaired.
Back Up and Restore Center	This starts the much improved system backup facility in Vista.
Windows Vista Demos	For the new Vista user, these video demonstrations are well worth watching in full.
Control Panel	This is the main portal for all system administration and configuration tasks.

In the lower half of the Welcome Screen you'll notice the Offers from Microsoft heading. Microsoft uses this section of the Welcome Center to advertise new software or services Microsoft has to offer its users, such as free services covered by the Windows Live initiative.

Understanding the Start Menu

If you've been around Microsoft operating systems for a long time, you'll probably get the hang of the Start menu pretty quickly. It looks, at first glance, like not much has changed; however, you should be aware of a few small improvements to its functionality so you can get the most out of these changes. Figure 6-2 shows the new look of the Start menu.

Figure 6-2 *The Vista Start menu builds on the success of its predecessor.*

In general, the layout of the Start menu is much like that of Windows XP (why fix what isn't broken?), with familiar Internet and E-mail shortcuts in the topmost section on the left side—these icons start Internet Explorer and Windows Mail, respectively.

> **TIP** You can "pin" new applications to the Start menu in the same way as Internet Explorer and Windows Mail by creating a shortcut to the application, right-clicking the shortcut, and then selecting Pin to Start Menu. Selecting Add to Quick Launch will add the icon to the Quick Launch toolbar.

Beneath the Internet and E-mail icons is a dynamically produced list of applications that you have most recently accessed. As you progressively start using applications in Vista, this list will change and reorder itself based on the frequency that you access these applications. The most recently accessed applications will appear at the bottom of the list, progressively moving their way up until they drop off the top.

Similar to this process of displaying recently used applications, the Start menu also records any files you have recently accessed, making these immediately available beneath the Recent Items menu on the right side of the menu, known as the Start panel. This is particularly useful because it prevents you from having to navigate in Windows Explorer to files you often access. To clear the items stored in the Recent Items menu, right-click Recent Items, and then select Clear Recent Items List.

> **TIP** You can disable the Start menu's ability to remember the applications and files you have recently accessed if you are worried about your privacy. This might be sensible if the computer is a shared system and you are working on sensitive information. To disable either or both of these capabilities, right-click the Start menu button, and then select Properties. Under the Privacy section, uncheck Store and Display a List of Recently Opened Files, and uncheck Store and Display a List of Recently Opened Programs.

Vista introduces a new way of navigating from one folder to another, whereby the Start menu remains contained within the Programs list on the left side when you drill down through the various options. If you click All Programs, for example, the list of applications and subfolders appears within this section of the menu rather than sprawling across the screen to the right as it did in Windows XP. To return to the previous menu, click Back. Each time you click a new folder, the folder contents appear in this panel of the Start menu; and in each case, clicking Back returns you to the previous menu.

The Search box, at the bottom of the Start menu on the left side, is also new for Vista. When you start typing in the Search box, Vista immediately begins to look within the context of the Start menu for items you want to find. For example, if you type **Con**, you'll notice that you get results for Backup Status and Configuration, Control Panel, Contacts, and more. If you continue typing, getting to **Contr**, you'll see the search has narrowed to return only two entries, Control Panel and Parental Controls. This search feature makes it really easy to find Start menu items that may be buried inside a deep folder hierarchy that takes time to navigate.

> **TIP** If you are looking for a file rather than a Start menu application, you can still get to it using the Start menu search facility by typing your query in the Search box and then clicking See All Results. This will open a Windows Explorer window and perform a complete file system search against your query.

The icon on the top-right side of the menu represents the logged-in user (selected when you created the user account) but is dynamic and will change to reflect the Start menu option your mouse is hovering over when you move over the items in the Start panel. Try hovering over the Documents or Games item to see what happens. Neat, isn't it?

Immediately beneath the user/feature icon you'll see the name of the logged-in user (clicking this will open Windows Explorer focused on the user's profile directory). Documents, Pictures, and Music will drill into the respective user's profile folders for those categories, while Game, as you'd expect, opens the Games folder in Windows Explorer, as shown in Figure 6-3.

Figure 6-3 *Clicking Games from the Start panel opens the Games folder in Windows Explorer.*

You can grant access to configuration utilities and system management functions through the Control Panel, which you open by clicking the Control Panel item in the Start panel. The other default items listed on the Start panel are as follows:

- Search opens the full Windows Explorer–based search facility so you can search your entire system.

- Computer shows you a graphical Windows Explorer view of the top-level disk drives available on your system, allowing you to drill down into the contents of each in turn, as shown in Figure 6-4.

- Network provides a view of all the computers and devices connected to your local area network.

- Connect To opens the Connect to a Network Wizard, which allows you to create new wired or wireless connections.

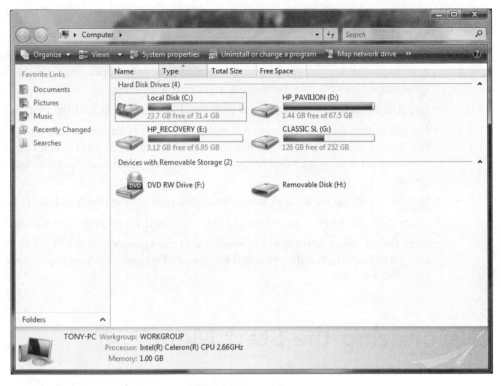

Figure 6-4 *Clicking Computer in the Start panel reveals a top-level view of system disk drives.*

- Default Programs allows you to change the applications to file extensions mappings, change your AutoPlay settings (for CDs, DVDs, or removable media), and set access controls on certain programs to limit their use.

- Help and Support starts the Windows Help and Support Center much like it did in previous versions of Windows, but Help and Support is now dramatically better than before with video demonstrations, walk-throughs, and direct access to online Help resources.

Finally, the options available for locking and powering off your computer are increased from the two available with Windows XP to include the new Vista Sleep mode, putting the system into a low power state yet still retaining system configuration and user state. Clicking the padlock (see Figure 6-5) will keep the user session active even though the system will present a username and password request to continue working after the system has been locked.

Figure 6-5 *Quickly place Vista in a Sleep state using the power icon.*

Other power and logout options are available by clicking the expand arrow to the right of the padlock. These are as follows:

- Switch User quickly switches from one logged-in user to another without the first user having to log out. This option is available only in Workgroup mode and is disabled when Vista is a member of a Windows domain.

- Log Off saves the user's profile to disk and logs the user out of the system.

- Lock retains the user session yet forces the user to log in again to access the system. If a system is locked, other regular users cannot log in; however, you can use an administrative account to force the session to close and allow the administrator to log in.

- Restart Power cycles the computer, closing the user session down and then rebooting.

- Sleep puts Vista into a power-saving state where the user session is still active.

- Shut Down closes down the user session and then powers off the PC. The PC will not automatically restart—you will be required to press the power-on button on your PC's chassis.

Customizing the Start Menu

You can add, remove, and modify practically everything you can see on the Start menu to best suit your own working arrangements. Start by right-clicking the Start menu and then selecting Properties. Click the Start Menu tab, and then click the Customize button next to Start Menu. You'll see the dialog box shown in Figure 6-6.

> **NOTE** If you really can't stand using the new Start menu layout, you can revert to the Windows XP version by right-clicking the Start button, selecting Properties, selecting the Start Menu tab, and then selecting Classic Start Menu.

The configuration interface is really easy to use, and as long as you know the difference between the following options, you can't go far wrong:

- Display As a Link is the default option for the majority of Start menu items, with the exception of Recent Items. Display As a Link makes the Start menu item in question open the appropriate Windows Explorer–style view for that item. In this way, clicking the Computer link, for example, will open the view shown in Figure 6-7.

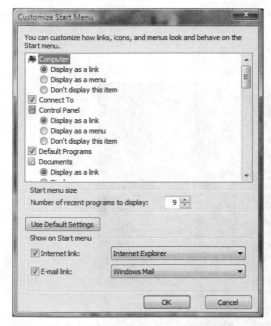

Figure 6-6 *Customize the Start menu to best suit your needs.*

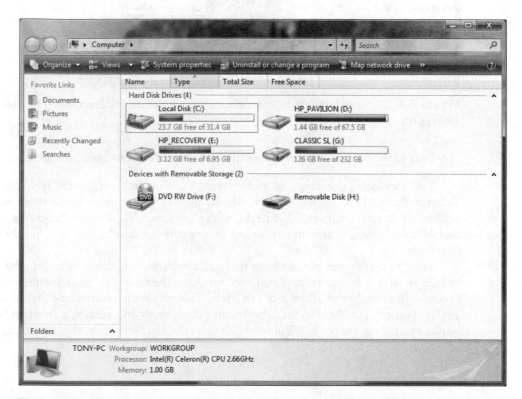

Figure 6-7 *When Start menu items are configured as links, they open Explorer-style windows.*

- On the other hand, opting to select Display As a Menu will offer you an extended menu off the Start menu that you can use to further drill into the option, as shown in the same Computer example in Figure 6-8.

Figure 6-8 *Displaying the item as a menu further extends the Start menu to display item content.*

- Don't Display This Item removes this item from the Start menu altogether.

You can configure many of the default Start menu items, such as Computer, Control Panel, Documents, Games, Music, and Pictures, using these three simple options. You can configure other items, such as Connect To, Default Programs, Help, and Network, simply as being on or off by selecting or deselecting the checkbox for that item.

You can set the number of recent programs to display, with the default being nine. If you regularly use more applications and want them on the Start menu, you can increase this number to allow more to cycle through the menu dynamically, or if you prefer, you can pin them to the Start menu permanently by creating a shortcut to the application (anywhere in Windows Explorer), right-clicking the shortcut, and selecting Pin To Start Menu.

TIP To remove an item from the Start menu that you've previously pinned there, right-click the item in question (on the Start menu), and then click Unpin from Start Menu.

Clicking Use Default Settings resets the Start menu to how it was when you first installed Vista.

Lastly, you can switch off the Internet and E-mail icons that are pinned to the Start menu by default by deselecting the checkboxes next to the appropriate item. The drop-down lists next to these items allow you to configure alternative Internet browser clients or email clients should you not be using the Vista defaults.

Finally, for all you enthusiasts who regularly use the Run command as a shortcut to starting applications, by default it's gone. Microsoft obviously thinks this Start menu command, for most users, is unnecessary; however, you can easily get it back, along with the Printers shortcut and Favorites menu, by checking the appropriate checkbox in the list.

NOTE You can still use Windows logo+R to start the Run dialog box.

Working with Windows Explorer

One of the most fundamental changes, and probably the one to confuse people the most, is the new look of Windows Explorer. Vista has completely changed the way it handles files and folders in order to make the interface more natural and ergonomic.

Having now dropped the *My* prefix from personal profile folders, you are left with the list shown in Figure 6-9.

Although Vista, under the hood, still uses the same folder naming structure that Windows XP used, the view you get through Windows Explorer has been abstracted away from the physical folder layout to better help you organize and group information in a more natural way.

In the following sections, we'll show the basic interface and how you can change how items appear within Window Explorer. To start Windows Explorer, right-click the Start menu button, and then choose Explore from the context menu.

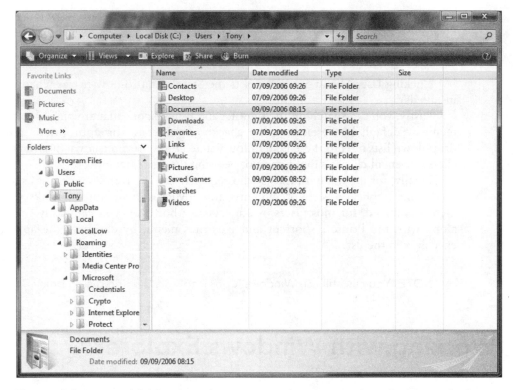

Figure 6-9 *Personal folders have been renamed in Vista to drop the* My *prefix from Windows XP.*

Following the Breadcrumb Navigation

At the top of the screen, you'll see the address bar. As you move from folder to folder, the address bar reflects each choice you've made so you can easily see exactly how you got there and what the parent folders are called. This information is known as a *breadcrumb trail*, named after the trail of breadcrumbs left by Hansel and Gretel to help find their way out of the forest when they were abandoned by their wicked stepmother. You can follow the breadcrumbs to find your way out of the file system.

You can click any of the breadcrumbs in the trail to instantly switch to that folder, and if you click the drop-down arrow next to a breadcrumb, you will see all the available subfolders beneath that folder.

> **NOTE** To see the physical path a folder lives in, click the down arrow to the far right of the address bar to reveal the absolute path, in the format `c:\folder`.

This breadcrumb navigation technique allows you to quickly get to a folder location without having to navigate up and down through hierarchies of folders to find the location you need. In this way, navigation is both vertical and horizontal and opens the file system up to lightning-fast navigation once you get the hang of it.

You can navigate back and forward through your selection history using the left and right arrows to the left of the address bar, much in the same way as you navigate through your web page history in Internet Explorer.

Using the Task Pane

Immediately beneath the address bar sits the Task pane. This is a dynamically configured set of options available for the folder Windows Explorer is focused upon at the time. For example, if you are viewing the contents of the Pictures folder in your profile, you'll see the Task pane shown in Figure 6-10. If you are viewing the Music folder in your profile, you'll see the Task pane shown in Figure 6-11.

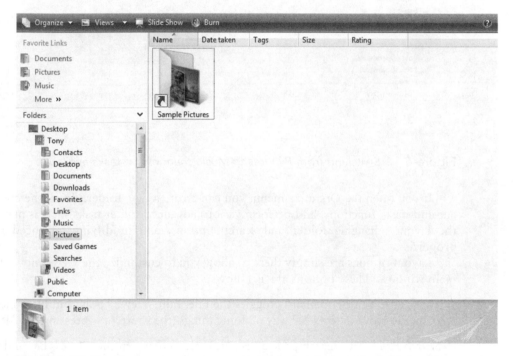

Figure 6-10 *The Task pane changes options depending on the folder contents.*

> **TIP** If you miss the old menus of File, Edit, View, Tools, and Help as they used to appear in Windows XP, you can press the Alt key to have these appear immediately beneath the address bar. Pressing the Alt key again hides them.

Although some of these options change depending on the folder content, such as the Slide Show application available in Pictures and the Play All and Burn options in the Music folder, all folders have the Organize and Views options available.

Figure 6-11 *Switching from Pictures to Music changes the tasks available.*

If you open the Organize menu, you can create a new folder, do all the common cut-and-paste functions, and perform various advanced folder tasks such as managing the layout, changing folder and search options, and modifying advanced folder properties.

Layout options are simply there to allow you to customize the views shown in the main window. These options are as follows:

Menu Bar: This permanently toggles the File, Edit, View, Tools, and Help menus from the old Windows XP way of doing things (the shortcut is pressing the Alt key).

Search Pane: The Search pane adds a new menu between the address bar and the Task pane for advanced searching.

Details Pane: This opens an area at the bottom of Windows Explorer that reports metadata details about files and folders if it finds any. To see a good example of this kind of metadata, select pictures or music files in the main window, as shown in Figure 6-12.

Preview Pane: The Preview pane displays videos, images, cover art for music, and even the first page of text from within documents.

Navigation Pane: The Navigation pane is a tree view of your files and folders shown on the left side of the screen.

Figure 6-12 *The Details pane shows metadata information pertinent to the selected file.*

If you click Folders and Search Options in the Organize menu, you'll be presented with a new configuration dialog box (much like the Tools ➤ Folder Options dialog box in Windows XP) where you can modify how folders are presented and what information is imparted about them.

> **TIP** A useful addition available through the Folder Options dialog box is Use Check Boxes to Select Items. Switching this feature on places a column of checkboxes to the left side of your files; you can use these checkboxes to select multiple and noncontiguous files in the same way you would have held down the Ctrl key and clicked each file individually. The improvement means it's now harder to mess up what you've selected since it's a matter of simply scrolling down the file list and checking what you're interested in—not having to keep the Ctrl key pressed during the entire operation.

On the General tab you can opt to switch on classic folders, transforming the new look of Vista back into something more akin to Windows XP. You can configure how new folders are handled, either opening in a new window or opening within the existing window. You also have the option of changing how mouse clicks are handled, with single-click or double-click options depending on whether you prefer the hyperlink approach or the more familiar double-click style used in Windows XP.

On the View tab, you can configure a whole variety of settings that describe exactly what will and will not be presented to the user within the context of the Windows Explorer window. Many users like to switch on Show Hidden Files and Folders to get a better idea of exactly what's installed on their systems.

On the Search tab you'll find options for defining exactly what's indexed by default in Vista—generally all documents in the Documents folders for each user and their respective email libraries—with the most comprehensive search options of indexing all files and content not being the default. If you do a lot of work on documentation, you should consider turning this option on and allowing Vista to catalog your entire system. This will undoubtedly help you locate content that may be buried inside any number of disparate files.

Clicking the Properties option in the Organize menu will expose the general Folder Properties dialog box where you can access more advanced options for folder encryption and compression; define the type of content the folder holds, such as pictures and videos or documents (on the Customize tab); and set the access control and share settings for securing the file system.

The second menu common across all folders is Views. If you open this one and take a look at what you can do, you'll immediately see the point of this menu item is to allow you to change the size of the file details shown in the main window. This ranges from the more traditional views of Tiles, Details, List, and Small Icons to the graphically enhanced Medium through Extra Large icons, which, in the same way as taskbar thumbnails work, dynamically show some of the contents of the folder or a preview of the file contents.

Searching in Windows Explorer

You can search in two ways within Windows Explorer. You can use the instant search box located in the top-right corner of the Windows Explorer screen, or you can switch on the advanced search feature by clicking the Organize drop-down menu, selecting Layout, and then turning on the Search pane. On the right side of the Advanced search toolbar, click the down arrow to expand the advanced search interface, as shown in Figure 6-13.

Instant searching of your file system is immediately available through many of the interfaces provided in Vista, with search boxes available in Windows Explorer, Media Player, and Photo Gallery as well as in the more obvious places, such as the Start menu.

In these instantly available search windows, Vista returns its findings as soon as you start typing your query (previously covered in the earlier "Understanding the Start Menu" section), and as you continue typing, the search will focus in on the specific item for which you are looking. In this way, even if you know only a partial filename or you are possibly guessing at what a tag might be that classifies a photograph, you have a better chance of getting the result you want.

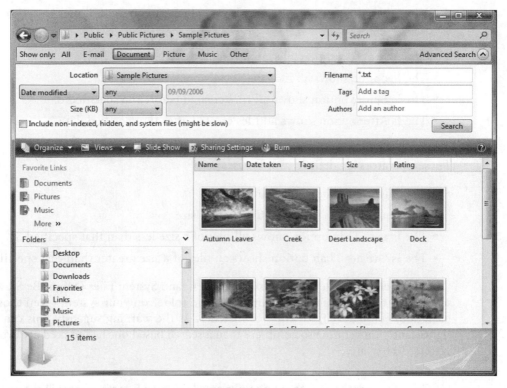

Figure 6-13 *Use the advanced search option to focus your search on specific metadata.*

Advanced searching, on the other hand, is useful when you are searching through many hundreds of gigabytes of information on devices such as Network Attached Storage (NAS) systems where you have millions of items stored within countless folders. You can target advanced searches at specific tags, authors, and filenames, and you can ask the search to take place within a certain collection of file types, such as email messages, documents, or pictures.

For example, to search through your photo collection for all photographs taken with a specific digital camera (as long as you have already tagged them), you can click the Picture button at the top of the Advanced Search window, type **Cannon EOS 10D** in the Tags field, and then click Search. The results will be all the digital photographs taken with your EOS 10D.

To change the location of where the search will take place, open the Location drop-down menu, and select from the list of available folders and drives. The Everywhere option, as you'd expect, searches your entire system.

Open the Date Taken drop-down menu to select from the following date options:

- Date Taken
- Date Modified
- Date Created
- Date Accessed

The Operator menu next to the date field offers you the following ways of better targeting your search:

- The Any option shows all search results.
- The Is option shows all files specifically created on that date.
- The Is Before option shows all files created before the specified date.
- The Is After option shows all files created after the specified date.

Beneath the date field you'll see the Size fields and the operators that support it. These operators are defined as follows:

- The Any option shows all search results.
- The Equals option shows all files of that size.
- The Is Less Than option shows all files of a size less than that specified.
- The Is Greater Than option shows all files of a size greater than that specified.

If you click Include Non-indexed, Hidden, and System Files (Might Be Slow), the search will trawl through every single file and folder on your system (even those that have not been indexed) looking for matches. As the warning suggests, this can take a significantly longer time to complete than a search based on the indexed areas of your system, so beware.

> **TIP** If you opt to search inside your email (clicking E-mail), Vista will return query hits from the message store held inside Windows Mail. You can also perform a similar search from inside the Windows Mail application if you prefer.

Increasing the Scope of Your Index

Vista, by default, will not create indexes of your entire system, instead limiting this processor-hungry activity to folders on your main system disk (with the exception of the Program Files, ProgramData, and Windows folders), as shown in Figure 6-14.

To increase the scope of what's indexed or to add a new drive to the regime, click Start ➤ Control Panel ➤ System and Maintenance ➤ Indexing Options. Click the Modify button, and then click Show All Locations. When you see the dialog box shown in Figure 6-15, you can check any of the drives not automatically indexed in the top pane, and if you expand each drive node, you can also choose which folders you don't want included in the index.

Figure 6-14 *The indexing service indexes your system drive with just a few exceptions.*

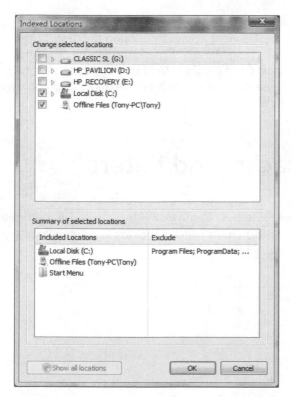

Figure 6-15 *Add drives and folders to the list by checking the appropriate hierarchies.*

If you click the Advanced button in the Indexing Options dialog box, you'll see the Advanced Options dialog box. In this dialog box, you can instruct Vista to index encrypted files (not done by default) and to index words with diacritics as different words.

> **NOTE** *Diacritics* are letter modifiers that change the way a word or letter is pronounced, such as the acute and grave accents commonly used in French.

If you are having trouble with your index, sometimes rebuilding it will solve the problem, whereby Vista discards the previous index and redoes the entire system from scratch; remember, however, that this might take a long time if you have a lot of content that needs indexing.

The last advanced option to mention is that of the index location. You can move the index from its default location on the system drive to a drive that is quicker or has more available space. The best way to achieve this is to click the Select New button, choose the location from the file explorer, and then click OK. You'll have to restart the indexing service to switch the index to the new location—typically you can achieve this by rebooting your system or stopping and restarting the service using the administrative Services applet.

> **TIP** Access the administrative Services applet by clicking the Start button, right-clicking Computer, and then selecting Manage. Expand the Services and Applications node, and then select Services. On the right side of the screen, scroll through the list of services until you find the Windows Search service. Right-click the service name, and then select Restart.

Using Groups, Stacks, and Filters

When you are viewing files and folders in Windows Explorer, you can use three techniques to help you process the information you are looking at as quickly as possible. These are grouping, stacking, and filtering.

Take a look at Figure 6-16.

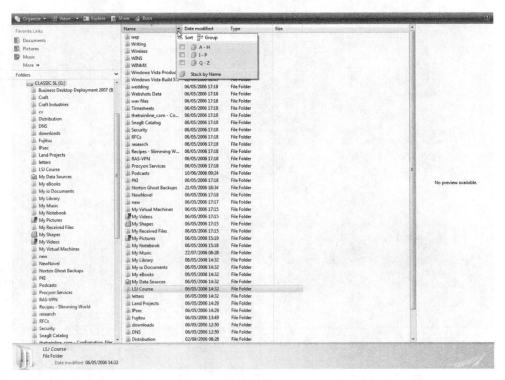

Figure 6-16 *Change the order of the files being displayed by clicking the column headings.*

At the top of the screen you'll see, as with Windows XP, a list of headings that you can use to order the way information is presented. If you click Name, for example, Windows Explorer will alphabetically order the items in the chosen folder with *A* at the top and *Z* at the bottom. Clicking Name again will reverse the order of the list with *Z* at the top and *A* at the bottom. This ordering works for all listed column headings, with Date ordering the list by the date that the file was created or modified (ascending or descending), Type grouping files of similar extension, and Size ordering by file size. You could do all this in previous versions of Windows, and it's also inherent in Vista.

Now for the clever part: click the down arrow next to any of the column headings, and you'll see a new context menu, as shown in Figure 6-17 (for Type in this case).

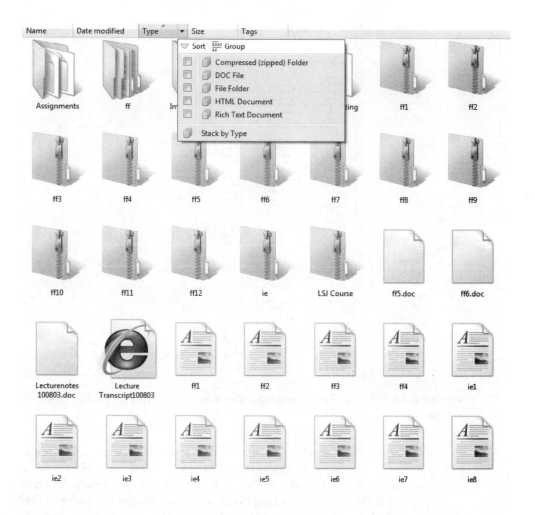

Figure 6-17 *Use the context menu to group, stack, and filter what's displayed.*

The command in the top-left corner of the menu, Sort, is what you've been doing when you click the column heading. You've been sorting the view as an ordered list based on the criteria listed in the column header.

Now, try clicking Group. You'll see that the files are immediately rearranged by file type into split sections in the main window (see Figure 6-18).

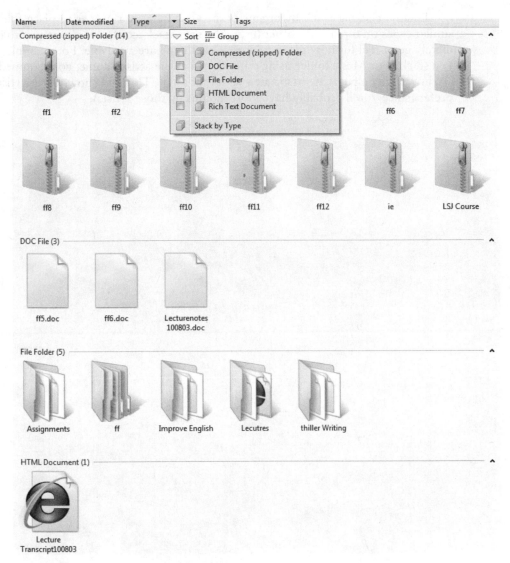

Figure 6-18 *Grouping files is useful to immediately process sets of similar file types.*

Next, try clicking any of the checkboxes listed in the Type context menu, such as File Folder, for example. This is what's known as Filtering and will display only the files you have selected. Clearing all checkboxes is the same as ticking all of them—this is simply because you would never need to filter out all of your files, thus leaving the display blank.

Finally, clicking Stack By organizes the view in such a way as to place folders of similar types on top of each other (using the new Stack icon); this allows you to immediately get a feel for how many folders of each type are available. For example, when you stack your Music folder using criteria such as the artist's name, you'll immediately see how many albums are associated with that artist. This will show which artists you prefer (since you'll probably have more albums by those artists).

CHAPTER 7

Administering Windows Vista

Many of the facilities available to you in Vista for system administration have been improved. Access to these facilities, however, is still in keeping with the Windows legacy style, so this chapter teaches you how to do things the Vista way, covering how to get at the tools hidden in the Control Panel, how to use the new Backup and Restore Center (including system restore points), how to control system services, how to change User Account Control (UAC) settings, and how to use Network Access Protection (NAP).

Using the Control Panel

The Control Panel (Start ➤ Control Panel) has been a fundamental part of Windows computing since the days of Windows 3.11, and in Vista, it remains the epicenter for all things remotely administrative.

The main difference between the Windows XP version of the Control Panel and the Vista one is that now 48 separate applets are available from a vanilla installation of Vista, not including any OEM applets that might have been installed to support bespoke hardware.

Like its predecessor, you can access the Control Panel using two independent views:

- Category view
- Classic view

Category view will group administrative functions into ten categories to better assist you in finding the applet you need to perform a function; for example, the Appearance and Personalization category contains the following applets: Personalization,

Taskbar and Start Menu, Ease of Access Center, Folder Options, Fonts, and Windows Sidebar Properties, as shown in Figure 7-1.

Figure 7-1 *Category view will group administrative applets that have similar functions.*

If you switch to Classic view (clicking the link in the top-left corner), the Control Panel reverts to the pre–Windows XP look where all the applets appear in single-dimensional windows. Some users prefer Classic view when they get more familiar with the range of functions available through the Control Panel because it takes a single click to open the Control Panel rather than multiple clicks through subsections to get where you want to be. From an aesthetic perspective, Classic view demands you double-click an applet to start it, while Category view icons act as links and so require only a single click to open a particular applet.

> **TIP** If you switch to Classic view but think you'd prefer to stick with Category view, click Control Panel Home in the top-left corner of the Control Panel window.

Figure 7-2 shows the top-level Control Panel in Category view, where you can easily see from the descriptions what each category is for and which applets it contains.

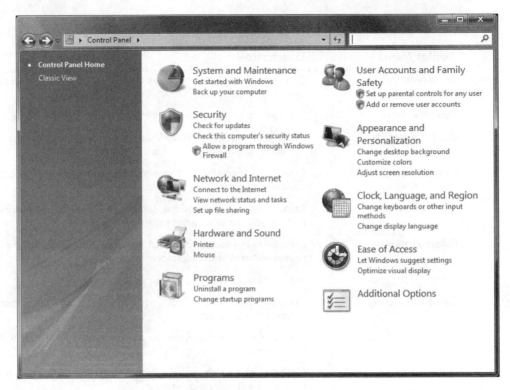

Figure 7-2 *The Control Panel shows ten administrative categories with a description for each.*

To help you understand what each of the Control Panel applets will do for you, Table 7-1 describes each one.

Table 7-1 Control Panel Applets

Applet Name	Description
Add Hardware	Manually install hardware that is not plug and play compliant.
Administrative Tools	Access a menu of advanced system management tasks such as the Local Security Policy and the Event Viewer.
AutoPlay	Modify the default behavior of CDs, DVDs, and removable media when Vista detects they have been inserted or connected to the PC.
Backup and Restore Center	Manage your system backup regime and restore previously recorded backup images using this applet (you'll learn more about this in the "Using System Administration Tools" section).
BitLocker Drive Encryption	Switch on or off and manage the characteristics of this disk-based encryption solution.

Table 7-1 Control Panel Applets (Continued)

Applet Name	Description
Color Management	Change the way Vista manages color translation for different devices, such as monitors, scanners, and printers.
Date and Time	Change the system date and time for your local time zone.
Default Programs	Manage the default program Vista uses for tasks such as browsing the Internet and opening email.
Device Manager	Directly manage the hardware and associated device drivers installed in your PC.
Ease of Access Center	Manage accessibility options, such as the Narrator and Magnifier, making your system easier to use if required.
Folder Options	Customize the look and feel of the default way folders are presented in Windows Explorer.
Fonts	Add or remove fonts from your computer.
Game Controllers	Configure the way joysticks or other game controllers buttons are mapped by Vista.
Indexing Options	Add or remove folders from the default index to optimize Vista's search times.
Internet Explorer	Configure the multitude of options available for changing the way Internet Explorer operates.
iSCSI Initiator	Connect Vista to remote iSCSI devices, and modify specific connection settings.
Keyboard	View and customize the behavior of your keyboard, concentrating on character repeat, cursor blink rate, and the ability to update drivers if necessary.
Mouse	View and customize the behavior of your mouse, including the pointer style, click speed, button mappings, and hardware drivers.
Network and Sharing Center	Monitor and change network settings, and view the current network status.
Offline Files	Configure how you handle offline files, which files and folders are cached, and how you treat duplicates.
Parental Controls	Apply controls to individual user accounts, so either permit or deny certain actions.
Pen and Input Devices	Configure pens and other input devices for Table PCs.
People Near Me	Manage your system in such a way as to allow the use of collaboration tools, such as Windows Meeting Space.
Performance Information and Tools	Monitor how your system is performing, and view the Windows Experience Index.
Personalization	Modify Vista's theme settings.

Table 7-1 Control Panel Applets *(Continued)*

Applet Name	Description
Phone and Modem Options	Configure modem hardware, manage connections, and enter local dialing rules.
Power Options	Administer how Vista handles various different power scenarios, such as balanced, power saver, and high performance.
Printers	Add, remove, and configure printers attached to your PC.
Problem Reports and Solutions	Check the Microsoft web site for the solution to problems you may be experiencing with Vista and view exception reports generated on your PC.
Programs and Features	Modify or remove installed applications from your computer.
Regional and Language Options	Customize the way Vista handles different language and regional options for your system, such as how currency is displayed, how the date format is handled, and the keyboard layout.
Scanners and Cameras	Add or remove scanners and digital cameras from your system, and configure scan profiles to apply tags to imported images.
Security Center	Monitor the security and integrity of your system, getting a rating for how safe you are from a variety of threats.
Sound	Configure audio input and output devices or change the sound scheme your system is currently using.
Speech Recognition Options	Manage how speech recognition works on your computer.
Sync Center	Create or manage existing synchronization pairings with removable devices, and resolve synchronization conflicts.
System	Access Device Manager, modify remote access settings, and change advanced system settings such as virtual memory, processor scheduling, and user profiles.
Tablet PC Settings	Configure Tablet PC settings and screen settings for Tablet PC users, such as setting pen calibration, informing Vista about which hand you write with, and deciding which screen orientation your prefer (landscape or portrait).
Taskbar and Start Menu	Customize the Start menu and the taskbar.
Text to Speech	Customize the way Vista provides text to speech, including the voice used for narration, the reading speed, and the preferred audio device used for output.
User Accounts	Add, remove, and modify user accounts on your system or perform administrative functions such as changing the user's password.
Welcome Center	Start the Windows Welcome Center.
Windows CardSpace	Create and manage information cards to help you identify yourself to web sites, passing on credential to trusted web sites.
Windows Defender	Examine your system for unwanted spyware and adware.

Table 7-1 Control Panel Applets *(Continued)*

Applet Name	Description
Windows Firewall	Configure your settings, allowing or denying application access to resources outside your local area network.
Windows Sidebar Properties	Change the way the Windows Sidebar operates, and add or remove gadgets.
Windows SideShow	Change how gadgets send information to SideShow-enabled auxiliary display devices.
Windows Update	Modify your system settings for how Vista acquires software updates and security patches.

We'll look a bit more in-depth at some of the more commonly used Control Panel applets to get you started in managing your Vista system.

Using System Administration Tools

From the Control Panel Category View, click System and Maintenance to see a list of tasks available for the typical Vista administrator. We'll cover the most important of these in the following sections, starting with the Backup and Restore Center.

Backing Up Your Files

You can use the Backup and Restore Center to both back your system up and restore previously saved data from backup media. Both operations use Vista's new imaging technology to make the processes simpler, less error prone, and quicker.

Figure 7-3 shows how the Backup and Restore Center looks when you first start it.

> **TIP** You'll need to make sure you are using an account that has administrative privileges if you want to back up or restore data using the Backup and Restore Center.

Before you begin, you'll need to decide where you are going to store your backup files, be it on a fixed hard disk or tape drive, on a removable hard disk, or on a DVD or CD.

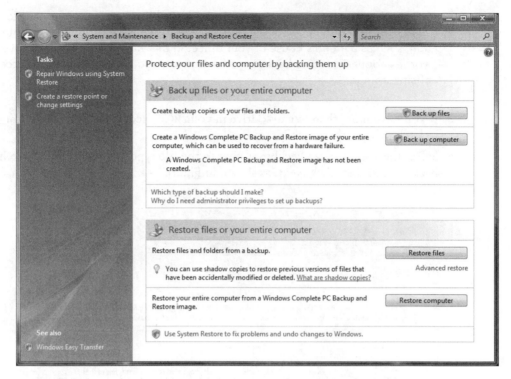

Figure 7-3 *The Backup and Restore Center presents a simple and intuitive interface.*

> **TIP** Although an internal hard disk might sound like a good option (and it's by far the fastest), you should seriously consider using a removable hard disk since it can be secured either offsite (at a friend's house) or in a fireproof safe. When backing up your system, especially if you have personal, private, or valuable information on your system, it's always worth safeguarding against disaster. If there is a fire, the second hard disk in your system box won't seem like such a good idea.

You can perform two types of backup:

- A backup of files and folders
- A backup of your entire system (image backup)

The first option, backing up files and folders, allows you to choose specific files or folders from the file system, such as your digital photograph library or your MP3s, and save them to your target backup media. To complete a file or folder backup, do the following:

1. Click Back Up Files.
2. Vista now checks for available backup devices. When asked where you want to save your backup, select your target media from the list, and then click Next.

> **NOTE** You can opt to save your backups on a network share. If you want to store a backup offsite, think about backing up over a VPN connection to a remote location, such as a friend's house or your office. In this way, you not only remove any worries about damaging backup media, but you also provide immediate access to offsite storage.

3. If you have more than one disk drive in your PC, select the disk or disks you want to back up, and then click Next.

4. Select the appropriate checkboxes next to the file types you want to include in the backup, and then click Next, as shown in Figure 7-4.

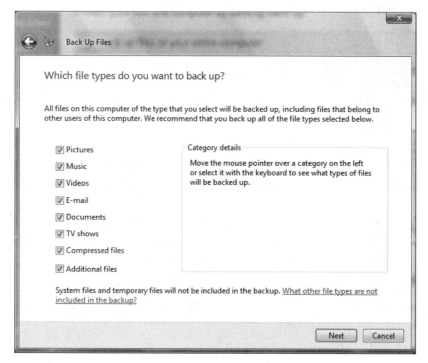

Figure 7-4 *Select the file types you want to include in the backup.*

5. Create a schedule of how frequently you'd like this backup to run, selecting from daily, weekly, or monthly and specifying the day of the week and the time you'd like it to occur. When you're done, click Save Settings and Start Backup.

> **TIP** The first time you perform a backup using the Backup and Restore Center, Vista will force you to do a complete backup. In this way, it can baseline your system and then start incremental backups thereafter.

6. A progress box will open and then automatically minimize, allowing you to continue what you were doing while the backup completes. To stop the backup at any time, click Stop Backup beneath the progress box.

To switch off the automatic backup feature, you should click the Change Settings link immediately beneath the Back Up Files button and then click Turn Off (down at the bottom of the screen).

To create an image backup (you probably won't need to do this often), run the Complete PC backup by clicking Back Up Computer and then following the wizard as before. Complete PC backups are not available with the Home Basic or Home Premium SKUs.

Restoring Files, Folders, and System Images

If you run into problems, such as accidentally deleting a set of files or folders from your system, the primary way of restoring those files will be from a backup. To start the Restore Wizard, click Restore Files in the Backup and Restore Center. If you have had a hardware failure and lost your entire system, you should use the latest image backup, following the wizard triggered by clicking Restore Computer.

Another (and somewhat slicker) way to restore files or folders that have been accidentally modified is to restore a shadow copy. *Shadow copies* are copies of files or folders that are automatically saved by Vista as part of a *restore point*. If you are using System Protection (covered next), Vista will automatically store copies of all files and folders that change over time. In this way, you can use the Windows Explorer context menu to restore from shadow copies by right-clicking the file or folder in question and then selecting Restore Previous Versions, as shown in Figure 7-5.

> **NOTE** If you accidentally delete a file or folder rather than just modify it, you can recover it by highlighting the parent folder, right-clicking it, and selecting Restore Previous Versions from the context menu. When you see the previous versions listed in the dialog box, select the one that corresponds to the time closest to the point where you deleted the file or folder. Highlight it in the list, and then click the Restore button.

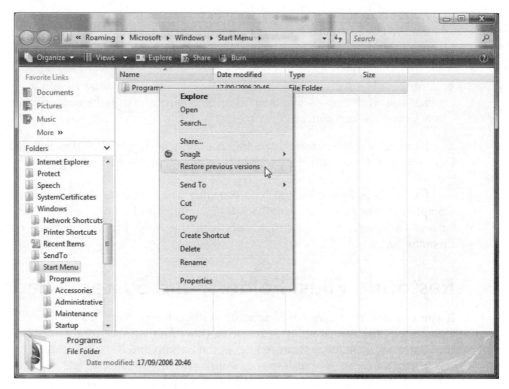

Figure 7-5 *You can easily restore shadow copies using Windows Explorer.*

Starting and Stopping Vista Services

System services are the main components of Vista that perform operating system–specific tasks such as the Parental Controls feature, which polices who does what on your system, and the Windows Firewall, which monitors inbound and outbound connections from your PC, blocking unauthorized access where necessary.

Sometimes you'll have to stop or start services, depending on how your system is behaving, and in the event you are trying to diagnose a problem with a specific aspect of Vista, it always helps to ascertain whether the appropriate services are running.

To access the system Services management console, open the Control Panel, switch to Classic view, and then double-click Administrative Tools. When you see the list of Administrative Tools, double-click Services. This starts the Services management console, as shown in Figure 7-6.

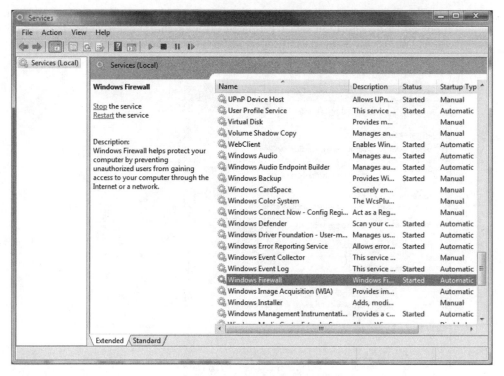

Figure 7-6 *Use the Services management console to change Vista service characteristics.*

Looking in the Status column, you'll see whether a service is currently active (started). If a service you are expecting to be working is not, right-click it, and select Start from the context menu.

The Startup Type column tells you how Vista handles a service when it boots up. You can set a service to one of the following start-up types:

- Automatic (Delayed Start)
- Automatic
- Manual
- Disabled

NOTE Automatic (Delayed Start) is a new start-up type and is useful if a service is not fundamental in the startup process and can be activated when the main body of services that are really required for login and network start-up have begun. In this way you can ensure you get your system up and running in the slickest possible way.

To change the start-up types for a service, right-click the service in the management console, and then select Properties. Open the Startup Type drop-down menu, and select the appropriate setting from the list, as shown in Figure 7-7.

Figure 7-7 *Select the most appropriate way for a service to start when Vista starts.*

If you look on the Recovery tab in a service's Properties dialog box, you can specify how Vista handles service failures. You can create a policy that dictates how these failures are handled over subsequent service failures (during the allocated time period set using the Reset Fail Count After: *xx* Days counter) and specify how Vista handles the first failure, the second subsequent failure, and all further failures of that services.

In each case, you have four possible options:

- Take No Action
- Restart the Service
- Run a Program
- Restart the Computer

Take No Action will leave a failed service alone and not try to restart it or deal with the problem. Restart the Service attempts to start the service as soon as the failure is detected. You can use Run a Program to trigger another application to try to handle the error, maybe starting a system-reporting tool or system-monitoring application. Restart the Computer will instigate a full Vista power cycle.

You can also build in a time delay before Vista attempts to restart the service, specified in the Restart Service After: *xx* Minutes box.

Using the System Applet

Another useful administration tool, available via the Category view, is the System management console, which is available by selecting System and Maintenance ➤ System.

From the screen shown in Figure 7-8, you have immediate access to a multitude of system-related information, such as the Windows Experience Index, the processor type you are using, the amount of memory you have available, and a list of computer and domain/workgroup-related settings, such as the computer name and workgroup name. To change any of this information, simply click the Change Settings link on the right side of the screen.

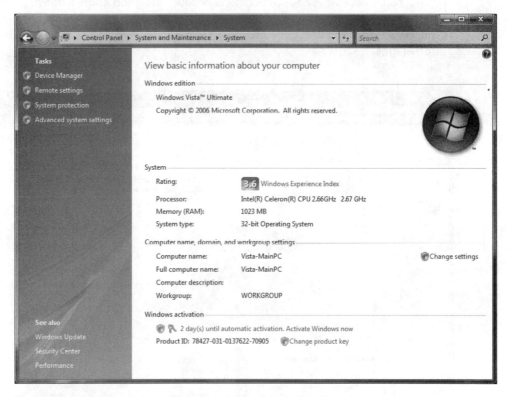

Figure 7-8 *Use the System management console to change your computer name and workgroup.*

Adding or Removing User Accounts

To add or remove user accounts from your system, open the Control Panel home page (in Category view), and click User Accounts and Family Safety ➤ Add or Remove User Accounts.

> **NOTE** You'll have to be logged in with an account with administrative privileges before you will be allowed to add or remove user accounts.

To add a new user account, when you see the screen shown in Figure 7-9, click Create a New Account, and then give the account a meaningful name. Select the appropriate option next to the account type (whether it's a standard user or an administrative user), and then click Create Account.

After a short delay, you'll return to the previous screen where you'll see that the new account has been added to the window. You can click any account visible in this window for more actions, such as renaming the account or deleting it.

> **TIP** You must always have at least one account assigned administrative privileges on your system. If you want to delete the user account you created when you first installed Vista, you'll first need to create another account and give it administrative privileges.

Figure 7-9 *Adding new accounts to Vista is a simple three-step process.*

Using System Restore

System Restore is the Vista component that creates the protection points discussed earlier. System Restore is also responsible for recording enough system state information in order to allow you to return your entire system to the state it was in prior to a problem occurring.

It's a good idea to create a restore point before you add any new hardware or drivers to your system since these type of system updates are notorious for causing system problems. To create a restore point, complete the following procedure:

1. Click the Start button, right-click Computer, and then select Properties.
2. Click System Protection (on the left side of the screen).
3. In the System Properties dialog box (on the System Protection tab), click the Create button shown in Figure 7-10.

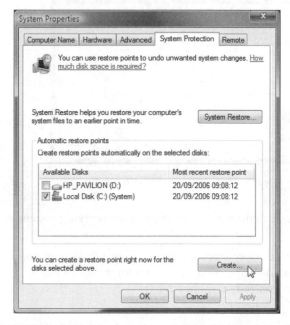

Figure 7-10 *Create a restore point before installing new hardware or updating drivers.*

4. Give the restore point a meaningful name, such as Hardware Update (the date and time are automatically appended to the name), and then click Create.
5. After a short time, you'll see a message stating "The restore point was created successfully." Click OK to finish.

If you experience a problem and think System Restore will help, it's a simple matter of returning to the System Properties dialog box, selecting the System Protection tab, and clicking System Restore. The following procedure should safely get you through the ensuing System Restore Wizard:

1. When you see the System Restore Wizard's Welcome screen, click Next.

2. You'll immediately see the Choose a Restore Point screen, as shown in Figure 7-11.

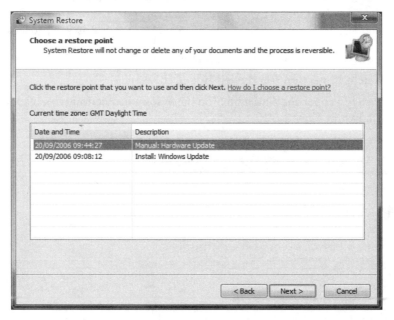

Figure 7-11 *Select the latest system restore point from the table.*

3. Select the restore point that corresponds to your latest working system state, and then click Next.

4. On the Confirm Disks to Restore screen, select the hard disks containing the Vista system files and any other disk drives on which you might have installed system files or device drivers. When you're ready, click Next.

> **TIP** To create and recover restore points on any disks other than your primary system disk, the disk must have System Protection enabled. You turn this on in System Properties on the System Protection tab—just select the checkbox next to each disk you want protected, and then click Apply. You can now create restore points using information on all protected disks.

5. On the Confirm Your Restore Point screen (shown in Figure 7-12), check that you have selected the correct restore point. When you are satisfied, click Finish.

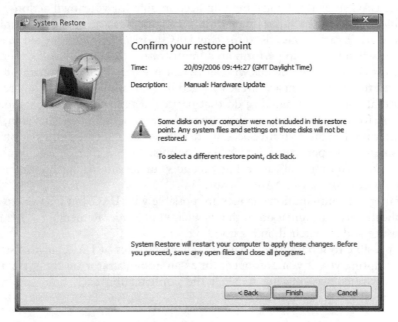

Figure 7-12 *Make sure you have selected the correct restore point before clicking Finish.*

CAUTION You'll need to confirm that you want to proceed with System Restore and that you are aware that the process must complete before you can do anything else. This is a critical system restore, and you must not power off your system or interrupt the process in any way.

Using User Account Control

Probably the most controversial and least liked of all of Vista's new features (unless you are a hardened security nut) is that annoying pop-up dialog box that prompts "Windows needs your permission to continue." You know the one—when you try to do just about anything clever with Vista, you have to acknowledge that it was you and not some third-party hacker who wanted to do that particular task.

Well, User Account Control (UAC), as it's known, has a valuable role to play in the overall security of your system, since many exploits lurking in cyberspace rely on that they can operate behind the scenes and get access to system resources without you knowing. UAC stops this by making you accountable for your own actions, allowing you to block access to facilities if you didn't instigate this access in the first place.

There are in fact two levels to the way UAC works. If you are logged in as a standard user, when you try to perform an administrative (protected) task, you are asked by UAC for account login details with sufficient privileges (an administrator account) to perform that task. If you are already logged in as an administrator, you are asked to confirm that you really wanted to do that particular task. In this way, standard users can still perform administrative tasks without having to log out and in again, with the act of entering the administrative account details as enough of a confirmation that you indeed intended to perform this task. The premise here is that of accountability and authorization. You must always acknowledge your intentions are honorable, and in this Vista is basically saying "Are you sure?"

A variety of configuration changes are possible with UAC, but it's wise to consider the implications of turning it off, if that is what you decide. Remember, UAC is a security measure and is switched on for good reason.

It's possible to modify the behavioral characteristics of UAC, such as stopping it from prompting you if you are logged in as an administrator on the system and are getting frustrated with having to click the confirmation each time you try to do anything.

> **CAUTION** If you decide to switch UAC off, make this a temporary measure rather than a permanent change, operating only for the duration of you performing administrative tasks.

To access the UAC settings in your local security policy, do the following:

1. Click Start ➤ Control Panel, switch to Classic view, and then double-click Administrative Tools.

2. Double-click Local Security Policy to start the Local Security Policy console.

3. In the left pane, expand Security Settings, expand Local Policies, and then highlight Security Options, as shown in Figure 7-13.

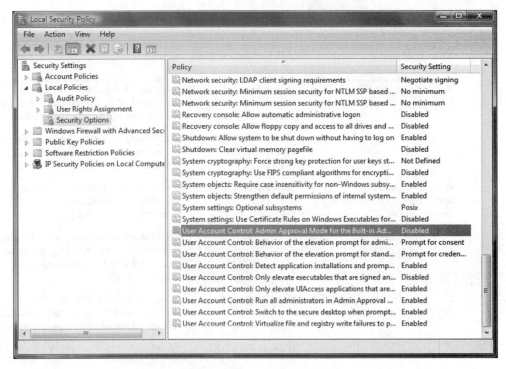

Figure 7-13 *Open the Local Security Policy management console.*

4. Now, referring to Table 7-2, open the policy setting you are interested in, and set the characteristics appropriate to your needs.

5. When you're done, close the console, and reboot your system.

Table 7-2 Local Security Policy Settings Affecting UAC Behavior

Policy Setting	Options (Default in Bold)	Effect
Admin Approval Mode for the Built-in Administrator Account	**Disabled**	Stops the built-in administrator from being asked to confirm actions.
	Enabled	Prompts the built-in administrator account to confirm UAC bound actions.
Behavior of the Elevation Prompt for Administrators in Admin Approval Mode	**Prompt for Consent**	Asks the administrative (logged-in) user to confirm her actions.
	Elevate Without Prompting	Stops UAC from issuing an authorization prompt.
	Prompt for Credential	Asks the administrative user to retype his credentials to proceed.

Table 7-2 Local Security Policy Settings Affecting UAC Behavior *(Continued)*

Policy Setting	Options (Default in Bold)	Effect
Behavior of the Elevation Prompt for Standard Users	**Prompt for Credentials**	UAC asks for the username and password of an administrative account before the action can proceed.
	Automatically Deny Elevation Requests	Stops all UAC bound administrative tasks from being performed in a standard user's session.
Detect Application Installations and Prompt for Elevation	**Enabled**	If the user is installing an application and requires elevated privileges, UAC prompts for administrative credential.
	Disabled	Stops users from ever being prompted to enter elevated privileges (useful in a managed Windows domain environment).
Only Elevate Executables That Are Signed and Validated	**Disabled**	Does not enforce the rule whereby unsigned and nonvalidated executables cannot be installed on the system.
	Enabled	Enforces the rule whereby unsigned and nonvalidated executables cannot be installed on the system.
Only Elevate UIAccess Applications That Are Installed in Secure Locations	**Enabled**	Allows only those applications installed in secure file system locations to execute.
	Disabled	Allows applications installed anywhere on the system to run.
Run All Administrators in Admin Approval Mode	**Enabled**	Governs how all other UAC policy settings work. If this is enabled, all other settings are ignored and this is enforced.
	Disabled	Allows the finer-grained control from previous settings to be applied.
Switch to the Secure Desktop When Prompting for Elevation	**Enabled**	Prevents users from doing anything else when the UAC prompt kicks in.
	Disabled	Makes the UAC prompt available on an interactive desktop.
Virtualize File and Registry Write Failures to Per-User Locations	**Enabled**	Redirects application and registry write failures to specified user locations.
	Disabled	Specifies that applications that write data to protected locations will fail as they would have with Windows XP.

Working with the Command Line

The command line has been a fundamental component of Windows systems since the early days. With its roots growing from the earliest incarnations of MS-DOS, the use of the command line for running administrative commands, getting inside the system, and performing more esoteric functions has always been there. In fact, system administrators nearly always resort to using the command line for targeted administrative tasks since the immediacy of information available through the plethora of commands is unparalleled in the world of the graphical user interface.

Access to the command line has always been, and still is, through the command shell windows, accessible in Vista through the Start ➤ All Programs ➤Accessories ➤ Command Prompt. This will start a new command shell window (as shown in Figure 8-1) with the user's top-level profile directory as the active folder.

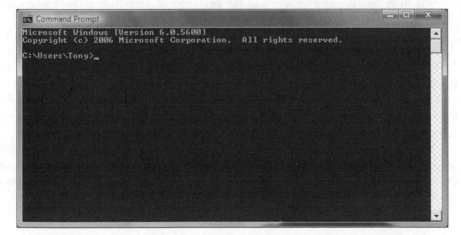

Figure 8-1 *When you start the command prompt, the default folder is your profile.*

As with every new version of the Windows operating system, the command-line capability has been extended. New commands have been added (some more useful than others), and some of those commands are inescapable. As a power user, you need to familiarize yourself with running commands in this environment, getting help about commands that are available, and making sure you understand the implications of running commands with switches that will affect how your system performs.

> **NOTE** Although the command prompt has its roots in MS-DOS, in Vista it's simply another Windows application living in the %SystemRoot% directory (commonly C:\Windows), called cmd.exe.

Customizing the Command Shell

The place where you type Vista command-line commands is known as the *command shell*. When you first start the command shell, you can enter commands next to the command prompt (shown as the folder name followed by a >) by simply typing the command, adding control switches or variables (altering how the command performs), and then pressing the Enter key to execute.

If you mistype an instruction, before you press Enter, you can use the arrow keys on your keyboard to backtrack across the text and then use a combination of the Delete and Backspace keys to edit it. Pressing the Insert key will toggle between insert mode or overtype mode.

Notice also that when you first start the command shell window, you'll see the Windows version displayed in the first line of text, immediately followed by a copyright statement.

To clear the screen, removing all the previous text, including the version number and copyright statement, type **CLS**, and then press Enter.

You can copy commands to the Clipboard from another application and paste them onto the command line simply by highlighting the target command and pressing Ctrl+C to copy the text; then, in the command shell window, right-click, and select Paste from the context menu.

If you press the up and down arrows on your keyboard, you can scroll back and forward through your command history, saving you time if you need to repeat a command.

You can also change the characteristics of the command shell window for this session and all future sessions by right-clicking the title bar (where it says Command Prompt) and then selecting Properties from the context menu. This will expose the "Command Prompt" Properties dialog box shown in Figure 8-2.

Figure 8-2 *Configure the command shell properties to best suit your needs.*

On the Options tab, you can alter the cursor size from the default underscore to the largest setting, which is a flashing character-sized block. The Command History settings allow you to adjust how many previous commands the buffer will remember (the default is 50, with a total of four buffers).

The Font tab will allow you to alter the character sizes of the text within the command shell window, ranging from a scaled font in a tiny 4×6 window to a massive font in a 10×18 window.

The Layout tab allows you to adjust the size of the command shell window without affecting the font size, so any dimensional changes here scale only the window, leaving the font as the default.

Finally, the Colors tab lets you adjust the color of the text, the background, the pop-up text, and the pop-up backgrounds.

> **NOTE** The default settings for the command shell are designed to specifically make the window appear as if it were still an MS-DOS window.

Understanding Commands

Almost 100 independent commands are available from the command shell; some are extremely complicated administrative functions, and others are simply navigational commands for working within the command shell environment. In this chapter, we won't go into the details of every command, but we'll cover a few of the useful ones (and some of the new ones in Vista) to get you started.

If you want to find out more information about a particular command, type its name, add a space, and then type /?. Then press Enter. For example, to see the Help for the "clear screen" command, type the following:

Cls /?

To see a complete list of all the commands available through the command shell, type **Help**, and then press Enter.

> **TIP** Since many of the commands have quite a lot of Help information associated with them, it might be wise at this point to resize the windows to maximize the amount of information you can see. If something has scrolled off the top of the screen, you can use the scroll bar on the right side to look back at what has gone through.

Two types of commands exist—those built into the command shell executable (cmd.exe) and those that exist outside this executable as executable files in their own right. The example command cls that you've already seen is an internal command, whereas a command such as bcdedit has its parent executable in the %SystemRoot%\System32 directory. In this case, bcdedit calls the bcdedit.exe executable file.

Internal and external commands both have Help information stored in the same way. Figure 8-3 shows how the Help information is presented for bcdedit.

> **TIP** If you have a set of commands you regularly run in sequence, you can create a text file with a .bat extension (known as a *batch* file), with each command written on a separate line followed by a carriage return and line feed. (Pressing the Enter key in the Notepad application should do this for you automatically.)

Figure 8-3 *The command shell Help system lists command-line iterations and switches.*

Table 8-1 describes some of the most commonly used commands for navigating your system and performing simple file-related actions. As with all commands, for more information about syntax and switches, type the command's name followed by /?, and then press Enter.

Table 8-1 A Selection of Commonly Used Commands for File System Navigation

Command	Description	Example Usage
cls	Clears the screen of text, leaving only the command prompt	cls
dir	Lists all files and folders in current directory	dir /p
cd	Changes the current directory to a new one	cd \windows\system32
copy	Copies a file or folder from one place to another	copy cmd.exe d:\backup\cmd
prompt	Changes the command prompt text	prompt "%computername%>"

Understanding the syntax of how commands are used is vital to understanding how to use them both on the command line and within a batch file. Take, for example, the "change directory" command, cd, shown in Figure 8-4.

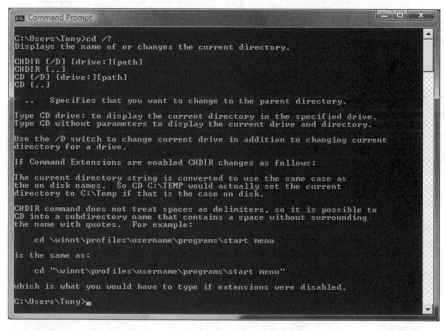

Figure 8-4 *Help information for the cd command*

The top line of the Help information explains in simple terms what you can use the command for; in this case, it displays the name or changes the current directory. Immediately beneath the description, you'll see options for how the command works, with two ways of accomplishing the "change directory" task, using either the cd command or the chdir command. Listed after each command line, you'll see a range of switches, usually shown in square brackets. The description of what each switch does appears beneath the command lines and switches.

Working with Batch Files

Creating batch files is easy using a text editor; for the examples discussed here, assume we are using Notepad (Start ➤ All Programs ➤ Accessories ➤ Notepad).

When you create a batch file, you should give it the file extension of .bat since these files are always processed using the Windows command shell.

You'll no doubt find the idea of simple batch files quite easy; it's no different from simply typing the commands at the command prompt one at a time. These simple batch files are sequentially handling a list of commands, saving you time and effort in retyping.

But this is not where the real power of batch files lies. The real strength of the batch file comes from the extra commands and operators available to help with program control, variable handling and processing, sequencing, report errors and handling exceptions, and in some cases even more complex loops and subroutines.

Administrators have used batch files for the past 15 years to create custom logon scripts, to automatically map network drives when users log in, to start stopped or stalled services, to check the status of security patches and hotfixes, to automatically start user applications, and to check error logs.

Starting Out with a Simple Example

To create a batch file that automatically maps a network drive with the letter Z to a share on a remote system, open Notepad, and start typing commands. It might look something like this:

```
Echo off
Title Batch File for Mapping User's Data Drive
Net Use z: \\server\data\%username%
Echo on
```

What this batch file does is this:

1. It suppresses any output from the batch file execution from going to the screen with Echo off.

2. It adds a meaningful title to the top of the command shell windows, in this case, Batch File for Mapping User's Data Drive.

3. It maps the network drive to the local drive, Z:.

4. It turns screen output back on again.

This is obviously a simple batch file, but it is extremely useful to highlight how you can put these commands together. You might, for example, want not only to map a drive, but you might want to automatically create a new local directory based on the date the user logged in and copy all the remote system files to that folder by way of a backup.

Some other useful commands that you can use in batch files are as follows:

• You can use rem to add a remark or comment to the batch file so that you can describe in plain English what a command is doing.

• You can use color to change the color of the foreground and background in the command shell window.

As you can see from this brief introduction to batch files, they are versatile and can easily grow to be complex and functionally rich. To learn more about batch files and scripting, there are many good books on the subject; alternatively, you can get good information on Microsoft's web site (try searching for *batch files* or *command line*).

Creating Advanced Batch Files

When you get familiar with how commands are structured and how switches (optional and mandatory) affect command-line operations, you're probably ready to proceed to more advanced batch file creation. This is where it gets really clever. Within the confines of a batch file, you have the following features available to you:

• Conditional functions such as IF THEN pairings

• Variables (known as *environment variables*) to save information and use it elsewhere in the batch file

• Arithmetic expressions

• Exception handlers

• File handlers and redirection

• Subroutines (*procedures*) that can be called as functions

Furthermore, you can pass information into batch files (known as *arguments*) from the command line, much in same way you do with extant commands, allowing you to process whatever information you need it to within the bounds of the script. The syntax for passing arguments into batch files is as follows:

```
Batchfilename [arg1] [arg2]
```

In this case, `Batchfilename` is the name of the script, and [arg1] and [arg2] represent data passed into the script for processing. To use an argument within a batch file, the arguments are referred to as numbers, sequentially listed from left to right, with the name of the batch file itself being argument 0 and all other arguments being 1, 2, 3, 4, and so on. To reference an argument, you must precede the argument number with a percent symbol. So if you had a batch file called `CopyUserFiles` and the script copied files from the first argument to the second argument, you would use `CopyUserFiles c:\tony\pictures z:\backup\picture`.

Within the batch file (aside from comments and the typical `Echo Off` statements, and so on), you would see the following embedded command:

```
Copy %1\*.* %2\*.*
```

> **TIP** Arguments that can be called range from 0 to 9. You might think this is some-
> what limiting, and the truth is, it is. However, you can pass more than nine arguments
> into a batch file and use the `shift` command to shift the addressable window right
> and left down your argument set. In this way, using simply `shift` moves the window
> one notch to the right, meaning argument %1 becomes addressed as argument %0,
> and the one off the right side, previously inaccessible as 10, becomes %9. You can
> also opt to shift from a particular place in the argument list, leaving the previous
> arguments intact. This is useful if you have, for example, four set arguments and
> then an indeterminate number of further arguments that need processing in a
> loop. To do this, use `shift /4` (in this example).

You can use batch files to call other batch files, and by using environment variables (variables that exist in the context of the existing command shell or permanent variables that exist outside the command shell), they can share information between each other or even back to GUI tools.

To see a complete list of all environment variables already present within the command shell, type **set**, and then press Enter. This will return a list like the one shown in Figure 8-5.

If you look at the list, you'll probably see some of the more familiar environment variables discussed earlier in this chapter. Variables such as `systemroot` and `path` are commonly quoted, and when shown in context, they are usually contained within a pair of percent symbols, for example, `%SystemRoot%`. The percent symbols are required to identify them as environment variables.

Figure 8-5 *Default environment variable set on a typical Vista system*

To create your own environment variable either from the command line or from within a batch file, you would use the set command. The format for the set command is as follows:

```
SET [variable=string]]
```

When using this command, variable is the name of the new or existing variable you are creating a value for, and string specifies the string of characters (remember that this is always character based) to be assigned to the variable name.

> **TIP** Don't think the command shell can tell the difference between data types. Unlike programming languages such as C or Visual Basic, variables are all stored as characters, even if you set a variable as a number, such as set count=1.

Now that you understand variables, you need to know how to use them. You've already seen the list of environment variables available on a typical installation of Vista, shown previously in Figure 8-5. If you want to change a system variable, for use somewhere else, it's a good idea to use a new variable derived from the system variable rather than changing the default. For example, to create a new HOMEPATH variable for use in a script, you could use the command set temphomepath=d:\users\tony\temp and use that variable within the context of the script. This saves you from having to reset a system variable on exiting the batch file, and it's especially useful in case the batch file terminates without completing the tidy-up job.

You can create tests within a batch file for checking arguments. The syntax for this test, like in many other programming languages, is to use an `if` command:

```
If "%3"=="%username%" (echo this is the logged in user)
else (echo this user is not logged in)
```

In this example, the statement has tested whether the third command-line argument passed to the batch file is equal to %username%, and if it is, it reports "this is the logged in user"; otherwise, you'll see the message "this user is not logged in."

You can add multiple commands in the brackets, separated by an ampersand. For example:

```
If "%3"=="%username%" (echo this is the logged in user)
else (echo this user is not logged in &
echo you cannot continue with this operation & pause & exit)
```

Now the test reports that both the batch file and command shell will terminate when the user presses a key and then does so using the `exit` command.

Within batch files, you can also create loops using the `for` command, and you can jump to subroutines using the `goto` command. These are all powerful scripting tools, and the combination of using all these techniques can lead to an extremely useful facility that's worth delving into in detail.

The final note on batch files is that you can easily pass arguments from one batch file to another using the `call` command followed by the batch file name and its argument list. For example:

```
If "%3"=="%username% call UserScript YES
```

This simple example will test whether the current batch file's third argument is the same as the environment variable %username%, and if it is, it will call another batch file called UserScript with the argument YES.

We hope this has given you enough of a flavor of what the command line is all about and how you can use this scripting interface to easily automate quite complex tasks. The rest of this chapter is dedicated to educating you about the purpose of some of the most useful commands available through the command-line interface, including some old and some new to Vista.

Commands to Add to Your Admin Arsenal

This section covers the ten most popular commands issued from the command shell (or from batch files, for that matter), explaining the purpose and context of each one. More information is available for each of these commands than is covered here, and you can do some more research if you are interested.

BCDedit

BCDedit allows you to look inside the boot configuration store and modify existing entries should you need to do so. If you are planning to install a copy of a previous version of Windows after you've installed your Vista system, you'll have to use bcdedit.exe to get Vista to recognize the existence of this operating system.

Using bcdedit.exe, you can delete entries from the database, export entries from the database, install imported entries from another system, perform queries on the database for particular entry types, and (the most commonly used function) change the boot selection timeout.

You can obtain command-line Help for the entire set of bcdedit.exe's functionality in the usual way—by using the command-line bcdedit /?.

Here are a few tips for using BCDedit:

- Operating systems are identified using a GUID, so you'll need to take note of any GUIDs you want to change before running the commands (try piping the contents of the database into a text file before you start by using bcdedit /enum all >bcd.txt).

- To change the default operating system (the one that is selected if the countdown expires), you can use bcdedit /default {GUID}. Remember, the GUID must be inside a pair of braces!

- To change the boot loader timeout, use bcdedit /timeout time, where time is the number of seconds the boot loader will wait for a decision on which operating system to select. If the timeout expires, the default operating system is selected (see the second point).

- To remove an entry no longer required, use bcdedit /delete {GUID} [/f]. The [/f] switch is necessary in this case to force the deletion of a known operating system, such as Window XP.

BCDedit can do much, much more than what we've covered here, but this should get you started with the boot configuration database.

ipconfig

Extremely useful in determining information about your network connections and adapters, ipconfig is one of the power user's best friends.

Typing ipconfig on its own and then pressing Enter will display only the IP address, subnet mask, and default gateway information for each network adapter you have installed in your system that is using TCP/IP.

Further details about these connections, including DNS server IP addressing, Media Access Control (MAC) addresses, and DHCP details, are available using the /all switch as follows:

```
ipconfig /all
```

Further switches are available that control DHCP leased addresses, such as /release and /renew, where an adapter can relinquish its IP address and then request a new one if there is a problem with the lease. Sometimes with dial-up connections this is necessary if you are dialed in over a long period of time.

ping

If you are troubleshooting a network problem and have exhausted all the GUI facilities available to you, the ping command can help ascertain where the connection problem may be. Simply typing ping followed by an IP address or host name will send out a network packet that effectively bounces off the target system and reports whether it's working—much in the same way as radar works in a submarine (where the name came from):

```
ping 192.168.0.1
```

The result of the ping being issued is that three IP packets are sent to the target system, and then the resultant time taken for a response is reported in milliseconds. The lower the number (called the *network latency*), the better the connection quality. If there is no response, you'll be informed that the target system is unreachable.

If you are having trouble reaching a target system, work backward from the target through each hop of the route to determine where the problem lies.

pathping

pathping works much in the same way as the standard ping command works except for the subtle difference that it also reports the number and identity of the network hops used to get to the target. A *hop* is literally each routing stage that the IP packet has to traverse to get to its target.

```
pathping 192.168.0.1
```

systeminfo

systeminfo is a new command in Vista that displays a full set of information related to your computer. Figure 8-6 shows a typical output for this command.

You have the option, using the /s switch, to connect to a remote system over the network and access its system information.

Figure 8-6 *Output from the* systeminfo *command*

net

The net command is extremely versatile with many varying uses, from creating accounts on your system to starting and stopping services. Using net /? will give you a full list of what the net command is capable of, but for convenience, here are some of the highlights.

The following will start the DNS client service if it is not already started. net stop acts in reverse, stopping the cited service:

```
net start DNS Client
```

> **TIP** net start on its own, without listing a service name, lists all services available on your system.

The following will create a network available share with the name userdata, mapped to the local drive c:\users\data. Network users will be able to browse for this share in their network explorer.

```
net share userdata=c:\users\data
```

| **TIP** net share on its own will return a full list of all available shares on the system.

ImageX

ImageX is a command-line tool used to take complete system image copies of Vista for use in a WinPE deployment environment. Chapter 3 covers this command in detail.

robocopy

robocopy is the most robust (which is where it gets its name) file-copy utility available on Windows system. Used simply, its syntax is as follows:

```
robocopy [source] [destination]
```

The source and destination arguments are simply the location of the source files and the location of where you want them copied to; for example:

```
robocopy c:\tony\*.* d:\backup\*.*
```

However, robocopy is extremely flexible and can cater to pretty much any eventuality of what might happen during a copy transaction; for example, you can instruct it to apply security settings to the files it's copying, to specify the copying of subdirectories (or not as the case may be), to alter the destination filenames to 8.3 file format (for compatibility with legacy Windows systems), and to do much more. robocopy /? will reveal all.

shutdown

You can issue the shutdown command to shut down your own system or a remote system in a variety of ways. To perform a standard shutdown, use the following command:

```
shutdown /s
```

You can add a further /t xxx switch (where xxx is the time in seconds) to the argument list if you want to specify a timeout on the shutdown. This is useful if you need to delay the shutdown while another operation completes.

Other useful iterations of the shutdown command are as follows:

- shutdown /i displays a graphical user interface for shutting the system down.
- shutdown /f forces applications to terminate without issuing a user warning.
- shutdown /h hibernates the computer rather than shutting it down completely.

diskpart

diskpart offers a rich set of commands you can utilize in managing and configuring hard disk partitions.

If you type diskpart at the command prompt and press Enter, a new command shell opens from the application. This is necessary because the functionality operates in a low-level system context and cannot perform its duties from the standard command shell.

For a full list of what diskpart can do, type **help** at the command line, as shown in Figure 8-7.

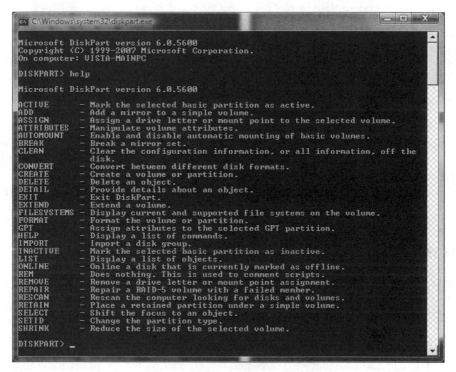

Figure 8-7 Use diskpart to manipulate physical and logical disk partitions from a command line.

CHAPTER 9

Understanding the New Folder Structures and Elements

Windows Vista has several new folder structures and elements that will make organizing and finding files, folders, and objects on your system even easier. In this chapter, we cover creating and using search folders, enabling and managing symbolic file system links from the command line, and using the Preview pane in Explorer windows.

Introducing Search Folders

Search folders are essentially shortcuts in Windows Vista to groups of files, folders, and other items that meet certain criteria. The main attraction of search folders is their nonreliance on absolute paths—that is, search folders can aggregate items without you worrying about their physical locations on the hard disk.

Why are search folders so useful? Well, you can organize files based on more than one set of absolute criteria, which eliminates the need for a complex physical folder organization system on your disk. Have you ever struggled when saving a file? You've probably asked yourself whether you should save a document relating to a project under a client's name, under your High Priority folder, alphabetically by manager's name, or by any other system. Organizing files based only on folders on your hard disk limits you to one classification system. Search folders, however, remove that limitation by allowing you to create more than one search folder, each with a different set of criteria. So, if you're a mortgage lender and working with a set of documents, you can store the set in one physical place on your hard drive but then create search folders that can include the set in various searches you define. The file you seek could then pop up in one search folder that searches by client name, in another separate search folder that searches by the name of the lender to which that loan has been sold, and so on. Search folders are flexible to accommodate you and your needs.

It's really easy to create a search folder. You simply perform a regular search, refine your criteria and tweak the result set using filters, and then save that search to a folder. To create a search folder, follow these steps:

1. Perform a search using the search feature. Enter your criteria, and add any sort of filters you need.

2. Once you have your result set established, click Save Search in the toolbar, as shown in Figure 9-1.

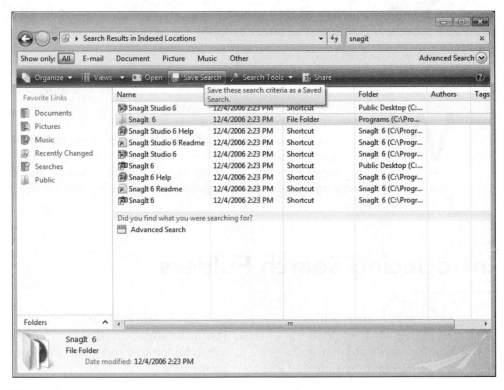

Figure 9-1 *Saving a search to create a search folder*

3. Type a name for your search folder, navigate within the window to where you want to store the folder, and then click Save.

To test the folder, go to the location to which you saved the search folder, and open it. The dynamic search is run, and the folder contents are populated automatically.

If you use the Windows Sidebar and the slide-show gadget, you can actually direct the gadget to a search folder, which is a great way to see only a specific set of pictures you'd like and a great way to expand the resulting set of pictures to other users' picture folders, network volumes, and so on. First, search for all the pictures you'd like to see.

Then, save that search to a folder somewhere. Next, go to the slide-show gadget, access its properties screen (right-click it, and select Options; see Figure 9-2), and point it to the search folder you just created. Check the Include Subfolders option, and then click OK.

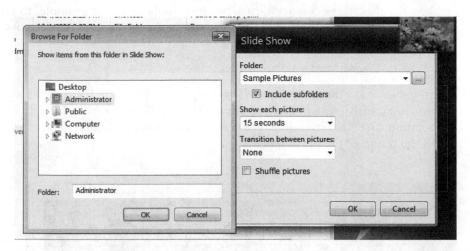

Figure 9-2 *Configuring the slide-show gadget to pull images from a search folder*

Introducing Symbolic Links

Just like in Linux and UNIX, you can create symbolic links from the command line in Windows Vista. Here is the official Microsoft definition of *symbolic links* as they relate to Vista:

> *A symbolic link is a file-system object that points to another file system object... Symbolic links are transparent to users; the links appear as normal files or directories, and can be acted upon by the user or application in exactly the same manner. Symbolic links are designed to aid in migration and application compatibility with UNIX operating systems. Microsoft has implemented its symbolic links to function just like UNIX links.*

Essentially, symbolic links are convenience tools that let you store links to other objects from within one folder and maintain the façade to programs and the operating system that the link you create is actually a real file.

You might have been familiar with the junctions functionality afforded by the Windows Server 2003 Resource Kit tools or through the Sysinternals toolkits, but they were restricted to NTFS 5.0 volumes, and you had to have the extra software installed; plus, those junctions worked only with directories—you couldn't link files. Symbolic links in Windows Vista work with both files and folders (or directories, if you're old-school), and you need no extra software; they're built in.

By default, only administrators can create links, but you can adjust this by tweaking the local security policy through secpol.msc. See Chapter 26 for details on configuring the local security policy using security templates.

You use the mklink command to create a symbolic link. For example, to create a link for a file named np in the current directory to the Notepad executable, issue the following command:

```
mklink np c:\Windows\system32\notepad.exe
```

If you look at a directory listing for the current folder, you'll see the np symbolic link you just created, with its link partner encapsulated in brackets to the right of it and the notation <SYMLINK> in the file type column. For example, look at Figure 9-3, which shows the results of the dir command.

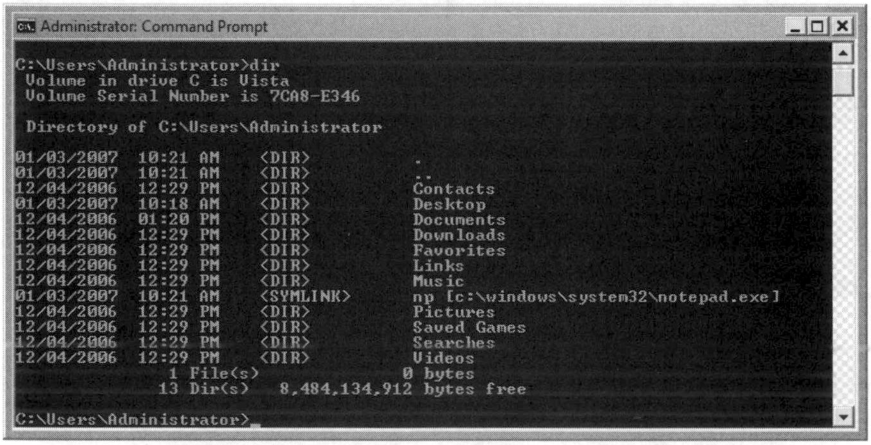

Figure 9-3 *Looking at a symbolic link to a file*

Next, you can use the /d switch to create a symbolic link to a specific directory. For example:

```
mklink /d win c:\Windows
```

After creating that link for the Windows directory, if you look at a directory listing for the current folder, you'll see the win symbolic link you just created, with its link partner encapsulated in brackets to the right of it and the notation <SYMLINKD> in the file type column, denoting it's a directory. For example, check out Figure 9-4.

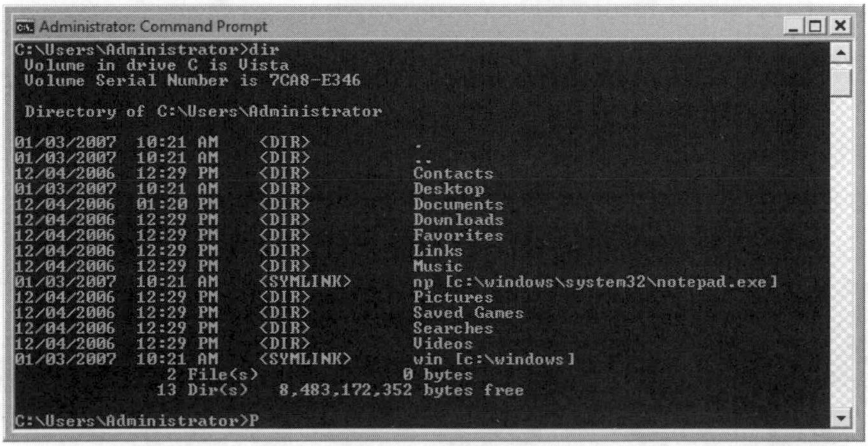

Figure 9-4 *Looking at a symbolic link to a folder*

Symbolic links can span volumes, and you can create symbolic links to network paths as long as they're delineated via the Universal Naming Convention (UNC). For instance, to link hd to a network home directory that resides at \\server\users\jon, you'd use the following command:

```
mklink hd \\server\users\jon
```

Using the Preview Pane

The Preview pane is a sliver of the regular Explorer window that shows the details of files within that window. It adjusts based on the file type you've currently selected in the window. For example, Figures 9-5, 9-6, and 9-7 show the Preview pane exploring a regular file, a graphics file, and a music file.

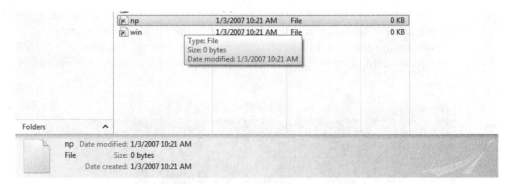

Figure 9-5 *The Preview pane when a regular file is selected*

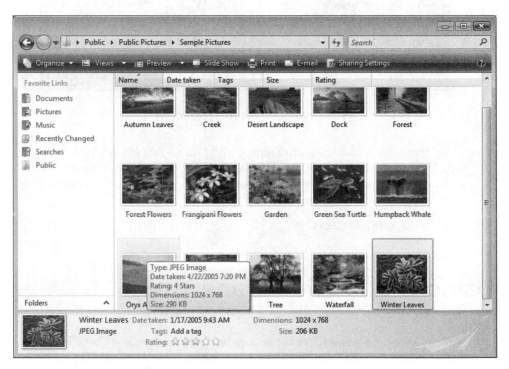

Figure 9-6 *The Preview pane when a graphics file is selected*

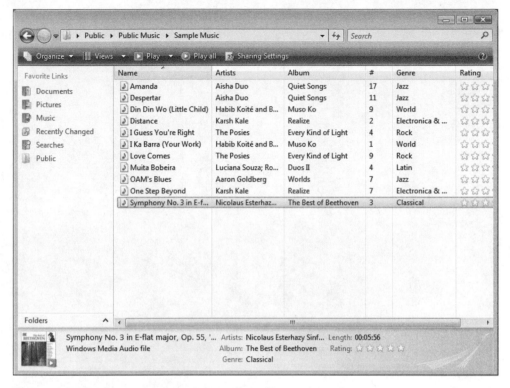

Figure 9-7 *The Preview pane when a music file is selected*

The Preview pane is a pure convenience feature that really doesn't allow for customization, but it is an easy way to get quick information about the properties of a file without having to right-click it and go to the Properties dialog box.

CHAPTER 10

Working with the File System

The file system tries to get out of your way, but it's still important to know how to control it. The two ways in which Windows Vista requires your attention are in setting permissions to restrict and filter access to a file and in restoring previous versions via the automatic backup system. In this chapter, we'll cover permissions and the Previous Versions feature and show you what you need to know.

Setting Permissions

One of the most dreaded and tedious but necessary tasks of system administration is file- and folder-level permissions; they are significant in protecting data from unauthorized use on your system. This is especially important if Windows Vista is serving files to others on your network.

If you have ever worked with UNIX permissions, you know how difficult they are to understand and set; with all those complex CHMOD-based commands and numbers that represent bits of permission signatures, it's so easy to get lost in the confusion. Windows Vista, on the other hand, provides a remarkably robust and complete set of permissions, more so than any common UNIX or Linux variety available today. It's also true that no one would argue about how much simpler setting permissions in Windows is than setting them in any other operating system. That's not to say, however, that Windows permissions are a cinch to grasp—there's quite a bit to them.

Introducing Standard and Special Permissions

Windows Vista, among other Microsoft operating systems, supports two kinds of permissions: standard and special. *Standard* permissions are often sufficient for files and folders on a disk, whereas *special* permissions break standard permissions down into finer combinations and allow more control over who is allowed to do what functions to an object on a disk. Table 10-1 describes the standard permissions available in Windows Vista.

Table 10-1 Windows Vista Standard Permissions

Type	Description
Read (R)	Allows a user or group to read the file.
Write (W)	Allows a user or group to write to the contents of a file or folder and also create new files and folders.
Read and execute (RX)	Allows a user or group to read attributes of a file or folder, view its contents, and read files within a folder. Files inside folders with RX rights inherit the right onto themselves.
List folder contents (L)	Similar to RX, but files within a folder with L rights will not inherit RX rights. New files, however, automatically get RX permissions.
Modify (M)	Allows a user or group to read, write, execute, and delete files, programs, and folders.
Full control (F)	Similar to M but also allows a user or group to take ownership and change permissions. Users or groups can delete files and subfolders within a folder if F rights are applied to that folder.

You should understand the following key points about how permissions work:

- First, file permissions always take precedence over folder permissions. If a user can execute a program in a folder, he can do so even if he doesn't have RX permissions on the folder in which that program resides. Similarly, a user can read a file for which he explicitly has permission, even if that file is in a folder for which he has no permission, by simply knowing the location of that file. For example, you can hide a file listing employee Social Security numbers in a protected folder in Payroll to which user James Smith has no folder permissions. However, if you explicitly give James R rights on that file, then by knowing the full path to the file, he can open the file from a command line or from the Run command on the Start menu.

- Second, permissions are cumulative: they "add up" based on the overall permissions a user gets as a result of his total group memberships. Deny permissions *always* trump Allow permissions. This applies even if a user is added to a group that is denied access to a file or folder that the user was previously allowed to access through his other memberships.

Windows Vista offers 14 default special permissions, shown in Table 10-2. The table also shows how these default special permissions correlate to the standard permissions discussed earlier.

Table 10-2 Windows Vista Special Permissions

Special Permission	R	W	RX	L	M	F
Traverse Folder/Execute File			×	×	×	×
List Folder/Read Data	×		×	×	×	×
Read Attributes	×		×	×	×	×
Read Extended Attributes	×		×	×	×	×
Create Files/Write Data			×		×	×
Create Folders/Append Data			×		×	×
Write Attributes			×		×	×
Write Extended Attributes			×		×	×
Delete Subfolders and Files						×
Delete					×	×
Read Permissions	×		×	×	×	×
Change Permissions						×
Take Ownership						×

The default special permissions are further described in the following list:

Traverse Folder/Execute File: Traverse Folder indicates the ability to access a folder nested within a tree even if parent folders in that tree deny a user access to the contents of those folders. Execute File indicates the ability to run a program.

List Folder/Read Data: List Folder indicates the ability to see file and folder names within a folder, and Read Data indicates the ability to open and view a file.

Read Attributes: This indicates the ability to view basic attributes of an object (read-only, system, archive, and hidden).

Read Extended Attributes: This indicates the ability to view the extended attributes of an object—for example, summary, author, title, and so on, for a Microsoft Word document. These attributes will vary from program to program.

Create Files/Write Data: Create Files indicates the ability to create new objects within a folder; Write Data lets a user overwrite an existing file. This does *not* allow the user to add data to existing objects in the folder.

Create Folders/Append Data: Create Folders indicates the ability to nest folders. Append Data allows the user to add data to an existing file but not delete data within that file or delete the file itself.

Write Attributes: This allows a change to the basic attributes for a file.

Write Extended Attributes: This allows a change to the extended attributes of a file.

Delete Subfolders and Files: Delete Subfolders and File allows a user to delete the contents of a folder regardless of whether any individual file or folder within the folder in question explicitly grants or denies the Delete permission to a user.

Delete: This allows you to delete a single file or folder but not other files or folders within that folder.

Read Permissions: This indicates the ability to view NTFS permissions on an object but not to change them.

Change Permissions: This indicates the ability to both view and change NTFS permissions on an object.

Take Ownership: This grants permission to take ownership of a file or folder, which inherently allows the ability to change permissions on an object. This is granted to administrator-level users by default.

Setting Permissions

To set NTFS permissions on a file or folder in Windows Vista, follow these steps:

1. Navigate to the file or folder on which you want to set permissions.
2. Right-click the file or folder, and select Properties.
3. Navigate to the Security tab.
4. In the top pane, add the users and groups for whom you want to set permissions. Then click each item, and in the bottom pane, grant or disallow the appropriate permissions. Figure 10-1 shows the Permissions For <objectname> dialog box.

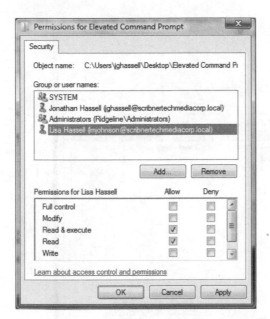

Figure 10-1 *Granting permissions on a folder to a user*

If a checkbox under Allow or Deny appears gray, this signifies one of two things: that the permissions indicated are inherited from a parent object (we'll discuss more about inheritance in the next section) or that further special permissions are defined that cannot be logically displayed on the basic Security tab. To review and modify these special permissions, simply click the Advanced button, if available on the object type for which you're trying to set permissions. (You can't apply special permissions to a shortcut, for example.) In this dialog box, by clicking the Add button, you can create your own special permissions other than those installed by default with Windows Vista. You can also view how permissions will flow down a tree by configuring a permission to affect only the current folder, all files and subfolders, or some combination thereof.

Introducing Inheritance and Ownership

Permissions also migrate from the top down in a process known as *inheritance*. This allows files and folders created within already existing folders to have a set of permissions automatically assigned to them. For example, if a folder has RX rights set and you create another subfolder within that folder, the new subfolder will automatically receive RX rights. You can view the inheritance tree by clicking the Advanced button on the Security tab of any file or folder. This will open the dialog box shown in Figure 10-2, which clearly indicates the origin of rights inheritance in the Inherited From column.

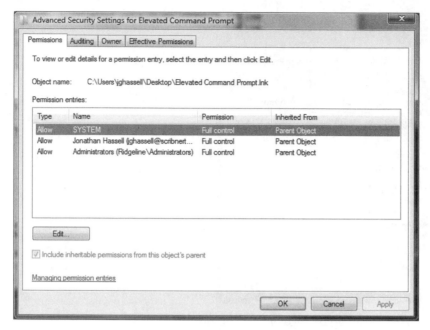

Figure 10-2 *Viewing the origin of permissions inheritance*

Windows Vista also establishes the concept of *ownership*. The specified "owner" of a file or folder has full control over it and therefore retains the ability to change permissions on it, regardless of the effect of other permissions on that file. Also, an owner can assign a standard permission called Take Ownership to any other user or group; this allows that user or group to assume the role of owner and therefore assign permissions at will. The high-level administrator account in Windows Vista has the Take Ownership permission by default (subject to passing a User Account Control acknowledgment, of course), allowing IT representatives to unlock data files for terminated or otherwise unavailable employees who might have set permissions to deny access to others.

To view the owner of a file, click the Owner tab on the Advanced Security Settings For <objectname> dialog box, shown in Figure 10-3. The current owner is enumerated in the first box. To change the owner—assuming you have sufficient permissions to do so—simply select a user from the box at the bottom, and click OK. Should the user to whom you want to transfer ownership not appear in the box, click Add, and then search for the appropriate user. Click OK when you've finished.

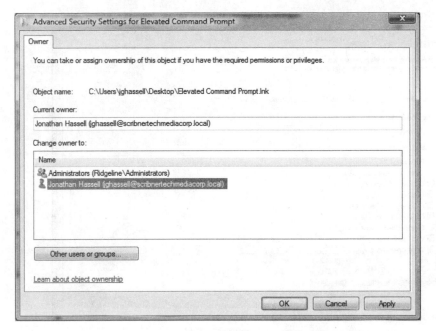

Figure 10-3 *Viewing the current owner and changing ownership*

Determining Effective Permissions

You can use the Effective Permissions tab on the Advanced Security Settings screen you just saw in the previous section to view what permissions a user or group, from within either the local user store or the Active Directory domain of which the current machine is a member, would have over any object. Windows Vista examines inheritance, explicit, implicit, and default access control lists for an object; calculates the access that a given user would have; and then enumerates each permission in detail on the tab. Figure 10-4 demonstrates this.

The Effective Permissions tab has two primary limitations. First, it does not examine share permissions. It concerns itself only with NTFS-based ACLs and, therefore, only file system objects. Second, it functions for users and groups only in their default accounts—it will not display correct permissions if a user is logged in through a remote access connection or through Terminal Services, and it also might display partially inaccurate results for users coming in through the local Network service account. Although these are reasonably significant limitations, using the Effective Permissions tool can save you hours of head scratching about why a pesky "Access Denied" message continues to appear. It's also an excellent tool to test your knowledge of how permissions trickle down and how Allow and Deny permissions override such inheritance at times.

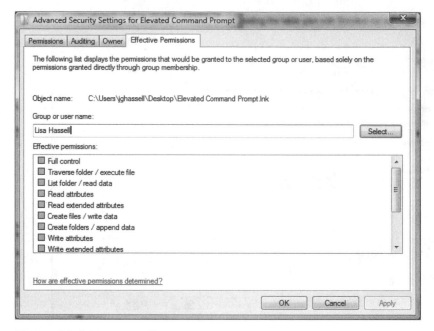

Figure 10-4 *Viewing effective permissions*

Using Previous Versions

Previous Versions is a feature within Windows products, based on shadow copy technology, that allows a machine to take snapshots of documents on a disk to record their states at certain points in time. If a user accidentally deletes or otherwise overwrites a file, she can open a version that was saved by the machine earlier in time, thereby eliminating the need for her to either re-create her work or contact the help desk to get them to restore the file from the most recent backup. Clients connecting to a share on that disk will be able to view and access previous point-in-time copies of either individual files or entire directories.

To access this tool, go to the Previous Versions tab in the Properties dialog box of almost any data object. It looks like Figure 10-5.

To restore a previous version of a file, all the user has to do is select the appropriate version and either copy it to a different location by clicking the Copy button or restore it to its location at the time the snapshot was taken by clicking the Restore button. Note that viewing an executable file will run that file.

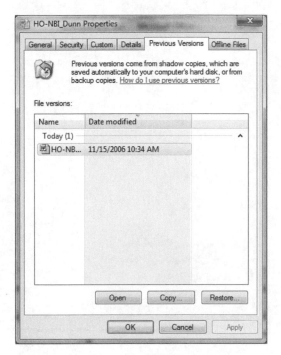

Figure 10-5 *The Previous Versions tab*

You should note three important points about how shadow copies might and (most notably) might not rescue you or your users from catastrophe:

- Only one previous version of a file is kept, and that is the version of a file that consisted of the oldest modification since the most recent snapshot. Even if multiple changes are made to a file throughout the day, the only previous version available for rollback is the one that was made directly after the most recent snapshot. This can be somewhat counterintuitive to understand, but it's crucial that your users not rely on the Previous Versions feature as a crutch and that they learn to use it only when a major disaster strikes.

- If you delete a file, you must create an empty file with the same name. This is quite obviously because you can't navigate to the Properties dialog box of an object if said object doesn't exist. In most cases, the workaround is simply to create a new file with the same name and then access the Previous Versions tab—Windows Vista will figure out what's happening. Obviously, the limitation here is that you must remember the exact name of a file. That is a simple task when the file is called 2007 Employee Dinner.doc but not when it's called ho_nbi_dunn_021x.doc.

- If you rename a file, you lose all access to previous versions of that file, even if some exist. Shadow copies are tracked exclusively by filename and state, so if the filename changes, Windows Vista isn't smart enough to follow the rename.

CHAPTER 11

Using BitLocker

The inclusion of BitLocker in Windows Vista is a "win" for those who continually fret over the security of data physically stored on hard drives that aren't in the relatively secure confines of a data center.

Data theft is a very real, very significant threat, and the consequences arising from the loss of data to unknown parties can be quite damaging—even catastrophic. Customers told Microsoft about this fear—in fact, Microsoft classifies a total hardware-based encryption system as one of its top requests—and therefore delivered BitLocker.

In this chapter, we'll cover BitLocker: its premise, how it works, how to enable it, how to recover data from it, and how to disable it.

Understanding the BitLocker Essentials

In a nutshell, BitLocker protects against someone booting another operating system or running a software-hacking tool and against breaking NTFS and system protections or performing offline viewing of the files stored on a drive it protects. BitLocker effectively provides sector-level encryption for your entire hard drive, with decryption less "coupled" with a user-level application running on the operating system than other drive protection solutions. BitLocker is baked into the core of Windows Vista, allowing the key that unlocks the drive to be stored either on secure removable media or in a specially designed module located on the motherboards of newer-model computers. By making the encryption persist independently of the operating system, BitLocker-secured drives are almost completely impervious to cracking, even when the original Vista installation is offline. Everything on the drive is encrypted: all system files, user data, and even swap and hibernation files.

The other aspect of BitLocker's defenses is its ability to check the integrity of key system and boot files during the power-on and boot processes. BitLocker can detect whether these elements have been tampered with—by a boot sector virus, a Trojan, or some other nefarious piece of code—and can lock the boot sequence and prevent such software from gaining access to the operating system. It also protects against encrypted drives being shifted around to different machines, which is a typical sign of drive theft.

At the heart of making the most of BitLocker is the Trusted Platform Module (TPM) microchip. A TPM chip offers a hardware-based capability to securely generate cryptographic keys and generate random numbers. BitLocker works with TPMs labeled as version 1.2 (and presumably later versions as well). The user doesn't know anything is different—the verification and decryption is all performed seamlessly, requiring no input from the user, assuming the TPM chip is present. BitLocker is also quite useful for computers that aren't equipped with a TPM chip, because it still supports encrypting a hard drive; however, TPM-less BitLocker is unable to validate the integrity of boot files. Instead, a user inserts a USB key or other removable media to verify his identity and presence at the machine during the boot process and to decrypt files for use during his Windows Vista session.

> **NOTE** You can also opt to simply use a USB key or PIN to use the computer with a TPM-equipped machine. You're not required to use the fully integrated capabilities of BitLocker.

Under the Hood: BitLocker

How does BitLocker actually detect whether boot files have been altered? The TPM on the computer's motherboard can finger and probe various places on the file system. These measurements are put together to form a "fingerprint" that is, of course, unique to the system—it's essentially a fancy hash. The fingerprint would remain the same unless critical files were altered, in which case the result of the measurements used to create the initial fingerprint would be different, signaling an intrusion. BitLocker interfaces with the TPM to restrict access to the secrets that are used to decrypt the drive; once the fingerprint has been verified, BitLocker unlocks the TPM and allows the boot process to continue. At this point, protection is handed off to Windows Vista.

The encryption itself is unique as well. A full-volume encryption key (FVEK) encrypts the entire contents of the drive, and that key is then encrypted by a volume master key (VMK). This results in a type of dual-layer protection, since the drive can be rekeyed with the VMK if other keys are lost, stolen, or cracked without necessarily having to decrypt the entire drive. Figure 11-1 demonstrates this concept.

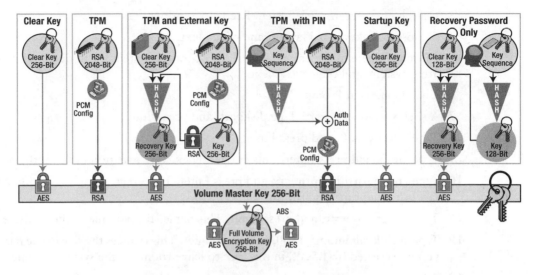

Figure 11-1 *Encrypting the drive using an FVEK and VMK*

Once Windows Vista is running, a file system driver in the Vista stack transparently encrypts and decrypts data on the disk, sector by sector, as data is read and written to and from the drive. Upon a hibernation event, the hibernate file is encrypted and saved to the BitLocker-protected volume. When the computer resumes from hibernation, the saved file is decrypted. BitLocker is designed to be seamless for the user; he shouldn't even recognize that BitLocker is enabled, and the encryption/decryption process should simply happen without any appreciable performance penalty or degradation of the user experience.

Partitioning Your Volume

BitLocker requires you to have two partitions on your hard drive. The system volume, which is the first partition, is unencrypted and stores boot information. The operating system volume, which is the second partition, is encrypted and contains all the operating system files and, presumably, user data as well. You must create the partitions before you install your copy of Windows Vista; you cannot create these partitions from a previously installed version of the operating system.

To correctly partition the hard drive of a computer on which you're installing Windows Vista, follow these steps:

1. Insert the Windows Vista DVD or CD, and restart your computer. Make sure you have backed up or otherwise safeguarded any data on the target hard drive.

2. The computer should boot from the media. The Install Windows screen will appear. Choose the appropriate responses for your installation language, time and currency format, and keyboard layout, and then click Next.

3. On the next screen, click System Recovery Options.

4. Choose your keyboard layout, and click Next.

5. Click anywhere in the empty area of the operating system list to deselect any operating system, and then click Next.

6. Click Command Prompt.

7. A shell window appears. Type **diskpart,** and press Enter.

8. Type **select disk 0,** and press Enter.

9. Type **clean,** and press Enter. This erases any existing partition table on the disk.

10. Type **create partition primary,** and press Enter. This creates a new partition and labels it as a primary partition.

11. Type **assign letter=c,** and press Enter. This names this volume as the C: drive.

12. Type **shrink minimum=1500,** and press Enter. This reduces the size of the partition you just created by 1.5GB, in this case to leave room for the system volume.

13. Type **create partition primary,** and press Enter. This creates another primary partition.

14. Type **active to select the newly created partition,** and press Enter.

15. Type **assign letter=s,** and press Enter. This volume can now be called the S: drive.

16. Type **exit** to leave the diskpart utility.

17. Type **format c: /y /q /fs:NTFS** to format the C: drive, and press Enter.

18. Type **format s: /y /q /fs:NTFS** to do the same for the S: drive.

19. Type **exit** to leave the shell window.

20. To continue the installation, close the System Recovery Options screen.

21. Click Install Now to proceed with the Windows Vista installation. Make sure the operating system is installed on drive C:.

Initializing the Trusted Platform Module

After you have partitioned your drive and installed Windows Vista, the next step to enabling BitLocker on your drive is to turn on the TPM on your machine—if it is equipped with one. TPM-enabled computers contain BIOS functionality that runs after the power-on self-test (POST) but before the actual operating system boot; the TPM Installation Wizard, part of Vista, can talk to this particular module and enable it. (The wizard works, however, only with BIOSs that are explicitly supported by Windows Vista. You may have a motherboard with a TPM but not a BIOS with Vista TPM support, in which case you will need to consult your computer manufacturer's instructions to turn on the TPM.) You also need to claim ownership of the TPM, which then allows you to turn it on and off securely and clear its contents when you dispose of the machine on which it's installed.

You need local administrator rights to perform both phases of the TPM initialization. To turn on the TPM, follow these steps:

1. Click the Start button, and then type **tpm.msc** in the search box.
2. The TPM Management Console will appear. Before this, you may need to acknowledge a User Account Control prompt.
3. Click Initialize TPM under Actions to start the wizard.
4. The TPM Initialization Wizard appears. If the TPM is off, the Turn on the TPM Security Hardware dialog box appears. Click OK, and then restart your system to continue the process. If the TPM is on, the Create the TPM Owner Password dialog box appears—in this case, skip ahead to the next set of steps.
5. Choose to shut down or restart, and upon reboot, follow the prompts your BIOS gives you to complete turning on your TPM.

To assign ownership of the TPM on your computer, follow these steps:

1. Click the Start button, and then type **tpm.msc** in the search box.
2. The TPM Management Console appears. Before this, you may need to acknowledge a User Account Control prompt.
3. Click Initialize TPM under Actions to start the wizard.
4. The Create the TPM Owner Password dialog box appears. Select Automatically Create the Password to let Vista choose a secure password for you. Click Next.
5. The Save your TPM Owner Password dialog box appears. Click Save the Password, navigate to a location on the file system where you can save the file, and then click Save again.
6. Click Initialize. It may take a few moments for this process to finish.
7. Click Close.

Your TPM is now enabled and ready for use with BitLocker.

Turning On BitLocker

Enabling BitLocker is easy once you have enabled and claimed the TPM. To turn on BitLocker, follow these steps:

1. Open the Control Panel.
2. Click Security, and then click BitLocker Drive Encryption. You may need to acknowledge the User Account Control prompt.
3. The BitLocker Drive Encryption screen appears. Click Turn on BitLocker.

4. Click Don't Use a Startup Key or PIN. (If you want to use a PIN, skip ahead to the next section.)

5. The Create Recovery Password screen appears; click the button to do so.

6. The Save the Recovery Password screen appears. You can choose from saving the password to a USB drive, saving it to a folder, showing the password on the screen so you can write it down, or printing the password to any configured printer. You can select more than one of these choices by clicking the Back button after completing the screens for that option. Next, you'll be presented some information about disk encryption.

7. The Encrypt the Selected Disk Volume screen appears; here, click the Encrypt button. The status bar appears, and encryption commences. You can expect the process to take about one minute per gigabyte of stored data.

After the process finishes, your disk is fully encrypted. This is transparent to the user—you won't notice any changes the next time you boot. Figure 11-2 shows this flow.

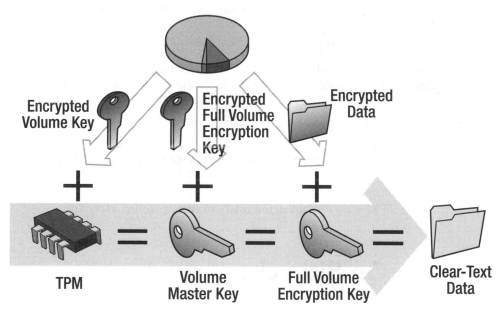

Figure 11-2 *The flow for using straight TPM with BitLocker*

But if the TPM changes, if it can't be accessed (for example, if the drive is moved to another computer, perhaps by a thief), or if someone tries to boot from removable media to "route around" the Vista installation on the drive itself, the computer switches to locked mode, and you'll need to provide the recovery key you selected earlier.

Using a PIN with TPM-Enabled BitLocker

Using a PIN with BitLocker is enabled in much the same way as a straight TPM installation. In practice, the next time you log in after the encryption process finishes, you will be prompted for your PIN. If the TPM associated with the drive is changed or if someone tries to boot from another disk, the machine will go into recovery mode until the appropriate recovery key is supplied. Figure 11-3 shows the flow in this process.

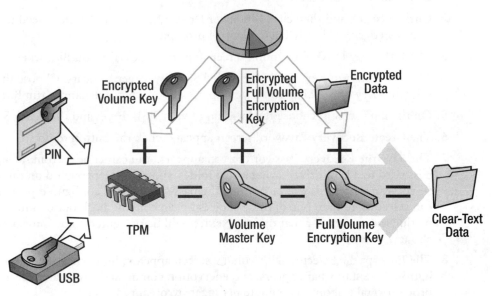

Figure 11-3 *The flow for using a PIN with BitLocker*

When you establish the PIN during BitLocker setup, it hashes the PIN using SHA-256. BitLocker then takes the first 160 bits of the hash and uses them as authorization data for the TPM to seal the VMK; at this point, the VMK is protected by both the TPM and the PIN for enhanced security.

To use the PIN option, in step 4 in the previous procedure, choose the option to use a PIN, then enter the PIN, and finally click Next. The remainder of the procedure is the same.

Using BitLocker Without the Trusted Platform Module

As we mentioned in the introductory section of this chapter, you can use BitLocker on a computer that does not have a TPM chip in it. The main differences in BitLocker's operation in this scenario are as follows:

- You will need to have the USB start-up key inserted into the computer whenever it boots.

- You will not be able to boot the computer without getting prompted for the key; thus, this is best for individual computers and not necessarily machines that have multiple users.

To use BitLocker with a start-up key, follow these steps:

1. Open the Control Panel.

2. Click Security, and then click BitLocker Drive Encryption. You may need to acknowledge the User Account Control prompt.

3. The BitLocker Drive Encryption screen appears. Click Turn on BitLocker.

4. The Use a Startup Key or PIN for Added Security screen appears. Choose the Save a Startup Key on a USB drive. If you do not choose this, you cannot run BitLocker.

5. On the next screen, choose the location of your USB drive, and then click Save.

6. The Create Recovery Password screen appears; click the button to do so.

7. The Save the Recovery Password screen appears. You can choose from saving the password to a USB drive, saving it to a folder, showing the password on the screen so you can write it down, or printing the password to any configured printer. You can select more than one of these choices by clicking the Back button after completing the screens for that option. Next, you'll be presented some information about disk encryption.

8. The Encrypt the Selected Disk Volume screen appears; here, click the Encrypt button. The status bar appears, and encryption commences. You can expect the process to take about one minute per gigabyte of stored data.

Recovering BitLocker-Protected Data

In BitLocker parlance, a partition is "locked" when its encryption key can't be automatically generated. Recall that upon boot, BitLocker looks for the key with the TPM or a USB key. If, for any reason, this key can't be accessed or has been tampered with, or if the user forgets his PIN that he selects during the BitLocker initialization process, the drive locks itself, and thus, a boot is prevented.

When a computer becomes locked, it can't accept regular keyboard input. You must use the function keys to enter the recovery password to gain access to your data; F1 represents the digit 1, F2 represents 2, and so on. F10 represents 0.

It's harmless to actually trip the TPM mechanism so you can test data recovery—all you need to do is turn TPM off and reboot the computer. With the TPM off, BitLocker can't access the key to decrypt the drive, and the computer will automatically lock. Open the TPM Management Console (type **tpm.msc** in the search box after opening the Start menu), and under Actions, click Turn TPM Off. You'll likely need to provide the password you implemented when claiming ownership of the TPM. Remove any USB drives that contain your key, and then shut down the computer. Upon restart, input your recovery password, and you'll gain access to your data.

Disabling BitLocker

Turning off BitLocker requires a choice: you can opt to temporarily disable BitLocker and its protection, which allows changes to the contents of the TPM and upgrades to the underlying Windows Vista installation, or you can choose to decrypt the drive, which of course disables BitLocker, except on a permanent basis. If you decrypt the drive, the recovery keys you generated are automatically voided, and if you choose to enable BitLocker again, you'll need to choose different ones.

You will need administrator rights to disable BitLocker, and you must be able to boot into Vista to perform the procedure. To turn off BitLocker, follow these steps:

1. Open the Control Panel.

2. Click Security, and then click BitLocker Drive Encryption. You may need to acknowledge the User Account Control prompt.

3. The BitLocker Drive Encryption screen appears. Click Turn off BitLocker Drive Encryption.

4. The What Level of Decryption Do You Want? screen appears. Choose either to disable BitLocker or to decrypt the volume. If you choose to decrypt, expect the process to take about one minute for every gigabyte.

CHAPTER 12

Hooking Up Wired and Wireless Networks

Choosing wireless networking over more traditional wired networking has always troubled users, more than likely because they've seen lots of bad press regarding the wireless technology over the past few years. Unfortunately, these stories were not unfounded; with security-enforcing technologies such as Wired Equivalent Privacy (WEP) being demonstrably insecure, it's little wonder it has taken wireless networking until now to penetrate the home PC marketplace as well as it has.

Recent improvements in the speed and security of wireless solutions have somewhat changed things, with new standards such as 802.11g and 802.11a allowing greater connection speeds whilst adding a new layer of security called Wi-Fi Protected Access (WPA), which affords a much higher level of assurance than its predecessor, WEP.

However, before you decide whether to use wireless or wired networking, you still have to consider some other issues. In many cases, you'd still be better off using traditional copper cabling since you'll get the maximum available bandwidth and much less noise on the line, for that matter—a fundamental requirement for services such as streaming digital video using Media Center.

Vista introduces a new range of networking features through its completely redesigned stack, known as the *next-generation TCP/IP stack*, with better and easier ways of configuring your systems and more secure ways of keeping the bad guys out.

This chapter introduces you to the fundamental components and principles that comprise the modern networking environment before covering more specifically how to set one up using Vista.

Going Wireless

Vista makes going wireless much easier than ever before by integrating wireless LAN (WLAN) drivers into the operating system. WLAN network cards automatically configure themselves, making it possible to install and configure a WLAN in a matter of minutes.

WLAN technology offers you many benefits: the flexibility to access your network from anywhere within range of the access point means you can use a PDA or laptop from anywhere in your home.

> **NOTE** WLAN NICs are like cabled NICs insomuch as both types are Ethernet based and both support IP. The central hub of a WLAN is called an *access point* but in essence performs the same job as the standard network hub or switch.

The minimum you need to set up a wireless network is two WLAN network cards (connecting in a manner known as *ad hoc*). These allow two computers to connect to each other.

However, it's strongly recommended that you use a wireless access point for all WLAN systems. Access points act as the police in managing the connections of wireless devices to your network and transmitting and receiving all network data from your wireless devices in the same way a regular network switch might. The added security features provided by an access point, as well as the ease of network management, make this a much better solution than the ad hoc, point-to-point setup.

Getting Connected

To get started, you'll first have to introduce Vista to the rest of your networking environment and configure it to talk the same language as the rest of your systems.

The following procedure should get you started:

1. Click the Start menu, and then select Connect To.
2. Click the hyperlink Set Up a Connection or Network.
3. Select the type of connection you are trying to set up from the list, and then click Next.

> **NOTE** The choices you have in making a connection are to connect the Internet directly from your PC, to set up a wireless network, to set up a dial-up connection, or to connect to a workplace using a virtual private network (VPN).

4. Depending on the type of network you decide to set up, you will be presented with a different route through the wizard. In each case, you will be required to enter the details appropriate to that connection, such as the wireless network name, your broadband username and password, or the telephone number of the dial-up service. When you're done and the wizard finishes, you can proceed to the Network and Sharing Center.

Working with Networks

If you are used to setting up a network in Windows XP or previous versions of Windows operating systems, Vista will seem somewhat different. But stick with it, and it will become second nature in no time.

It's worth remembering that although Vista is more functionally rich than any other desktop operating system under the hood, Microsoft's primary goal in design was to expose this power to the general user. This explains not only the complete redesign of the networking architecture to cater for new functionality and interoperability, such as the IPv6 stack, but also the total redesign of the interface to make it more intuitive to less informed users.

To help you get the most out of Vista's plethora of networking capabilities, the following section introduces three features for configuring, managing, and troubleshooting your network:

- Network and Sharing Center
- Network Map
- Network Connections

The Network and Sharing Center

The first port of call for network configuration is the Network and Sharing Center. To open the Network and Sharing Center, you need to do the following:

1. Click the Start button, and then select Control Panel.

2. Click the Network and Internet category, and then click Network and Sharing Center, as shown in Figure 12-1.

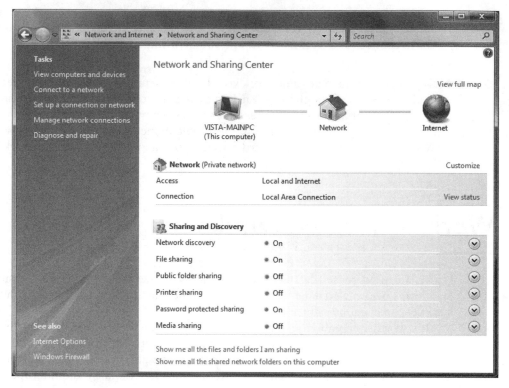

Figure 12-1 *The Network Center is the place to start when configuring a network.*

From the Network and Sharing Center, you get an instant feeling for how your network is functioning. If you have a fully operational connection to the network and onward to the Internet, the map at the top of the screen should show you the PC on the left, connected with a green line to the Network icon (the small house) and another green line to the Internet (the world icon).

If there is a problem in any stage of the connection, you'll see a red *x* marking where the problem is, as shown in Figure 12-2.

If you click the red *x*, Vista tries to diagnose what the root cause of the problem might be, and in the case of the example shown in Figure 12-3, it reports that the Local Area Connection network adapter (which is the default adapter) is disabled. It also, in this case, offers you the ability to enable it from this dialog box.

When your network connection *is* fully operational, you'll see three distinct panels on the Network and Sharing Center main screen. At the top, you'll see the network map (more about this in a moment); in the middle of the screen, you'll see specific network details; and at the bottom of the screen, you'll see Sharing and Discovery.

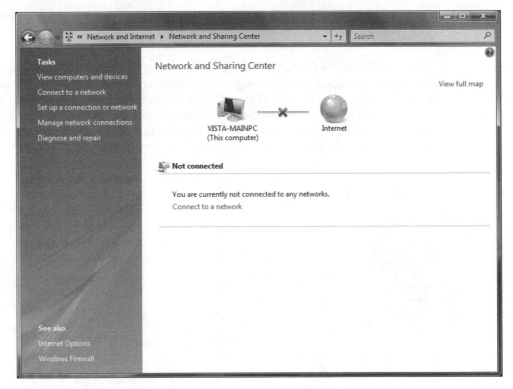

Figure 12-2 *Connection problems are highlighted on the map using a red x.*

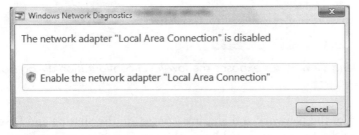

Figure 12-3 *The Network and Sharing Center diagnoses problems and offers a solution to try to fix the connection.*

You can click any of the icons in the network map to open a Windows Explorer window on that resource. Clicking the PC icon will open Windows Explorer to the main Computer folder view. If you click Network, you'll see a Windows Explorer view of all the PCs visible to Vista on your network. Finally, clicking the Internet icon will open Internet Explorer and go to your preconfigured home page.

Looking at the Network section, you'll see that your network is described as having access as Local and Internet and your connection as Local Area Connection. Clicking the View status link will open the Local Area Connection Status dialog box, as shown in Figure 12-4, where you can configure the details of how your connection is set up (you'll learn more about this in Chapter 13).

> **TIP** Try clicking the Customize option to the far right of the screen opposite Network. This allows you to change the network name to something more meaningful than the default name of Network as well as to instruct Vista whether this system is in a public or private location. If your computer is a kiosk in a library, for example, limit its visibility on the network by selecting Public. The Private setting is best used within the confines of your own home or office.

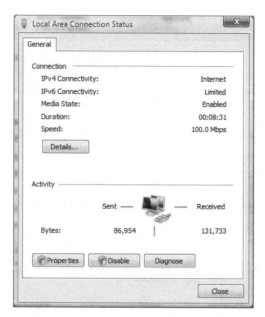

Figure 12-4 *Clicking View Status exposes the low-level configuration dialog box for your NIC.*

At the bottom of the Network and Sharing Center are the Sharing and Discovery settings. Next to each of the items listed here, notice an arrow pointing down on the right side of the screen. Clicking the down arrow will reveal further settings pertinent for each of the six configuration items. A status light indicator tells you immediately whether the capability is enabled or disabled. Table 12-1 describes the settings available for each list item.

Next we'll take a quick look at the functions available on the task pane on the left side of the Network and Sharing Center.

Table 12-1 Sharing and Discovery Settings for Vista Networks

Name	Options	Settings (Default in Bold)	Description
Network Discovery	Turn On Network Discovery	**Enabled**	Vista can see and access other systems on your network.
	Turn Off Network Discovery	Disabled	If you enable this, Vista cannot see and access other systems on your network.
File Sharing	Turn On File Sharing	**Enabled**	Vista shares local resources with other network hosts.
	Turn Off File Sharing	Disabled	If enabled, Vista will not share local resources with other network hosts.
Public Folder Sharing	Turn On Sharing So Anyone with Network Access Can Open Files	Disabled	If you enable this, anyone with network access can access files in your Public folder (not just users on your computer).
	Turn On Sharing So Anyone with Network Access Can Open, Change, and Create Files	Disabled	If you enable this setting, network users have full control over files in your Public folder.
	Turn Off Sharing (People Logged On to This Computer Can Still Access This Folder)	**Enabled**	The Public folder is not shared on the network but is still accessible to all local users on your PC.
Printer Sharing	Turn On Printer Sharing	Disabled	If this is enabled, other users on the network can access your locally connected printer.
	Turn Off Printer Sharing	**Enabled**	You cannot share local printing resources with network users.
Password Protected Sharing	Turn On Password Protected Sharing	Enabled (default)	Users can access shared resources on this computer only if they have a local user account.
	Turn Off Password Protected Sharing	Disabled	If you enable this, all network users have free access.
Media Sharing		Disabled	You can enable media sharing through Window Media Player for sharing pictures, MP3 files, and digital video.

> **NOTE** The Public folder is a quick and simple way to share files on your computer. Any other user on your computer can access any file or folder placed in the Public folder. If you share the Public folder on the network, users on other computers can also access these files and folders. The Public folder is accessible using Windows Explorer from within the Desktop node.

View Computers and Devices opens a Windows Explorer window showing the network devices discovered on your local area network, as shown in Figure 12-5.

Figure 12-5 *View all devices connected to your network, and browse available resources.*

Double-clicking the visible computers or network devices allows you to access their resources, such as shared folders and printers.

Clicking Connect to a Network opens the dialog box where you can select another network to which you'd like to connect. This is useful if you want to switch to a wireless network or move to a new wired network if you change locations, such as if you use your laptop in your office and your home.

If you select Set Up a Connection or Network, you will see the list of available network types you can select from to create a new connection.

Manage Network Connections displays a full list of the connections configured on your system, and by double-clicking any you are interested in, you can subsequently adjust its connection properties (covered in more detail in Chapter 13).

Diagnose and Repair tells Vista to determine what the cause of a problem might be and to offer some advice about how to fix it. You can usually fix simple problems by this method.

Network Map

Clicking Full Network Map will show you the full extent of your network. It uses the neighbor detection functionality built into Vista's new stack to show you the complete (as far as possible) picture of what's connected to what. Here you'll see computers, peripherals, and networking equipment such as routers.

From the network map interface, you can click any of the displayed icons to be taken to the associated network resource. If you click a router, for example, and that router has a configuration interface available for access over the network, you can access the interface in a new window (although you may have to authenticate yourself to that device before proceeding).

Network Connections

The Network Connections window displays every network connection configured on your computer, as shown in Figure 12-6.

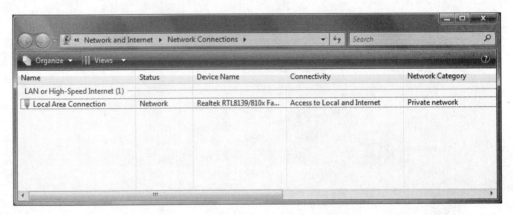

Figure 12-6 *Use Network Connections to view all the network interfaces configured on your system.*

To access Network Connections, you need to open the Network and Sharing Center as previously described and then, in the left pane, click Manage Network Connections.

You can right-click any available connection to get the following options:

- Disable allows you to stop access to the network interface. You can use this to isolate your system from the rest of the network in the event of, for example, a virus outbreak.

- Status will display a new window that shows some information about the connection, such as the number of bytes sent and received on that interface, the speed of the connection, and how long the interface has been active.

- Diagnose runs a small diagnostic routine to try to determine why a malfunctioning interface has failed. If it can fix the problem, it offers to do so.

- Bridge Connections allows you to select two network interfaces—for instance, a LAN connection to a wireless interface—and join them. This means network traffic is sent from one network to the other through this system. You need to have two independent interfaces available to use this facility.

- Create Shortcut speaks for itself.

- Delete removes the network interface configuration. To reverse this, you need to set it up again from scratch.

- Rename changes the name assigned to the interface, allowing you to give it a more meaningful name than the default.

- Properties, the contents of which are covered in detail in Chapter 13, takes you to the dialog box that forms the fundamental configuration settings for your system to interoperate on the network.

Understanding TCP/IP

You've no doubt heard of TCP/IP before now, but what really is it? It stands for Transmission Control Protocol/Internet Protocol and is the industry networking standard used most widely today. Other networking standards also exist, but with the advent of the Internet, which is solely based on the services provided by TCP/IP, and with Microsoft standardizing all platform development on the paradigm of "Internet readiness," then it's little wonder TCP/IP is removing all competition.

The protocol was designed as a global player, capable of routing many diverse networks together over a number of connection types (from slow dial-up to the staggering speeds of some of the modern SDSL connections, which can carry data up to 24Mbps (for example, ADSL 2).

Vista relies heavily on the underlying principles of TCP/IP to create the networked environment, and many of the services and applications you have come to rely on in the modern world, such as email and the Internet, would not be possible without TCP/IP.

> **NOTE** The TCP/IP stack (the software that makes TCP/IP work) has been completely rewritten in Vista to iron out some of the previous operating systems' deficiencies in operation. Fortunately, Microsoft has completely reengineered it and adhered more than ever to industry standards. This means Vista is the most interoperable of the Windows operating system family, now with built-in support for the next generation of TCP/IP systems based on an updated protocol called IPv6.

The standards for TCP/IP are published as open source documents on the Internet, all in the format of ratified documents known as Requests for Comments (RFCs). These RFCs detail the workings of every underlying TCP/IP service and can be used by system developers when they are creating new applications or operating systems that need to interoperate within a TCP/IP environment.

> **NOTE** To see a current list of the RFCs available, go to the Internet Engineering Task Force's home page, but be warned—they are not light reading. Everything you need to know about the configuration and administration of TCP/IP is covered in this chapter, but if you must start digging into the RFC database, take a look at the following web site: http://www.ietf.org/rfc.html.

Conquering the Jargon

Looking at a TCP/IP configuration dialog box for the first time can certainly be confusing. You have to get the hang of a whole collection of acronyms, and you must enter required information into lots of data fields. If you're not so familiar with networks, it might seem like you're about to embark on a long, grueling, uphill struggle before you are ready to set up a network.

However, never fear; Vista has been designed in such a way as to ensure you don't have to worry too much about any of the underlying network configuration if you don't want to, but to really get under the hood, it's worth digging just a little deeper into TCP/IP. First, though, we'll present a typical TCP/IP configuration dialog box, as shown in Figure 13-1.

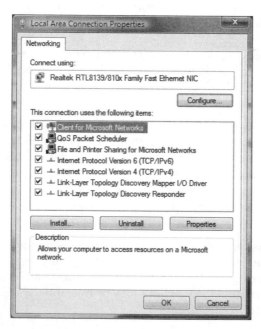

Figure 13-1 *Network connection properties for a typical Ethernet NIC*

Start by clicking Start ➤ Control Panel ➤ Network and Internet ➤ Network and Sharing Center. Click Manage Network Connections; then, in the list of interfaces, right-click the one you are interested in, and then select Properties.

For now, we're going to look at IPv4 settings; we'll cover the new IPv6 standard later in this chapter. Highlight Internet Protocol Version 4 (TCP/IPv4), and then click Properties. You'll see the dialog box used to configure the appropriate settings for your TCP/IP v4 network, as shown in Figure 13-2.

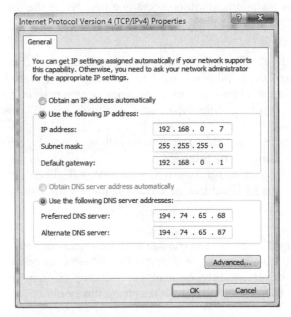

Figure 13-2 *Properties for a TCP/IP v4 network interface*

On this screen, you'll see the following terms:

- Dynamic Host Configuration Protocol (DHCP) is a method of address allocation used by network clients to obtain an IP address from an authoritative server, such as your ISP.

- The IP address is the unique address used by your computer to communicate within the TCP/IP networking environment. There can never be two systems configured with the same IP address on your network. You cannot enter your own IP address details if the DHCP radio button is selected.

- The subnet mask associated with your IP address identifies in which network the computer is participating. This can also be assigned using DHCP.

- The Domain Name System (DNS) translates meaningful names such as www.microsoft.com into reachable IP addresses. DNS servers operate across the entire Internet space, helping worldwide clients resolve names.

- The Advanced tab takes you further into the depths of TCP/IP, allowing you to configure other methods of name resolution or add IP addresses on each NIC interface.

Understanding the IP Address

Every single networked system in a TCP/IP environment has a unique address. This allows systems to locate and chatter with each other and is known as the *IP address*.

> **NOTE** Systems that participate in a TCP/IP network are known as *hosts*. This applies to NAS storage devices, workstations, printers, and any other device that requires an IP address.

An old analogy (but a good one) likens an IP address to a street address. The street address uniquely identifies the house, allowing mail to (mostly) be delivered from anywhere in the world. The same follows suit on a network: every system must be uniquely identifiable from every other; otherwise, data wouldn't get to where it's supposed to go.

The conventions for formatting host addresses must be followed closely, especially if the host system will be connecting to the Internet.

In most cases when you connect to the Internet, your ISP will allocate your IP address. ISPs maintain large pools of IP addresses and subsequently allocate these to their clients on connection.

> **NOTE** IP addresses assigned by an ISP can change each time you connect. This is because they are allocated from the pool held by the ISP. When your connection terminates, you lose your address, and someone else may end up using it. The next time you connect, you get the next available address from the pool.

Each IP address is a 32-bit number, written in decimal form as four numbers separated by full stops (also referred to as a *dotted-quad*). The notation looks something like this: 127.0.0.1.

Each section of the IP address (each of the four 8-bit numbers) is known as an *octet*. There are eight positions when translated into their binary equivalent, such as 100010101, and each octet has a decimal range of 0 through 255.

The address consists of two parts:

- The *network ID*, used to create a pool of addresses that can be allocated to hosts
- The *host ID*, identifying each individual host

Because this numbering system theoretically can support 4.3 billion combinations of IP addresses, a system had to be devised to control their allocation. To accomplish this, the *class system* groups IP addresses into varying sized networks.

You need to know about five address classes; each has a different number of hosts per network ratio:

Class A: These addresses are assigned to extremely large networks, such as international companies, that need to connect a large number of host systems. IP addresses with the first octet from 1 to 126 are part of this class. The other three octets are free to be used internally by the owner in whatever way they see fit. This means each of the 126 allocated Class A networks can have a total number of 16,777,214 hosts.

> **NOTE** In reality, most Class A network addresses have been allocated by being farmed off to network providers such as AT&T and Sprint. Many Class A addresses have been allocated at a regional level through national agencies for each Internet-enabled country (such as the United Kingdom, Australia, and Canada), and in each case, the Class A network would be further partitioned to allocate smaller network portions to controlling bodies such as ISPs.

Class B: Class B addresses are allocated to medium-sized networks, such as university campuses. IP addresses with a first octet from 128 to 191 are part of this class. Class B addresses also include the second octet as part of their assigned identifier. The other two octets identify the host. Class B networks (of which there are a total number of 16,384 possible) allow for 65,534 hosts.

Class C: These addresses are commonly assigned to small/mid-sized businesses with the IP addresses from 192 to 223 in the first octet. Class C addresses also include the second and third octets. There are a total of 2,097,152 Class C networks, each allowing 254 hosts to connect.

Class D: Class D addresses are special addresses used exclusively for network multi-casts. Multicasting is used for broadcast-style communications, such as that of streaming video or audio.

Class E: Class E addresses are reserved for experimental purposes and should be of no consequence to a small-business environment.

Small networks, such as Class C networks, are relatively easy to manage, but imagine trying to keep 16 million hosts under control if you owned one of those Class A networks—not an easy task. For this reason, a system known as *subnetting* was introduced to allow people to split large networks into smaller, more manageable ones.

A *subnet* is a defined portion of a network that allows systems with that subnet to directly communicate. To communicate with systems outside the subnet, information must be passed through a device that knows about the existence of the other network, with an interface on both networks. This device is known as a *router*.

Configuring IP Addresses in Vista

As soon as you've come to grips with the basic principles of IP addressing, it's easy to set up large, seemingly complicated networks in no time at all. First you need to understand three important aspects of configuration:

- The *IP address*, to recap, is the unique address assigned to each host on your network. This network might be a private network or an Internet-allocated one from one of the address classes A through C. This IP address contains all the information needed by your computer to allow it to recognize both the network ID and the host ID.

- The *subnet mask* determines on which portion of the network your host is communicating. (A complicated algorithm is used to mask the IP address against the subnet number.)

- The *default gateway* is effectively the doorway from your network to the outside world. Chances are it is your router's address.

> **NOTE** Certain ranges of addresses are reserved for private network use, starting with the first two octets, such as 192.168.x.x. These can be used within your business.

The three amigos: the IP address, the subnet mask, and the default gateway. Without the first two, nothing would work. Without the third, you'd never find anyone outside your own network.

Understanding DNS

So, if IP addresses uniquely identify hosts on the Internet, why don't you simply type the IP address when you want to connect to Amazon.com? Easy: because it's a pain in the neck. So, to get around this problem, you will be exploiting the system known as DNS.

> **NOTE** If you wanted, you could connect to Amazon.com by IP address only, but remembering these addresses would be nearly impossible. Humans need human-readable names, and that's why we use DNS.

When you surf the Web, you tend to type the universal resource locator (URL) for the address of the system, the first part of which is the DNS name of the server you are trying to contact.

Domain names consist of two or more parts separated by dots, with the piece on the left being the most specific, and the piece on the right being the most general—for example, Microsoft.com. Because IP addresses are numbers but humans work better with "real" names, some method was required to translate the numerical IP address into a more easily recognizable name—the domain name.

The sole purpose of DNS is to turn readable names into IP addresses so network systems can contact each other using the correct address. The deluge of computers that flood the Internet use a distributed database of domain names that maps all names to corresponding IP addresses. This database is available to all computers and users of the Internet, allowing your local business systems to perform DNS lookups anytime they need.

Understanding DHCP and Static Addressing

If you are connecting to an ISP for your broadband connection, chances are that your router or Vista interface will request an IP address from the ISP's DHCP server. In this way, you need do nothing at all, and the system will configure itself to work. However, if you are setting up your own local network, you might consider using static addresses so you know who has which address, allocating addresses from one of the private address ranges, such as 192.168.0.0. This way, you can configure sequentially each PC on your network with an address from this range, as follows (note that the only thing to change in each case is the IP address):

Here's the configuration for PC 1:

```
IP Address: 192.168.0.2
Subnet Mask: 255.255.255.0
Default Gateway: 192.168.0.1
Preferred DNS server: 194.73.23.34
Alternate DNS server: 194.73.23.35
```

Here's the configuration for PC 2:

```
IP Address: 192.168.0.3
Subnet Mask: 255.255.255.0
Default Gateway: 192.168.0.1
Preferred DNS server: 194.73.23.34
Alternate DNS server: 194.73.23.35
```

Here's the configuration for PC 3:

```
IP Address: 192.168.0.4
Subnet Mask: 255.255.255.0
Default Gateway: 192.168.0.1
Preferred DNS server: 194.73.23.34
Alternate DNS server: 194.73.23.35
```

From these examples, you can see that the hosts on your network start from 192.168.0.2, and the gateway (access to the Internet) is set as 192.168.0.1.

It's clear from this example that DHCP addressing would be much easier to implement, especially for security purposes (you might be scouting through event logs to look for unusual activity whereby it's easier to trace an IP address to a computer if it's static).

> **NOTE** If you don't want to configure IP addresses yourself, leave the settings as DHCP to force Vista to do it for you. If no DHCP server is discovered on your network, Vista uses what's called an automatic private IP address (APIPA), which allocates addresses from the range 169.254.0.1 to 169.254.255.254 with a subnet mask of 255.255.255.0. The APIPA does not allocate DNS server addresses, so if you need to contact Internet hosts by URL name, you'll still need to manually configure DNS addresses in the interface properties.

Gathering TCP/IP Information

You have no way to tell from the interface Properties dialog box what a DHCP-allocated IP address is. To find out what your IP settings are, you need to use the command-line interface.

To start the command-line interface, hold down the Windows logo key, and press the R key. In the text-entry box, type **cmd.exe**, and then press Enter. At the command prompt, type **ipconfig /all**, and then press Enter. Figure 13-3 shows the results.

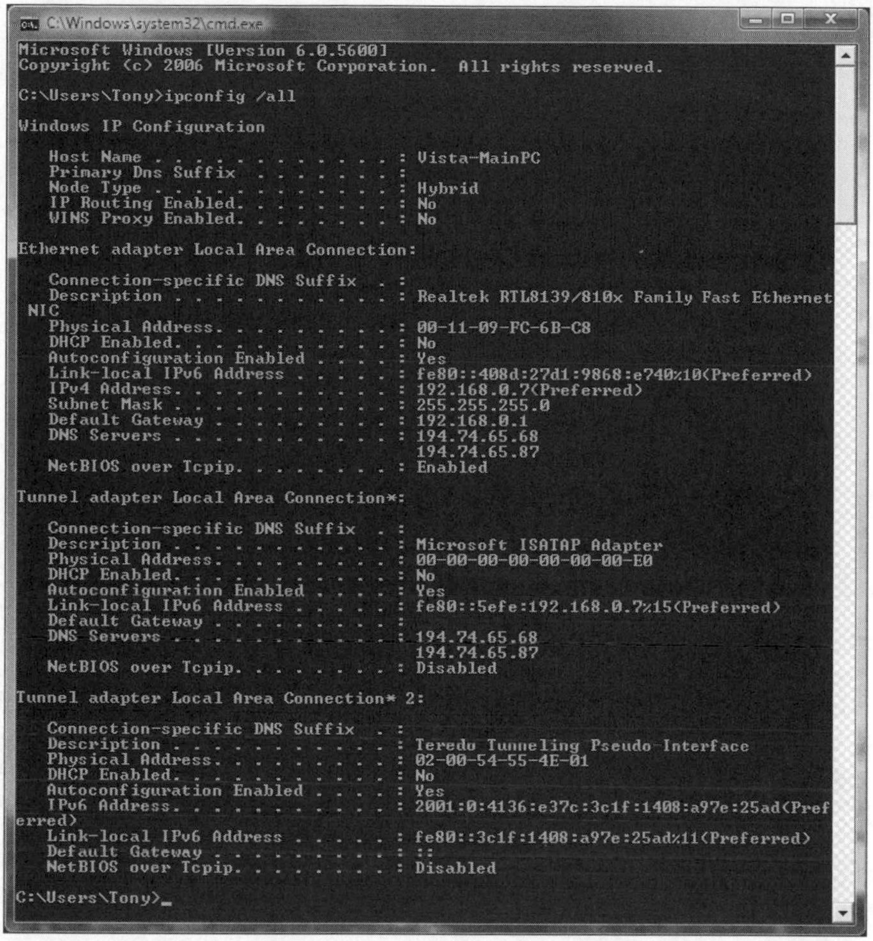

```
C:\Windows\system32\cmd.exe
Microsoft Windows [Version 6.0.5600]
Copyright (c) 2006 Microsoft Corporation.  All rights reserved.

C:\Users\Tony>ipconfig /all

Windows IP Configuration

   Host Name . . . . . . . . . . . . : Vista-MainPC
   Primary Dns Suffix  . . . . . . . :
   Node Type . . . . . . . . . . . . : Hybrid
   IP Routing Enabled. . . . . . . . : No
   WINS Proxy Enabled. . . . . . . . : No

Ethernet adapter Local Area Connection:

   Connection-specific DNS Suffix  . :
   Description . . . . . . . . . . . : Realtek RTL8139/810x Family Fast Ethernet
 NIC
   Physical Address. . . . . . . . . : 00-11-09-FC-6B-C8
   DHCP Enabled. . . . . . . . . . . : No
   Autoconfiguration Enabled . . . . : Yes
   Link-local IPv6 Address . . . . . : fe80::408d:27d1:9868:e740%10(Preferred)
   IPv4 Address. . . . . . . . . . . : 192.168.0.7(Preferred)
   Subnet Mask . . . . . . . . . . . : 255.255.255.0
   Default Gateway . . . . . . . . . : 192.168.0.1
   DNS Servers . . . . . . . . . . . : 194.74.65.68
                                       194.74.65.87
   NetBIOS over Tcpip. . . . . . . . : Enabled

Tunnel adapter Local Area Connection*:

   Connection-specific DNS Suffix  . :
   Description . . . . . . . . . . . : Microsoft ISATAP Adapter
   Physical Address. . . . . . . . . : 00-00-00-00-00-00-00-E0
   DHCP Enabled. . . . . . . . . . . : No
   Autoconfiguration Enabled . . . . : Yes
   Link-local IPv6 Address . . . . . : fe80::5efe:192.168.0.7%15(Preferred)
   Default Gateway . . . . . . . . . :
   DNS Servers . . . . . . . . . . . : 194.74.65.68
                                       194.74.65.87
   NetBIOS over Tcpip. . . . . . . . : Disabled

Tunnel adapter Local Area Connection* 2:

   Connection-specific DNS Suffix  . :
   Description . . . . . . . . . . . : Teredo Tunneling Pseudo-Interface
   Physical Address. . . . . . . . . : 02-00-54-55-4E-01
   DHCP Enabled. . . . . . . . . . . : No
   Autoconfiguration Enabled . . . . : Yes
   IPv6 Address. . . . . . . . . . . : 2001:0:4136:e37c:3c1f:1408:a97e:25ad(Pref
erred)
   Link-local IPv6 Address . . . . . : fe80::3c1f:1408:a97e:25ad%11(Preferred)
   Default Gateway . . . . . . . . . : ::
   NetBIOS over Tcpip. . . . . . . . : Disabled

C:\Users\Tony>_
```

Figure 13-3 *Use `ipconfig /all` to view your IP address, subnet mask, gateway, and DNS settings.*

Introducing TCP/IP Version 6

As you've already seen earlier in this chapter, Vista's next-generation network stack has dual support for both TCP/IP version 4 and TCP/IP version 6. You configure IPv6 settings using the same Properties dialog box you use for configuring IPv4, but you'll have to select Internet Protocol Version 6 (TCP/IPv6) rather than Internet Protocol Version 4 (TCP/IPv4).

The configuration dialog box is slightly different from that of IPv4, although principles such as DHCP and DNS remain extant, as shown in Figure 13-4.

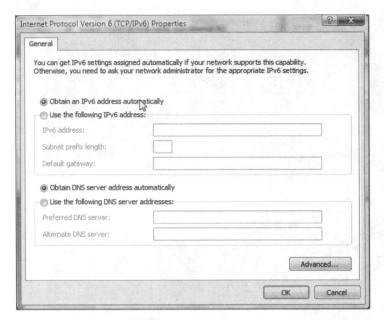

Figure 13-4 *IPv6 properties are slightly different from that of IPv4.*

Even though the next-generation TCP/IP stack has a split personality, it still automatically supports both the IPv4 and IPv6 protocols simultaneously. This is good news for both network administrators and regular users because it means nothing has to be done on the client (on Vista) to get the appropriate addressing information onto the PC, especially if your network infrastructure supports DHCPv6.

Who Needs More IP Addresses?

You might be wondering why you need IPv6 at all. What's wrong with IPv4? The major change in IPv6 is the vast increase in the number of available addresses for network hosts, whereby every single possible and perceivable device could have its own unique address. In comparison with IPv4 addresses where there are 4.3×10^9 available, IPv6 supports 3.4×10^{38} addresses.

> *[Ipv6 offers] 5×10 ^28 (50 octillion) for each of the roughly 6.5 billion people alive today, or almost 57 billion addresses for each gram of matter in the earth.*
>
> —Wikipedia

To provide such a vast number of network addresses, the length of the address has had to increase from 32-bits long as it was with IPv4 to a massive 128-bits long in IPv6, comprising a 64-bit subnet section and a 64-bit host section.

The notation for this 128-bit address is in the form of eight hexadecimal number groups, written like this: 1101:08ab:23c2:3abc:90ae:7654:23df:abcd.

You can address an IPv6 host in a URL form by embedding the address in the hyperlink as follows: http://[1101:08ab:23c2:3abc:90ae:7654:23df:abcd]/.

To find out more about IPv6 and how it might affect you in the future, take a look at the RFC posted on the Internet Engineering Task Force web site at http://tools.ietf.org/html/rfc2460.

CHAPTER 14

Connecting to the Internet

To connect your Vista PC to the Internet so you can begin consuming services such as email and web browsing, you'll need to set an account up with an Internet service provider (ISP).

> **NOTE** ISPs are effectively agents that act on behalf of (under license) the Internet authorities, offering domain name registration, DNS services, and IP address allocation. The added value an ISP offers comes from its unique service or cost model that provides the end user with Internet capabilities. Many ISPs specialize in cost-effective web hosting or ecommerce engines, while others, such as the telecom companies, specialize more in straightforward connectivity and basic services such as email. It is not unusual for computer users these days to acquire the services of multiple ISPs to ensure the best possible deals on each individual service required.

ISPs provide the following services:

- Physical Internet connectivity
- The connection device, such as an ADSL modem
- Email accounts
- Security advice
- Domain names and web hosting
- Advice on configuring the interconnectivity between your network and the Internet

When you are considering which ISP best suits your needs, check how wide-ranging and versatile its service portfolio is. You certainly don't want to be tied into a yearlong contract that prohibits you from upgrading a costly dial-up connection to a cheaper and faster ADSL alternative.

Gathering the ISP Account Details

When you sign up for an ISP account, your ISP will give account details for logging in, accessing email, acquiring web mail services, and doing whatever else you've signed up for. The key information you'll need to have in hand before proceeding to configure Vista to connect is as follows:

- You'll need your account name and password.
- If you are using a modem, you'll need a telephone number to dial.
- If you are using DSL or cable, you'll need to understand how to configure your router.
- You'll need the email server addresses.
- You'll need the email collection's configuration details.
- You'll need the web mail server's URL and password.
- You'll need the DNS server's IP addresses.

Although we cover Windows Mail in more detail in Chapter 18, Figure 14-1 shows an example of filling in the account details within the application so it can connect to your ISP.

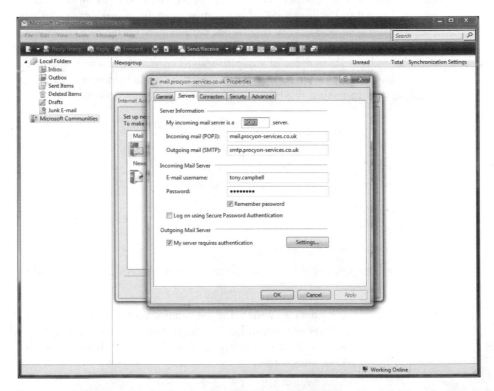

Figure 14-1 *Windows Mail requires ISP details to download email from the Internet.*

Creating the Connection in Vista

When you have everything set up and ready to go, the last stage is to run through the Connect to the Internet Wizard in Vista.

Click the Start button, select Connect To, and then select Set Up a Connection or Network. This will display the Choose a Connection Option dialog box, as shown in Figure 14-2.

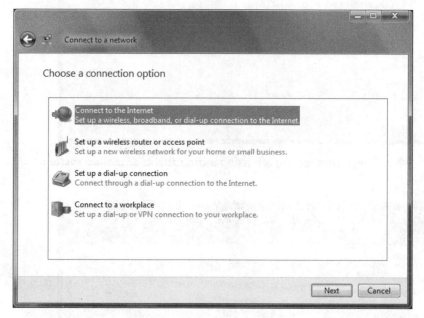

Figure 14-2 *Select the connection type you are using to reach your ISP.*

From here, you'll need to work through the following procedure:

1. To set up an Internet connection, click Connect to the Internet.

2. Select which connection type you are using from the list, either broadband or dial-up, as shown in Figure 14-3.

3. On the following screen, depending on which system you are using, you'll need to enter the account and connection details your ISP gave you when you set up your subscription. For a broadband connection, you'll need the username and password associated with the account. Alternatively, for a dial-up connection, you'll again need the username and password, but you'll also need the dial-up telephone number, as shown in Figure 14-4. When you're done, click Connect.

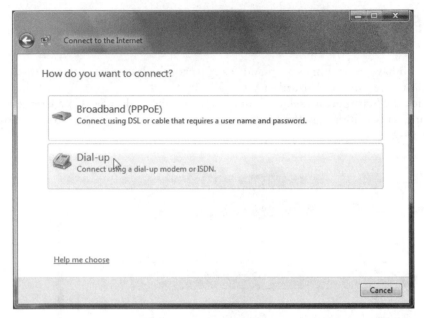

Figure 14-3 *Select whether you are using a broadband or dial-up system.*

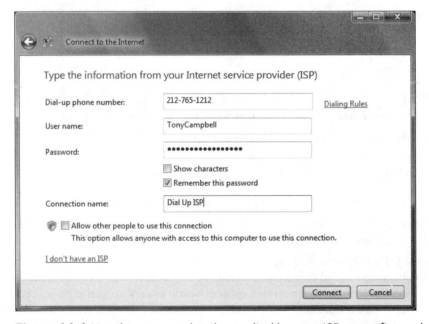

Figure 14-4 *Use the account details supplied by your ISP to configure the connection.*

4. Vista now tries to establish a connection to the ISP to test the new settings. If you are not physically connected at this stage, you can click Skip to complete the procedure. Otherwise, Vista will connect, using your preferred method, to the ISP and will present your account details. If successful, the connection will be established, and you should be able to start using the Web.

5. If there was a problem with the connection test and you expected it to work, you can ask Vista to try again or attempt to diagnose the problem. If you are happy that the connection details are correct and all is well, click Set Up the Connection Anyway.

In the future when you want to use this new connection, click the Start button, click Connect To, select the connection from the list (shown in Figure 14-5), and then click Connect.

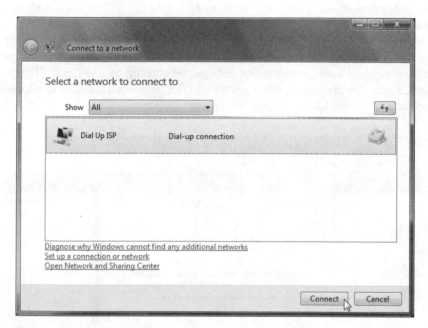

Figure 14-5 *Highlight a connection in the list, and then click Connect.*

Setting Up Internet Connection Sharing

It's possible to share an Internet connection with multiple PCs on your local area network using what's known as Internet Connection Sharing (ICS).

The PC being used for the primary Internet connection is always known as the ICS *host* computer, and it will have the physical connection to the ISP using the logon details and configuration information discussed earlier in this chapter.

To enable your ICS host to provide the necessary routing to the Internet for other PCs on your network, you should do the following:

1. Click the Start button, and then select Control Panel.

2. Click Network and Sharing Center; then, on the left side of the screen on the task list, click Manage Network Connections.

3. Right-click the connection you want to share with other users, select Properties from the context menu, and switch to the Sharing tab, as shown in Figure 14-6.

4. Under Internet Connection Sharing, check the Allow Other Network Users to Connect Through This Computer's Internet Connection checkbox, and then click OK.

> **NOTE** When you configure a system to become the ICS host, Vista will configure the LAN adapter with the new IP address of 192.168.0.1. The act of setting your system as an ICS host also allows it to operate as a DHCP server, allocating IP addresses to LAN systems automatically in the locally defined address range. If you have previously configured other systems with static addresses, you should return to their adapter configurations and change the settings to use DHCP. That way, the ICS host can update the other systems on the LAN when changes to addressing, such as the Internet DNS servers, take place.

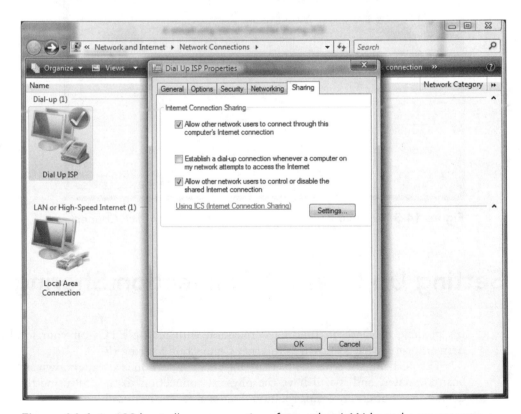

Figure 14-6 *An ICS host allows connections from other LAN-based systems onto the Internet.*

CHAPTER 15

Using the Remote Desktop Connection

The Remote Desktop Connection (RDC) allows remote computer systems to connect to Vista over a network connection. When a connection is established, it's possible to interact with the target system, obtaining a standard Vista desktop and working as if you were local to that computer.

> **NOTE** It may seem obvious, but to connect to a remote computer using the RDC service, you need to ensure the remote system is powered on and ready to accept incoming connections. An RDC might not work for a number of reasons, one of which has to do with the version of Vista to which you are trying to connect. RDC is designed to be used only in a business environment; hence, it is limited to being available in only the two business SKUs and the Ultimate edition.

Giving remote systems access to Vista is a two-stage process:

1. Switch on remote access on Vista.
2. Connect from the remote system using a Remote Desktop Protocol (RDP)–enabled client.

Switching On Remote Access

First things first—you need to configure Vista to allow remote-access users to log in. This process is straightforward and is completed as follows:

1. Click the Start button, and then select Control Panel.
2. Open the System and Maintenance category, and then select System.

3. On the left side of the screen, in the Task pane, click Remote Settings to open the System Properties dialog box, as shown in Figure 15-1.

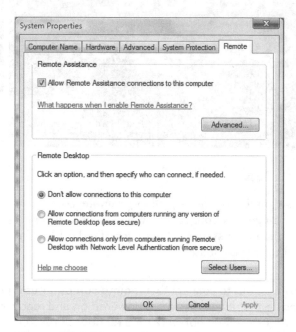

Figure 15-1 *You configure remote access and remote help from the System Properties dialog box.*

4. Look at the lower part of the dialog box under Remote Desktop. By default, remote access is switched off, with two options available for how it can be enabled.

TIP If you want to connect to this computer from a remote system also running Vista, you are immediately able to use the more secure version of remote access, Allow Connections Only from Computers Running Remote Desktop with Network Level Authentication. Network-level authentication is a new (for Vista) method of securing a network connection that relies on a user-based challenge response before you receive a login screen. In this way, only authorized users will even get a chance to form an IP connection with the host. An upgrade for the Windows XP RDP client is available from Microsoft that includes network-level authentication, which is the best option if you are accessing Vista from a legacy Windows operating system.

5. You should select the required level of protection, with the preferred and most secure being Allow Connections Only from Computers Running Remote Desktop with Network Level Authentication. The less secure but more accessible option, Allow Connections from Computers Running Any Version of Remote Desktop, is a better choice only if you are unsure of or cannot control the version of the client connection. For this example, we will assume you are using the more secure option.

6. Click the Select Users button to open the Remote Desktop Users dialog box, as shown in Figure 15-2.

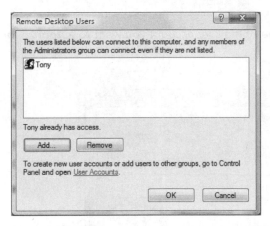

Figure 15-2 *Select the users who are authorized to remotely log in to your Vista system.*

7. When you first open the Remote Desktop Users dialog box, the list of authorized users is blank. To add a new user to the list, click Add.

> **TIP** It's a good idea, if you intend to audit a specific user's usage of your system over a remote connection, to consider setting up a new user account for remote access. In this way, in the Event Viewer you can easily differentiate and filter audit events generated by a remote user since they originate from a separate user account.

8. You are now asked to enter the object names to select. If you know the name of the user account you want to authorize, it's a simple matter of typing it in the dialog box and clicking Check Names, as shown in Figure 15-3.

9. If you are unsure of the user account details, you can click the Advanced button to open a search box that allows you to search through the local account database, as shown in Figure 15-4. If you click Find Now, you'll see a complete list of all user accounts and groups defined on your system. To add a user from the display to the authorized list, highlight the account name, and then click OK.

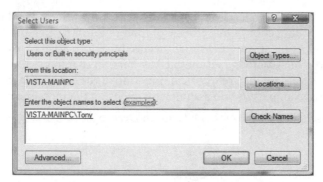

Figure 15-3 *Type the name of the user account you want to authorize for remote access.*

Figure 15-4 *Search for users or groups on the local system using the advanced search option.*

10. When you've added all the users you want to allow remote access to, click OK.

11. To remove users from the authorized list, highlight the name in the Remote Desktop Users dialog box, and then click Remove.

12. Finally, in the System Properties dialog box, click OK.

You are now ready to initiate a connection from a remote system using the RDP client.

Using the RDC Client

To instigate an RDC from another computer to your Vista system, you'll need to complete the following procedure:

1. In Vista, you can find the Remote Desktop Connection client by clicking the Start button, selecting Accessories, and then selecting Remote Desktop Connection. This starts the Remote Desktop Connection connection manager, as shown in Figure 15-5.

Figure 15-5 *Type the system name or IP address to which you are trying to connect.*

2. To form a connection with your Vista computer, it's a matter of typing in the system name or IP address and clicking the Connect button.

TIP You can find older versions of the Remote Desktop Connection client, such as the one used in Windows XP, for example, by selecting Start ➤ All Programs ➤ Accessories ➤ Communications.

When you click Connect (authentication permitting), the screen will change, and a new window will open (maximized at first) containing the Vista login screen. The name of the host computer appears at the top of screen. You can now log in to Vista and work as usual.

Setting the Remote Desktop Connection Options

The Remote Desktop Connection client is an extremely powerful interface and can do a lot more than meets the eye on first glance. Instead of clicking the Connect button, try clicking the Options button to expand the dialog box, as shown in Figure 15-6.

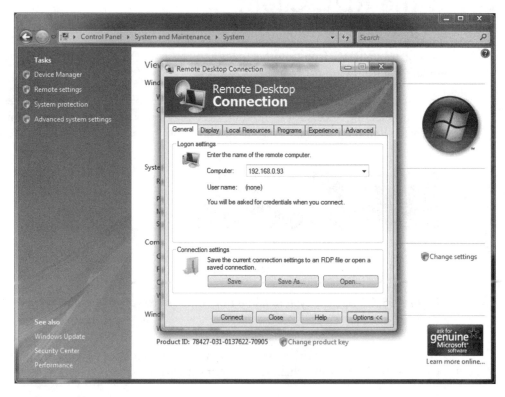

Figure 15-6 *Expand the Remote Desktop Connection options for greater control.*

> **TIP** It's possible to save remote connection configuration information and use it again in the future. You can also consider sending these configuration files to other users who need to connect to your system in order to make setting up the criteria as simple as loading the file. Use the Save, Save As, and Open buttons at the bottom of the dialog box to use these configuration files. You can identify a configuration file by its .rdf extension.

On the Display tab you'll find options for changing the available screen resolution and color handling, much in the same way you would find these options for your primary screen settings. The screen sizes will depend on your monitor, ranging from a relatively small window to a full screen.

The Local Resources tab, shown in Figure 15-7, will allow you to map resources on the remote computer to resources on your local computer. In this way, sounds generated on the computer you've connected to will be played through the local audio handler, and devices such as printers and the Clipboard will be transient over the network. Clicking the More button will allow you to select from a complete list of devices and drive letters and will allow you to authorize that all future connected devices also be mapped.

Figure 15-7 *Map remote system devices to the system running the RDC.*

The Programs tab allows you to specify an application that you would like to run automatically when you start the RDC. You can specify both the program path and its filename; you can also suggest a folder in which to start the application.

Clicking the Experience tab will reveal a variety of options that allow you to optimize the connection for the bandwidth you have available. In this way, you can cut back on functionality if you are connecting over a modem connection or increase functionality if you have a fast LAN speed or broadband connection.

Finally, the Advanced tab allows you to specify what happens when user authentication fails and also lets you specify settings for a Terminal Services gateway should you be using the RDC in an enterprise environment.

NOTE A *Terminal Services gateway* is a network server that allows authenticated/authorized users to connect to remote systems across a corporate network; it is a new Windows solution that allows access to remote desktop servers or workstations without the need to create a virtual private network (VPN). It can mediate connections from client computers through corporate firewalls as a proxy without having to allow direct access from the client.

CHAPTER 16

Setting Up a Network Presentation

In this chapter, we'll cover setting up a projector that you can access over the network, which allows you to give presentations without having to fuss with external monitor cables, connections, and all of the trouble that traditionally surrounds hooking your PC up to a projector.

Connecting the Projector

If you look in the Start menu under All Programs ➤ Accessories, you'll find an option called Connect to a Network Projector. Click this, and you'll see the dialog box shown in Figure 16-1.

A *network projector* is a video projection facility (much like you'd use to project movies onto a screen) that is connected either via a fixed cable system (a LAN) or a wireless solution to your network.

When you want to send a presentation to the projector, you simply stream the output over the network connection rather than the traditional way of sending it over fixed video cabling, which is more restrictive because of cable lengths than a network solution is.

When you first run the Connect to a Network Projector Wizard, the wizard can automatically search for and connect to a projector on the network—the projector's IP address and subnet must be configured to be contactable from your own LAN. Alternatively, if you already know the address of the network projector and want to type it, click Enter the Projector Address, and then follow the instructions to enter the host name. In both cases, if the projector requires a password (again, this is set up on the projector), you should enter it in the dialog box, as shown in Figure 16-2.

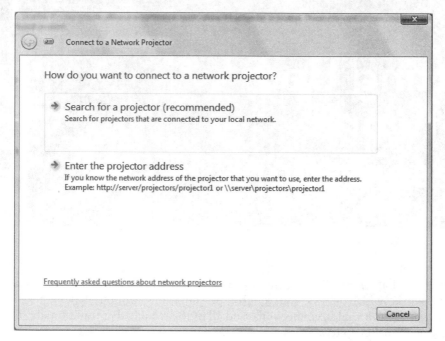

Figure 16-1 *Connect Vista to a network projector for a remote presentation.*

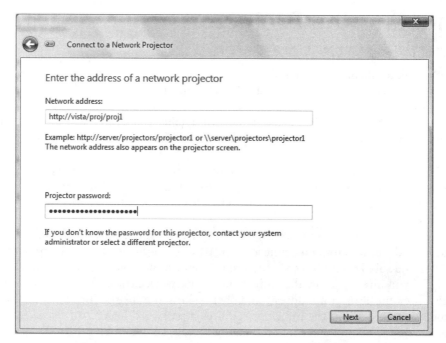

Figure 16-2 *Enter the projector's host name and password to initiate the connection.*

> **NOTE** Network projectors tend to use URL-style addresses, so they will always be prefixed by http://. Some also can be addresses using a universal naming convention address (a Windows host address) appearing as \\servername\projector. Your manufacturer's documentation for your projector should explain how to address your device.

A network presentation uses the same underlying networking technology as used by the Remote Desktop Connection (covered in Chapter 15) to communicate with the projector; in other words, it streams video output from the Vista PC to the projector using the Remote Desktop Protocol (RDP). For this reason, the encryption techniques leveraged by RDP apply also to the network presentation and secure sensitive data from network sniffers and hackers. If the presentation is delivered over a wireless networking solution, then the underlying network security, such as Wi-Fi Protected Access (WPA), encapsulates the network traffic and forces endpoint authentication. This means you can safely stream your presentation over the airwaves without any worry that you are being spied upon.

You'll find that many organizations will have meeting rooms where regular presentations are given to customers, staff, or investors. You can install network projectors in each of these conference rooms, allowing presenters to simply show up in the room, run the wizard, and start the presentation using the local hardware. Some offices may find that a fixed terminal with a wireless pointer and control for advancing the slides in a presentation is the best way, allowing users to work at their desk and then connect over the network from the presenter's terminal to a server for the presentation source (possibly a Microsoft PowerPoint file).

When you connect to a projector, the wizard will display an icon with or without a lock to denote whether it's secure.

The last step when you run through the wizard is to select whether to display your entire desktop or to extend your desktop in the same way you would extend it to attach a second monitor.

> **TIP** Consider the projector screen as a second physical desktop, and manage application distribution on the desktop accordingly.

Once you've established the connection with the projector and you have a working presentation, the wizard minimizes to an icon on the taskbar. At any time when the connection is active, you can click the icon and pause/resume the connection; if you are finished, you can click Disconnect.

> **TIP** You can connect to multiple projectors at once by running the Connect to a Network Projector Wizard multiple times. This is useful for giving corporate briefings where you have people physically located in different conference rooms but want them all to see the presentation simultaneously.

CHAPTER 17

Using Windows Internet Explorer 7

Despite all the controversy about whether Internet Explorer (IE) is a separate product or inextricably intertwined with Windows, or whether it should be bundled with the operating system, the fact of the matter is that millions upon millions of users load IE to view the Web each day. The next version of Internet Explorer, version 7, has a lot to offer these users, particularly when they're using IE 7 on Windows Vista.

In this chapter, we will discuss what's new and improved in Internet Explorer 7, and what the user-friendliest enhancements are and how to use them, and then we'll explore how to adjust just about every setting in IE. Finally, we'll discuss how to batten down IE's hatches a bit more than they already are to protect against unknown security vulnerabilities that exist in the wild.

Looking at the Major Areas of Improvement

The Internet Explorer 7 team focused on three areas of improvement over previous versions of IE: security, user experience, and the Internet Explorer platform. We'll examine those improvements in this section and also look at the differences in IE 7 between Windows XP and Vista.

Security

Of course, IE has been maligned in the press and on popular web sites over the past few years because of its many security flaws and vulnerabilities, some of which take three and four patches at a time to fully correct. It was impossible for IE 7 to be successful while still containing the many security flaws that its predecessors had. IE 7 is basically a rewrite from the ground up, offering all of the benefits of Microsoft's security initiatives, while bringing the fundamental code base up to a level of integrity that matches that of Windows Vista itself.

User Experience

The user experience in IE 6 left a lot to be desired. In the initial version of IE 6, there was no support for tabbed browsing, pop-up blockers, ad blocking, or many other conveniences that a more modern browser, like Mozilla Firefox, implements from the start. Another point of frustration for many web developers was IE 6's lack of comprehensive and consistent CSS support, making it very difficult to present a web page consistently to a user regardless of which browser he or she is using.

Internet Explorer Platform

Finally, Microsoft wanted IE to be more of a platform than a stand-alone web browser. In recent years, Microsoft has realized the value of creating software based on the web platform, and it recognizes that the large footprint of IE in terms of installed base gives the company massive leverage to deploy Web 2.0–based features. Additionally, the IE team wanted to include support for new technologies that are redefining the traditional web experience, like RSS feeds, transparent PNG support, and other, more modern mechanisms found on the Web.

The end result of the team's efforts is reflected in IE 7, which is available built into Windows Vista and as a stand-alone product for Windows XP with Service Pack 2. A lot has changed in this release. Some behind-the-scenes highlights include the following:

Protected Mode: In Protected Mode, IE runs in the lowest possible security context, limiting what dynamic add-ons and programs coming in through the browser can do to a system. Protected Mode is available only in the version of IE residing in Vista, as it relies on the operating system support in Windows to reduce the rights of a process. See the "Hardening Internet Explorer 7" section later in this chapter for more details on Protected Mode.

Printing: When printing web pages, IE now defaults to shrink-to-fit mode, which detects a particular page's width and adjusts it to fit on the type of paper you've selected to print. Orphan control also rids you of those annoying second pages that contain only a header and footer by shrinking content to one page where possible and where readability is not affected.

Standards Compliance

You might have heard a little bit about the brouhaha surrounding IE 7 and its compliance with popular web development standards. To make a long story short, many web designers build web pages that conform to popular web standards. The Acid2 browser test is a common test that determines a browser's ability to render correctly formatted HTML code that is built according to the specifications of the standard. There was some debate during IE 7's development about whether the product would actually pass the Acid2 test. Chris Wilson, Lead Program Manager for IE Core, wrote the following in the IEBlog in July 2005 (see `http://blogs.msdn.com/ie/archive/2005/07/29/445242.aspx`):

> *I've seen a lot of comments asking if we will pass the Acid2 browser test published by the Web Standards Project when IE7 ships. I'll go ahead and relieve the suspense by saying we will not pass this test when IE7 ships. The original Acid Test tested only the CSS 1 box model, and actually became part of the W3C CSS1 Test Suite since it was a fairly narrow test—but the Acid 2 Test covers a wide set of functionality and standards, not just from CSS2.1 and HTML 4.01, selected by the authors as a "wish list" of features they'd like to have. It's pointedly not a compliance test (from the Test Guide: "Acid2 does not guarantee conformance with any specification"). As a wish list, it is really important and useful to my team, but it isn't even intended, in my understanding, as our priority list for IE7.*

Examining the New Internet Explorer Features

In this section, we'll look at the most useful new features in this version of Internet Explorer, how to use and customize them, and how to get the most out of them.

Tabbed Browsing

For the longest time, perhaps the harshest criticism of previous versions of Internet Explorer was its lack of support for tabbed browsing. Available in Firefox, Opera, Safari, and other competitive browsers, tabbed browsing is a fabulously useful feature wherein different pages are loaded in different tabs within a single parent browser window, eliminating the need to have 17 different windows of your browser open at one time—a nightmare to navigate. While there have been some third-party IE add-ons that enabled this functionality, IE 7 is the first version of IE to have tabbed browsing functionality integrated natively.

Figure 17-1 shows the way tabs appear within the IE interface. Each tab contains a separate web page.

Figure 17-1 *Tabbed browsing within Internet Explorer*

To configure tabbed browsing, choose Internet Options from the Tools menu, and in the Tabs section, click the Settings button. The Tabbed Browsing Settings screen will appear, as shown in Figure 17-2.

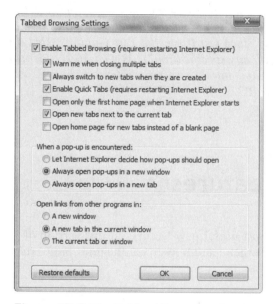

Figure 17-2 *The Tabbed Browsing Settings screen*

From this dialog box, you can enable tabbed browsing, configure how IE alerts you when you try to close a window with multiple tabs open, enable Quick Tabs (the multiple tab view I discuss later in this section), and so on. You can also configure how pop-ups are handled in the context of tabbed browsing—whether pop-up windows should be opened in a new tab or in a new window, or whether IE should decide what happens. Finally, you can also choose how links from other programs open in IE: in a new tab, in a new window, or in the current tab or window view.

One great feature of IE over the current version of Firefox as of the time of this writing is the tab view, which is accessible via the Tab Group icon, third from the left side of the IE window by default. When you click this button, you are taken to a view of all tabs and their respective web pages in a small preview graphic, much like a thumbnail (see Figure 17-3). To make any page the active tab, just click it.

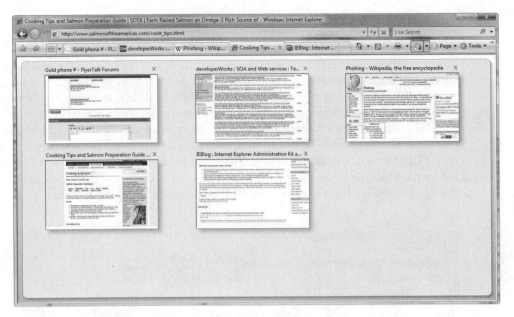

Figure 17-3 *Viewing multiple tabs and their respective web pages*

Here are a few more advanced ways to use tabbed browsing in IE:

Opening multiple home pages: You can use tabbed browsing to open multiple home pages each time you start IE. To do so, from the Tools menu, select Internet Options and then the General tab. Enter each page you'd like to open in the text box, separating multiple sites with a carriage return. This will effectively create a group of tabs that open on launch of the browser.

Saving a group of tabs to your Favorites folder: If you're in the middle of a browsing session and have a lot of tabs open, but they all relate to a central theme, or you just want to save them together, you can save the group of currently open tabs to your Favorites folder. To do so, click the star icon with the plus sign (the icon second from the left on the toolbar within IE) and select Add Tab Group to Favorites.

Phishing Filter

What exactly is *phishing*? According to Wikipedia (see http://en.wikipedia.org/wiki/Phishing),

> *In computing, phishing is a criminal activity using social engineering techniques. Phishers attempt to fraudulently acquire sensitive information, such as passwords and credit card details, by masquerading as a trustworthy person or business in an electronic communication. Phishing is typically carried out using email or an instant message, although phone contact has been used as well. Attempts to deal with the growing number of reported phishing incidents include legislation, user training, and technical measures.*

The Phishing Filter is a new feature in IE 7 that dynamically alerts users if they are visiting a site that Microsoft thinks is designed to steal personal information. The filter checks web sites that either aren't on a list of known "good" web sites or fail some heuristics tests and therefore appear suspicious. If IE sends a URL to the Phishing Filter server, the path of the URL is stripped down to its most basic level to prevent personal information from being transmitted within a URL, and then the stripped-down information is sent over an SSL-protected connection to the Microsoft server.

To configure the Phishing Filter, you can expand the Phishing Filter under the Tools menu from within IE 7, and then select Phishing Filter Settings. You'll be taken to the Internet Options dialog box and navigated to the Advanced tab. Scroll down the list to the Phishing Filter section, as shown in Figure 17-4, and then choose to disable the filter entirely, or turn on or turn off the automatic checking feature.

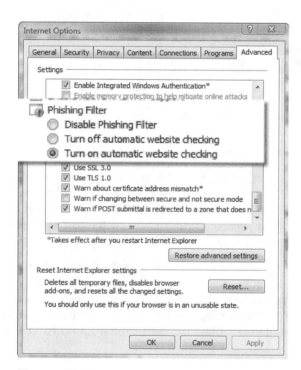

Figure 17-4 *Configuring the Phishing Filter*

If you stumble across a web site that you believe is phishing for information, you can submit that information to Microsoft for potential inclusion in the Phishing Filter suspect list. To do so, once you are on the suspicious site, expand the Phishing Filter submenu under the Tools menu and select Report this Website. You'll be taken to a web page where you enter the language in which the web site is written, and then check a box acknowledging that you believe said web site is a phishing web site. Click Submit once you're done.

Implementing RSS Feeds

Really Simple Syndication (RSS) is a very popular protocol by which items are pushed from web sites to users in a variety of convenient formats. IE 7 can discover and read items pushed via the RSS protocol, making IE a rudimentary but functional aggregator for news, blog posts, and other RSS-able information. Currently, IE 7 supports web feed formats RSS .9x, RSS 1.0, and RSS 2.0, as well as Atom 0.3 and Atom 1.0.

You can find out if a web page has an available web feed by clicking the standard RSS feed icon on the IE toolbar, which looks as shown in Figure 17-5 (the other icons are grayed out to emphasize the correct icon).

Figure 17-5 *The RSS feed icon*

Clicking the button takes you to the RSS view, which is a beautified version of the marked-up code that makes up the RSS feed. If you click the drop-down arrow beside the RSS icon on the toolbar, you'll get a list of all of the feeds available on a page. Sometimes there is more than one RSS-like protocol, such as an Atom feed, and you can choose which one to view.

When you are on the RSS feed page and viewing it within IE, you can click the Subscribe to this Feed link in the yellow box at the top of the page. This will bring up a dialog box, shown in Figure 17-6, that allows you to choose a friendly name for the feed and create the feed link in a specific folder for easy reference. Click the Subscribe button to confirm your subscription.

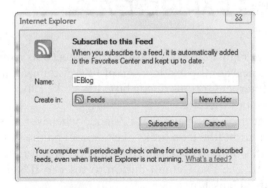

Figure 17-6 *Subscribing to a particular RSS feed*

By subscribing to a feed, Windows Internet Explorer will automatically check for updates to that feed, even if IE isn't running. You can configure this update sequence, along with several other options, by selecting Internet Options from the Tools menu, selecting the Content tab, and clicking the Settings button under the Feeds section. The Feed Settings dialog box is shown in Figure 17-7.

Figure 17-7 *Configuring RSS feed settings*

On this screen, you can choose to have IE automatically look for feeds to update and set the frequency for that update. You can also choose feed-browsing options and their related settings, including automatically marking feed items as read when viewing a feed, using the feed reading view at all, and playing a sound when an RSS or other feed is detected on a page being viewed within IE.

Customizing Internet Explorer 7

The Internet Options dialog box (see Figure 17-8), accessible from the Tools menu on the standard IE toolbar, is really the heart of the product. All of IE's customization and settings options are present in the Internet Options dialog box. Let's take a look at the areas one by one and discuss the options therein.

On the General tab, you can set the home page that is loaded whenever IE starts and also when you click the Home button (the icon looks like a house) on the standard IE toolbar. If you want to change this option, click the Use Current button to set the home page to the current page in IE, the Use Default button to reset to IE's default home page, and Use Blank to set up a blank home page.

In the Browsing History section, you can delete temporary files, history, cookies, saved passwords, and information from web forms by clicking the Delete button. Click the Settings button to configure caching functions and options, the location of the Temporary Internet Files folder, and how many days IE should save its list of sites you have recently visited.

Figure 17-8 *The General tab of the Internet Options dialog box*

In the Search section, you can click the Settings button to access the Change Search Defaults dialog box. Here, you can configure which search provider is used to return responses to queries typed in the search box in the main IE window, at the top-right corner. You can click the Find More Providers link on that dialog box to add other search engines and providers, like Google or Amazon. The default is Windows Live Search.

Finally, in the Appearance section, you can adjust the colors, languages, fonts, and accessibility settings for web pages as needed.

The Security tab is shown in Figure 17-9.

On the Security tab, you can select from a list of zones in which IE operates and configure the appropriate security settings for each zone. For example, most web sites operate in the Internet zone, in which IE restricts a lot of dynamic activity that could result in a security risk. By clicking a zone and adjusting the Allowed Levels slider in the bottom portion of the screen, you can set how tolerant Windows is of dynamic and installable elements on web pages, like automatic content downloading and ActiveX control installation. You can also choose to enable or disable Protected Mode from here. To add certain sites to a particular zone, click the zone to which you want to add a site, and then click the Sites button and type the URL of the site in the resulting screen.

The Privacy tab is shown in Figure 17-10.

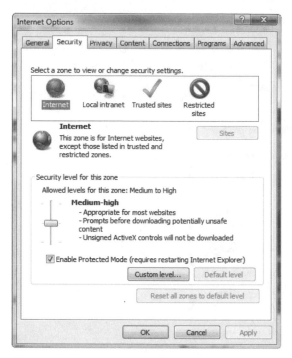

Figure 17-9 *The Security tab of the Internet Options dialog box*

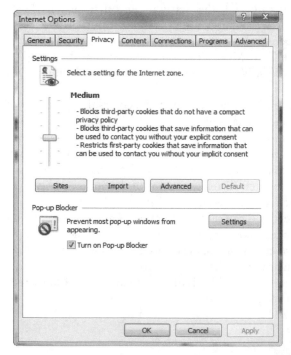

Figure 17-10 *The Privacy tab of the Internet Options dialog box*

On the Privacy tab, you can select the privacy settings for the Internet zone. Adjust the slider level to achieve different levels of privacy. These settings affect how cookies are stored and how personal information is saved and transmitted. Click the Advanced button to go to the Advanced Privacy Settings screen, which allows you to override automatic cookie handling and accept, block, or prompt first- and third-party cookies.

Back on the Privacy tab, you can also configure IE's built-in pop-up blocker and turn it on by clicking the appropriate check box. Clicking the Settings box results in the dialog box shown in Figure 17-11.

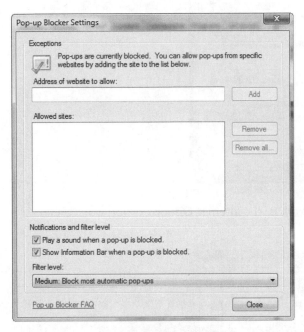

Figure 17-11 *The Pop-up Blocker Settings dialog box*

You can explicitly allow sites to use pop-up blockers by entering the URL and clicking the Add button. You can also set up how you will be notified when IE encounters a pop-up and how stringent the pop-up blocker filter is.

The Content tab is next, as shown in Figure 17-12.

On the Content tab, you can interface with the Parental Controls function in Windows Vista (see Chapter 6 for more information); enable the Content Advisor, which is a marginally useful tool that looks at web site ratings to decide whether content is suitable for the current user to view; look at the currently cached certificates for sites using Secure Sockets Layer; control the AutoComplete function, which prefills web site forms using information you have entered in previous sessions; and control RSS feed settings as discussed previously in this chapter.

If you need to delete AutoComplete history—for example, if you've mistyped something in a web form and it continues to haunt you every time you revisit the site— then click the Settings button in the AutoComplete section and follow the instructions.

The Connections tab is shown in Figure 17-13.

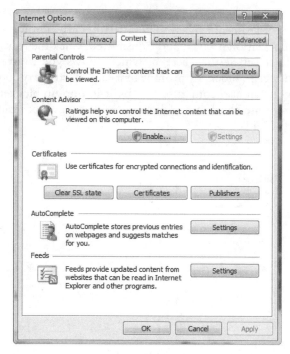

Figure 17-12 *The Content tab of the Internet Options dialog box*

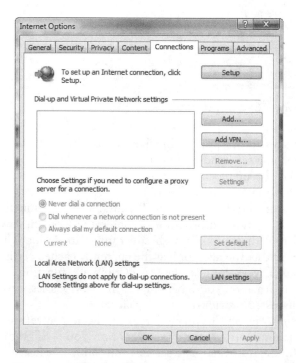

Figure 17-13 *The Connections tab of the Internet Options dialog box*

On the Connections tab, you can configure which temporary (i.e., not nailed up) dial-up connection is used by IE to view web pages. The Add, Add VPN, Remove, and Settings buttons take you directly to Windows networking screens, as covered elsewhere in this book. You can choose whether IE will never dial a connection, dial when a connection is not currently present, or always dial a connection. Clicking the LAN Settings button takes you to the Local Area Network Settings box, where you configure how IE detects a proxy and whether a proxy server is explicitly configured. If you need to add a web proxy server to IE, enter it in the Proxy Server section of that dialog box.

The Programs tab is shown in Figure 17-14.

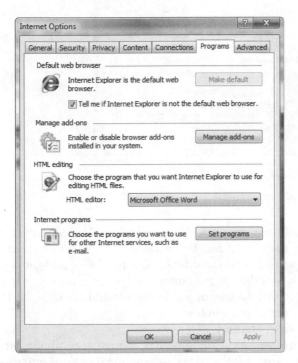

Figure 17-14 *The Programs tab of the Internet Options dialog box*

On the Programs tab, you can elect to make IE the default web browser of choice on your system. You can also manage add-on programs installed within IE on your machine, choose the default HTML editor as installed on your machine, and set default links to other programs on your machine as well (by clicking the Set Programs button).

To manage add-ons, click the Manage Add-ons button. You'll see the screen shown in Figure 17-15.

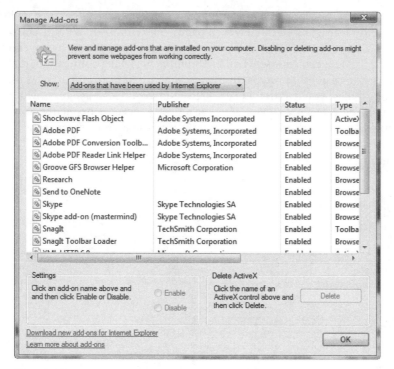

Figure 17-15 *The Manage Add-ons screen*

You can choose to show add-ons already used by IE, add-ons loaded in the current IE environment, add-ons that don't need ancillary programs in order to run, and any 32-bit ActiveX controls that were downloaded by IE. If a particular add-on is giving you trouble, click it in the list, and then at the bottom enable or disable it as needed. You can select the ActiveX control by selecting it in the list and clicking the Delete button at the bottom-right corner of the window.

The Advanced tab is shown in Figure 17-16.

On the Advanced tab, you can select options that control accessibility settings, browsing preferences, HTTP 1.1 protocol settings, international options, multimedia, printing, search, and security options. Scroll through the list—the feature names are self-explanatory, and some are advanced enough to be specifically prescribed in technical guidance, like in the upcoming "Hardening Internet Explorer 7" section—and set options as needed. Be careful, though, as options here typically affect the core browsing experience. On this tab, you can also elect to restore IE's entire collection on default settings. To do so, click the Reset button and restart IE.

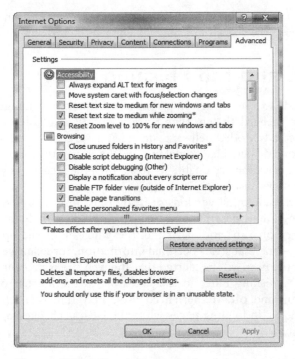

Figure 17-16 *The Advanced tab of the Internet Options dialog box*

Hardening Internet Explorer 7

In this section, we take a look at some features and recommendations for keeping IE 7 secure and hardened.

The MHTML Hole

In late 2006, Secunia, a security firm based in Denmark, discovered a vulnerability in IE 7 that is not exactly critical but at the same time still important enough to pay attention to. Essentially, the vulnerability involves the potential for web sites with malicious code to steal data from other sites opened in a copy of IE 7. It's debatable how serious this is, and Microsoft claims that the vulnerability exists in Outlook Express rather than IE. Whatever the reason, the vulnerability exists as demonstrated at this sample site hosted by Secunia: http://secunia.com/Internet_Explorer_Arbitrary_Content_Disclosure_Vulnerability_Test.

To work around this vulnerability, disable the ability for ActiveX content to run automatically. The setting is covered in the checklist coming up a bit later in this section.

Protected Mode and the Phishing Filter

Rarely is it advisable to upgrade to a new operating system just to take advantage of a new feature, but if you are a diehard IE fan, then a feature in IE available only in Windows Vista, called Protected Mode, helps create what is arguably the safest browsing environment, bar none. It's enabled by default on Windows Vista, and if you refuse to use Firefox or for some reason are unable to do so, then the security is worth the price of admission to Windows Vista.

Another feature that is available in all versions of IE (not just in IE coupled with Windows Vista) is the Phishing Filter, described earlier, which works with a database of suspect web sites that Microsoft runs and alerts the user when he or she opens a potentially malicious web site—one that steals personal information, for example. The address bar will turn red and the user will be alerted that the web site is problematic. You can see the status of the Phishing Filter in the status bar at the bottom of the window; click it to turn it on and off. (Experienced users may find the behavior annoying, and there is a slight lag in loading pages while the URL is checked against Microsoft's phishing site database.)

Settings Checklist

Here is a list of recommended settings for a custom level within IE 7. To implement these recommendations, select Options from the Tools menu in IE 7, and then navigate to the Security tab. Click the Custom Level tab after ensuring the Internet zone is selected, and then make the following selections from the list (some less important settings can be left alone).

In the ActiveX Controls and Plug-ins category, choose the following options:

Binary and script behaviors: Disable

Run ActiveX controls and plug-ins: Disable

Script ActiveX controls marked safe for scripting: Disable

In the Miscellaneous category, choose these options:

Allow Web pages to use restricted protocols for active content: Disable

Display mixed content: Disable

Installation of desktop items: Disable

Launching applications and unsafe files: Disable

Launching programs and files in an IFRAME: Disable

Navigate sub-frames across different domains: Disable

Software channel permissions: Maximum Safety

Submit non-encrypted form data: Disable

Web sites in less privileged Web content zone can navigate into this zone: Disable

  In the Scripting category, choose these options:

Active scripting: Disable

Scripting of Java applets: Disable

CHAPTER 18

Setting Up Windows Mail

Windows Mail, the replacement to the venerable Outlook Express, is the mail and newsgroup client bundled with every version of Windows Vista. Windows Mail has improved incrementally over its predecessor, with some minor improvements and user interface tweaks here and there. There's nothing major in this product—it's a simple mail client, designed for people who don't need the full-blown power of Outlook or other email solutions.

In this chapter, we'll briskly walk you through the initial Windows Mail setup, and then we'll dig deeper into personalizing the program, using it to read NNTP-based newsgroups, taking advantage of its security features, and maintaining the message store.

Setting Up Accounts

The wizard-based interface makes short work of setting up mail, newsgroup, and directory service accounts. You'll be greeted with the wizard when you first launch Windows Mail, but if you need to access it again (to add another account, for example), you can find it by clicking Add on the Tools/Accounts window.

Setting Up a Mail Account

Setting up a mail account using the wizard is simple. Launch the wizard as described, and then do the following:

1. On the first screen, select a mail account, and click Next.

2. Enter your display name, and click Next.

3. Enter your email address, and click Next.

4. Select the type of incoming email server you have (POP3, IMAP, or HTTP). Consult the information your provider has issued to you for the correct selection here. Enter the incoming email server name, enter the outgoing server name (your SMTP server), and then select whether authentication is required. Click Next.

5. Enter your incoming email server's username and password combination. Choose whether to remember the passwords, and then click Next.

6. Click Finish to finish the wizard.

Setting Up a News Account

A news account accesses newsgroups, like the old USENET forums from the early days of the Internet. Setting up a news account is almost identical to setting up a mail account, except instead of specifying incoming email and outgoing email addresses, you're specifying one NNTP server name instead:

1. On the first screen, select a mail account, and click Next.

2. Enter your display name, and click Next.

3. Enter your email address, and click Next.

4. Enter the name of your NNTP (newsgroup) server, and indicate whether you have to use a username and password to log in. Click Next.

5. If you chose authentication on the previous screen, enter the appropriate username and password combination. Choose whether to remember the passwords, and then click Next.

6. Click Finish to finish the wizard.

Setting Up a Directory Service Account

Directory service accounts allow you to check for people, businesses, and other entities listed on a directory. Corporations sometimes have an Active Directory service running on their network, which is a common directory service, and there are other directory services with a wider audience, such as Bigfoot and VeriSign.

To set up a directory service, follow these steps:

1. On the first screen, select a directory service account, and then click Next.

2. Enter the name of the directory server, and indicate whether authentication is required to use that server. Click Next.

3. If you chose authentication on the previous screen, enter the appropriate username and password combination. Choose whether to remember the passwords, and then click Next.

4. Indicate whether you want to check the address of intended recipients in your messages against this directory server. This may help catch misspelling and other typos, but it causes a slight performance penalty, since a network directory lookup is required. Click Next.

Working Within Windows Mail

Windows Mail works like any other mail program you've ever used. The message list appears in the top-right corner of the window, a preview of the body appears below it, and the navigation pane appears to the left and shows a tree of your various mail and news accounts and the folders and groups therein. Figure 18-1 gives you a preview.

Figure 18-1 *The main view of Windows Mail*

Personalizing Windows Mail

In the Options dialog box, available from the Tools menu, several tools allow you to personalize your experience with Windows Mail:

Setting an interval to check mail: You may want Windows Mail to automatically perform a send/receive operation at regular intervals. On the General tab, choose the Check for New Messages Every box, and then enter the number of minutes between checks that you would like.

Configuring delivery and read receipt behavior: On the Receipts tab, you can define how Windows Mail will handle receipt requests—never send them, send them when requested, or send them always (with or without a request). You can also choose whether you want to send a read receipt request by default with any messages you send.

Setting the default outbound mail format: On the Send tab, you can indicate the default format for outbound mail and news messages—either HTML, which allows for different fonts, embedded pictures, emphasis techniques, and so on, or plain text, which is efficient for transmission but lacks pretty features.

Composing a signature: On the Signatures tab, you can choose whether to automatically append signatures to outbound messages, including replies and forwards. You can also compose signatures directly on the tab. By clicking the Advanced button after you have defined a signature, you can set the mail account to which that signature should correspond—useful if you have multiple jobs and want to have unique signatures for each email address you use in Windows Mail.

Identities

The predecessor to Windows Mail, called Outlook Express, introduced a feature known as identities, which was designed to make it simple for families and users who share their computers to each have an individual, and semiprivate, configuration for sending and receiving their Internet email and newsgroup postings. Identities created separate message stores for each person configured to use Outlook Express, and the feature was a great help until Windows XP. Windows XP introduced a feature called fast-user switching, which basically took the concept of identities and increased the scope from Outlook Express to the entire operating system, creating compartmentalized accounts for each person using a particular machine.

Identities have been retained in Windows Mail, but Windows Vista has also improved the fast-user switching experience. Since by default new users on a machine get a fresh copy of Windows Mail, which can then be configured exactly to that user's liking, there is little reason to use the identities feature of Windows Mail. This is why we won't cover it.

Creating separate user accounts is vastly superior to identities in every way, with virtually no drawbacks. Check out Chapter 7 for more information about creating user accounts.

Using Newsgroups

Newsgroups are a relic from the old days of the Internet, where USENET forums were the place people came together to exchange ideas in a bulletin-board style format. Perhaps unsurprisingly, newsgroups are still fairly popular, and they have been embraced by corporations looking to provide sales and support information to their customers in a friendlier interface format than just a web page.

Windows Mail supports downloading, subscribing, reading, and monitoring newsgroups. After you've added your newsgroup account (covered earlier in this chapter), click the account in the left pane of Windows Mail. You'll be prompted to download a list of the newsgroups available on the server you configured; acknowledge it, and after a brief period you'll see the Newsgroup Subscriptions window, as shown in Figure 18-2.

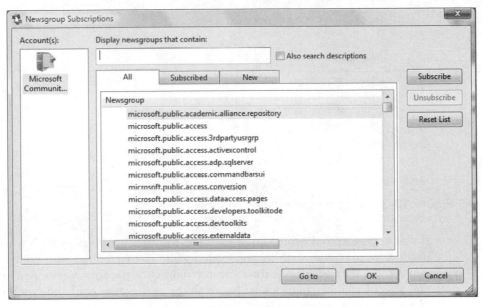

Figure 18-2 *The Newsgroup Subscriptions window*

Subscribing to a newsgroup means that Windows Mail will add the newsgroup to the folder pane and download its messages when you click it. To filter the list of newsgroups to groups that contain a certain phrase—for instance, say you want to subscribe to all groups with the word *vista* in them—simply type the phrase in the textbox; the list will dynamically adjust. To subscribe to a group, click it, and then click the Subscribe button. By clicking the appropriate tabs at the top of the list, you can toggle between a listing of all groups on the server, just those groups to which you've subscribed, and groups added since your last listing download.

Strategies for Managing Newsgroup Reading

Windows Mail includes several features that make it easy to download newsgroup headers and messages, read them on your portable computer or while you're otherwise away from your primary network connection, and then synchronize when you reconnect to the newsgroup server. Here's how to set downloading and synchronization options:

- To tell Windows Mail to download headers only, new messages only, or all messages, click the account name in the folder pane, and select the newsgroup you want to modify in the listing pane on the right. Right-click it, and then select the appropriate option on the Synchronization Settings submenu, as shown in Figure 18-3.

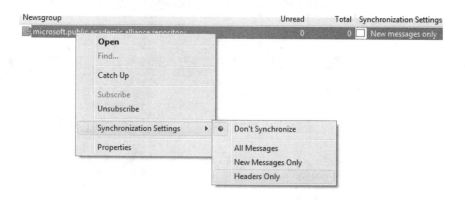

Figure 18-3 *Setting synchronization options*

- If you've chosen to download new messages only but you're away for a while and don't want to read everything you missed while you weren't at your computer, you can use the Catch Up feature. Simply right-click the appropriate newsgroup, and select Catch Up. Outlook will note all the messages as read and synchronize as appropriate the next time.

- Synchronization is just that—messages are downloaded by Windows Mail as they're added by the NNTP server, and they're removed simultaneously as well. If a message contains vital information for you, for instance, and you want to save it, you need to do so through the File/Save As menu item. The message likely will disappear from the newsgroup view after some period, and you won't be able to retrieve it otherwise.

Creating Message Rules

Windows Mail includes a reasonably hearty set of rules, and you can define actions based on those rules to help you manage the flow of incoming email or newsgroup messages; for instance, you can tell the program to sort all incoming mail from a specific person to a certain folder or to automatically forward messages with, say, a certain text string in the subject to another person or department. Rules are especially useful for people who subscribe to multiple high-volume mailing lists or those people who get a lot of email each day and need to whittle down their inbox to only the most important messages requiring their attention.

> **NOTE** Rules apply only to POP3-based email accounts. You cannot use Windows Mail rules with IMAP services or HTTP-based services, such as Windows Live Mail or Hotmail.

To create a new rule, select Tools ➤ Message Rules ➤ Mail. The New Mail Rule window will appear, as shown in Figure 18-4.

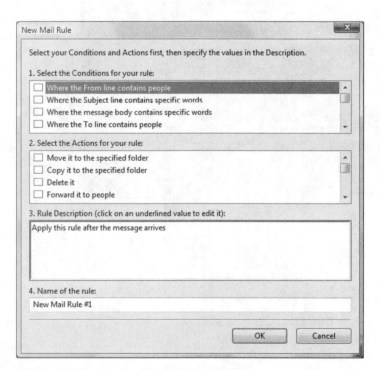

Figure 18-4 *The New Mail Rule window*

As you can tell, you can choose from many options and criteria. Generally, to create a rule, select the criteria for which the rule should apply in the first box, and then in the second box, select the specific actions Windows Mail should take when those criteria are met. You can edit the variables in the third box by clicking the underlined links. Finally, name the rule something meaningful to you, and click OK.

You can include negative criterion in your rules when you drill down a bit further into the conditions of a rule you're setting up. You do this by setting up a standard rule with positive conditions and then editing those conditions. For instance, suppose you are performing some action to messages from a specific person. Choose the appropriate criteria, and then in the Select People window, click the Options button; you'll see the Rule Condition Options window appear, as shown in Figure 18-5. Here, you can choose whether the rule applies when messages do or do not come from the selected recipient.

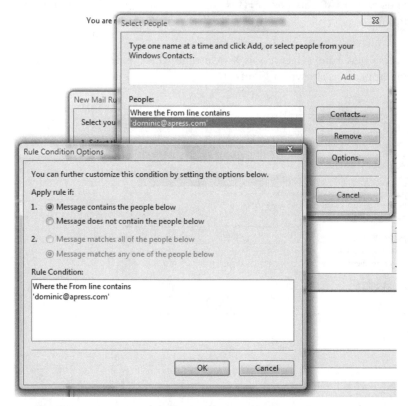

Figure 18-5 *The Rule Condition Options window*

Protecting Against Unwanted Email and Attachments

Currently, spam, viruses, and other nasty messages regularly arrive in your inbox. To manage your email on a daily basis is to spend significant amounts of time sorting and deleting spam and dangerous messages from the legitimate email that requires your attention or that you otherwise want to receive. Windows Mail recognizes this issue and provides several protections against unwanted email wasting your time:

- Windows Mail includes the Junk E-mail filter, which is designed to scan incoming messages and heuristically determine whether they have a high likelihood of being unsolicited commercial email (UCE). If so, Windows Mail automatically routes them into the Junk E-mail folder, a special location available in the folder pane. You can customize the filter so you can adjust thresholds of detection, making the filter stronger or weaker as you deem necessary.

- Two lists, the Blocked Senders list and the Safe Senders list, further protect your time and machine by allowing you to define senders from whom you either never want to see email again or always want to see email no matter what. Messages originating from senders on the Blocked Senders list will be deleted before they ever hit your inbox, whereas messages from so-called safe senders will always be immune from any filtering or detection.

Changing the Junk Email Protection Level

To change the thresholds for the junk email detection mechanism, do the following:

1. From within Windows Mail, select Tools ➤ Junk E-mail Options.

2. Select the Options tab, which is shown in Figure 18-6.

3. Select from one of the choices. No Automatic Filtering will disable the detection mechanism, although Windows Mail will continue to check senders against the Blocked Senders list. Low blocks only the most obvious junk mail. High sets the filter into high gear, as you might expect, and is useful if you regularly get a lot of spam at one address. Some legitimate messages may be classified as spam. Finally, Safe List Only blocks all mail except messages from senders on your Safe Senders list; everything else is relegated to the Junk E-mail folder.

4. If you trust the filter implicitly and simply want junk email deleted automatically and not shunted off to another folder, click the checkbox.

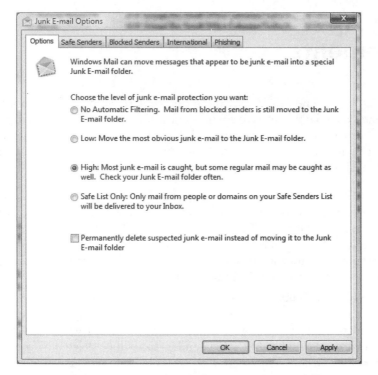

Figure 18-6 *Setting thresholds for the Junk E-mail filter*

Adding and Removing Senders to the Blocked Senders and Safe Senders Lists

If you receive a message and you want to add the sender of the message to the Blocked Senders list, it's easy to do so from within your inbox. Just right-click the message, hover over the Junk E-mail option, and click Add Sender to Blocked Senders List (Figure 18-7 shows this menu). If you want to block out the entire business, corporation, organization, or other entity—not just the single user—select Add Sender's Domain to Blocked Senders List.

Similarly, if you receive a message from a trusted person and want to ensure you will receive all future emails from that person, you can use the same context menu described earlier. Right-click the message, hover over the Junk E-mail option, and click Add Sender to Safe Senders List. If you want to trust everything coming from that domain, select Add Sender's Domain to Safe Senders List.

Additionally, you can add addresses to either list manually, which comes in handy if you know someone's address or domain but don't have a message handy. Select Message ➤ Junk E-mail ➤ Junk E-mail Options, and then navigate to the Blocked Senders tab. Click Add, and then type the email address or domain of your target. Click OK to finish. You can use the same procedure to add a sender or domain manually to the Safe Senders list—just use the Safe Senders tab instead.

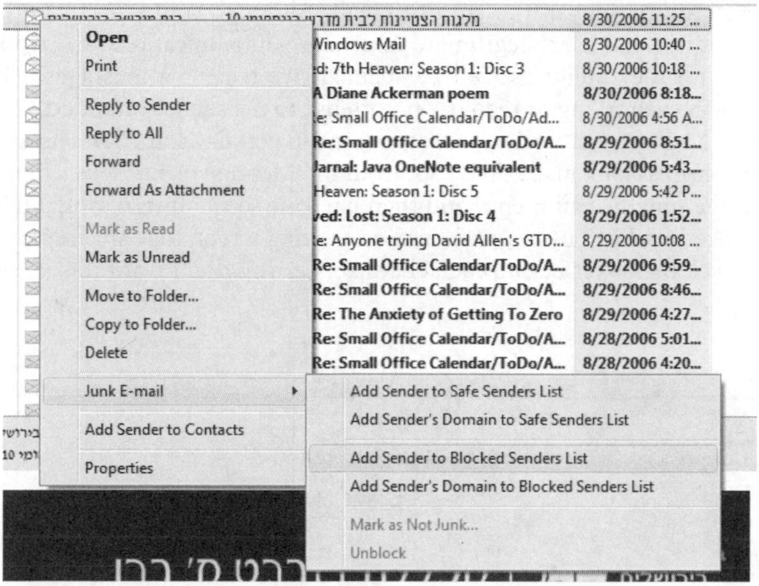

Figure 18-7 *Adding senders to the Blocked Senders or Safe Senders list*

You may also want to automatically trust people to whom you send emails or people you have added to your Windows Contacts list. Windows Mail can automatically add your intended recipients to the Safe Senders list after you send a message. To turn on this option, from the Message menu, select Junk E-mail Options from the Junk E-mail menu, and then navigate to the Safe Senders tab. Click the Automatically Add People I E-mail to the Safe Senders List box. Windows Mail can also trust emails from people you have in your address book; to turn on this option, click the Also Trust E-mail from My Windows Contacts box, as shown in Figure 18-8.

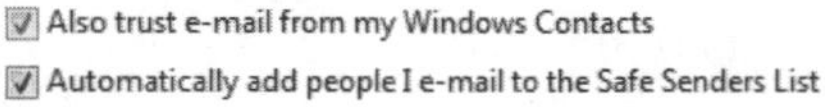

Figure 18-8 *Automatically trusting email from certain people*

Removing senders and domains from either list is just as easy. From the Message menu, select Junk E-mail Options from the Junk E-mail menu, and then navigate to the Blocked Senders or Safe Senders tab as appropriate. Click the name you want to delete, and then click Remove. Click OK to finish.

Managing International Messages

Many languages are present in the land of email. Although some—even most, arguably—emails not in English are legitimate nonspam communications, to people who speak only English they might as well be spam. If we receive a message in Korean, there's no point in even trying to read it—no offense to the sender intended, of course. With Windows Mail, you can select messages sent in certain character sets and automatically mark them as junk mail. To do so, from the Message menu, select Junk E-mail Options from the Junk E-mail menu, and then navigate to the International tab. Click the Blocked Encoding List button, and on the resulting screen that appears (shown in Figure 18-9), click the boxes beside each character set you don't want to see, and then click OK.

Figure 18-9 *The Blocked Encodings List window*

You may also correspond with a limited set of people who are in only a couple of countries; therefore, you don't care to see any email originating from a sender whose domain is internationalized in another country. You can automatically block these messages from the same menu location; just click the Blocked Top-Level Domain List button, and check the boxes beside the domains you'd like to block—you can see an example in Figure 18-10. Click OK when you are finished.

Figure 18-10 *The Blocked Top-Level Domain window*

Guarding Against Phishing

Much like the integrated Junk E-mail filter, Windows Mail includes the Phishing filter. Microsoft defines phishing as follows:

> *...a way to trick computer users into revealing personal or financial information through a fraudulent email message or website. A common online phishing scam starts with an email message that looks like an official notice from a trusted source, such as a bank, credit card company, or reputable online merchant. In the email message, recipients are directed to a fraudulent website where they are asked to provide personal information, such as an account number or password. This information is then usually used for identity theft.*

The Phishing filter in Windows Mail will try to detect attempts as described earlier, and if it finds a potentially offensive message, it will disable any hyperlinks within the message and display a warning to you in the message bar; it will also color the message red in the message list window and display the familiar red shield instead of an envelope icon. If you discover a message you really want to see that the filter has blocked, you can choose to enable the links in the message simply by clicking the Unblock button.

In this release of Windows Mail, the Phishing filter is not very customizable: it's more of an on-or-off affair at this stage. Message ➤ Junk E-mail ➤ Junk E-mail Options, and then navigate to the Phishing tab, as shown in Figure 18-11. Click the box to turn on the filter, and optionally click the box to move potential phishing messages to the Junk E-mail folder.

Figure 18-11 *The Phishing filter configuration tab*

Blocking Potentially Problematic Attachments

In the previous versions of Windows Mail, called Outlook Express, Microsoft introduced a security feature that blocked users from accessing mails with attachments that had extensions common to executable programs or other vectors through which malware could enter the system. Although it was a good idea in theory to block .exe, .pif, .bat, and other files, in practice users found the feature so frustrating they wanted to turn it off.

Windows Mail continues to include the attachment-blocking feature. If you'd like to turn it on or off, follow these steps:

1. From within Windows Mail, open Tools ➤ Options.

2. Navigate to the Security tab.

3. Uncheck the Do Not Allow Attachments to Be Saved or Opened That Could Potentially Be a Virus box.

4. Click OK to finish.

Performing Windows Mail Maintenance

Any software requires a bit of upkeep if used regularly, and Windows Mail is no exception. Although the program cares for itself in most cases, it has some knobs for you to turn. You can find them on the Maintenance window (shown in Figure 18-12), which you access through the Options dialog box available from Tools ➤ Options. Click the Advanced tab, and then click the Maintenance button.

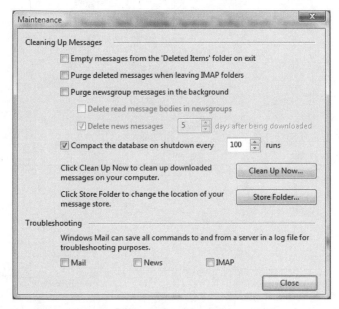

Figure 18-12 *The Maintenance screen*

Most of the options on this screen are self-explanatory, but a couple are worth highlighting:

- When you delete messages permanently, the space within the file that stores your messages—appropriately called the *message store*—isn't automatically reclaimed. If you regularly delete a lot of messages, you'll find your store size ballooning, which makes Windows Mail's performance deteriorate. To reclaim this space, you will need to compact the store, which is referred to as *cleaning up* the store in Windows Mail–speak. Click the Clean Up Now button to reclaim the space.

- Windows Mail by default puts your message store in a relatively buried location—typically `C:\Users\username\AppData\Local\Microsoft\Windows Mail`. Although nothing is inherently wrong with this location, you may want to move the store to a more central location so that it's included within your regular backup scheme. To change this location, click the Store Folder button, and then click the Change button. Specify the new path for the store, and then click OK.

CHAPTER 19

Collaborating with Windows Meeting Space

C ollaboration is king these days. However, starting a meeting is difficult. How do you share notes, files, or other documents? How do you get everyone on the same page? What if you need to meet with someone but no network is available? Or how do you meet with people who might not be in the same state, or even country, as you?

Windows Meeting Space can take care of all these problems. In this chapter, you'll learn about what the application can do for you, and you'll walk through all the features of Windows Meeting Space.

What Is Windows Meeting Space?

Windows Meeting Space allows peers on the same network, or even on different networks but with clients that all have wireless cards, to open ad hoc *spaces* in which they can collaborate. If you're familiar with the old Windows NetMeeting application, you know it was mainly designed as a videoconferencing application, with the ability to share your screen with other parties, use a shared virtual whiteboard, and so on. Although you might not have known you were running NetMeeting, in Windows XP whenever you loaded Windows Messenger, MSN Messenger, or Windows Live Messenger and tapped into each program's application and desktop sharing and whiteboard features, you were hooking directly into NetMeeting for that functionality.

In Windows Vista, NetMeeting has been deprecated and is no longer available; Windows Meeting Space takes its place. Windows Meeting Space builds on the foundation that NetMeeting provided and adds the ability to set up an ad hoc network. If Windows Meeting Space can't detect an existing wireless network, it will offer to set up a "scratch" network between computers with active wireless cards and use it only for sharing and collaboration—a great way to pass information and data between computers in a team environment wherever you are, not just around a hotspot.

Using Windows Meeting Space

Windows Meeting Space is a simple application in that it has few features and not much room to mess up. (Perhaps Microsoft took a page from Apple's playbook.) In fact, it's quite easy to get started with the program. From the Start menu, choose All Programs, and then click the Windows Meeting Space icon to load the application.

The Windows Meeting Space Setup screen appears, as shown in Figure 19-1. Choose to continue setting up Windows Meeting Space, and acknowledge the User Account Control (UAC) prompt if necessary. This step automatically pokes a couple of necessary holes through your firewall—TCP ports 801 and 3587 and UDP ports 1900, 3540, and 3702—that are necessary for the application to function, including allowing desktop sharing and file collaboration. Then, look for the People Near Me screen to appear (shown in Figure 19-2).

Figure 19-1 *The Windows Meeting Space Setup screen*

The People Near Me feature helps detect when other users of Windows Meeting Space are in the general vicinity of your computer. If you put your display name here, other users can find you and invite you to their meeting spaces. You can also choose to allow invitations from anyone using Windows Meeting Space, from only contacts you trust (you can set up this up once you get into the program for the first time), or from nobody. Click OK when you are finished with the initial configuration.

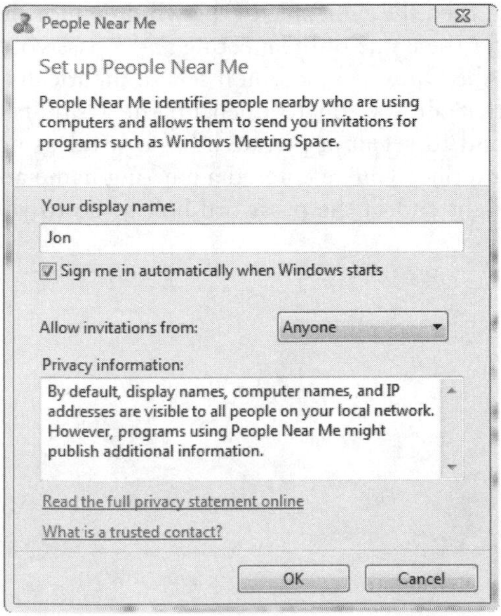

Figure 19-2 *The People Near Me screen*

Once the setup is finished, you'll see the main Windows Meeting Space screen, as shown in Figure 19-3. From here, you have two main choices—either start a new meeting of your own or join an existing meeting that you can access via your current network or an ad hoc network.

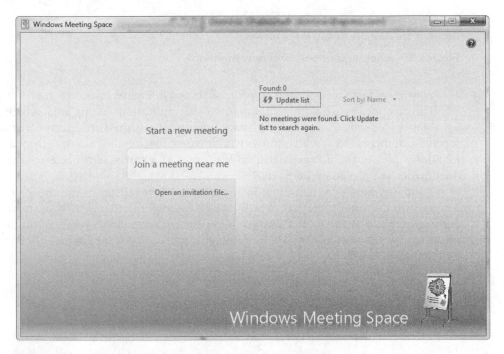

Figure 19-3 *The Windows Meeting Space main screen*

If you click Start a New Meeting, then the right side of the window morphs into a data-entry screen, where you can enter the name of the meeting and a password to use for joining the meeting. If you click the Options link, you'll see an identically named screen—depicted in Figure 19-4—that allows you to open up the visibility of this particular meeting space to others and to set up a private ad hoc wireless network. Click OK to finish setting options, and once you've entered a meeting name and password, click the green arrow at the right end of the password box to go to your new meeting space.

Figure 19-4 *Setting options for a new meeting*

Your meeting space will then appear, as shown in Figure 19-5.

The meeting space has three main areas—the application sharing area, which takes up about two-thirds of the meeting space window itself; the Participants area in the top right of the window, which shows who is currently attending this meeting; and the Handouts area at the bottom right, which serves as a convenient place to distribute documents and files to participants.

To invite more potential attendees, click the Invite button in the top menu bar. The resulting Invite People screen will be populated with other nearby users on your current network or the ad hoc network you elected to establish when setting up the meeting. If you want to invite still more people, you can click the Invite Others button and then choose either to send the invitation via email to someone else or to create an invitation file that you can place on a shared network location or send over an instant messaging program.

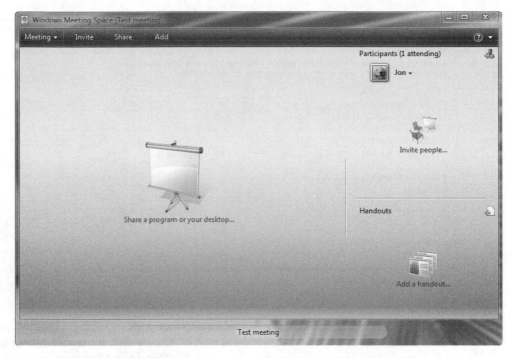

Figure 19-5 *A new meeting space, waiting for attendees and collaboration*

Most people want to share a program on their desktop during a meeting—either a Microsoft PowerPoint presentation, a Microsoft OneNote note, or even a message within Microsoft Outlook with points to talk about during the meeting. To share a program or your entire desktop to all participants in a meeting, click the Share a Program or Your Desktop link, and acknowledge the warning. The Start a Shared Session screen appears, as shown in Figure 19-6; here, you can choose the application to share, browse for a file or program to open and subsequently share, or share your entire desktop. In this example, we'll simply share our Microsoft Office OneNote 2007 window with meeting notes, which presumably we would use as a framework for discussion with all the participants of the meeting.

Windows Vista will probably switch itself to the Aero Basic color scheme, depending on what you're sharing and what your desktop wallpaper is, so you'll lose window transparency, any rich desktop wallpaper you have enabled, and a couple of other aesthetic niceties in order to save bandwidth and transmission time over a network connection. But at this point, the OneNote window is shared and is being transmitted to all other meeting participants. You can tell sharing is active by looking in the right corner of the title bar of the shared application—it should have a green dot with the message "Currently Sharing." If you're curious about how your session looks to participants, you can click the Show Me How My Shared Session Looks on Other Computers link. To shop sharing, click the aptly named link in the Windows Meeting Space main window.

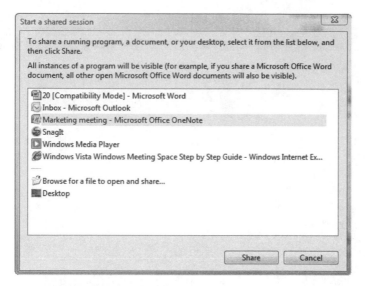

Figure 19-6 *Starting a shared session*

Additionally, you can add virtual *handouts* (simply files to share among all participants) to the meeting space via the Add button on the top menu bar. The warning box when you click the button is simply telling you that Windows Meeting Space will copy the handout document you choose to each participant's computer. One attendee at a time will be able to edit that document, and then the changes will be reflected in each participant's copy of the document, so everyone stays up-to-date. You can see how this looks in Figure 19-7.

Figure 19-7 *A handout loaded into the meeting space*

To open the handout, double-click it in the Windows Meeting Space window, and acknowledge the warning. The file will open on your computer.

To leave a meeting, from the Meeting menu, click the Leave Meeting option. You'll be prompted to save any handouts.

CHAPTER 20

Using Windows Fax and Scan

Windows Fax and Scan is a unified application that allows you to enter, send, and receive faxes from your computer, as well as manage scanned images from an attached scanner. The interface is decidedly like Microsoft's Outlook email software, and chances are you'll be able to get started right away with the familiar interface.

Faxing

You can send and receive faxes in one of two ways: using a modem to directly dial target fax machines and answer incoming fax calls and using a network-based fax server.

Sending and Receiving Faxes Using a Modem

Before you can use Windows Fax and Scan to send or receive faxes using a modem, you'll need to have a modem installed on your computer with the drivers configured appropriately. Most modems these days are plug-and-play modems and some are even built in to the motherboards of computers, so chances are your modem, if one is installed, has already been detected and configured properly by Windows Vista. You do need analog phone lines to send receive faxes using a modem, because digital-based phone lines like those you would find in an office or connected to a PBX won't function properly unless you install a digital-to-analog converter.

Figure 20-1 shows the basic Windows Fax and Scan interface, which is the same whether you are using a modem or a fax server to manage your faxes.

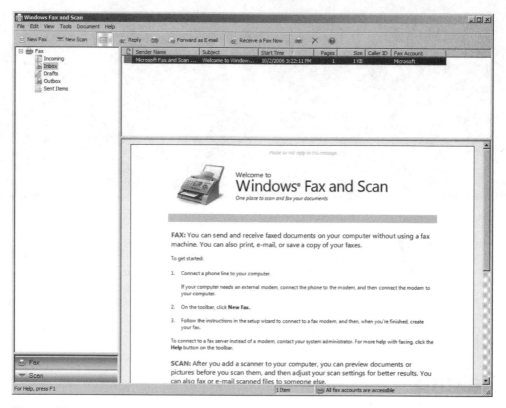

Figure 20-1 *The Windows Fax and Scan interface*

Sending Faxes

The first time you send a new fax, you'll be prompted to set up the fax program:

1. In Windows Fax and Scan, choose the New Fax button at the top-left corner.

2. The Choose a Fax Modem or Server screen appears; for the purposes of this section, choose Connect to a Fax Modem.

3. On the next screen, type a name that will help you identify the modem you're using to send a fax.

4. The Choose How to Receive Faxes screen appears; on this screen you can choose to have Windows Fax and Scan answer all incoming calls as faxes automatically, notify you when incoming calls are received in order to begin receiving faxes, or defer the decision and move on with sending a fax right now. Choose the Notify Me option for the purposes of this section.

You may have to acknowledge a UAC prompt, and you'll probably have to enable access through the Windows Firewall for the Windows Fax and Scan program.

Finally, the New Fax dialog box will appear, as shown in Figure 20-2.

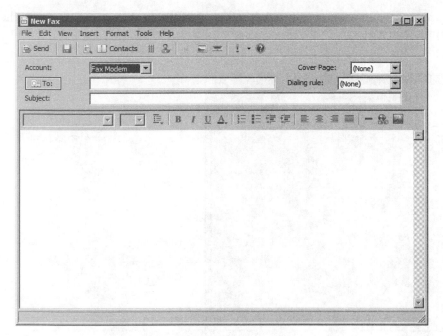

Figure 20-2 *The New Fax dialog box*

You can select an appropriate cover page from the drop-down menu; there are options for confidential faxes, "FYI"-type faxes, a generic fax cover page, and one labeled urgent. Next, enter the destination fax number in the To line. You can search the Global Address Book, if you have one configured, by clicking the To button beside the textbox. This feature also interacts with the Outlook Address Book, so you can use the fax numbers already stored in your address book in order to address faxes using this applet. Select a dialing rule, which is useful if you have a laptop and usually dial from several different locations that might have different patterns for reaching outgoing lines, and then enter a subject to appear on the cover page. Finally, in the textbox, enter any text that should appear in the body section of the cover page.

Once you have prepared your fax, you can save the fax to send later by clicking the disk icon in the toolbar, or you can send it immediately by clicking the Send button in the toolbar. You can also mark a message as high priority, insert a picture or a scanned document into the facts, check the recipient names against your Outlook or global address list, and get a preview of what the fax will look like once it's sent.

Receiving Faxes

Receiving faxes operates in much the same way. Received faxes from a fax modem are stored in the Windows Fax and Scan inbox. You can then take them from the inbox and save them in another location that you prefer.

When you first sent a fax, you were taken through a wizard that configured incoming fax settings. You can change those settings by selecting Tools ➤ Fax Settings.

(You may need to acknowledge a UAC prompt to do this.) Figure 20-3 shows the Fax Settings dialog box and the appropriate options to configure.

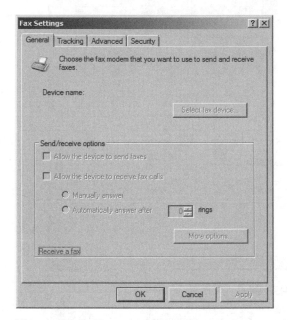

Figure 20-3 *Changing fax receipt options*

If you have configured Windows to notify you about incoming calls so you can choose whether to receive them as faxes, Windows will open a notification window in the corner of your screen alerting you to an incoming call. You can receive the fax by clicking the notification bubble. Or, during the time in which the incoming call is ringing, you can click the Receive a Fax Now button in the toolbar at the top of the window.

> **TIP** You can tell Windows Fax and Scan to automatically save a copy of each received fax. Choose Tools ➤ Fax Settings, acknowledge the UAC prompt if necessary, and click the More Options button on the General tab. Check the Save a Copy To checkbox, and then enter the path to the folder where you want to store received faxes.

Sending and Receiving Faxes Using a Network Fax Server

To send and receive faxes using a fax server, you'll need to know the address of the fax server. To configure a fax server in Windows Fax and Scan, follow these steps:

1. From the Tools menu, select Fax Accounts.

2. Click the Add button.

3. The Fax Setup dialog box appears. Click the Connect to a Fax Server on My Network option.

4. On the Type the Fax Server Location dialog box, type the network path to the fax server you want to use. Click Next.

5. On the next dialog box, type a friendly name that will help you identify this fax server. Then choose whether this should be the default server for sending faxes. Click Done.

Sending Faxes Through Other Applications

Windows Fax and Scan also supports receiving documents from a printer stub configured in Windows Vista. This allows you to fax directly from other applications that might not support direct faxing themselves.

If you've ever used Adobe Acrobat, chances are you have printed to a PDF printer, which then created a PDF document for you to use. This works in the same way. When you print to a fax printer, the item being printed is converted into a TIF file to be received by any fax device.

Figure 20-4 shows the default Fax printer installed in Windows Vista. Use this printer to fax directly from applications.

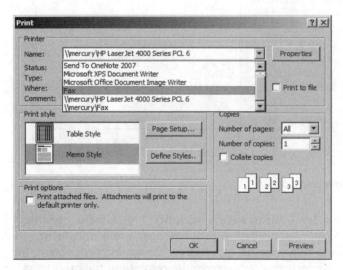

Figure 20-4 *Printing from within other applications*

Scanning

Windows Fax and Scan excels at scanning text documents, although it can also scan photographs and other pictures. To scan, you obviously will need a scanner attached to your machine and the appropriate drivers installed.

Once you've placed the document you want to scan in the scanner's feed slot, click the Scan toolbar at the bottom-left corner of the Windows Fax and Scan interface. Then, click New Scan on the toolbar. Windows Fax and Scan will try to establish a connection with the scanner attached to your machine and, if successful, will open the New Scan dialog box, which is shown in Figure 20-5.

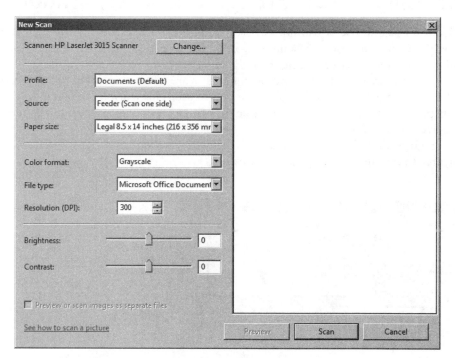

Figure 20-5 *Creating a new scan*

Windows Fax and Scan automatically includes a document "profile," which contains all the typical settings needed to properly scan a text document. Adjust the settings as necessary including selecting a source for the scanned document, the size of the paper used, the color format, the file type, the resolution, the brightness, and the contrast, and then click Preview. The scanner will make a quick scan of the document and populate the preview box, which allows you to select certain portions of the image or the entire scanned image. Once your selections are complete, click the Scan button to make a final scan.

By default scanned items are placed in the Documents folder under a directory named Scanned Documents; you can move them and copy them from there, just like any other file system object. From within Windows Fax and Scan, you can choose any individual scanned item and forward it either as a fax or as an email to a particular recipient by clicking the appropriate buttons on the toolbar within the scan area of the program.

Tips for Advanced Scanning

Here are a few tips and tricks for scanning various types of documents or pictures in Windows Fax and Scan:

- If you're trying to scan several images in a document, you can instruct the program to scan them separately and save them as distinct files. Simply check the Preview or Scan Images As Separate Files box in the New Scan dialog box.

- TIF images are the format to choose if you have some old documents in a scanner's sheet feeder and want to save them as a single file.

- You can automatically forward scanned items on a network by using scan routing tools. To configure this, from the Tools menu, select Scan Routing (Figure 20-6 shows the resulting dialog box). Choose the scanner for which you want to configure routing, and then enter an email address to which to forward scans and the requisite email server information. Alternatively, you can choose to save all scans in a network folder; check that box, and enter the path to the network folder you want to use.

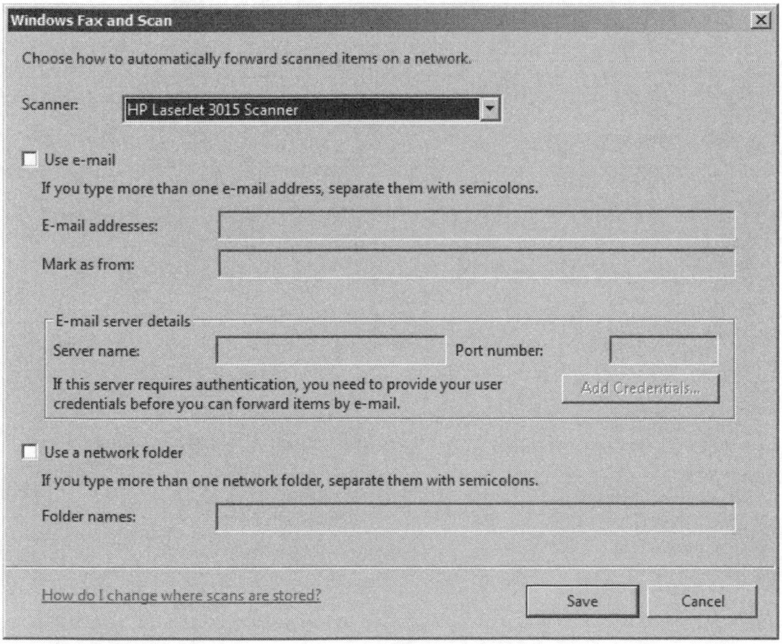

Figure 20-6 Scan routing options

CHAPTER 21

Working with Windows Media Player 11

The Windows Media Player has been part of Microsoft's digital media capability for quite some time; it's always cited as one of the main players (no pun intended) in the digital content–processing arena. Version 11, shipping as a core component of all the Vista editions, delivers a total facelift for Media Player, with new capabilities for supporting the latest video and audio formats as well as a much-improved interface and a whole set of new metadata search and organizational features.

Setting Up Media Player for the First Time

The first time you run Media Player from the Start menu (Start ➤ All Programs ➤ Windows Media Player), you need to complete a short setup routine that configures how Media Player will look, what it will be responsible for playing, and how it handles issues of security and privacy.

The first screen to appear allows you to choose Express or Custom setup; for completeness, this section will cover all aspects of the Custom setup as a way of introducing the topics covered throughout this chapter (see Figure 21-1).

To start customizing Media Player, you should select the Custom radio button, and then click Next. When you see the Select Privacy Options screen, shown in Figure 21-2, you need to carefully consider some of the settings.

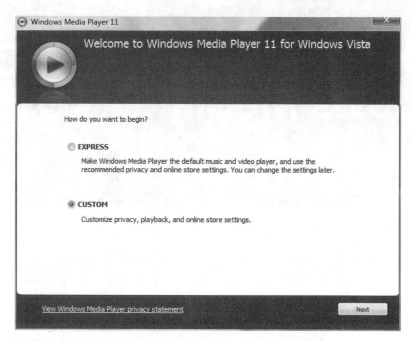

Figure 21-1 *You can select Express or Custom setup.*

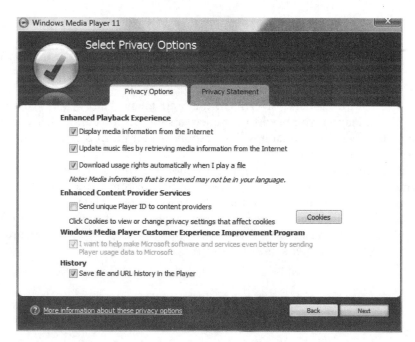

Figure 21-2 *Customizing Media Player to suit your needs is easy using the setup wizard.*

Understanding Privacy

Privacy refers to your ability to keep personal information about you, your family, or your computer system from public consumption. Information directly related to your bank account or credit card is an obvious candidate for what you might want to protect; however, you have many more items of data pertaining to your life that should remain under your direct control. Take, for example, your email address. You might consider this to be publicly available information since you send it over the Internet every day. Nevertheless, spammers would happily buy this information from an email collection source to help in targeting their spam. If your email address never gets on a spammer's list, you won't get spam. That sounds simple, doesn't it? You should realize, however, that many web sites capture your email address as part of registration and can, without your knowledge, sell this to third parties. The protection of this data falls under the catchall banner of *privacy*.

For this reason, applications that interact with third parties on the Internet (corporations, web stores, or individuals) should be able to offer you, the user, the ability to select which information you deem private and which information you deem public.

Throughout this book, you'll see various references to privacy (especially in the context of working on the Internet), and Media Player is no different. With the latest features in downloading content, online shopping, and digital rights management, privacy has become a hot topic in Media Player.

Table 21-1 lists the privacy settings available in Media Player; all but two are available to configure during the setup stage. To locate these privacy settings in Media Player later, select More Options from the Library drop-down menu, and then switch to the Privacy tab. The table shows the default privacy settings and a more secure alternative where available.

Table 21-1 Privacy Settings for Consideration Within Media Player

Setting	Description	Default	Most Secure
Display Media Information from the Internet	Media Player requests information about digital content from an online store. For this to work, Media Player sends the store an ID tag from the CD or DVD. This could allow the music store to determine which CDs and DVDs you have in your collection. Take note, this setting does not only display information (as the name suggests); it also interfaces with online services.	Permit	Deny
Update Music Files by Retrieving Media Information from the Internet	Media Player will automatically search online for any missing information from your library, such as album cover art or track listings, and download it. This setting works in harmony with the previous setting. If you deny the previous one, you should deny this one also.	Permit	Deny

Table 21-1 Privacy Settings for Consideration Within Media Player (Continued)

Setting	Description	Default	Most Secure
Download Usage Rights Automatically When I Play or Sync a File	Media usage rights determine how you can use content you have purchased online. If you opt to permit this setting, Media Player automatically downloads the rights, and the playback experience should be seamless. If you choose to deny this capability, you will have to obtain the license another way. It's not a good idea to deny this functionality, unless you have a good reason; hence, both default and more secure settings remain as permitted.	Permit	Permit
Automatically Check If Protected Files Need to Be Refreshed	If you have licensed content with an expiry date, where the license is renewable, Media Player can automatically detect this and request an updated license from the issue authority. Denying this capability will mean licensed digital content will no longer be usable when the license expires. For this reason, both options remain as permitted.	Permit	Permit
Set Clock on Devices Automatically	Media Player can synchronize the clock on portable media devices, such as MP3 players. This is important if you are playing licensed content since the license can be time-dependent. If you have licensed content and you want to synchronize with a portable device, you should permit this setting.	Permit	Deny
Send Unique Player ID to Content Providers	This setting means Media Player will send a unique identifier to online providers to allow them to identify you and adjust their service according to this unique identifier. This setting could be seen as a privacy violation; hence, its default is denied. Nevertheless, some content providers might require this, so it's your own decision whether to turn it on.	Deny	Deny
I Want to Help Make Microsoft Software Services Even Better by Sending Player Usage Data to Microsoft	If you want to take part in Microsoft's Customer Experience Improvement Program, you should permit this setting. This will anonymously notify Microsoft as to how you are using Media Player with a guarantee that no personal information will be transmitted over the network.	Permit	Deny
Save File and URL History in the Player	This setting permits Media Player to keep a record of the files you have most recently opened using Media Player. If you permit this setting, anyone using your Media Player can see what you have been playing.	Permit	Deny

You can also determine how cookies are handled by your system, although you should evaluate this setting in the wider context of Internet Explorer and how your privacy settings are configured there. Clicking the Cookies button (shown in Figure 21-2) will take you to the Internet Properties dialog box, usually accessed by selecting Internet Explorer ➤ Tools ➤ Internet Options and going to the Privacy tab.

> **NOTE** To read Microsoft's comprehensive statement about how it is approaching privacy, you can view the statement on the Microsoft web site at `http://www.microsoft.com/windows/windowsmedia/player/vista/privacy.aspx`.

When you have finished configuring your privacy settings, click Next to continue.

Selecting the Default Music and Video Player

Figure 21-3 shows the next screen in the setup routine, where you can select whether to allow Media Player to take over the role of playing all digital media content it knows about or whether you prefer to use a third-party product for some files and Media Player for others.

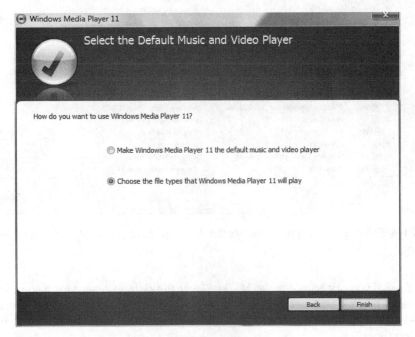

Figure 21-3 *You can instruct Media Player to be responsible for a subset of your content or all of it.*

If you select the topmost option, Make Windows Media Player 11 the Default Music and Video Player, all digital music and video content on your PC will be played by Media Player. If file associations for other players existed, such as for .avi files or .mp3 files, this option will remove the old associations and associate those file types with Media Player. In the future, running the content from Windows Explorer (double-clicking it) will automatically fire up Media Player.

If, on the other hand, you want to use your other media player for specific file types, you should select Choose the File Types That Windows Media Player 11 Will Play and then click Finish. This will fire up the Set Associations for a Program screen (shown in Figure 21-4) where you can select each of the file types for which you want Media Player to be responsible. Don't forget to save your selections when you're done.

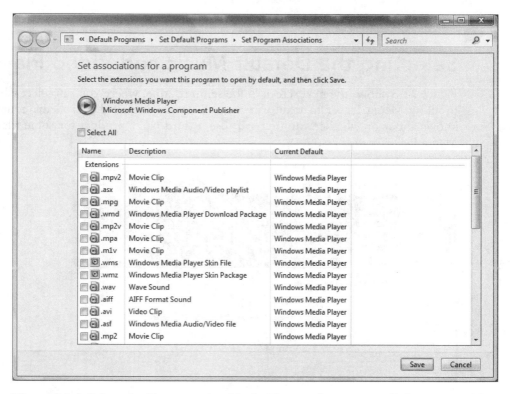

Figure 21-4 *Select the file types that Media Player will automatically be responsible for playing.*

> **TIP** Even if you opt to not make Media Player the default player for a specific file type, such as .mp3, you can still have Media Player play these files by simply pressing Ctrl+O and then locating the file in the file system through the file browser and clicking Open.

When you have saved your selection, the window will close, and you will have your first view of what Media Player looks like. If you want to adjust any of the settings you've entered during the setup process, you can do this using the Welcome

Center. Select Start ➤ All Programs ➤ Accessories ➤ Welcome Center, select Show All 12 Items, select Windows Media Player Set Up, and click Start (located in the top right of the Welcome Center).

The Media Player interface, like most other Vista products, has been significantly improved to make it more ergonomically acceptable and easier to navigate. To make this possible, a lot of the underlying power of the player is hidden beneath the menu system, leaving the main interface, shown in Figure 21-5, purely for finding, playing, and manipulating your digital content.

Figure 21-5 *The new Media Player interface is optimized for searching through the library.*

Starting at the top of the screen and working down, we'll cover each component that composes the interface.

First, the crossbar menu at the top of the screen, as with most Vista applications, is where you control what's displayed in the main window (directly beneath the crossbar) and where you switch primary functionality from one feature to another. Each button on the crossbar is split into two parts. The topmost part switches the main screen to the capability shown on that button. However, if you hover the mouse pointer over the bottom of the button, you'll see a highlighted arrow that allows you

·to open a drop-down menu of options for that capability; for example, if you open the Library drop-down menu, you'll see options for creating playlists, selecting genres, and adding music to your library.

The buttons on the crossbar are as follows:

- Now Playing
- Library
- Rip
- Burn
- Sync
- Online Stores

What's Playing?

The Now Playing tab is by far the most straightforward of the Media Player tabs. If you switch to the Now Playing tab, by default you will see one of the many visualizations available through the drop-down menu (for example, Now Playing ➤ Visualizations ➤ Battery ➤ Cottonstar). If you click Download Visualizations (in the Now Playing ➤ Visualizations menu), Media Player launches Internet Explorer and directs you to the Microsoft Media Player Visualizations web page where you can choose from plenty of custom-made visualizations. Follow the online instructions for installing and optimizing the visualization to suit your Media Player needs.

> **NOTE** From the Microsoft Media Player web site, available from the Visualizations page we just described, you can download custom skins (custom look-and-feel interfaces for Media Player), extra visualizations developed either by Microsoft or third-party vendors, and plug-ins to add functionality to Media Player.

If you click Show Enhancements (in the Now Playing menu), a graphic equalizer appears at the bottom of the main screen. You can use this facility as you would a physical graphic equalizer on a typical piece of a HiFi kit, adjusting balance and level for each of the ten available frequency ranges. If you click the small arrows in the top-left corner of the graphic equalizer, you can scroll through interfaces that allow you to adjust the playback speed (great for speeding up speech podcasts where the interviewee might be talking too slowly for your liking) and switch on Media Player's quiet mode, whereby frequency suppression compresses the sound to make the average volume of the output more consistent. Another enhancement, called SRS WOW Effects, offers audio enhancement techniques that allow you to scale your audio output to suit your physical speaker arrangement and boost your system's bass representation to your output device.

> **NOTE** For more information about SRS WOW and how it integrates with Media Player, visit `http://mediaplayer.srswowcast.com`.

The Video Settings enhancement menu lets you adjust the hue, saturation, brightness, and contrast of video played in Media Player and is really useful for adjusting home movies or videos that are not represented that well on the PC. Cross-fading allows you to add a fade-out/fade-in effect between items in your playlist, and, as its name suggests, the Auto Volume Leveling option allows Media Player to have consistent playback volume even if the source content output level changes from one track to the next.

Notice also that the List pane (on the right side of Media Player when using the Now Playing view) lists all the tracks to be played in the current playlist. If you have simply selected a single track to play directly from the library, you'll see all the tracks in the library that follow the current, playing track. You can switch off the List pane from the Now Playing drop-down menu. You can select a new track to start playing from the List pane by double-clicking the track.

Beneath the List pane, you'll see two small blue buttons:

- Full Screen
- Switch to Skin Mode

Clicking Full Screen allows Media Player to take over the entire screen, removing toolbars, the Start menu, and taskbars. This is a great party mode for playing on a big screen when entertaining.

To revert to a windowed view, press Escape or move the mouse (to reveal the taskbar at the bottom of the screen), and click the blue button on the bottom-right corner of the screen entitled Exit Full-Screen Mode.

At the bottom of the screen, you'll see a common set of controls that you'll recognize from many of the Vista-based applications; you'll see buttons that represent playing/pausing, stopping, going to the next and previous tracks, repeating, and shuffling.

> **NOTE** If you press the Shuffle button, the order of the songs played from your library will be random. If you click the Shuffle button again, the player will revert to playing the tracks in the order presented in the library. Clicking Repeat will force a replay of the track to which you are currently listening.

If you select Now Playing ➤ Plug-ins ➤ Download Plug-ins, you are redirected to the Microsoft Media Player web site where you can download new functionality to augment Media Player's current capabilities. This site contains downloads of DVD decoder software, new MP3 encoders, and Media Player PowerToys and utilities, such as new autoplaylists.

> **TIP** To really get under the hood of Media Player, download TweakMP. This PowerToy (capable of working on all Media Player versions since 9) enables you to get into all the hidden Media Player settings, whereby you obtain total control over everything Media Player could possibly be configured to do.

Finally, under Now Playing ➤ Plug-Ins ➤ Options, you can alter the properties (where possible) of installed plug-ins and visualizations. With the Options dialog box, you can perform much of the advanced media player configuration that we cover later in the "Using the Advanced Library Options" section.

Introducing the Media Library

The library is the main screen for viewing and manipulating digital content. From the Library drop-down menu, you can create new playlists of content and switch the view between music, pictures, video, recorded TV, or miscellaneous content items (under the Other heading). Each of the categories of content type, such as Music or Pictures, will focus the display on the library containing content of that nature. By default, the user's profile directories, such as your own Music and Pictures folders, will be displayed; however, you can add files to the library from other folders (or network locations), and these will all appear as one consolidated library resource in Media Player.

On the left side of the screen (in the Navigation pane), you'll see two top-level folders: Playlists and Library.

Playlists are predefined lists of songs that you can select to play as an ordered list. You can find more detail about using, creating, and deleting playlists throughout this chapter, but for now, you can click a preinstalled playlist (such as All Music) to see how it presents information in the library.

The library folders are actually used to change what's displayed in the main view on the right, with each option changing the content displayed in Library view. For example, selecting Songs, beneath the Library node, displays every album and track listing (this is the default view). Alternatively, to aid you in searching for a specific album or artist, selecting Album will display the cover art of all your albums in alphabetical order oriented around the album name, while selecting Artist will display the cover art for all albums in alphabetical order oriented around the artist's name (see Figure 21-6).

Figure 21-6 *Use the categories on the left to determine how your library appears.*

Above the Navigation pane, you'll see three overhead drop-down menus running from left to right. Each drop-down menu controls what is displayed in the Library view, with each item to the right being more specific in grouping that category than the previous. For example, if you select Music ➤ Library ➤ Album, you will see all your album art shown in the library in alphabetical order; however, selecting Video ➤ Library ➤ Folder will display all your library folders that contain video items, again in alphabetical order oriented around the folder name.

The search box to the upper-right side of the screen allows you to perform fast interactive searches of your entire library using media information known as *metadata*.

> **NOTE** Metadata is used extensively by Vista to help users of applications better manipulate and categorize data files for use in the real world. Date, time, tags, and star ratings are all forms of metadata that you can use in Media Player.

You can search on any textual information associated with your content, such as album name, artist's name, or the date the album was released. If you've added extra tagging information about the track using the Advanced Tag Editor (see Figure 21-7), you can search on additional track information you've added about the artist, song lyrics, pictures associated with the track, or any additional comments you might have added, such as a review of the album that you sent to Amazon.com. To start the Advanced Tag Editor, right-click a track, and then select Advanced Tag Editor from the context menu.

Figure 21-7 *Use the Advanced Tag Editor to add information into your library.*

To the left of the search box are two drop-down menus worth discussing. The left-most of these offers a number of options for changing the layout of the screen; you can toggle on and off the Navigation pane and the List pane, add the classic menu bar to this version of Media Player to align it with previous versions (File, View, Play, Tools, and Help), and modify the columns displayed at the top of the Library view.

Between the Layout Options menu and the search box is the View Options menu. Using this menu, you can change the library layout to show a detailed view (with no album art), to show a less detailed view with album art (the default), or if you prefer, to show only an icon.

Use the arrow to the right of the search box to expose the List pane if it has previously been hidden.

The Media Player controls at the bottom of the screen are consistent throughout each of the menu tabs and always perform the same functions (play/pause, stop, next/ previous track, repeat, shuffle, and volume up and down).

Working with Different Types of Content

Using the Library view, you can search for a variety of different content types: music, videos, recorded TV, and various other types of uncategorized content. Changing from one form of digital content to another is as easy as opening the Library drop-down menu and selecting the appropriate content library from the list.

Music, pictures, and video are fairly self-explanatory, with the default file locations being in your user's profile under the Pictures, Music, and Videos folders.

More interestingly, you can now play recorded TV shows that have been recorded in the Microsoft Recorded TV Show format (files ending with the extension .dvr-ms) directly through this interface without having to run Media Center (you'll learn more about Media Center in Chapter 25). If you have Media Center running on the same computer as you are running Media Player, the file is automatically recorded in your user profile and can be played back using Media Center; or, if you are working and want them shrunk into a small window, you can view them in Media Player. Furthermore, if you want to take your recorded TV shows with you on a machine not capable of running Media Center, you can simply copy the files from the Media Center computer (using removable media or a wireless or wired network) and put it in your profile's Recorded TV folder.

The Other category is for files that do not fall into any of the categories already discussed. These might be digital media files that rely on a proprietary codec to play them, or perhaps you want to store files that you have paid and licensed using digital rights management (DRM) in this separate category.

Creating and Using Playlists

As mentioned, playlists are collections of digital media that you have grouped for a specific purpose, such as party songs, driving music, or classical music for your mother-in-law, for example. The other great reason for creating playlists is that you can use a playlist as the unit of synchronization when copying media to a portable device; for example, you can create a synchronization with a media device with a lot less space than your hard drive, synchronizing your favorite tracks as your tastes change.

Playlists are really easy to create, either by using the Library drop-down menu and selecting Create Playlist or by pressing Ctrl+N. This will expose the List pane on the right side of the screen and offer you a blank playlist with the name Untitled Playlist. The first step is to rename it to something more meaningful. Click the arrow next to the playlist name to expose the drop-down menu, and select Rename Playlist. To add tracks to the playlist, it's a simple matter of dragging them from the Library view to the List pane where it says Drag Items Here.

Once you are happy with the selection of songs in your playlist, you can right-click any song shown in the List pane and use the context menu items Remove from List, Move Up, and Move Down to delete that track or change the play order. When you are happy with the contents of a playlist and its order of play, click the Save Playlist at the bottom of the List pane. Your playlist will have an extension of .wpl and will, by default, be stored in the My Playlists folder in your profile under the Music folder.

To view all the playlists you have stored on your system or select a playlist for use, expand the Playlists node in the Navigation pane and then select the one you recently saved from the tree, as shown in Figure 21-8. There will be a whole collection of playlists already created by default on your system, based on criteria such as when the files were added to your library, their star ratings, and favorites (based on the number of times you have listened to the track). Also, it's worth noticing that you can create playlists of photos, video, and TV using the same technique. This is important since portable media devices are now capable of playing so much more than simple MP3 music files.

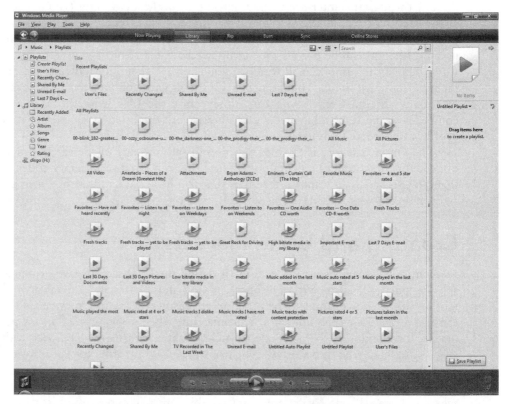

Figure 21-8 *You'll notice that a whole bunch of playlists are already included by default.*

Autoplaylists are even more useful, dynamically updating themselves from metadata associated with items in your library. Autoplaylists use rules to determine membership, and these rules are extremely flexible.

To create an autoplaylist, open the Library drop-down menu, and then select Create Auto Playlist. In the dialog box shown in Figure 21-9, give the autoplaylist a meaningful name, and then proceed to create the rules that automatically populate that playlist with content.

Figure 21-9 *Use content filtering rules to determine which content is included in a playlist.*

To set a rule, do the following:

1. Click the green plus sign under the topmost item in the rules list, Music in My Library. This will open the criteria drop-down menu and offer an initial selection of 20 criteria to choose from (although there are more available if you select More at the bottom of the list). Choose the criterion that best matches the content you want to include in this playlist, such as Genre.

2. You will see the Genre criterion listed as Genre Is [click to set] (notice the Is is actually underlined). Click this Is to change the logic being applied by this operand, selecting Is, Is Not, or Contains. In this example of Genre, you might use Contains if you wanted all rock music but there were many genres associated with rock, for example, soft rock, heavy rock, glam rock, and so on. If you are planning to create the playlist by exclusion, you can use Is Not as the operand and, in the genre example, exclude all dance music.

3. When you've set the operand, click [click to set], and select the item from the drop-down list that matches your requirement; for example, in the case of genre, you might select Blues.

4. To add more criteria to the list, you can add as many of these rules as you like. You might start by creating a genre rule, and then you might add another rule for the Release Year. This way, you could start building up a playlist of 80s soul music, for example.

5. Use the And Also Include criteria to include other content types in the playlist, such as music, pictures, and video.

6. Finally, add a restriction, if required to the playlist, such as a maximum number of tracks or a size limit. This is particularly useful if you are using this playlist as the one you synchronize with a portable device with limited space.

7. When you have added all the criteria necessary to filter your library the way you want, click OK. This adds the new playlist to the list in the Navigation pane.

From now on when new music is added to your library, if it meets the criteria specified by the rules in the playlist, Media Player automatically makes those tracks members of that playlist. Each time you synchronize with a portable device, the updated playlist is automatically transferred to the remote device.

Adding Content to the Library

You can add new digital content to your library using two methods. You can manually copy the content into your default library, such as the Music folder in your profile, or you can connect a new device (or create a new folder) on your PC and add the folder path to the Monitored Folders list to force Media Player to look in that new folder each time it starts.

> **TIP** If you add multiple albums from a single artist to your library, Media Player will start stacking the items in the library so that when you view them by artist, you immediately see how many albums by that artist you have.

To access the interface for configuring how content is added to the Media Player's Monitored Folders list, click the Library drop-down menu, and select Add to Library.

You will see the screen shown in Figure 21-10. Make sure to click Advanced Options to view the list of monitored folders.

You can add or remove folders from the list using the Add and Remove buttons. Folders can be local to your computer, or they can exist on another PC accessible over your network. In the case of a folder being under the control of another user or PC, that folder will need access rights that allow you to connect to and read the content before you can use it.

If you select the Add Files Previously Deleted from My Library checkbox, Media Player will automatically enter content in the library if you have previously deleted the entry.

> **CAUTION** Adding files back into the library if they have been removed is possible only if the file still exists on your hard disk. If you physically delete the file rather than just the library entry, Media Player cannot recover it from the Recycle Bin.

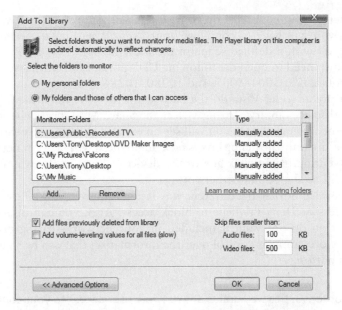

Figure 21-10 *To add new folders to the Monitored Folders list, use the advanced options.*

If you want to apply volume leveling to the tracks as they are imported into your library, the time taken to integrate each track takes much longer since each track's volume is assessed against an average, and then the track is suppressed or enhanced to align it with that average.

You can also limit Media Player from incorporating audio and video files beneath a certain threshold. This is particularly useful for stopping fragments of songs and video from being imported into your library and cluttering it up.

Sharing Your Library

Sharing data and collaborating is a common theme when you look across the Vista product set, and it's no less so in Media Player. If you have a network with more than one PC, you can share your Media Player library from a single location or distribute the libraries across any number of PCs and open access to each shared library to the rest of the network.

Your network makes sharing your content really easy and offers the benefits of being able to consume content from any location your network reaches.

> **CAUTION** If you want to use library sharing on a PC, it must be part of the same physical network as another computer, connected with IP addresses in the same subnet. Library sharing cannot be used in a domain environment; it's possible only when you are operating Vista in a workgroup.

It is possible to set up library sharing on your system without using the option in this menu; however, you will have to configure your firewall settings to permit the following TCP ports, all with a defined scope in the local subnet: 554, 2177, 2869, and 10243. You will also need to open the following UDP ports, again with a scope of local subnet only: 1900, 2177, 5004–5005, and 10280–10284.

If, however, you prefer to let Vista do the hard work for you, open the Library drop-down menu, and select Library Sharing. Select the Share My Library checkbox, and then click OK. When you click OK, you will see an expanded dialog box showing the same options as before only the dialog box is now augmented with a list of network devices available for sharing. Right-click any of the devices shown in the window to configure how they will be shared on the network.

You can configure each device in a different way if you require, using Allow Privilege to authorize access or Deny Privilege to block access. Also, you can disable or remove the device if you do not want it included in your network-sharing profile. Finally, you can gain more granular control over the information that can be shared if you click the Settings button.

> **NOTE** Sharing content in this way grants any network user access to your content. Consider whether you want this to happen before allowing sharing to be used.

Getting Album Art and Media Information

If you want Media Player to check the Internet for updates of media information, including album art and track listings, you can use the Apply Media Information Changes option in the Library drop-down menu.

This is quite slow because the process must check the track and album identifiers contained in your library against an online database, and then where it finds new information, it must download that information to your computer. If you have a large media library with a lot of untagged content, prepare for this process to take up to a few hours to complete.

Using the Advanced Library Options

A few more options are available for configuring how Media Player handles the information contained in the library and how files are kept or deleted, depending on your preference.

To access the advanced options for your media library, click the Library drop-down menu, and select More Options. This will open the Options dialog box shown in Figure 21-11.

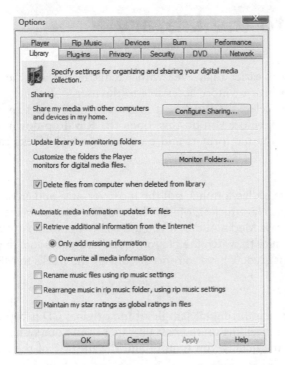

Figure 21-11 *Use the Library tab of the Options dialog box to configure advanced library options.*

By default the Delete Files from Computer When Deleted from Library checkbox is selected. This means when you right click a track in the library and select Delete, the file is sent to the Recycle Bin. If, however, you prefer to delete a track from the library but keep the source content file on the hard disk, you should deselect this checkbox. If you want to keep files on the hard disk but don't want them in the library, it's also a good idea to move them to another location that is not automatically scanned as a monitored folder. This way, you can permit the monitored folders functionality to automatically add all the files it finds in the Monitored Folders list without having to toggle that setting on and off.

Further configuration items at the bottom of the dialog box allow you to override Internet information downloaded for a file using settings predefined as specific Rip Music settings. These are not checked by default since most people are happy to use Internet-supplied information since it tends to be effortless and mostly accurate.

You can also instruct Media Player to always update the entire library's metadata rather than just look at new files. Be warned, however, that this can take a long time and should be done only when you don't need to do anything else with Media Player for a few hours.

Ripping Content to the Library

Ripping music to your library is easier than ever with Media Player 11; the most important update is that the settings are more accessible to the user.

You'll notice that when you select the Rip tab, it instructs you to insert an audio CD into the CD drive. However, before you do this, open the Rip drop-down menu to see how easy it is to change the file formats and bit rates to which tracks can be ripped.

> **NOTE** You can choose from six file formats, but the most versatile and cross-plat-form of these is certainly MP3. Nevertheless, Media Player defaults to the Microsoft proprietary format of Windows Media Audio. If you are using a portable media device that plays MP3s, be sure to switch the file format before you begin ripping CDs to your library; otherwise, you'll have to rerip or convert the tracks to MP3 in the future.

The bit rate is the rate at which the digital sample of the original CD is copied to its new ripped file format. When deciding on the best bit rate to suit your system, you must strike a balance between the quality you require and the file size of the ripped track.

The default bit rate in Media Player is 128Kbps, offering a good halfway compromise with relatively small files and virtually undetectable loss on the original track's CD quality.

If, however, you are a connoisseur of music and demand the best quality available, you can switch the bit rate to sample at 192Kbps, giving you a virtually lossless conversion to the new file format. On the other hand, to preserve disk space or to fit more tracks on a portable device with limited memory, you can compromise on quality for the smallest file size and select 48Kbps.

If you want to speed up the ripping process, cutting down on the number of clicks needed to start the process, you can follow the Rip menu item Rip CD Automatically When Inserted, and select Always. This option will start the ripping process immediately as you insert a CD into the drive, even if Media Player is not focused on the Rip tab. The default setting is to start automatically if you are focused on the Rip tab. Lastly, there is an option to never start automatically; if you select this, you have to click the Rip [album name] item in the Rip menu or click the Start Rip button in the bottom-right corner of the interface. If you want to stop the ripping process, click the Stop Rip button in the bottom-right corner.

If you want the CD automatically ejected from the CD drive when it has copied your library, select the Eject CD After Ripping menu item from the Rip menu. If you are ripping a lot of music, this can be a great reminder that the rip has completed and it's time to put in the next CD. In this case, you might want to have the system start ripping automatically when you put a new CD in the drive also.

NOTE Before you start ripping CDs, you have to decide how you will be handling copy protection. Media Player allows you to protect the music you rip to ensure that you don't infringe any copyright laws if your media files end up finding their way into the public domain. Nevertheless, be warned that copy protection will prohibit your media being played on other devices that you own, and this is perfectly acceptable within the bounds of the law. Whatever you decide, you will have to check the disclaimer checkbox, thereby relinquishing Microsoft of any copy protection or copyright infringement liability as a result of your own misuse of the digital content.

Select whether you want to use copy protection on your music, and check the disclaimer before clicking OK. You should now see the track listing and the album information in the Rip view, and as each track is copied to your library, you'll see a notification that it is ripped to library. A progress bar appears for the track currently being ripped, as shown in Figure 21-12.

Figure 21-12 *Watch the progress as tracks are copied one at a time to your library.*

Take a look in the Options dialog box for the Rip function (Rip ➤ More Options); Figure 21-13 shows the Rip Music tab.

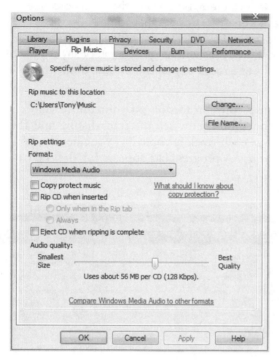

Figure 21-13 *Use the Options dialog box to change advanced ripping settings.*

You can change the default location where new music is ripped to; the default is the Music folder in your user profile (C:\Users\<username>\Music). To change the file location, click the Change button in the Options dialog box on the Rip Music tab.

You can alter the way the filename for each track is created by using different metadata information available when the track is found on the online information services. Click File Name to see the full list of information that can be used to create the filename for ripped music.

Creating CDs and DVDs from Your Library

Creating (*burning*) CDs using Media Player is really easy. Click the Burn tab, and open the drop-down menu to see the options available for CD creation. If you have not inserted a blank CD that is writable using Vista, you will see a message in the main interface window stating "To begin, insert a blank disc into the drive."

You have the option of creating two distinctly different kinds of CD:

- An audio CD for playing in a standard CD player
- A data CD containing exact copies of the source files, such as your MP3s

If you opt to create a data CD, you will effectively be doing a straight copy of the files in your library to the CD. Creating an audio CD forces the reformatting of the source files into the appropriate digital format necessary to be played on a regular CD player. Because this file format is substantially larger than the MP3 format, for example, you'll find that although 50 MP3s might fit easily on a data CD, only 18 will fit on the audio CD.

> **TIP** It's worth checking to see whether the CD player supports MP3. If this is the case, you can create a data CD of MP3 files that are playable by the CD player.

The first step when you want to create a new CD is to place the blank CD in the CD writer. Media Player should automatically recognize it as a blank CD and report this through the interface. In the List pane, you'll see the Burn list initially with no items beneath it. This is where you add tracks that you want copied to the CD. The trick here is to switch back to the Library tab and find the music you want to burn. Next, click back to the Burn tab, and start dragging the tracks you are interested to over to the Burn list.

> **TIP** To select multiple tracks from the library, hold down the Ctrl key, and click each track you want copied to the CD. When you have selected a group of tracks, release the Ctrl key, and then drag any one of the selected files to the Burn list. You'll notice that all the other follow along quite obediently.

As you drag each track to the CD, Media Player reports how much space is left to copy more files. When you are ready to commit the tracks to the CD, select Burn ➤ Burn, or click the Start Burn button in the bottom-right corner of the main interface. This will take a little time, so be patient. A green progress bar shows the status as each track is burned, as shown in Figure 21-14.

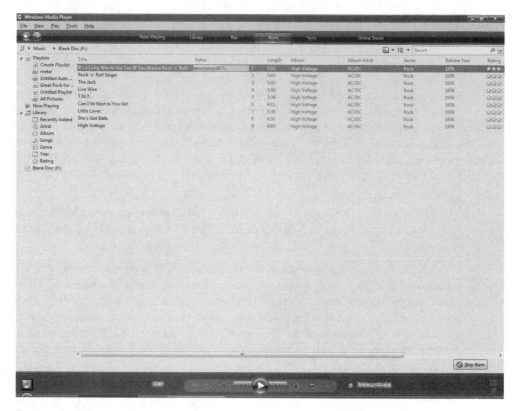

Figure 21-14 *Burning can take some time, but you can still use Media Player to play other tracks.*

If you access the Options dialog box for advanced burning settings, you will see the Burn tab, as shown in Figure 21-15.

It is rare that you would ever have to change this burn speed from its default of Fastest; however, if you are experiencing problems with the CDs you are creating, it's a good way of testing the writer's burning mechanism. If the problem is fixed by reducing the speed it burns at, it might be that the drive has a hardware fault that needs repairing.

The Automatically Eject the Disc After Burning setting is fairly obvious, but it's worth remembering that you can switch off this option if you don't want the CD taken offline once it's created. Some people like sharing their CD drive on the network, and this might be a good way of quickly sharing information with others on your network without going through the process of library sharing.

Volume leveling will ensure that all the tracks on your CD have the same audio output levels. This makes for a consistent level in the playback, something that is essential for a comfortable listening experience.

Data CDs are always copied with an associated playlist, either in WPL (standard Media Player playlist format) or in M3U (a standard MP3 playlist format). This means that another media player, capable of using playlists, can exploit this data and display it on its own interface.

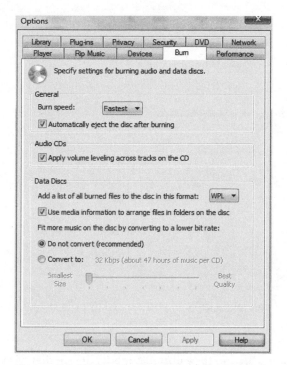

Figure 21-15 *You have a variety of advanced options to configure how CDs are created.*

If you allow Media Player to arrange the files according to the metadata in your library, the files will be stored in folders ordered by the artist's name, then by the album name, and finally by the track. If you clear the checkbox for using media information, all files will be stored in the root folder of the data CD. This is unadvisable since it's little overhead to make the final CD ordered and more organized.

Lastly, you can adjust the bit rate for the copied files to fit more of these files onto the destination CD. In this way, you can keep high-quality files on your PC yet write low-quality files to your CD to maximize its capacity to hold more tracks.

Synchronizing with Portable Devices

As soon as you connect a Vista-compatible portable media device, you can configure Media Player to synchronize with it. First, you need to go through a short configuration process for that device before it becomes an automatic function.

The first time you connect a portable device, you are presented with a dialog box that allows you to authorize Media Player to overwrite any existing files on that device or leave any existing files intact and augment them with new files from your library, as shown in Figure 21-16. In this case, we chose to leave the files intact on the device.

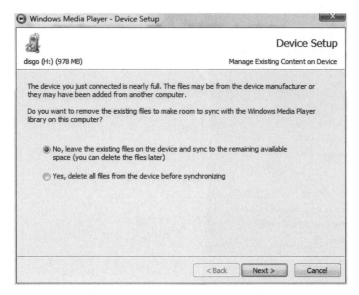

Figure 21-16 *The first time you connect a device, you can ask Media Player to wipe it clean.*

> **NOTE** When you are shopping around for a portable media device that will seamlessly integrate with Media Player 11, make sure to look for the PlaysForSure logo on the hardware you invest in. This logo is Microsoft's seal of approval on devices that have been tested and authorized as fully compliant with Media Player.

If you are happy to overwrite the files on the portable device, select Yes, delete all the files from the device before synchronizing, and then click Next. You are then asked to confirm you are happy for Media Center to delete any content on the device (it's your last chance to save your data). Clicking Yes will delete everything on that device and leave it fresh and clean for synchronizing with your Media Center library.

Finally, you are asked to name your portable device. Choose a name that is meaningful, and then click Finish.

> **NOTE** The first time a new device is connected to Media Player (one that is new to Media Player, that is, not necessarily one that is just out of the plastic carton), Media Player will select what it thinks is the best way of synchronizing with that device, either automatically or manually. If your portable device has enough memory to hold an entire copy of your library, Media Player will synchronize with it automatically, copying everything. If the capacity of the drive is less than that of your library size, Media Player reverts to a manual mode, which allows you to select which songs and playlists are transferred. When you click Finish in the device setup routine, Media Player selects the synchronization mode, either starting the sync automatically or passing control to you to do it manually.

When the device setup routine finishes, you can switch to the Sync tab to see the device in the List pane. You'll see an icon representing the device and some information about the device's capacity and how much space is left to copy data onto it.

Shuffling Music Content on a Portable Device

A great feature of this version of Media Player is the ability to shuffle content onto the device. You can shuffle content using either the Click Here link on the List pane or the Sync drop-down menu where you select Shuffle [device name]. When you select Shuffle, Media Player will copy a random selection of tracks onto the device to fill its capacity. This is great for MP3 players with, say, 1GB of space when your library is an order of magnitude greater. Each time you select the Shuffle option, Media Player will replace the files on your device with a whole bunch of new ones.

As Media Player synchronizes with your device, you will see the progress mapped out, as shown in Figure 21-17.

Figure 21-17 *Media Player sends a whole set of new tracks to the device each time you shuffle.*

Setting Up Synchronizations

To get down into the weeds of setting up a clever and customized synchronization regime for each of your portable devices, open the Sync drop-down menu, select the device's name from the menu, and then select Set Up Sync. This opens the Device Setup screen shown in Figure 21-18.

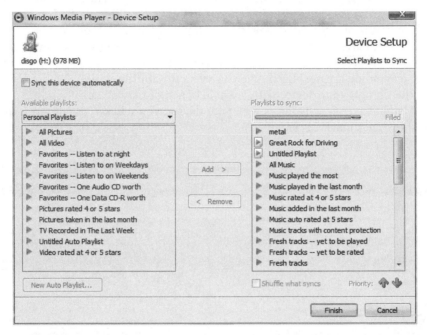

Figure 21-18 *Select custom playlists to autosync with small-capacity portable devices.*

If you are currently manually synchronizing this device, because of capacity constraints, you can now instruct Media Player to switch to automatically synchronize with whichever playlists you want.

> **NOTE** The trick to making this work is to use autoplaylists that you have developed rules specifically for when you're on the road. You can easily create a custom autoplaylist that contains rules to limit the size of the playlist it creates. Remember the constraints you can build into autoplaylists at the bottom of the filters screen.

To make all this work, you need to select Sync This Device Automatically. There is a shortcut at the bottom of the screen to take you to the New Auto Playlist screen where you can immediately create a playlist that matches the criteria imposed by the constraints of your portable device.

> **TIP** Double-click a playlist to see the tracks contained within it. On the View Play-list screen, you can double-click a track to listen to it in Media Player.

You can change the order of what is synchronized using the priority arrows beneath the Playlists to Sync list, and if you want the songs to shuffle when they arrive on the device, select the Shuffle What Syncs checkbox. Click Finish when you're done.

When you exit from setting up the sync, Media Player will start synchronizing automatically with your device.

Using the Advanced Options for Portable Devices

You can access advanced options for synchronizing your portable devices in two places, through the Sync drop-down menu (selecting the device name and then Advanced Options where you specify options for each individual device) and through the regular Options dialog box (specifying the option for the Media Player end of the synchronization).

First we'll cover the Advanced Options dialog box particular to this functionality of each individual portable device.

Click Sync ➤ [device name] ➤ Advanced Options.

The Advanced Options dialog box here is specific to this device. You'll see the synchronization name for this device (by default this is the same as the device name as recognized when you first plugged it into Vista), which you can change if you so desire. If you check the Create Folder Hierarchy on Device checkbox, the synchronization will use library metadata, such as the artist's name and album names, to create a folder hierarchy on the device much in the same way as you would in your library or when you create a data CD. If you want all the tracks copied to the root directory of your device, uncheck this box.

> **TIP** You might wonder why you would ever want to synchronize into the root directory of your device without folders, but some devices require this. For example, some FM transmitter devices—the sort you use to transmit from an MP3 player to your car-stereo system—allow you to plug in memory sticks with no real playback capability of their own. Although this is particularly useful and a cost-effective way of taking music with you on the go, they have only simple play, next/previous track, and stop controls. You can't navigate folders, and you get no clever display.

You can choose to start the synchronization as soon as the device connects, or you can wait until you click the Start Sync button. The default for Start Sync When Device Connect will depend on the initial setup of that device—if the device has high capacity and can take your entire library, it will be automatic; otherwise, it will be manual.

If the device is a picture storage device, you can ask Media Player to automatically delete pictures from that device once they have been transferred into your library. Select Delete Pictures from Device Once Copied to Computer. This stops you from having to manually delete images from a digital camera, for example, after you've copied them into your library.

Finally, on this screen, you can ask Media Player to reserve some of the capacity of the portable device for use by other information. You might also use the device to back up your Documents folder or keep copies of data not related to Media Player. Use the slider to change the percentage of the portable device that remains preserved for other use.

Now switch to the Quality tab. It's advisable you leave the topmost checkbox— Convert Music, Pictures, Videos, and TV Shows As Required—selected as the default. This ensures that Media Player will make the best effort to make your content play on the portable device, even if this required a format change from .wma to .mp3 or a downgrade in quality.

You can also opt for a downgrade of content based on the settings of the two sliders, applying to both music and video content.

When you're done, click OK.

On the other side of the synchronization, you can configure some Media Player– specific options using the main Media Player Options dialog box (Sync ➤ More Options); then, on the Devices tab, click Advanced (see Figure 21-19).

Figure 21-19 *Convert files before you start synchronizing to speed things up.*

The background conversion of files will occur for synchronization when the portable device is not plugged in. Your system must also be idle (no user input from the keyboard or mouse) for at least ten minutes before background conversion will begin.

> **NOTE** If your portable device is plugged in, files are converted as the transfer happens, not in the background.

By default, background synchronization is enabled only for video files, but you can also switch it on for audio content. You can also instruct the conversion process to deinterlace video files on conversion (some media content players require this—you should look at the manufacturer's instruction for your device). Through this interface you can also improve the quality of converted video, change the folder used for temporary file conversions, and specify the amount of temporary disk space used to hold the converted files. The default upper limit of disk space that is utilized by the conversion process is 3225 MB, but you might want to increase this if you have a lot of music and video to convert. This is your call and is best optimized through trial and error.

> **NOTE** You can use an Xbox 360 as a remote media player, using its built-in media capability to connect to your shared library over your network. The Xbox 360 can also act as a Media Center extender and can stream content from your Vista PC over the wireless or wired network to anywhere it is connected. You can find more information about using an Xbox 360 as a Media Center extender in Chapter 25.

Buying Music Online

You can obtain two kinds of content from an online store: subscription content and purchased content. Subscription content can either come at a cost or be free, but it is usually associated with regular updates of content, such as weekly radio shows or television shows.

When you click the Online Stores tab, you can access a massive variety of content provided through the online MSN interface. Digital content (audio and video) can be sourced from these online services and will be downloaded to your library in the same way as ripped CD content. The only difference between your own ripped content and content sources from an online service is that it might have media usage rights for copy protection downloaded with it, limiting its use to your PC and prohibiting distribution.

As more and more content providers wake up to the new world order of digital content on the Web, new applications and plug-ins are shifting the way we listen to and use digital content. Take, for example, MTV's URGE service. URGE installs as a plug-in for both Media Player and Media Center, and it has a small subscription charge (paid monthly). Much in way you subscribe to a pay-per-view movie service, you have access to millions of audio tracks, music videos, and other kinds of digital content. URGE also acts as a portal to a whole bunch of online radio channels that are free to connect and listen to. You can also opt to pay for and download tracks in the more traditional way. Whichever way to choose to use URGE, the integration of these technologies opens up the doors to a whole new way of viewing the digital world of multimedia content.

For more information about using URGE or to download and install the URGE plug-in for Media Center, go to http://www.urge.com. When you successfully install URGE on your system, you'll see a new URGE tab appear on the top menu crossbar.

Using the Classic Menus

You can access the classic menu bar containing File, View, Play, Tools, and Help at any time by right-clicking the blank space to the left of Now Playing. If you want to lock the classic menu onto the interface, select View ➤ Classic Menus. (You can always reverse this procedure by toggling the Classic Menus option.)

The classic menu offers options that align this new version of Media Player with its predecessors. This is convenient for those of us who fear change. However, some functionality of the new player is not available any other way than through this menu system, namely, the Skin Chooser and skins download interface.

TIP Toggle the classic menus on and off using the shortcut Ctrl+M.

Using the Mini Player

At any time whilst running Media Player, you can minimize it so it docks onto the taskbar, offering the same playback controls as before but in a much more compact and unobtrusive way for the rest of your desktop, as shown in Figure 21-20. This is known as the Mini Player.

Figure 21-20 *Use the Mini Player when you need access to other applications on the desktop.*

In the bottom-right corner of the Mini Player, you will see the Maximize icon used to return Media Player to its original size.

If you hover the mouse pointer over the Mini Player, you will see some additional information about the current track being played, and if you click the small icon above the Maximize button, it switches on the Mini Player's Visualization window.

TIP You can use the Mini Player visualizations to display a small video screen attached to the taskbar when you are playing TV or video. In this way, you can watch video content without the player taking up a significant amount of desktop space.

Customizing Windows Media Player

We'll finish this chapter with a quick look at the settings available for best optimizing the way Media Player operates in your environment.

Open the Options dialog box, and click the Player tab. At the top of the page, you can select how often Media Player checks the online update service for software updates. Available options are Once a Day, Once a Week, and Once a Month. Media Player updates will certainly appear occasionally. You'll probably find that the setting Once a Month is more than acceptable—if there is some specific update you hear about online that you need immediately, you can always download it manually from the Help menu by right-clicking the blank space beside Now Playing, selecting Help, and then selecting Check for Updates.

If you leave the Download Codecs Automatically checkbox selected, Media Player will try to find a codec for content it doesn't know about before telling you there was an error. If you don't want Media Player going to the Internet if you try to play content of an unknown format, uncheck this box. From a security perspective, you might prefer to maintain full control over what is and is not installed on your system.

Another convenient feature in the Options dialog box is the ability to make Media Player go into Mini Player mode when it starts playing content with a particular piece of metadata associated with it. In this way, you could use a playlist name (called Tunes to Work To, for example), and your desktop is automatically cleared for word processing or email.

You can revisit privacy settings (configured the first time you ran Media Player) through the Privacy tab. You'll recognize many of the settings you selected previously, but you'll also find that convenient shortcut to Internet Explorer for changing cookie privacy settings and the ability to clear the Media Player history file and clear cached content from your system.

On the Network tab, you can limit the protocols and ports used by Media Player when communicating over the network. You can also change the proxy settings for HTTP, mms, and RTSP used in case you are behind a proxy server.

Finally, on the Performance tab, you can use the controls to adjust how Media Player communicates over your network connection (although the default setting where it detects the connection speed for you is by far the best). You can also adjust the amount of content buffered by Media Player before starting playback, although, again, you'd need a pretty good motive to change this setting from the default.

CHAPTER 22

Working with Windows Movie Maker

This latest version of Windows Movie Maker (version 6.0) has a multitude of interface and capability enhancements, such as an improved Preview pane and enhanced transitions and effects, but more important, the inherent support for the high-definition video (HDV) format coupled with the integration of DVD-burning facilities (Windows DVD Maker) has elevated the package from a low-ranking amateur to a fully fledged movie production and publishing facility.

Three versions of the Windows Vista family come with Windows Movie Maker 6.0 by default; these are the versions primarily focusing on the home entertainment market. If you are using any of the following Windows Vista editions, you will have immediate access through the Start menu to Windows Movie Maker 6.0:

- Windows Vista Home Basic Edition
- Windows Vista Home Premium Edition
- Windows Vista Ultimate Edition

NOTE If you are using one of the other editions of Windows Vista, you will still be able to install Windows Movie Maker; however, you'll have to download it (free of charge) from http://www.micosoft.com/moviemaker.

This chapter looks at Windows Movie Maker 6.0's features and takes you through the following stages of preparation and movie production:

- Assessing hardware requirements
- Shooting your movie
- Capturing video content
- Editing your movie
- Adding effects and transitions

- Mastering the final cut
- Burning a DVD

Examining the Interface

To make sure you get off to the best possible start with Windows Movie Maker, this brief introduction to the interface will explain the principles and facets of the software before we move on to the details of video capturing, editing, and production.

To begin with, you will need to start the Windows Movie Maker application. To start Windows Movie Maker, perform the following steps:

1. Click the Start menu.

2. Click All Programs.

3. Click Windows Movie Maker.

Figure 22-1 shows how the interface appears when you first start Windows Movie Maker.

Figure 22-1 *The interface is easy to use with the simple, task-based layout.*

Understanding Windows Movie Maker Projects

In Windows Movie Maker terms, a *project* is the name for an entire production. A project includes all the information pertaining to the way you have arranged your movie footage, including the order in which your clips appear, the timings of effects and transitions (more about that later), and any overlaid audio or commentary that might be part of the final production.

When a project is saved in on your hard disk, it will have the file extension .mswmm, unlike the final production movie, which will be an .avi or a .wmv file.

To create a new movie project, select File ➤ New Project. If you then click File ➤ Project Properties, you can type in the name of the movie, your own name (as director), a copyright message, a movie rating, and some comments about the content (if you desire).

During production, it's a good idea to periodically save your entire project. You should also make a copy of the .mswmm file when you complete a project, since the final .avi or .wmv file will not be editable. In this way, you can return to a production and modify it without having to start from scratch.

Introducing the Tasks Pane

On the left side of the screen, you will see the Tasks pane, situated neatly beneath the application's main menu. The Tasks pane is a quick-launch menu offering a range of single-click facilities under three major headings: Import, Edit, and Publish To. Using the Tasks pane, you can easily import digital media into Windows Movie Maker and edit existing footage, adding effects, transitions, titles, and credits to the production; when you are ready, you are just a few clicks away from publishing the footage in a variety of formats.

Introducing the Collections Pane

The Collections pane is situated in the center of the screen and contains thumbnail representations of content clips, video effects, and transitions, depending on the choice selected from the drop-down list immediately above the pane.

> **TIP** You have many ways to add and remove clips from the Collections pane. The easiest way is to go through the Import Media Wizard, accessible through the Tasks pane. However, if you want, you can also drag and drop media content (audio and video) directly into the Windows Movie Maker application from any open folder.

You can have more than one Collections folder, giving you a great way to arrange your movie clips and photographs for a production.

To add a new Collections folder, select View ➤ Collections. You will see the Tasks pane replaced by the Collections pane, containing three items: Effects, Transitions, and Imported Media. If you right-click Imported Media and then select New Collection Folder, a new folder called New Folder will appear beneath Imported Media. The name (New Folder) will be highlighted at this stage. Click the highlighted text, and rename the folder to something more meaningful; for example, if the folder will contain still photographs of a holiday trip, you might call the folder Disneyland06 Stills.

Introducing the Preview Pane

Using the Preview pane, you can review any aspect of your movie production before you commit to a full production. You can preview each clip by simply selecting it from the Collections pane and then pressing the Play button situated beneath the preview player. If you apply video effects or scene transitions to your movie, you can test their effectiveness using the Preview pane.

You can drag the Preview pane's horizontal and vertical alignment bars to increase and reduce its size. It is also possible to resize the Preview pane by right-clicking in the middle of the screen area and selecting Small, Large, or Full Screen from the context menu.

> **NOTE** You use effects to change the way a particular clip, title, or credit appears in your movie. When you apply an effect to a clip, the entire clip is affected. If you want only a section of a clip to be affected, you will have to split the clip into three pieces: the part before the effect, the part where the effect will be applied, and the remaining part of the clip. Windows Movie Maker has a total of 49 effects that you can apply to your movie footage. You can also layer effects so more than one applies at a time to a clip. Transitions are similar to effects but instead of applying to the clip itself, a transition will bridge the gap between clips. When you join clips together with transitions, you have 63 different transitions you can apply.

Introducing the Storyboard and Timeline Panes

When you begin to assemble your clips into a single production, you will use a combination of the Storyboard and Timeline panes to piece together clips, effects, and transitions and to ensure that soundtracks, credits, and titles all appear in the production at the right point in time.

> **TIP** You can toggle the interface between the Storyboard pane and the Timeline pane by pressing Ctrl+T.

Introducing AutoMovie

The last feature we should discuss before going into detail about Windows Movie Maker is AutoMovie, as shown in Figure 22-2. AutoMovie provides a great means for getting an idea of what Windows Movie Maker is capable of; however, the rigorous application of effects and transitions based on just five preset styles means you have little flexibility in what the final product looks like. You will find that once you become more familiar with the Windows Movie Maker interface, you will never use AutoMovie.

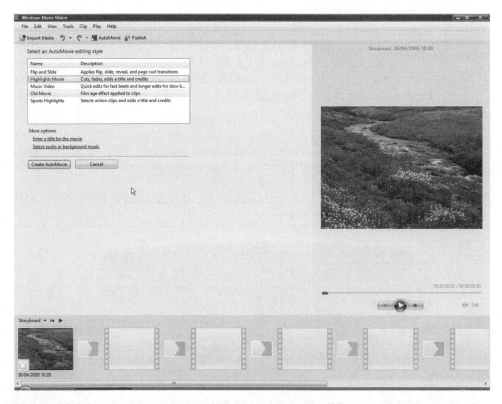

Figure 22-2 *You can use AutoMovie to create any one of five preset movie styles from your clips.*

Capturing and Importing Content

You can import four kinds of content into Windows Movie Maker for use in your production: content streamed from your camcorder, videos stored on your PC, digital still images stored on your PC, and audio tracks (music or dialog) for overlay onto the final production.

Capturing Content from a Camcorder

To transfer content to Windows Movie Maker from a camcorder, you first need to connect your camcorder to your PC's interface port (USB 2.0 or FireWire) and wait for the device to be recognized by Windows Vista.

> **NOTE** The first time you connect your camcorder to Windows Vista, you will see a pop-up message that informs you the hardware driver is being installed for your device. This may take a few seconds to complete, so be patient. After the device is installed, a new message stating "Your devices are ready to use" will appear, and a new Import Video: Microsoft DV Camera and VCR window will appear. For now, close that dialog box since we will show how to import the video through the Windows Movie Player interface.

Once the hardware is recognized and made available to the operating system, navigate to the Tasks pane, and select the menu option in the Import section called From Digital Video Camera.

If there is a problem with connecting your device to Windows Movie Maker, you will see the error message shown in Figure 22-3.

Figure 22-3 *Follow the hyperlink to the Help menu to find out more information about connecting your camcorder to Windows Movie Maker.*

Follow these steps to extract digital media content from your camcorder:

1. From the Tasks pane on the left side of the screen, click From Digital Video Camera under the Import heading.

2. This launches the Import Video: Microsoft DV Camera and VCR window. Make sure to type a meaningful name for the video content you are importing, and select the folder where you want the content to be stored. You can change the folder to any on your system by clicking Browse. Also, you must select how the content will be encoded on your PC. Finally, you should select the format the content will be stored in. When you have finished, click the Next button.

> **NOTE** Windows Media Video (WMV) or Audio Video Interleaved (AVI) files—
> which to choose? WMV is a lot more compressed than AVI, and you'll find that one
> hour's worth of WMV content will take about 1GB of disk space, whereas one hour's
> worth of AVI content will consume a whopping 13GB. If you desire, you can have
> each clip recorded on your camcorder imported as a separate file; this makes for
> much easier editing when you are working with clips on Windows Movie Maker.

3. On the following screen, you have the option to select whether the entire contents of the video will be imported to your PC, or if you prefer, you can ask Windows Vista to import only a selection of the content appropriate to your needs. Select the appropriate radio button, and then click Next. If you selected the entire videotape, proceed to step 6; otherwise, proceed to step 4.

> **TIP** If you select the option to import only a selection of the content from the
> camcorder, you will be able to cue the video to the right point using the PC
> controls and then download only that piece of footage. This gives you the best
> control over the content you are importing. Often there are pieces of content you
> really don't need recorded on the raw footage, and it's best to avoid copying
> these to your hard disk in the first place since they take up valuable space and
> waste a lot of processing time.

4. Shortly after clicking Next, you will hear your camcorder start, and you'll see the first frame on the videotape in the Preview pane. A few seconds after that, a new window appears, where you are able to cue the tape to the point you would like to start importing content. Use the digital video camera controls shown in Figure 22-4 to move the tape to the position you would like to start importing. If you have a widescreen camcorder, you can select the Preview Widescreen checkbox beneath the Preview pane to have your content represented in the appropriate aspect ratio. If you know how long after the start position you want to stop importing (in minutes), select the Stop Importing After (Min) checkbox, adding the duration of the import in the numeric entry box. When you have cued up the first frame and are satisfied you know when to stop importing content, click Start Video Import.

5. When you have collected all the footage you want from your camcorder, click the Finish button. After a few seconds, control will return to Windows Movie Maker, and your clip will appear in the Collections pane.

> **TIP** If you don't see your newly imported clip appear in the Collections pane when
> control returns to Windows Movie Maker, this may be because you are displaying
> the wrong selection. Make sure you have selected Imported Media in the drop-
> down list above the Collections pane. Your new clip will appear at the bottom of
> the list.

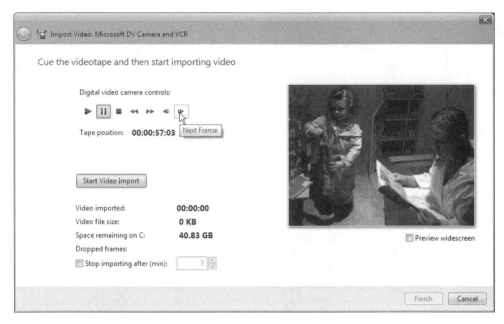

Figure 22-4 *Use the camera control buttons to cue the tape to the right position.*

Importing Videos

You can import video content into Windows Movie Maker that is already stored on your computer by navigating to the Tasks pane and clicking Video in the Import section. The following walk-through will help you get video clips presented in the Collections pane for use in your productions:

1. Click the Videos link beneath the Import heading in the Tasks pane.

2. The Import Media Items window will appear. The default location for searching for a video file is C:\Users\<username>\Videos, shown automatically on the screen. You can, however, search any other file location on your system by clicking the links on the left side of the window to look in Computer, look in the Desktop folder, or perform a context-sensitive search. When you see the file you want to import into Windows Movie Maker, highlight it, and then click the Import button.

> **TIP** You can experiment with the sample video files that come with Windows Movie Maker to hone your talents with cutting and editing before starting to mess with your own video files. The sample video files are in the Sample Videos folder, accessible from the Import Media Items window.

3. Your newly imported video file will appear in the Collections pane as the last item in the list. You might have to scroll down to see it if the list is long.

Importing Pictures

A movie production can include both video footage and digital still images. Digital stills are great for the backdrop to opening titles and the backdrop for rolling credits, or you could create a picture gallery, edited with music and credits to display a complete photograph album.

To import digital photographs into Windows Movie Maker, you'll need to complete the following steps:

1. Click the Pictures link beneath the Import heading in the Tasks pane.

2. The Import Media Items window will appear focused on the Sample Pictures folder that comes with Windows Vista. You can experiment with these images before using your own pictures in a movie production. Select a picture from the folder (or search for other images on the PC by navigating the folders on the left side or using the Windows Vista search option), and then click the Import button.

3. You can access the newly imported image from the Collections pane in the same way as you would a movie clip.

You can use still images for a variety of purposes in a movie production. Many modern directors have used the artistic merit of freeze-frame images combined with atmospheric music overlays and digital effects to really enhance their message; you can create a literary metaphor using these modern techniques.

Importing Audio Content

Audio content comes in the form of music, sound effects, or even simple dialogue. If a movie is shot outdoors, for example, or in a crowded, noisy place, such as a train station, dialogue can become drowned out in the background din.

Windows Movie Maker allows you to import audio clips and soundtracks from any PC source and easily overlay them onto your video footage. Windows Movie Maker renders the video and audio tracks together as a whole, adding emotion and atmosphere where necessary.

To import sound clips and audio files into Windows Movie Maker, you should perform the following actions:

1. Click the Audio or Music link in the Import section in the Tasks pane.

2. The Import Media Items window will appear focused on the Music folder in the user's profile. You can experiment with the sample audio files in the Sample Music folder by double-clicking Sample Music, then selecting any of the displayed files, and finally clicking the Import button. Remember, you can search for other audio files on the PC by navigating the folders on the left side or using the Windows Vista search option.

3. Audio tracks will appear in the Collections pane alongside the video clips and still images.

> **TIP** When you are using the Import Media Items Wizard, you can drag a select box around as many media items as you like; then when you click the Import button, your entire selection will be transported into the Windows Movie Maker Collections pane.

Producing Your First Movie

The following sections take you through the complete process of creating your first movie, including the following tasks:

- Getting to know the Storyboard and Timeline panes
- Adding clips to the Storyboard pane
- Splicing video footage
- Adding transitions
- Adding effects
- Adding a soundtrack
- Adding opening titles and closing credits
- Creating the final cut

Getting to Know the Storyboard and Timeline Panes

The Storyboard/Timeline pane at the bottom of the screen (see Figure 22-5 for an example of the Storyboard pane) is used for a multitude of purposes and will become the primary interface to the movie creation process.

When you select the Storyboard pane, you will be assembling your clips in the order you need them to appear in the final movie production. You can also use the Storyboard pane to place effects and transitions on and between your clips to enhance and bond them. The Storyboard pane is a great way of quickly assembling clips, effects, and transitions in a relatively rough manner, without the aggravation of critical timings and overlays playing any part in the production at this stage.

> **TIP** You should use the Storyboard pane to test how clips appear in sequence before applying any further editing or cutting. As soon as you are happy your scenes are appearing in the right order, you can move into the more focused Timeline pane to really start the editing process.

Figure 22-5 *Use the Storyboard pane to quickly assemble your movie clips in the correct sequence.*

Switching Windows Movie Maker into the Timeline pane (Ctrl+T) allows you, as the director, to do all sorts of clever stuff. You can remove sections of footage that you no longer require (such as trimming off the overlap between scenes), adding a soundtrack, and overlaying other audio tracks such as sound effects; if you desire, you can also add opening titles and closing credits. Figure 22-6 shows an example of the Timeline pane. Notice that all of the menu nodes, where possible, have been expanded to reveal the sublayers that make up the entire composite movie.

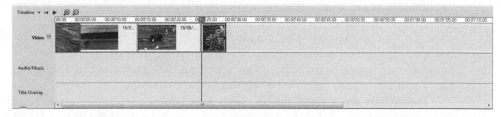

Figure 22-6 *Most of your detailed editing will take place using the Timeline pane.*

> **TIP** At any time you can press Ctrl+W to preview the content of the Storyboard/Timeline pane as it currently stands. All effects, transitions, and overlays will appear as they would in the final cut in the Preview pane on the right side of the screen.

Thing You Can Do in the Storyboard Pane

When you are using the Storyboard pane, you can click the Storyboard drop-down menu, which allows you to switch to the Timeline pane. Two further options are presented beneath Timeline: Narrate Timeline and Audio Levels. You cannot narrate over the Storyboard pane, so if you select this option, Windows Movie Maker will force you into the Timeline pane. To narrate over the Timeline pane, you should have a good-quality microphone set up and the input levels adjusted for your system. If you select Audio Levels on the Storyboard pane, you can adjust the balance between the audio played directly from the clip and any audio track you have layered over the top. In this way, when the final production takes place, you can have background music playing throughout scenes, even when there is dialogue taking place.

If you right-click any individual clip, you can remove it from the Storyboard (Ctrl+X), copy it for pasting into another part of the movie (Ctrl+C), or remove it (Delete).

> **CAUTION** Cutting a clip is not the same as removing it. If you cut a clip from a time slot, you can paste that clip somewhere else since it is stored in the Clipboard. If you remove it from the Storyboard, it's gone for good.

Things You Can Do in the Timeline Pane

If you change to the Timeline pane (Ctrl+T), you get a much more detailed breakdown of how your movie is constructed. The Timeline pane is where you will perform most of your fine, detailed editorial functions, such as adjusting your effects and transitions and properly aligning your audio tracks. When you preview your production using the Timeline pane (Ctrl+W), a position marker moves along the Timeline showing how the clips, transitions, video audio, overlay soundtrack, and titles will appear in the final production.

When you first start using the Timeline pane, you should expand the Video element to reveal the transition and audio elements that reside beneath it. Working with these subelements is key to ensuring your final production will be just right. If you want to add a new transition to the movie in the Timeline pane, you can drag the transition from the Collections pane to the Video element and drop it beneath the two clips in question on the Transition element. When the transition is dragged to the correct spot (beneath and between two video clips), a vertical blue inset line will appear letting you know you can release your mouse button.

Transitions are a fixed length when first added to a production; however, by selecting any transition on the Timeline pane, you can drag the trailing edge to change its duration. Dragging a transition to the left will increase the time it takes for that transition to complete in the following frame.

Adding Clips to the Storyboard

This is the easy part. To add a clip to the Storyboard, it's simply a matter of dragging the clip from the Collections pane onto one of the available Storyboard time slots.

It's possible to add clips in a collection to your Storyboard at the same time by dragging a selection box around all clips you require, then right-clicking, and selecting Add to Storyboard from the context menu. To select all clips in the Collections pane, you can select Edit ➤ Select All, or you can press Ctrl+A when you have selected one clip, and the rest will automatically become selected.

> **TIP** You can use multiple copies of the same clip by right-clicking a clip in the Storyboard pane, selecting Copy, placing your mouse pointer in an available time slot in the Storyboard pane, right-clicking again, and selecting Paste.

Splitting Video Clips

If a clip is too long or you want to split it into distinct scenes, you can split the clip easily in the Preview pane. To split a clip, perform the following steps:

1. Highlight the clip you want to split in the Collections pane. You should see the first frame of the clip appear in the Preview pane on the right side of the screen.

2. Press the Play button beneath the Preview pane, and watch the clip. When you are happy you know when you would like to split the clip, watch it again, but this time, click the Pause button just before the point you want to make the cut.

3. Now you should use the Next Frame and Previous Frame buttons (on either side of the Play button) to locate the exact point in the footage you want to make the cut. When you are happy, click the Split button to the right of the Play button.

Your original clip will now be split into two separate clips, both available in the Collections pane for adding to your Storyboard pane.

> **NOTE** If you suddenly decide you don't want the clips split in this way, you have two options. You can place both clips next to each other in the Storyboard pane and have no transitions or effects binding them. In this way, the first clip will seamlessly flow into the second one, and when you cut the final movie to DVD or publish it to the Internet, no one will be any the wiser. However, if you are quick enough, you can also press the Undo button (Ctrl+Z) to splice the two clips back together.

Adding Transitions

Transitions are effects that are used to join movie clips together. Rather than clips simply bumping together with the scenes appearing to jump around, a carefully placed transition, such as a fade, will soften the scene change for the viewer.

If you select Transitions from the drop-down list above the Collections pane, you will see the entire set of available transitions displayed as thumbnail images in the Collections pane, as shown in Figure 22-7.

To preview the effect a transition will have on your footage, you can double-click any one of them to see an example in the Preview pane of how it would look. Two sample still images of flowers are used to show exactly the effect of the transition.

To add a transition to the Storyboard, you can drag it (in the same way you drag a clip) to the smaller time slots between the clip time slots.

> **TIP** When you apply a transition to your movie, you will always see the ending of the previous clip untainted. The transition will be applied to the leading few frames of the flowing clip.

Figure 22-7 *Transitions can bind clips together, offering an artistic cut between clips.*

If you right-click a transition in the Storyboard, you have the options of playing the entire movie, cutting the transition from the movie (with the intention of being able to paste it somewhere else), and copying the transition to another time slot; or, indeed, if it is not required, you can entirely delete the transition.

> **TIP** Don't overuse transitions. It may seem like great fun to fade in every scene or shatter from one clip to another, but the art comes from using them sparingly, at the right time. Otherwise, they become trite. Imagine if the only time in an entire movie you use the shatter transition is when a football hits the camera. This is a much better effect than using it to cut in the credits.

Adding Effects

In Windows Movie Maker terms, *effects* are digital modifications to the footage that apply to the entire duration of a clip. Movie Maker has 49 effects you can apply to your footage, many of which you will never use. However, they are great fun to experiment with. Still, you should use them sparingly so not to overpower the footage itself. As with transition, effects should be subtle and helpful to the movie production. If an effect seems to detract in any way from the message of the underlying footage, remove it.

In the Storyboard pane, you simply drag the effect from the Collections pane to the clip to which you want to apply it. You can preview the effect of the effect as soon as it is applied in the Preview pane (Ctrl+W).

When you have applied a new effect to a clip, the Effect icon (as shown in Figure 22-8) will be highlighted.

Figure 22-8 *The Effect icon appears darker when an effect is applied to a clip.*

You can apply multiple effects to a single movie frame, and you can preview the cumulative effect in the Preview pane. When you have applied multiple effects to a clip, the Effect icon changes yet again to layer multiple stars on top of each other.

Once you have applied a number of effects to a clip, you might decide you want to change the order they are applied in, or you might want to remove one that dominates the set. If you right-click the Effect icon in the clip you are editing, you will see the Add or Remove Effects dialog box, as shown in Figure 22-9.

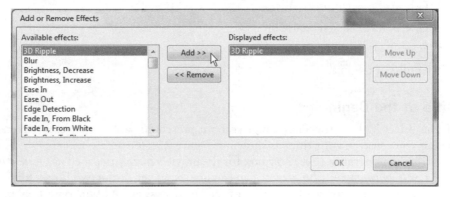

Figure 22-9 *Rearrange the order effects are applied to your clip or remove unwanted clips.*

You can add new effects from the list on the left side by selecting the one you want applied and clicking Add. To remove an effect, highlight it from the list on the right side, and click Remove. To change the order the effects are applied, select any one of them from the list on the right, and click Move Up or Move Down.

NOTE Since effects are applied to a clip and do not affect the timings of your production, you will not see effects appear in the Timeline pane. To work with effects, you will need to be in the Storyboard pane.

Adding a Soundtrack

When you have added audio tracks, sound effects, or commentary to your project and imported them into the Collections pane, you can switch to the Timeline pane and drag thee audio files into your production. You should drag all audio content into the Audio/Music component of the Timeline pane.

When an audio track is added to the Timeline, the entire duration of the track appears on the chart. If you click the track, you can then trim it to suit the clip to which you want it applied. To trim the audio track, hover your mouse pointer over either the leading or the trailing edge of the audio track; then, when you see the double-headed arrow, drag the slider to the point on the Timeline you would like the track to finish.

Adding Opening Titles and Closing Credits

Opening titles and credits can certainly add a professional-looking touch to your final production. You can lead into the main footage with some music, fade in from a still image and over the top, and complete the movie with some outtakes, overlaid with some choice music and rolling credits.

To add titles and credits to your movie, on the Tasks pane, select Titles and Credits. The screen changes to ask, "Where do you want to add a title?" You have four options:

- Title at the Beginning
- Title Before the Selected Clip
- Title Overlay on the Selected Clip
- Credits at the End

Title at the Beginning

If you select Title at the Beginning, you are presented with a text-entry dialog box where you can type your title, as shown in Figure 22-10.

Use the uppermost text entry box for the movie's main title, such as *Gone with the Wind* or *Nightmare on Elm Street*. You can use the lower of the two boxes (divided by the thin blue line) for a subheading or slogan if desired. As you type text in these boxes, you will see how it will appear in the Preview pane automatically. Notice that the lower of the two textboxes will generate title text in a smaller font size than in the upper box.

You can change the animation used for introducing the title and also modify the font and text color used in the display. You can use the two options presented beneath the textbox to change the title's display characteristics.

When you are happy with the title, click Add Title, and you will be returned to the main production screen.

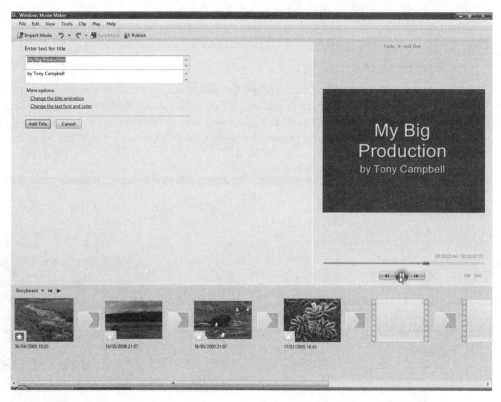

Figure 22-10 *The top textbox is the main title, and the lower textbox can be a slogan or subheading.*

> **TIP** You can change the timings of your titles by changing to the Timeline pane and dragging the end trim handle back or forward toward the required part of the movie.

Title Before the Selected Clip

If you would like to introduce clips using title screens, you can do this using both the Storyboard and Timeline panes. Select the clip you want introduced by the title, and then click Titles and Credits on the Tasks pane. Next, click Title Before the Selected Clip.

You can now create your title in much the same way as you did in the previous step; however, when you click Add Title, the title is now inserted into the movie in the position you selected.

Title Overlay on the Selected Clip

This option is much the same as the other title options; however, the difference is that the title is overlaid on the clip's footage rather than appearing in a new clip of its own. This way, you can start layering titles over clips, with background music and sound effects all coming together in the way a Hollywood production would appear on the big screen.

Credits at the End

And finally, we can talk about credits. Credits usually appear at the end of a movie and contain, as you might expect, actor names, dedications for music and composition, your own name as director, and anyone else who deserves a mention. When you click Credits at the End, you are presented with a table, as shown in Figure 22-11.

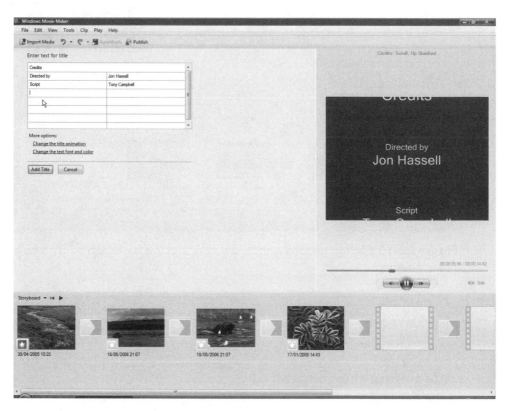

Figure 22-11 *Fill in the name and role of each person involved in your movie production.*

You should now fill in the name and the role of each person you would like to credit for their involvement in your production. The layout of the default credits is straightforward: you use the topmost cell in the table for the title (repeat the movie title or perhaps put in a dedication, such as "Thanks to the following...") and then use the left column to state the person's role (such as sound engineer) and the right column to state their name.

When you are finished entering text in the Credits table, click Add Title.

Creating the Final Cut

When you have completed your editorial function, placing your clips in order and adding transitions and effects, soundtracks and commentary, and titles and credits, take a final pass through the entire movie in the Preview pane before proceeding to the next stage of production. If you right-click in the Preview pane before you start your preview and then select Full Screen, you will get the best possible impression of how the movie will appear when it has been cut to hard disk or DVD.

Setting Advanced Movie Maker Options

If you select Tools ➤ Options, you will see a dialog box offering some extra configuration controls. If you select the General tab from the top of the dialog box (this is the default tab to be displayed the first time you open the Options dialog box), you'll see various options for changing the way Movie Maker functions.

The temporary storage location (the topmost item on the General tab) is where new movies are generated from their component parts before being finally published using the Publish Movie Wizard. If you prefer to have Movie Maker work in a different folder than the one shown, you should type the new folder location into the text-entry box and click OK.

If you check the Open Last Project on Start-Up checkbox, Movie Maker will open your most recently edited movie when it starts, offering it in the same state it was in when you last used it.

You can also modify the AutoRecover interval (the default is ten minutes) in case your system crashes. AutoRecover will record information about your movie production on a schedule determined by this interval so that, in the event of a system crash, you lose only the last ten minute's worth of production and editing. If ten minutes is unacceptable, you can change the value to as low as one minute; however, you should realize that AutoRecover operations take time themselves, and you'll need to seek the best balance between safety and usability.

If you do not want your published movie to contain information pertaining to the properties you might have defined for the movie, you should select the Do Not Include the Title, Author Copyright, Rating, and Comments Information in the Published Movie checkbox.

By clicking the Reset Warning Dialogs button, you will reinstate any warning pages you previously discarded. In Windows Vista, warning pages are displayed by the operating system until you decide not to display them.

If you click the Advanced tab, the topmost settings are related to the duration still pictures are played before moving to the next clip. The default is five seconds, although you can change this to be as long as you require. You can also modify the transition time (the time it takes to play the transition effect from one clip to the next). The default transition time is 1.25 seconds.

Video properties are next in the list. You can adjust the format between NTSC and PAL (NTSC is used in the United States for analog television broadcasting, while PAL is used in most of the rest of the world except Russia and some parts of Africa), and you can adjust the aspect ratio of your output to suit standard 4:3 monitors or televisions or, if you prefer, the widescreen ratio of 16:9.

At the bottom of the Advanced page, you can set a maximum size for movies that are published to be emailed. The default is 10MB.

Finally, if you click the Compatibility tab, you can manage video filters installed on your system, disabling any that might be troublesome in the Movie Maker environment. Unfortunately, it's hit and miss when troubleshooting filters, and it's simply a matter of experimenting with the ones you have to see what works best.

> **NOTE** Video filters are code modules installed by third-party video software and are used to help play video and audio content that has been encoded in a proprietary format. Sometimes video filters can conflict with the playback of your movie and should be deactivated within the context of Movie Maker.

Mastering Your Production

You have various ways to publish your movie to your eagerly awaiting fans. You can use the Publish Movie Wizard, use the File menu, or select any of the following five options from the Publish section in the Tasks pane:

- This computer
- DVD
- Recordable CD
- E-mail
- Digital Video Camera

All these options, except for DVD, will launch the Publish Movie Wizard. Publishing a movie to your computer will create an `.avi` or a `.wmv` movie file on your computer's hard disk that can be played using a suitable software video player, such as Windows Media Player 11. You'll find that the best-quality movie output will be in `.avi` format; however, you can also encode your movie in a number of other supported formats, including three HD formats (one of which is suitable for playback on an Xbox 360).

> **TIP** If you select the Digital Video Camera option from the Publish Movie Wizard, you can record your movie to your camcorder. This allows you to watch the final cut on your camera or even play it back through the normal camcorder AV-out port, directly to your television. Doing this will record the movie onto your camcorder's storage media (MiniDV or DVD) and is great for archiving and backing up your footage.

To publish a movie to your computer, you should follow this procedure:

1. In the Tasks pane, click This Computer in the Publish To section. This launches the Publish Movie Wizard.

2. Type a name for the movie file, and then, using the drop-down list or the Browse button, select a folder in which to store the movie file.

3. On the Choose the Settings for Your Movie page, the default selection is to create the movie using the best-quality format (creating an .avi file). Alternatively, you can instruct Windows Movie Maker to create the movie based on the size of file you want, such as a maximum of 10MB, or you can select the format from the drop-down list next to the More Settings option. When you have selected the most appropriate format, click Publish.

> **TIP** The higher the quality of the output, the better the movie will look on the screen; however, you should be aware that .avi files are huge—four times the size of even HD 1080–formatted files. You should experiment with the equipment you have on hand to find the lowest resolution you can get away with in your environment. Sometimes it's worth creating a master .avi file and then cutting a new version of the movie in a different format for distribution.

4. Now you will see a progress bar showing how long it will take to create your movie; in addition, it shows the movie filename and the folder in which it will be saved. When the movie has been successfully published to your hard disk, the wizard gives you the option to watch your new movie when you click Finish. If you don't want to watch the movie in Windows Media Player 11, uncheck the box, and click Finish. If you want to watch the final production, shortly after clicking Finish, Windows Media Player 11 will start to play your new movie.

If you select DVD from the Publish To menu, Windows Movie Maker launches Windows DVD Maker. You will need to ensure you have placed a blank, writable DVD in your optical drive before selecting this option, or you will receive an error stating there is no DVD in the drive.

When you see the Windows DVD Maker, your movie will appear in the list as a single item, as shown in Figure 22-12.

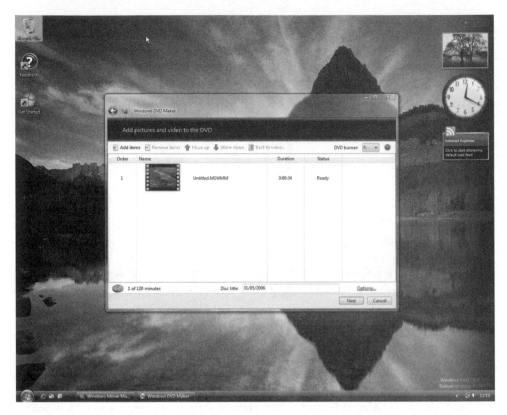

Figure 22-12 *Windows Movie Maker sends your entire movie to Windows DVD Maker.*

You need to perform the following steps to burn your DVD:

1. When you see your movie file listed in the Windows DVD Maker, click Next.

2. If you want to preview your movie in the Windows DVD Maker, click the Preview button; however, this option is fairly unnecessary when using Windows DVD Maker alongside Windows Movie Maker.

3. On the right side of the screen, select the kind of DVD menu you would like at the beginning of your DVD from the Menu Styles list. If you select a new style, the Preview pane on the left will change to reflect your menu option. For more information about working with Windows DVD Maker, see Chapter 24. When you are ready, click the Start Burn button.

4. You will now see a dialog box showing the progress of the DVD's creation. This can take a while to complete, so be patient. When you are finished, close Windows DVD Maker to return to Windows Movie Maker.

Creating a video CD is much the same as creating a movie on your computer (as long as you have a writable CD in your optical drive). The Publish Movie Wizard expects a filename, a name for the CD, and your choice of quality for the final product. As with publishing to your computer, you can select the required format from the list of available choices.

If you opt to create a movie for sending via email, the movie will be compressed so that it is easily transmittable over the Internet. This will obviously reduce the quality but make the final product much more distributable over a network.

Finally, if you opt to publish your movie onto your camcorder, you can select Digital Video Camera from the menu (making sure your camcorder is connected to your PC) and follow the wizard to create an .avi file that is recorded onto your camcorder's media (MiniDV or DVD).

CHAPTER 23

Working with Windows Photo Gallery

Windows Photo Gallery is a great addition to the Vista family; it integrates well with other digital media products, such as Windows Movie Maker and Windows DVD Maker, and it offers a great range of capabilities for manipulating digital photographs and home movies.

The product forms an integral part of the Vista operating system and is installed by default with all editions. Whether you are an amateur enthusiast or a professional photographer, Windows Photo Gallery offers a rich range of services that you will find invaluable to your photography. However, professionals will probably be inclined to exploit the viewing and publishing features of Windows Photo Gallery and leave picture manipulation to a third-party product, such as Adobe Photoshop.

Using Windows Photo Gallery, you can perform the following functions:

- Import images from an external device, such as a camera or USB-connected hard drive

- Tag photographs or movie clips to order them into themed sets

- Add further metadata to images, such as the date and time they were taken

- Run a slide show of sets of images (this can be based on tags)

- Edit images with basic digital tools, such as removing red eye and adjusting contrast

- Print images using the Photo Print Wizard

- Move images and movies seamlessly between other Vista applications

TIP When you import photographs from a digital camera or other such removable device, you should always apply a tag to the pictures. You have the option of doing this when the import process begins. This ensures all imported photographs have appropriate metadata applied to each image, grouping them in a way that permits easy identification later.

Getting Started

To start Windows Photo Gallery, click the Start menu, select All Programs, and then choose Windows Photo Gallery from the menu. This starts the application and automatically imports photographs and movies from both the public and personal Pictures and Videos folders on your PC.

Figure 23-1 shows the Windows Photo Gallery interface. First we'll start with a little orientation.

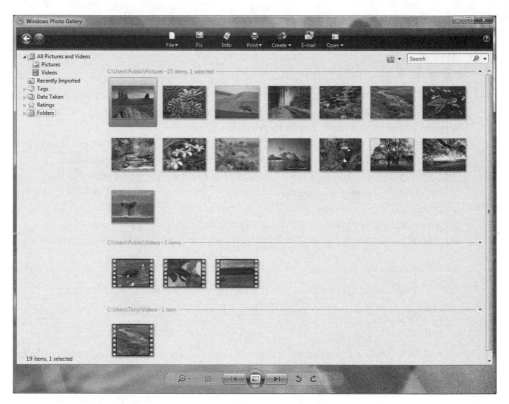

Figure 23-1 *Photos and movies are arranged in a way to make them easy to work with.*

Starting at the top of the screen, you will see the top menu bar, featuring the File, Fix, Info, Print, Create, E-mail, and Open buttons. We'll explore this menu in detail in the next section, but for now it's sufficient to say it contains all the features for importing, touching up, and exporting your digital content. On the far right side of the menu bar, you will see the Help icon (a blue circle with a question mark inside).

On the left pane, you'll see a list starting with All Pictures and Video and ending with Folders. You can use this list for organizing your content. From here, you can add metadata to images or movies, give your content star ratings, and arrange pictures and movies into appropriate folders.

> **NOTE** Star ratings are a great way of collecting your favorite photographs together for ease of viewing. If, for example, you had 200 holiday photographs but your favorite 30 were the ones you consistently liked showing to the relatives, you can rate those 30 with a five-star rating and give the others a lower mark. When you want to look through the entire collection, you can browse the holiday folder and cycle through all 200. When your relatives come over, you can easily run a slide show of only the five-star images, cycling through the best 30.

In the top-right corner of the main screen, you'll see a small, four-panel icon to the left of the search box. Clicking this icon opens a drop-down list of menu items that allow you to change how the content is presented within the Windows Movie Maker application. The choices you have available are as follows:

- The Thumbnails option displays the images as small versions of the main image.
- The Thumbnails with Text option displays the images with the date and time the image was acquired.
- The Tiles option shows the image thumbnail, the date and time it was acquired, the star rating, and the size.
- The Group By option allows you to collect images by a whole range of differing attributes.
- The Arrange By option orders the images inside a group.
- The Table of Contents option provides a new menu on the left of the main viewing screen in date order.
- The Refresh option refreshes the viewing screen in case changes are not automatically applied.

> **NOTE** You should experiment with finding the best combination of Group By and Arrange By to suit your own needs. For example, you can select to group your images using their tags and then arrange them using the star ratings. This means you can have all your holiday snaps together (using the grouping) and have all the best photographs at the top of the list (based on their star ratings).

The next item on the screen to discuss is the search interface, located in the top-right corner of the main image-viewing screen. As with all Vista applications, the search function forms a fundamental component of Windows Photo Gallery, allowing you to trawl through the contents of your existing gallery for data that is associated with your images. Searching begins as soon as you enter a character in the search window, and this can be based on any of the character-based metadata connected with your images, such as the tag, the date, the image name, or even the photographer's name.

TIP To see a full list of all the metadata associated with an image, right-click the item, and select Properties. Select the Details tab at the top of the Properties dialog box, and scroll through the list. You can alter some of the properties by clicking to the right of the item and then typing a new value. However, you cannot change some properties since they are fixed at the point the image was captured on the camera; for example, you cannot alter the resolution of an image by simply typing a new value. Professional photographers will find many of the properties at the bottom of the list useful for capturing information about the camera, the lens, the metering used when taking the photograph, the exposure settings, and a whole range of other manual values. This is useful when trying to ascertain the reason why a particular image turned out the way it did.

If you have performed a search and subsequently want to return to a compete view of your gallery, you need to clear the search information from the search field (by deleting it) or click the curved back arrow displayed to the right of the search box (see Figure 23-2).

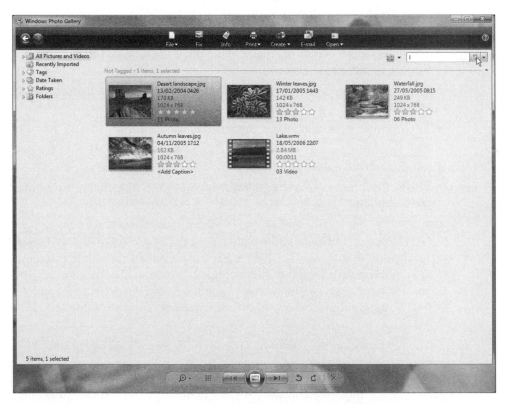

Figure 23-2 *Click the orange back button next to the search box to restore the entire gallery.*

In the middle of the screen, you will see your pictures and movies in the display. If you hover your pointer over an image for a short period of time, you will see a slightly larger version of the image displayed as a preview (see Figure 23-3). Once you are in this preview mode, you can point to any other image in your gallery to see the image in this expanded window.

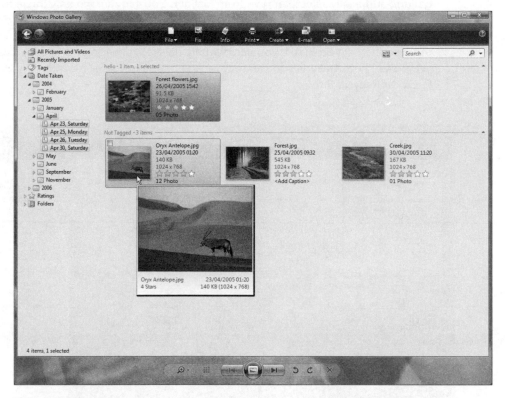

Figure 23-3 *Hover the mouse over an image to get a better look at the picture.*

At any time you can double-click an image to blow it up to a larger preview screen, as shown in Figure 23-4. From here you can right-click the image to perform a variety of functions, such as making the image the Vista desktop, rotating the image clockwise and counterclockwise, copying or deleting it (affecting the file itself and not the gallery object), and modifying the image properties.

CAUTION Deleting images will not only remove them from the gallery, but it will also remove them from the file system. If you want images removed from the gallery, you should manually remove them from the folder using Windows Explorer; alternatively, if you have an image folder you have added to Windows Photo Gallery but no longer want it displayed in the gallery, on the left side of the main screen expand the Folders item, then right-click the folder you want removed from the gallery, and finally select Remove from Gallery. You can remove only those folders you have added yourself. You cannot remove default folders such as Pictures and Videos in this way; however, you can delete them using Windows Explorer (sending them to the Recycle Bin). If you accidentally delete an image or a folder using Windows Photo Gallery, you can recover the image or folder from the Windows Explorer Recycle Bin.

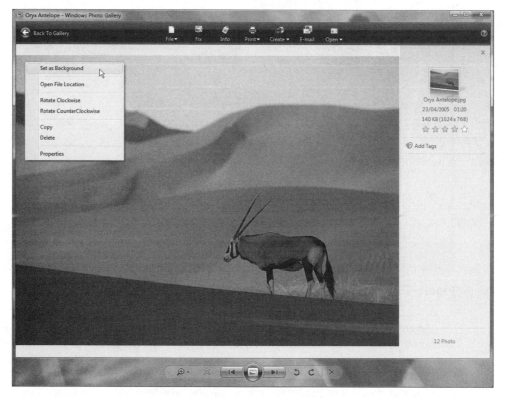

Figure 23-4 *Double-clicking a thumbnail blows up the image and offers new functionality.*

The last component of the interface to look at in basic orientation is the control bar situated beneath the main image-viewing window. You can use this control bar to change the way pictures are viewed in the main viewing window (the size of each thumbnail), to control how the slide show runs, to select an image to manipulate (the current image is the one that is highlighted by the shaded box), and to spin the image on its central axis by 90 degrees at a time, in a clockwise or counterclockwise manner. The final button to mention on this control bar is the Delete button. This will remove the image both from the gallery and from the file system, placing the deleted image in the Recycle Bin.

Capturing and Importing Images

You have two methods of importing images and videos into Windows Photo Gallery:

- Directly from the file system
- From an external device such as a camera or scanner

> **NOTE** The first time you connect a new device to your PC, you will see an information balloon in the bottom-right corner saying that Vista is installing a new device. In most cases, the device will automatically install, and after a few seconds you will see a message saying something like "Canon DIGITAL IXUS 430 Device driver software installed successfully." When the device has installed, you will see an AutoPlay dialog box offering you various options. The one to choose in this case is Import. Make sure you uncheck the Always Do This for This Device checkbox since you might want to select one of the other options next time.

Importing Photo and Video Items from the File System

Importing photographs from the file system is easy. Click File ➤ Add Folder to Gallery, and then browse the file system for the location of your images. When you've located your images, highlight the folder, and then click OK. You will see a dialog box stating that the folder has been added to Windows Photo Gallery, and all photographs within will now be available in the main Windows Photo Gallery interface.

Importing Photo and Video Items from a Digital Camera

Connect the digital camera to your PC, and click the Import button in the AutoPlay dialog box. This starts the Importing Pictures and Videos Wizard. When you see the text-entry box awaiting an image tag, you can click the Options link in the bottom-left corner of the dialog box. You will see the Import Settings dialog box that allows you to modify the default characteristics of how images are imported into Windows Photo Gallery, as shown in Figure 23-5.

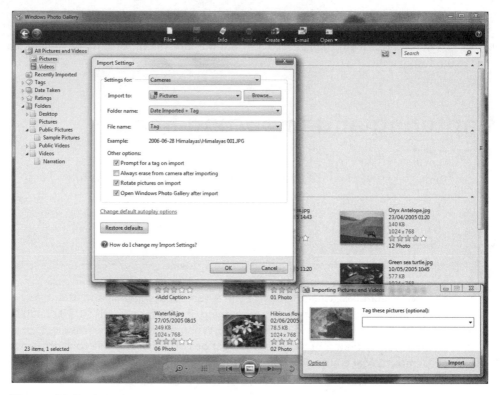

Figure 23-5 *The import settings used by the wizard determine how your images are stored.*

You'll notice that in Import Settings, the drop-down list for the Settings For field has three profiles for which you can configure default characteristics:

- Cameras
- CDs and DVDs
- Scanners

You should select the profile appropriate to the device you are setting the options for and enter the appropriate details. You can adapt profiles to suit your needs based on folder names, tags, and options that determine the following:

- Does the wizard prompt you for a tag each time you connect the external device?
- Will images be erased from the camera after they are transferred to Vista?
- Should images be rotated when they are imported—this might be more appropriate for images transferring from an A4 scanner than from a camera; however, if you are a portrait photographer, you might want all images rotated to be easily viewed on the screen.
- Should Vista automatically open Windows Photo Gallery after the wizard completes the import?

> **TIP** You can create a separate profile for each of the device types in the drop-down list. This allows you to treat images from each source in a different way; for example, you might want to create a separate subfolder beneath the Pictures folder for images imported from a scanner while saving all photographs from a camera, CD, or DVD source to the Pictures top-level folder. You can modify all options available in the Import Settings dialog box for each of the three import profiles.

You can modify the import settings at any time, either by clicking the Options link the next time you connect a device or, from the Windows Photo Gallery main menu, by clicking File, selecting Options, and then clicking the Import tab.

OK, let's return to the import wizard. When you see the text-entry box asking for the name of a tag (if the profile demands one), enter the name, and click Import. This will start the import process. If you have a lot of images, it can take some time for this to complete. At any point during the process you can check the Erase After Importing checkbox. This will ensure all images are deleted from your camera after successful importation into Windows Photo Gallery.

> **NOTE** If you see an information dialog box pop up during the import process asking if you want to correct picture rotation every time you import images, you have the option of allowing Windows Photo Gallery to take this initiative for you. Or, if you prefer, you can wait until the images have been imported and then manually manipulate the images to your taste. This information dialog box will stop the import until you decide to have it continue. If you opt to allow Windows Photo Gallery to automatically correct your image rotation but later want to cancel this selection, you can do this from the Import Settings page as previously discussed.

When all the images have been successfully imported into Windows Photo Gallery, you can start working with them by cataloging them, tagging them, and creating slide shows.

Working with Your Photos

A variety of tools and options are available for manipulating and modifying photographs to best suit your requirements. The following sections deal with the two menus at the top of the screen: File and Fix.

Using the File Menu

The File menu is the menu you will use to import photographs and other content into Windows Photo Gallery; modify, copy, and delete images already present in the gallery; and set up a feature called *library sharing*, whereby you make your photograph library available to other users on your network.

Select the File menu to see the drop-down list shown in Figure 23-6.

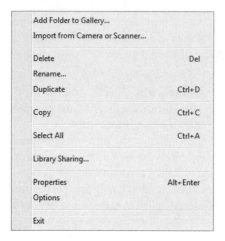

Add Folder to Gallery...	
Import from Camera or Scanner...	
Delete	Del
Rename...	
Duplicate	Ctrl+D
Copy	Ctrl+C
Select All	Ctrl+A
Library Sharing...	
Properties	Alt+Enter
Options	
Exit	

Figure 23-6 *You can use the File menu to add, modify, and configure gallery items.*

Most of these menu options (such as Delete, Rename, and Duplicate) are self-explanatory, or we have already covered them (Add Folder to Gallery and Import from Camera or Scanner); however, three menu options available here are worth delving into a little deeper:

- Library Sharing
- Properties
- Options

Library Sharing

The sharing of digital media content throughout the entire Vista product set is pervasive. Your digital media library could comprise music, photographs, videos, TV content, and movies, and on any single instance of Vista this content is stored under a standard set of folders in your user profile.

Where you are running a networked environment with more than one PC connected, you can have your digital content served from a single location to save the duplication of high volumes of disk-hungry information across multiple systems. Networking computers together permits collaborative information sharing with the benefits of being able to enjoy your digital content from any location to which your network extends. This means you can have the same content stored on your main computer in the office serving photographs across your network to a laptop running Vista Media Center in your living room.

> **CAUTION** All systems wanting to share information must be part of the same physical network and connect with IP addresses in the same subnet. Library sharing is really only a means to support the sharing of information in the home or small-business environment where no central server system is present.

It is possible to set up library sharing on your system without using the option in this menu; however, you will have to configure your firewall settings to permit the following TCP ports, all with a defined scope in the local subnet: 554, 2177, 2869, and 10243. You will also need to open the following UDP ports, again with a scope of local subnet only: 1900, 2177, 5004–5005, and 10280–10284.

If you prefer the easy method for setting up library sharing, use the option in the Windows Photo Gallery File menu. When you see the dialog box shown in Figure 23-7, select the Share My Library checkbox, and then click OK. You'll also see a convenient shortcut to the Vista Network Center (Networking) in case you need to check your network configuration before proceeding.

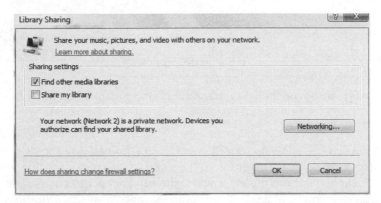

Figure 23-7 *Library sharing makes sharing digital content easy with just one mouse click.*

> **NOTE** Library sharing is not supported when Vista is operating as part of a Windows domain. If you are connected to a domain, the Share My Library checkbox is not available when you enter the Library Sharing menu option. In a domain environment, you can use a digital content server to provide digital media to network users.

When you click OK, you will see an expanded dialog box showing the same options as Figure 23-7, augmented with a list of devices available for sharing and a Settings button.

At this stage, you can right-click any of the devices shown in the window and select how they will be considered in your shared environment.

You can set each device to be authorized to share information (the Allow privilege), or you can opt for that device to not be authorized to participate (the Deny privilege).

You can also disable or remove the device if you do not want it to be displayed.

More granular control over the information that can be shared is possible if you click the Settings button (see Figure 23-8).

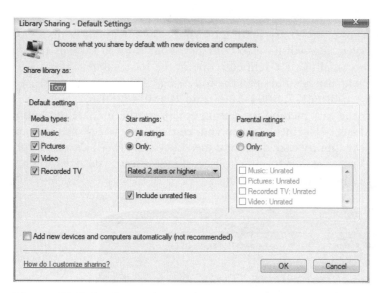

Figure 23-8 *Configure the media types, star ratings, and parental settings of shared content.*

> **NOTE** On the surface, allowing new PC systems to automatically access shared digital content in your library might seem the simplest way of configuring your system, but bear in mind this means anyone who can connect to your subnet can now gain access. If you have a wireless network, someone outside your home or small business could be ripping off your content.

Library Item Properties

Photographers typically have vast quantities of notes and scribbles associated with their photographs. The properties page for each photo in the gallery contains an extensive amount of data pertaining to each photo and makes a great replacement (or at least a place to consolidate) your photo notes.

A lot of the information you'll see in there is populated automatically from the device capturing the image (in a lot of cases this comes from the digital camera itself); however, many fields are blank so you can make your own production notes and keep your own records.

Take the time to scroll through the list of image properties that you can modify to see which might be useful for you. For example, scroll down to the Advanced Photo section where you can enter information particular to your lens maker and model, and if you have used a flash gun, you can list its manufacturer and model.

Options

The Windows Photo Gallery Options dialog box has two tabs you can choose from: General and Import. We already covered the Import tab earlier in this chapter, so now we'll cover the General tab.

Under the Tooltips heading, you can select one checkbox: Show Picture and Video Previews in Tooltips. If this checkbox is selected (the default), when you hover the mouse pointer over a gallery item, Windows Photo Gallery will magnify the image and display some extra metadata. Clearing this checkbox switches off this functionality.

When you use the Fix capability in Windows Photo Gallery, a copy of the original picture is also kept in case you decide the fix did not achieve what you wanted. In the drop-down box at the bottom of the dialog box, you can specify how long Windows Photo Gallery keeps the original photograph before sending it to the Recycle Bin. The default is to never delete any original images, but once you get better at using the tools, you might decide that it's actually OK to delete these originals if you haven't used them for a while. Available options range from one day to one year.

Using the Fix Controls

Quite often, you can make digital photographs look a lot better through some simple adjustments of exposure, color, and contrast manipulation that would not be easily accomplished using traditional film. This is what makes digital media so attractive these days and why film, for most, is becoming a thing of the past.

Windows Photo Gallery comes with a set of tools that can adjust critical settings in your digital photographs, such as color and contrast, and these can make photos that might at first seem unusable actually great shots.

To start the process of fixing an image you are not quite happy with, highlight the image in the gallery, and then click the Fix button in the menu bar at the top of the screen. The image will be blown up to fit the full screen, and you will be presented with a new task pane on the right side with the following options:

- Auto Adjust
- Adjust Exposure
- Adjust Color
- Crop Picture
- Fix Red Eye

Auto Adjust will allow Windows Photo Gallery to attempt to automatically correct any problems with image exposure (brightness and contrast) or image color. Sometimes an autocorrection of this type is all an image needs to make a great improvement. Nevertheless, you should always be prepared to adjust these settings manually if Auto Adjust does not quite do as you intend.

> **TIP** With all image corrections, you can undo each fix in turn should you find it is not what you intended. To undo a correction, click the Undo button at the bottom of the task pane. To put an image correction back if you have undone it but decided you liked it after all, click the Redo button. If you have committed the image modification to the image by clicking Back to Gallery, you can easily retrieve the original photograph by selecting the image, clicking the Fix button, and then clicking the Revert button at the bottom of the task pane.

If you click Adjust Exposure, you will see two slider controls—one for brightness and one for contrast—that you can move to increase or decrease these two components of exposure.

Adjust Color allows you to adjust the *color temperature* (the balance between blue at the bottom end and red at the top end to make the image seem cooler or warmer), *tint* (whereby a color cast can be removed or added to an image by removing or adding a green tint), *saturation* (whereby the intensity of color in the image can be varied from none at all, giving you a grayscale image), and *full saturation* (where the colors begin to impinge on each other).

If you choose Crop the Picture, you can drag the box around the outside of the image using the pick-up points on each of the four straight edges to contain only the part of the image you are interested in keeping. When you are happy your image is better framed, click the Apply button. This will zoom in on the image to fit the full viewing pane.

Finally, if you want to reduce the reddening effect of flash photography on the subject's eyes (where the subject ends up with bright red eyes), click Fix Red Eye, drag a box around the affected area, and then release the mouse. The problem with red eye will be removed.

In each case, when you have fixed the image the way you want, click Back to Gallery (in the top left) to commit the change to the image and return to the gallery.

Working with Metadata

Metadata is data used to describe data. In Windows Photo Gallery, metadata comes in many forms, such as the date an image was taken, the star rating attributed to that image, and the photographer's name. To see a complete list of all metadata associated with an image, look in the image properties, available through the File menu.

Metadata is extremely useful for a variety of reasons: indexing your pictures, grouping them into easily recognizable collections, and searching through your image collections on criteria that are not searchable in the raw image format. In essence, metadata turns digital image data into something meaningful in the real world.

Three important items of metadata are used in Windows Photo Gallery that will be invaluable in helping you keep your library organized:

- Tags
- Captions
- Star Ratings

You can think of tags as identifiers that group images with something in common. A suitable tag might be Holiday in Florida or Baby's First Steps. By tagging your images when you import them into the gallery, you can easily search across a whole range of folders and groups based on this one simple identifier.

To create a new tag, right-click the Tags node of the menu tree on the left side of the main gallery, and select Create Tag. When you see New Tag appear beneath the Tags node, click it, and type the tag name. Windows Photo Gallery will automatically add all images with that tag to this new container. To add a tag to an image (or a group of images), select the image in the gallery, right-click, and select Add Tags. Type the tag for the image in the text-entry box, and press Enter.

Captions are specific to individual images. Captions are displayed in both the thumbnail view of the image in the gallery and in the bottom-right corner of the image in the full-screen mode (when you double-click the image). To add a caption, click Add Caption in the thumbnail for the image in question, or click Add Caption in the bottom-right corner of the gallery.

> **TIP** Once you start developing good practices with metadata, tagging and captioning your images so they are easy to locate and sort, you can use the search box (top of the screen) to locate your images effectively. Many people use a system of tagging and captioning that allows them to group and then home in on images in a matter of seconds, even when their gallery contains thousands of digital photographs.

Finally, the star rating is a great way of assessing your images, running from Not Rated up to five stars (the highest award you can give). A good example of how you would use the star rating is shooting a wedding. You might shoot 1,000 photographs over the course of the day, 500 of which you think are passable and might consider giving to the bride and groom. However, they have asked that you also put on an after-dinner slide show during the speeches and you want to make sure you impress everyone there (who knows, this could muster up some more business). Using the star rating system, pick the best photographs from the collection (say the top 50) and rate them with five stars. Subsequently, go through and rate the rest with four, three, two, and one star (simply clicking the relevant star beneath the thumbnail will do the trick). Now, when it comes to the slide show, click the five-star Ratings node on the left side of the screen, and start the slide show. Later, when the bride and groom want to look through the rest of the images that you are willing to show them, you can run another private slide show for them, this time clicking the four-star or three-star Ratings node.

You can change the rating of an image at any time simply by clicking the new value.

Printing and Online Ordering

Two options are available for you to obtain hard-copy prints of your digital images:

- Print on your home printer
- Order prints from an online printing service such as Kodak

If you decide to print your own photographs, you will need to install a suitable printer that will work with Vista. Select the image (or images) you want to print, click the Print menu, and then select Print (you can also press Ctrl+P to skip the menu). This launches the Print Pictures Wizard (see Figure 23-9).

Figure 23-9 *Choose how you want your pictures formatted when they are sent to your printer.*

You must select the printer, paper tray, and quality of the image before you click Print; then select (from the scrollable list on the right) the number of prints you want printed on each page of output. If you are printing more than one image, the images will be printed in the order they appear in the gallery. Finally, before you click the Print button, specify the number of copies of each picture in the entire output cycle that you want; enter this number in the box at the bottom of the screen. You can increase the number by clicking the up arrow and decrease the number by clicking the down arrow.

> **TIP** If you want Vista to manipulate the output so it ensures as much of the canvas you are printing is covered by the image, check the Fill Each Frame box. Be aware, however, that this option can often lead to losing the edges of an image where the aspect ratio has been perfectly maintained and the image expansion makes certain parts of the image outsize the available printable space on the page.

Online ordering, from companies such as Kodak, Fujifilm, and Shutterfly, is easy. Select the images you are interested in having professionally printed, click the Print menu, and select Order Prints. The first time you do this, Windows Photo Gallery requests a list of online companies that specialize in this service before offering you the choice of who will finish your photographs.

Creating a DVD, Movie, or Data Disc

On the top menu bar, click the Create button to reveal three options available for producing media-specific output from Windows Photo Gallery:

- DVD
- Movie
- Data Disc

If you want to make a DVD slide show of the items contained in your gallery, select the images you are interested in from the gallery, and then click DVD. This automatically imports your selection into Windows DVD Maker and allows you to process them using this facility. For more detailed information about how to use Windows DVD Maker, see Chapter 24.

> **NOTE** You need to make sure you have a blank DVD in the optical drive before selecting this option since the Movie Maker application requires a writable disk to be available before it will start.

In keeping with the tightly integrated model of Vista applications, you can also opt to export gallery items to Windows Movie Maker to create a richer and more elaborate movie production. For information about using Windows Movie Maker to create your own digital movie production, see Chapter 22.

> **NOTE** If you decide to create a movie using Windows Movie Maker, your final production can also be written to a DVD using the integration between Windows Movie Maker and Windows DVD Maker.

A data disc is simply a direct copy of the digital photo files to a writable CD or DVD. To start the process, first place a writable CD or DVD into the optical drive on your PC, click Create, and then select Data Disc.

You will need to enter a meaningful title for the disc, such as the kind of photographs you are copying onto it or the date you are making the copy—this is really important if you are using this CD or DVD as a backup of your photographs. You can use this option if you want to pack as many photographs on a CD or DVD as possible since the images will be copied without the overhead of compiling them into multimedia experiences. If all you want is to simply share the raw material or archive it in your fireproof safe, this is by far the best way.

Sending Photos by Email

The ability to share photographs by email has been around for a while, but the new interface available by clicking the E-mail option on the top menu bar makes it really easy.

When you first click this menu item, you are presented with a dialog box that allows you to select how your pictures are resized when sending them over the Internet. This is to make sending pictures by email a more practicable option since most email users are constrained to relatively small attachment sizes (some as low as 10MB imposed by their ISPs).

You should also be aware of constraints the recipient might have if you are sending large files and attachments—if the recipient is using a dial-up connection and you send 10MB of information to them, it will take significantly longer to download the email from the ISP than if they have a 1MB broadband pipe.

> **NOTE** You'll be surprised at how good digital photographs can still look, even at low resolutions. If you are sending your photos by email, try experimenting with sending the lowest-quality downgrades available (the Smaller: 640×480 setting) to see how they appear on the screen.

Using the drop-down list, select the picture size you'd like to send, and then click the Attach button. Windows Photo Gallery will resize selected images from your gallery and then create a new email in your default email client (Windows Mail is the default mail client in Vista).

> **CAUTION** If the person you are sending the images to wants to have them printed, you should really look at transferring the raw data file to them rather than resizing it in any way. The printing process demands that the image quality be of much higher resolution than that required to view the same picture on the screen.

Running a Slide Show

You use the control bar at the bottom of the Windows Photo Gallery window to run your slide shows. A *slide show* is an automatically cycling screen representation of selected gallery images, displayed in a predefined theme.

To start a slide show, select the images you want included, using either tags, folders, or search criteria such as photographer's name, and then click the center button (the square in the circle) on the control bar. Your photographs will automatically appear in the default theme and start cycling.

Once the slide show is playing, moving the mouse will reveal the control bar at the bottom of the screen, leaving the slide show running in full-screen mode.

Using Themes

If you click the Themes button on a running slide show, you have the option of changing how the pictures are displayed, frame by frame. A *theme* determines how the picture is framed on the screen and instructs the slide show about how to transition between frames and how many photographs should be displayed on each frame.

> **NOTE** Windows Movie Maker users will see that far fewer themes are available in Windows Photo Gallery than in Window Movie Maker; however, these themes are optimized for digital still images and have been specifically designed to be soothing and complimentary to your shots. Also, they offer that digital photo frame effect that was previously missing from Windows XP slide shows.

You should experiment with the 15 available themes, trying each in turn to evaluate their merits and drawbacks and matching them to your needs and style of photography. The simple themes, such as Frame, add a white-and-brown frame around the image, cycling your photograph inside that container. Others, such as Sepia, significantly alter the image being displayed to add a sepia tone to the pictures—this one is particularly effective for viewing pictures of old buildings or subjects in period fancy dress. If you try the Travel theme, you might be surprised to see the image rotate, dissolve, fade, overlay other images, and show multiple images side by side. It's a matter of taste and choosing what suits you best at the time.

Setting Options

The small cog wheel next to the Themes button permits moderate control over how the slide show operates, offering the following options for configuring how it performs:

- Slow
- Medium
- Fast
- Shuffle
- Loop

The three speed controls affect the duration an image stays on the screen, with the default Medium being five seconds between transitions. If you select Shuffle, the images will not be played in the order they appear in the gallery; instead, they will appear in a random order. Finally, if you selected Loop (selected by default), the images in the slide show will continually play until you physically intervene by pressing a key or clicking End Slide Show.

Manually Controlling Slide Shows

When the slide show is running, you can click the Pause button in the center of the control bar to freeze-frame on the image currently on your display. To start the slide show again, simply click the Play button.

To manually move through the gallery, forward and back, click the corresponding arrows on either side of the Play/Pause button.

Setting Audio Controls

If you are playing a soundtrack over the top of your slide show, you can alter the volume output by clicking the + and – signs next to the audio speaker symbol. If you click the speaker button itself, this will instantly mute the audio track. Clicking the speaker again will switch the audio back on at the volume level previously set.

Ending a Slide Show

If you want to exit from a slide show and revert to the regular gallery view, you can press any key, or click End Slide Show on the control bar.

> **NOTE** You might think it strange that Microsoft included the End Slide Show button when any key on the keyboard will stop the pictures looping and return you to the gallery. However, more and more people connect their PCs to large television screens and use remote mouse or pointer controls that don't have keyboards.

Integrating with Other Applications

The last menu item to cover is the top menu bar item labeled Open. If you click this item with any image in the gallery highlighted, you have the option of sending the image to that application, such as Microsoft Paint or Adobe Photoshop. This is useful if you want to regularly edit in other applications yet still manage the photo library from Windows Photo Gallery.

CHAPTER 24

Working with Windows DVD Maker

Previously, because of licensing restrictions, the Windows operating system family contained no inherent support for creating your own MPEG-2 formatted DVDs—the only way to author such creations was to purchase an additional authoring package that included the necessary MPEG-2 encoder.

When Windows XP Media Center Edition 2005 emerged from Redmond, original equipment manufacturers (OEMs) started including third-party DVD-authoring packages in the Media Center PC build, making sure it was capable of authoring DVDs from anywhere within the Media Center menu system. This was a big step for multimedia users.

However, Vista has taken DVD authoring one stage further. With a fully licensed MPEG-2 encoder built into the operating system, you are free to use the new Windows DVD Maker software to create and publish MPEG-2 formatted DVD movies that are compatible with any stand-alone DVD player that supports your DVD hardware.

> **NOTE** You'll come across four main DVD hardware formats when you start delving into discs and writers: DVD-R, DVD+R, DVD-RW, and DVD+RW. Some systems also support a combination of these formats. DVD-R (DVD-Recordable) can record data onto a DVD, creating a fixed, permanent copy of the movie. Anything on DVD-R cannot be removed. The disc cannot be reused. The following companies support DVD-R: Toshiba, Hitachi, NEC, Pioneer, Samsung, Sharp, Panasonic, and Apple Computers. DVD+R (DVD+Recordable) provides the same functionality as DVD-R but comes from a different set of hardware vendors, namely, Hewlett-Packard, Dell, Ricoh, Yamaha, Philips, Sony, and a few others. DVD-RW (DVD-ReWritable) discs can be erased, and the disc can be reused again and again. Manufacturers supporting DVD-RW are Toshiba, Hitachi, NEC, Pioneer, Samsung, Sharp, Panasonic, and Apple Computers. DVD+RW (DVD+ReWritable) provides the same functionality as DVD-RW but has been adopted by different manufacturers, namely, Hewlett-Packard, Dell, Ricoh, Yamaha, Philips, Sony, and a few others. Many manufacturers now produce multiformat drives that support all four of these formats. If you have the choice, you should look for the combination of letters and symbols on the specification sheet for the system you are buying; the best choice, for maximum compatibility, is DVD±RW. DVD±RW will ensure you can record and play back any DVD created on another writer and create content that is extremely portable.

Understanding the Interface

To launch Windows DVD Maker, perform the following steps:

1. Place a writable DVD disc in your optical drive, and close the bay.
2. Click the Start menu, and select All Programs.
3. Click Windows DVD Maker.

The Windows DVD Maker interface has been designed to be as simple as possible to use. Figure 24-1 shows how the interface looks before you start creating a DVD project.

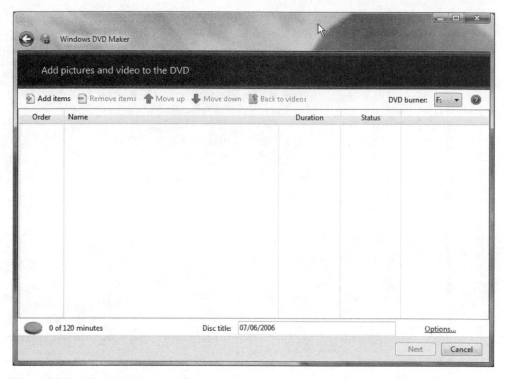

Figure 24-1 *The Windows DVD Maker lets you add, remove, and reorder content in one place.*

Working from the top of the screen to the bottom, the first feature to note is the toolbar that resides just beneath the Add Pictures and Video to the DVD area of the screen. Clicking Add Items allows you to select the type of multimedia files you want added to your DVD from the folder view, as shown in Figure 24-2.

Figure 24-2 *Navigate the Vista folder structure to locate the files you want included in your DVD project.*

Select the files you want to add, and click the Open button. You can add as many files at once as you require, and if you prefer, you can also add them one at a time, each time returning to the main Windows DVD Maker menu and clicking Add Items.

When you have added your files to your DVD project, they appear in the list in the order you added them, as shown in Figure 24-3.

If you highlight any of the content in the list, you will see the rest of the top toolbar becomes available. You can now change the order the clips are presented (the topmost clip represents the first clip to be played in the sequence) using the Move Up and Move Down buttons, as well as being able to delete clips that you have decided you no longer require (clicking the Remove Items button).

At the far right side of the toolbar you will see the DVD Burner drop-down list. Make sure you have selected the device you want to create the DVD.

> **NOTE** Most people have only one DVD burner available on their system; however, some users might have DVD burners of more than one format or multidisc burners for mass DVD production. The DVD Burner drop-down list allows you to select to which device you want your movie sent.

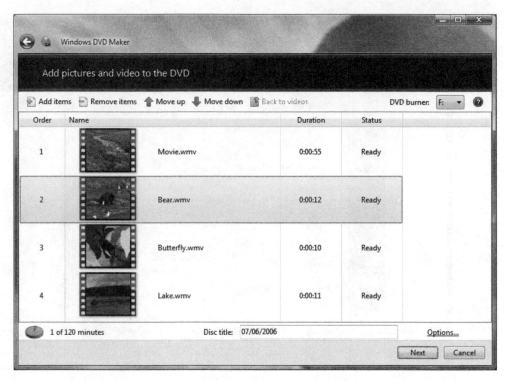

Figure 24-3 *Multimedia content clips will appear in the order you added them to the project.*

In the bottom-left corner of the screen, you are informed about how much of your DVD is left for you to write content. In most cases, you will have a total of 120 minutes of writable disc time, but this depends on both the disc capacity and the writing capabilities of your burner.

The disc title at the bottom of the screen is filled in by default with the date you created the DVD project. To edit this, click it, and type whatever you want the project title to be. You are limited to 32 characters for the title.

If you click the Options link in the bottom-right side of the screen, you will see the DVD-Video Options dialog box, as shown in Figure 24-4.

The topmost setting, Choose How Your DVD Is Played Back, allows you to change the default behavior of how the DVD menu is presented to the viewer. By default, the DVD will be created in the traditional way, with the menu system at the beginning of the disc; you also have the options of playing the movie first and then presenting the viewer with the DVD menu after the film completes or not bothering with a menu and playing the DVD content on a continuous loop.

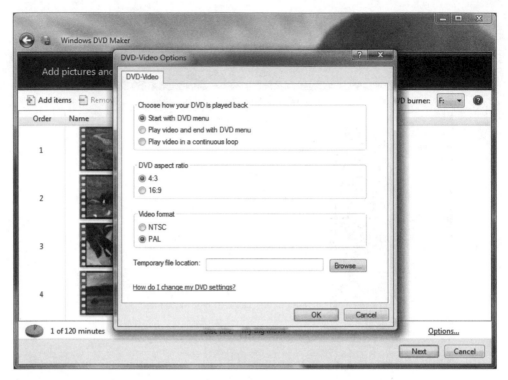

Figure 24-4 *Change the output characteristics of the final DVD production to best suit your needs.*

> **NOTE** You might consider using continuous loop playback for a DVD that plays in an entrance hall or at an exhibition. This is useful since no operator input is required to start the footage playing again once it has completed.

Next in the DVD-Video Options dialog box, you can modify the aspect ratio of the output format for either standard 4:3 television or monitor playback, or if you prefer, you can have Windows DVD Maker create the disc in 16:9 widescreen format.

The video format used (NTSC or PAL) will determine which devices the content will play back on. NTSC is primarily a North American format, whilst PAL is used in many other countries around the world, including the United Kingdom and Australia.

If you desire, you can specify the temporary file location used by Windows DVD Maker in the production of the DVD, but unless you are really short of disk space or prefer this work carried out on a specific hard disk, it's best to leave well enough alone. To change the location used for temporary files, click the Browse button, and select the appropriate folder.

When you are finished with the DVD-Video Options dialog box, click OK.

Creating a DVD Project

The rest of this chapter will take you through the process of creating a professional DVD.

Arranging Movie Items in Order

As stated earlier in this chapter, you can change the order that items appear in the interface using the Move Up and Move Down buttons on the main toolbar at the top of the screen. One additional tip for arranging your movies or multimedia clips into the most appropriate order is that you can gather a collection of clips into a set and manage them as a single item. To do this, hold the Ctrl key when selecting items. When each item is selected, it will be cast in a light blue shadow. If you subsequently right-click any of the selected images in your collection, you'll see a context menu (see Figure 24-5) that allows you to move the entire collection up, move it down, or delete it from your project.

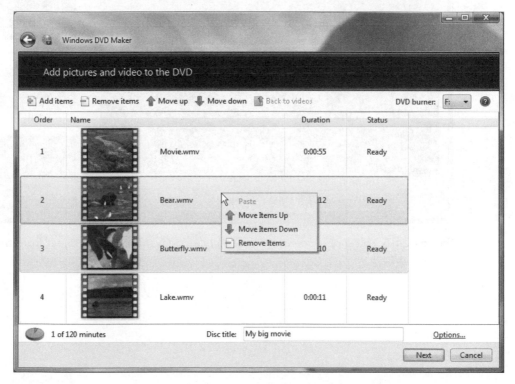

Figure 24-5 *Manipulate a collection of clips as if they were a single item.*

Choosing Menu Styles and Viewing Previews

When you have successfully arranged your clips in the order you want them presented on the final DVD product, click the Next button at the bottom of the screen.

The screen will go blank; then after a few seconds, you will see the Ready to Burn Disc dialog box, as shown in Figure 24-6. You are now at the stage where you can create the DVD menu, modify the menu style, and choose to create a slide show from digital stills if you so desire.

Figure 24-6 *You should select the menu style you want for your project from the list on the right.*

Notice that the movie title you created in the previous section appears as the title on the DVD menu.

You can preview any of the menus shown on the right side of the screen. Simply scroll down the list until you find one that appeals to you, and click it. The new menu will be immediately shown in the Preview pane, as shown in Figure 24-7.

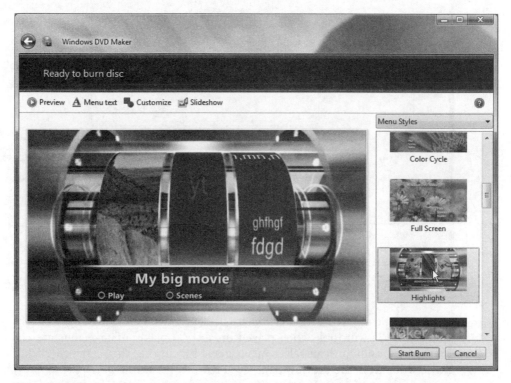

Figure 24-7 *Use the menu styles selection taskbar to change the look of your DVD project.*

At any time, you can click the Preview button on the toolbar to generate a software version of the final product. When you click Preview, it takes a few minutes to compile the movie as it will be presented on the final DVD production, so be patient. You will see a progress bar showing how long you have to wait, as shown in Figure 24-8.

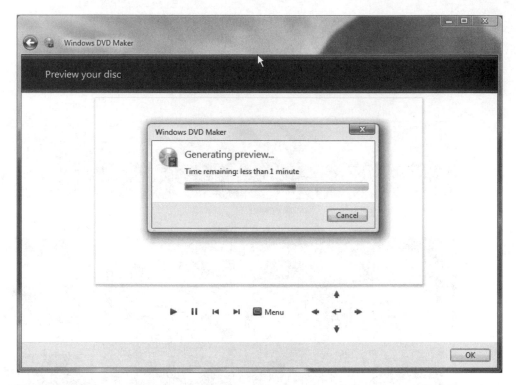

Figure 24-8 *If your movie is quite big, it could take a few minutes to compile the preview.*

When the preview is ready, you are presented with an exact copy (in software) of how the DVD will look when played on a DVD player. The menus are completely operational, and you can select menu items by clicking them. If you click Play, the movie will play in the Preview pane (see Figure 24-9) as if it were playing on your television, including any sound and effects you have included in the footage.

You can use the buttons immediately beneath the Preview pane to play, stop, pause, and skip chapters, as well as to return to the main menu once the DVD is playing. These buttons are similar to the buttons on your DVD player's remote control. You can use the arrows to move around the menu system to simulate what the remote control will be able to do.

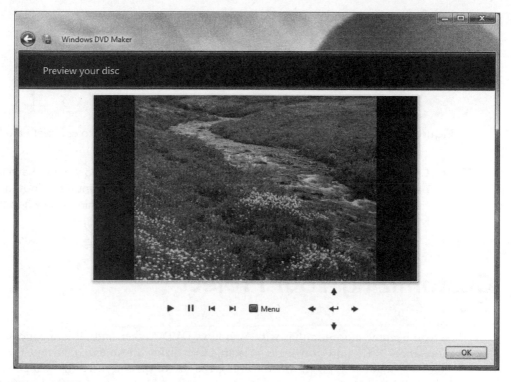

Figure 24-9 *You can preview your project as if it were a final production.*

Burning a DVD

As soon as you are content with your menu selection (using the style you like the best), all you do is click the Start Burn button in the bottom-right corner. This will start the process of committing your project, as previewed, to the DVD in your optical drive.

> **NOTE** After previewing your DVD, if you are unhappy with any aspect of it, you can return to the Preview menu, where you can start adding, removing, or changing the order of your clips. To return to the previous step, click the Cancel button in the bottom-right corner of the window.

When you click Start Burn, a small progress bar will appear in the bottom-right corner of the screen (see Figure 24-10), and the main Windows DVD Maker window will disappear.

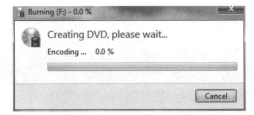

Figure 24-10 *The progress bar shows how much longer it will be to complete the burn.*

CAUTION Progress can be slow when encoding MPEG-2, so you will have to be patient. Even the smallest DVD production (even just a few minutes of footage) can take ten minutes to complete. Be prepared to go do something else when the burning begins.

Customizing Your Project

As you become more familiar with Windows DVD Maker and all its nuances, you'll more than likely find you want to start customizing the menu text and the menu styles—it might be appropriate to increase the size of the font used in the menu text to help the visually impaired, or you might decide to add some background music to the menu style to make the menu experience more appealing. If you want to modify a style, you can save your modifications for later use, or you can opt to leave the existing styles alone and create a new one.

Setting DVD Menu Text

From the main menu, in the Ready to Burn Disc dialog box (refer to Figure 24-6), click the Menu Text button to change the styles and words used to describe your menu items. You will see the Change the DVD Menu Text dialog box, as shown in Figure 24-11.

You can select any of the fonts installed with Vista by clicking the drop-down list next to the current font. The default font is Segoe UI, and the text will appear in bold. Using the buttons to the right of the font selection field, you can change the text color (useful if the background picture of the menu is drowning your text), as well as turn off and on bold and italics.

You can also modify the DVD title on this screen, which is somewhat more convenient than having to backtrack to the initial movie clip item selection window.

You can also change the text used for the Play, Scenes, and Notes buttons, and you can add notes that will be displayed when the Notes button is clicked. You might change *Play* to *Play Movie*, for example.

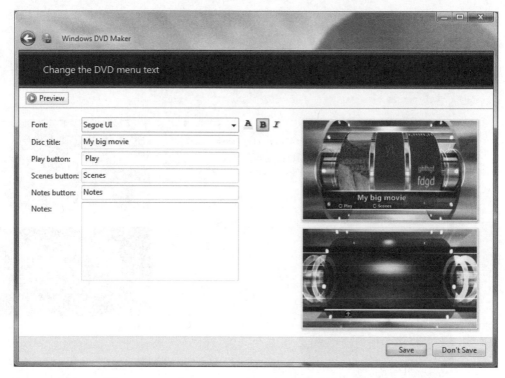

Figure 24-11 *Change menu button labels and text style for your DVD project.*

Working with Menu Styles

You can customize any of the menu styles included in Windows DVD Maker.

From the Ready to Burn Disc dialog box (refer to Figure 24-6), click the Customize button. This will open the Customize the Disc Menu Style dialog box, as shown in Figure 24-12.

Customizing style is limited to the following:

- Changing the text font used for the menu items
- Adding foreground video to the menu
- Adding some background footage to the menu
- Adding an overdubbed audio track to the menu
- Changing the animation scheme used in the menu (this is limited)
- Changing the shape of the menu item buttons

Figure 24-12 *Change fonts, add video, overdub music, or change buttons on your DVD menu.*

> **NOTE** If the menu style you have selected does not permit you to add foreground or background video footage, you will not be able to click the Browse button next to that field to add the clip. Some of the styles, such as Rolling Hills, permit you to add only foreground video, with the background being fixed to the scene built into the style.

Adding foreground video, background video, and audio tracks is as simple as clicking the Browse button and then navigating to the folder where the clip is located. When you find the clip you want to use, click it, and then click the Open button. When you add video footage or an audio file, you should preview it (see Figure 24-13) before going any further to make sure it looks OK and does not impair the menu function.

> **TIP** If you want to add a clip from your DVD movie as a rolling clip to be played behind the main DVD menu, it's a good idea to use Windows Movie Maker to extract an appropriately small clip (see Chapter 22)—maybe ten seconds of footage—and have that clip available as a separate file on your hard disk.

Figure 24-13 *Make sure the menu items are not drowned out by the video content.*

You can save your modified style as a new style by clicking Save As a New Style. If you prefer your modifications to apply to the style you are working with rather than creating a new one, click the Save button in the bottom-right corner of the screen.

To exit the window without applying any changes to your style, click the Don't Save button.

Creating Slide Shows

Back in the first window where you add pictures and video footage to your project, click Add Items (refer to Figure 24-3), and select the digital photographs you would like to use in your slide show. You'll notice that digital images are displayed in this window differently than video clips are, as shown in Figure 24-14.

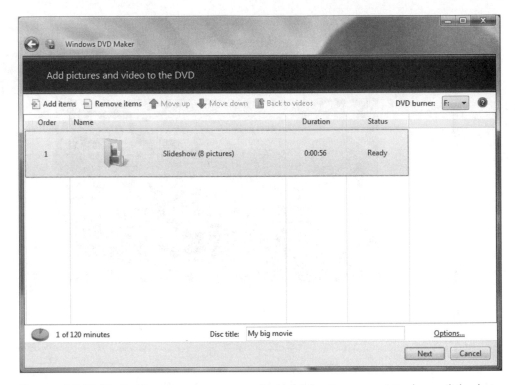

Figure 24-14 *Digital images appear as a single folder item annotated as a slide show.*

The item description in this window shows the folder to be a slide-show folder and tells you how many images are included in the folder. As you add new digital images to the slide show, they are added to this folder and the number increases.

If you double-click the slide-show folder, it will expand the contents so you can reorder or delete individual images. When you want to return to the video clip–editing page, you can click the newly highlighted button Back to Videos.

When you have added all the images you want included in your slide show, click the Next button.

Select your preferred menu style from the list on the right side of the screen (the Photographs style is quite nice for a slide show), and then click the Slideshow button on the toolbar at the top of the screen. This takes you to the screen where you set the attributes specific for this slide show and how it will be presented when it is played on the DVD (see Figure 24-15).

From here, you can add music tracks to be played in the background as your photographs are cycled through in the slide show, and you can change the characteristics of how each photograph is displayed, that is, how long the picture is displayed (for picture length, the default is seven seconds) and how the pictures transition from one picture to the next (options available are Cross Fade, Cut, Dissolve, Flip, Inset, Page Curl, Pixelate, Random, and Wipe).

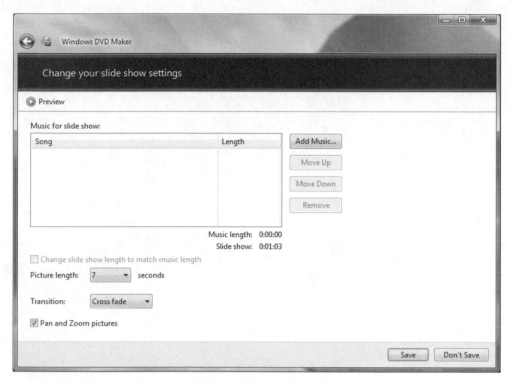

Figure 24-15 *Add backing music to enhance your slide show.*

> **NOTE** Picture transitions apply to the entire slide show. If you want more control over the slide show, where different transitions and times apply to different photographs, you should consider using Windows Movie Maker because it offers a lot more flexibility in how you construct your movie.

If you select the Pan and Zoom Pictures checkbox, each picture will artistically pan and zoom across your screen before transitioning to the next photograph.

You can add multiple music tracks to your slide show, and if desired, you can stretch the time taken to complete the slide show to allow the music to complete. To do this, you should check Change Slide Show Length to Match Music Length.

CHAPTER 25

Working with Windows Media Center

Media Center is a software extension to Vista that offers a central controlling function for all your home theater and multimedia entertainment needs. Media Center provides the following:

- Analog and digital television playback and recording
- An Electronic Program Guide (EPG) for easy program scheduling and viewing
- Internet and FM radio
- Integrated DVD playing and recording
- Video playback with support for a wide variety of standards and formats
- Digital still photograph gallery for easy viewing and manipulation
- Digital music playback and recording
- Extensible Vista programming API for developing add-ons and enhancements

The goal of Media Center has, from the beginning, been to create a user-friendly interface that doesn't have the complication or intricacies of a typical PC interface. More important, the system will more often than not be installed in the living room, so every function proffered through the user interface must be optimized for use with a remote control.

> **NOTE** The living-room PC is a relatively new phenomenon with the latest systems such as those from Sony that have the look and feel of a hi-fi system rather than a standard desktop or laptop PC. Coupled with high-quality internal components and configured for silent running, these PCs are fast replacing the need for stand-alone devices such as DVD players and CD players.

This was a challenge to say the least, but the problems faced by users of the Windows XP version of Media Center have mostly been addressed, with Vista sporting a highly streamlined and improved UI.

Needless to say, the functionality from the Windows XP version is all still there, only presented slightly differently.

Because of the hardware extensibility of the PC platform, it's easy to integrate a wide array of functional components into your system to add to Media Center's overall capability. This will allow you to dispose of discrete hi-fi components as they reach the end of their natural life, thus saving space and cutting down on the number of remote controls you have to own and understand how to use.

Using Media Center PCs

You can turn practically any PC that runs Vista (Home Premium or Ultimate) into a Media Center PC. All you need are a few extra pieces of low-cost hardware (if you don't already have them) and your PC connected to your TV source (cable, satellite, set-top box, or analog), and you're ready to get going.

> **NOTE** The licensing for this version of Media Center is a lot more flexible since it comes as part of the standard operating system package rather than with previous versions that were OEM only. For this reason, AV enthusiasts were previously unable to easily build their own systems since the Media Center operating system components were available only to official system builders. However, the market is about to change since Media Center is now included with Vista. AV enthusiasts can now purchase a Vista upgrade license (through their regular supplier), which gives them immediate access to Media Center. And so, the world changes for the better.

The differentiator between a so-called Media Center PC and a non–Media Center PC has become somewhat blurred. Most PC vendors are now leveraging the selling power of an integrated home theater to increase sales, but what does this mean for you? Basically, a Media Center PC is any PC that can support the functions offered by the Media Center software. However, to get the most out of Media Center, you should aim to have the best possible hardware setup to create the perfect home theater.

Buying a Media Center PC

The chassis design of your Vista Media Center is critical when you make a purchase. You can get three different types, all with their own merits and purposes.

Using a Standard Desktop

A standard desktop is one that fits best into your office and connects to your monitor (flat panel or CRT) in the usual way. You should consider a standard desktop PC if you are not installing it in your living room, requiring instead standard PC operations, such as word processing. The downside of these standard desktops is that the internal engineering of the motherboard and cooling system has not been optimized, so the same computer in a living room environment would produce a lot of noise and heat. These systems are usually bundled as a complete PC package, including a monitor.

Using a Laptop

A laptop chassis offers an extremely mobile solution that can easily be transported to the location where you are working. A laptop easily doubles as an office system, allowing all the features you might expect from standard Vista; the main downside is that expandability and hardware upgrades are often impossible to come by (unless externally connected using USB 2.0). Laptop PCs are usually limited on expansion slots and upgrade bays and in some cases can get hot and might, in the wrong environment such as a hi-fi cabinet, shut down.

Using a Living-Room PC

The living-room PC is a PC that looks like a piece of hi-fi equipment. As well as this aesthetic outward appearance, the internal components have been carefully selected to take account of the intended environment. Complex cooling systems allow for silent running, and integrated LCD screens display program information and functional messages that mean you don't need to dip into Vista to use the system. Quite often, living-room PCs come without a monitor included in the package because it's expected you will be using your own television set to view output.

Networking a Media Center PC

To get the most out of Media Center, you will require an Internet connection. This is not to say Media Center will stop working if you don't go online, but some of the features require an uplink of some kind or another to perform critical and functional updates, such as updates to the Electronic Program Guide.

You can directly connect your PC to the Internet or, like any other system, go through an Internet Connection Sharing host. If you are connecting directly, you will need to configure this underlying Internet connection in Vista before running through the Media Center setup. This allows the setup program to optimize Media Center for your network infrastructure and set up the services needed to keep the software up-to-date, acquire media information, and download program information.

Many Media Center PCs (especially the living-room and laptop models) come with an onboard wireless network card. You can use a wireless network in a number of ways:

- To connect your PC to your wireless Internet router
- To network your PC with other systems in your home
- To allow network access when you're moving the Media Center system from one location to another (most often when you have a laptop system)
- To stream content over your network to an extender, such as an Xbox 360 (you can also accomplish this using a wired network)

Using Extenders

Although Media Center is a great solution for consolidating your multimedia systems into one simple-to-use box, you certainly don't want to buy a new PC for each room you want to use its services in. So, what should you do? You should use an extender.

An *extender* (of which there are a few different models on the market, including Microsoft's own Xbox 360) is a hardware device that allows your primary PC running Vista to send its output to a remote device in another room. Extenders take the output from your Media Center PC and broadcast it (TV, videos, pictures, and music) to another location using either wired or wireless networking.

> **TIP** If you want to connect an Xbox to your Media Center PC using a wireless network, you should use the latest, dual-band 802.11a+g wireless technology. This ensures you get optimum performance and that the content won't be degraded when sent across the network.

A number of manufacturers specialize in extender technology with both wireless and wired networking support. Microsoft has its own gaming console, the Xbox 360, which is the easiest and by far the best extender around. This is an extremely good value option since you also get the extensive gaming capabilities offered in the same package.

Setting up the Xbox 360 with Vista Media Center is easy, and if you're interested in more information on the Xbox, take a look at Microsoft's product web site: http://www.microsoft.com/windowsxp/mediacenter/extender/default.mspx.

If you're not interested in buying an Xbox 360 but still want to extend the reach of your Media Center, companies such as Linksys are always offering multimedia components in this market.

Setting Up Digital TV

When you first run the Media Center application (Start ➤ All Programs ➤ Windows Media Center), you are presented with the Welcome screen, as shown in Figure 25-1.

Figure 25-1 *The Welcome screen*

The easiest way to get up and running is to use Express Setup. Use the remote control to select Express Setup, and then click OK.

On the following screen, you'll see the Media Center top-level menu, with the TV + Movies item selected by default. If you have a TV card in your system that you want to set up, click the right arrow on your remote control twice, and select Set Up TV, as shown in Figure 25-2.

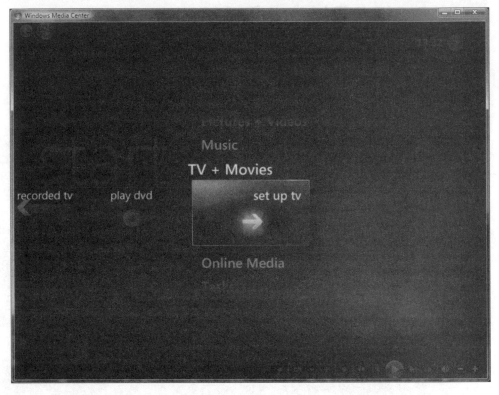

Figure 25-2 *Use the Set Up TV function to tune in and configure analog and digital TV receivers.*

The following procedure shows you how to set up a standard digital TV tuner card:

1. On the first screen, entitled Set Up Your TV Signal, click Next.

2. You are now asked to confirm your region. The region should be automatically detected from the system registry; in this case, as shown in Figure 25-3, the region is the United Kingdom, but if it's not, you have the option of choosing a different region. When you have selected either the Yes or No option, click Next.

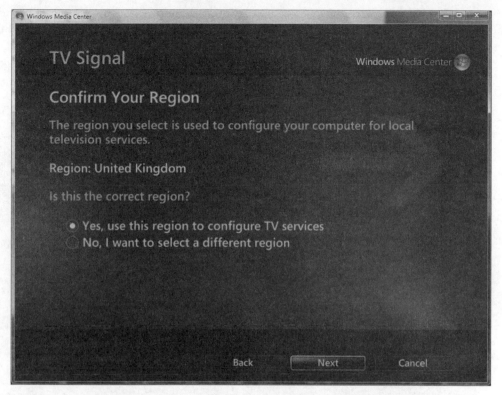

Figure 25-3 *Choose the region in which you will be watching television broadcasts.*

3. The setup process now downloads TV setup options from the Internet. This will take a few minutes on a slow connection, so you'll have to be patient. When it has finished, click Next to set up the guide (this is the Electronic Program Guide you'll be using for surfing, recording, and scheduling your viewing).

4. On the Guide Privacy screen, select Yes, and then click Next.

5. Read the terms and conditions on the Guide Terms of Service screen, then click I Agree, and then click Next.

6. Enter your postal code in the space provided (use the remote control like you would the text buttons on your cell phone). Click Next when you're ready.

7. Media Center now connects to the Internet and presents a selection of broadcast providers available in your area. Select the one nearest your location, and then click Next.

8. Media Center again connects to the Internet to download the Electronic Program Guide information for your area, as shown in Figure 25-4. When it's done, click Next.

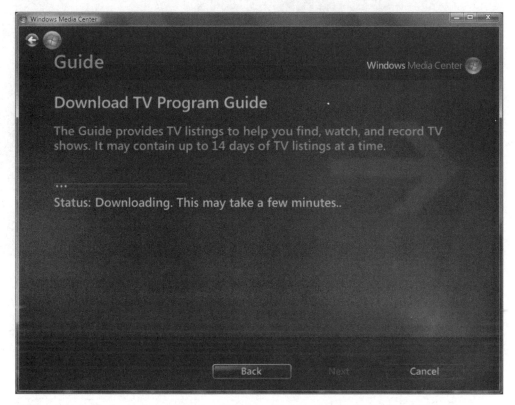

Figure 25-4 *Choose the region in which you will be watching television broadcasts.*

9. The next part of setup is to scan for services. *Services* are channels in your area broadcast over your selected medium. Click Start Scan to have Media Center perform a frequency scan for all available channels. This can take a few minutes, so go have a coffee. When it's done, it displays all the channels it discovers in the list box. If you think there should be more channels than those displayed, click the Scan for More button. When you're done, click Next.

That's it. You are now ready to start using the guide to watch and record TV shows.

Setting Up the Music Library

Using the top-level menu (if you're ever stuck, simply click the green button on the remote or in the top-left corner of every screen), select Music Library. The first time you go into this menu you are prompted to point Media Center at your music library location (if it's not in Vista's Music folder in your profile). The Library Setup Wizard is simple and intuitive to follow:

1. Select Add Folder to Watch, and then click Next (see Figure 25-5).

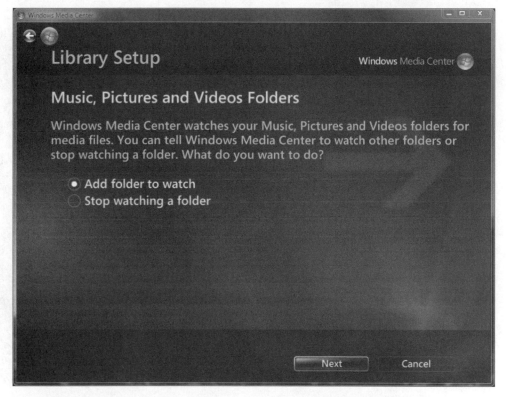

Figure 25-5 *Add folders containing music to your Media Center library.*

> **NOTE** To remove a folder from your "watch list," you can right-click anytime in the music library and select Library Setup. To remove the folder, select Stop Watching a Folder, and follow the instructions. Folders that are being watched automatically update the library as new songs are added.

2. You can add folders from your local computer, from a computer over the network, or from both. Select which folders you'd like to add at this stage, and then click Next.

3. Locate the folders in the Windows Explorer–style folder view, and select each one by pressing your remote control's OK button next to the folder name. When you've selected all the folders you'd like added at this stage, click Next.

4. Confirm you selection, and then click Finish.

Once you've added folders to Media Center, you can scroll through all the available music by genre, looking at cover art and track listings at the click of a button, as shown in Figure 25-6.

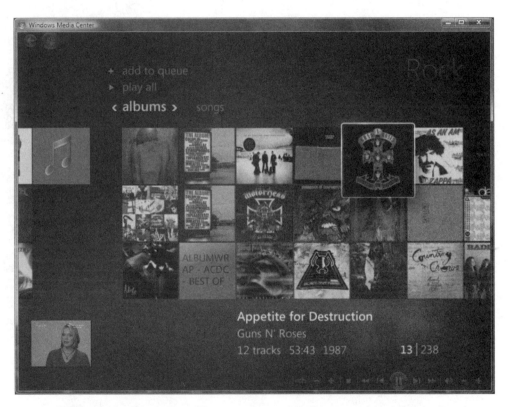

Figure 25-6 *The horizontal scrolling menu system allows you to see immediately what's available.*

Setting Up Pictures and Videos

From the top-level menu, select Picture Library. The first time you enter the picture library you are prompted to point Media Center at the location on your system where you store pictures and videos (if it's not in Vista's Pictures folder in your profile). The Library Setup Wizard is simple and intuitive to follow, and the process is the same as setting up your music folder—in fact, there's no point in repeating the walk-through; it's simply a matter of instructing Media Center which folder (network or local) contains your pictures and videos.

Exploring More Setup Options

The beauty of Media Center is that it's easy to get started, and each option for setting up separate functionality is driven by a simple-to-use wizard. To access the full range of setup features available in Media Center, select the Tasks ➤ Settings menu, as shown in Figure 25-7.

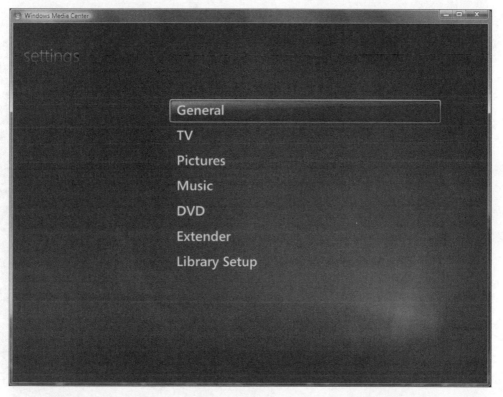

Figure 25-7 *Run through each of the setup wizards for the functionality you require.*

Using Media Center

Media Center is designed to be simple. The key to making the most of it comes from knowing how to get to the hidden features that live just out of sight. Once you start navigating the menu system and see what top-level features are available, it's time to start digging, and in most cases, you can do this by using the information button (the small *i* button on your remote) or right-clicking the option to reveal a context menu.

Making the Most of the Guide

The *guide* is Media Center's on-screen, interactive listing of TV shows available for viewing over the coming days and weeks. Figure 25-8 shows an example of what the guide looks like.

Figure 25-8 *The guide displays the programming schedule for the coming weeks.*

This guide is in fact a powerful interface used not only to display the coming days of scheduled programming but is also the primary interface for getting to the added value Media Center offers. Getting more information about a program is easy. If you navigate to the program listing in question using your remote control and highlight its name, you'll see a description of the show at the bottom of the screen.

If you press the OK button on the highlighted show, you'll start watching that channel if the program is currently being broadcast. If it's scheduled to be shown later, you'll have the option to record it or look in the guide to see whether it's repeated at a later date, maybe on another channel.

If you press the information button on a highlighted guide entry, you can select from the context menu to get extra program information (a full description of the show), record the program (save the show to your hard disk for watching later), record a series (where you record the entire series of a selected show on all channels where it is shown), view categories (takes a look at popular viewing categories to search for a particular show), and finally, as with all context menus, get a shortcut to the Settings menu.

Searching through the content in the guide (the rightmost menu option from the TV + Movies top-level menu) is one of the most powerful features available. The search feature allows you to trawl through the information stored in the guide by show title, explicit keyword, or category. A title search looks through the guide for a specific show title you type in a search interface. Similarly, you can search for a keyword, which allows you to look for shows with a particular actor, for example, allowing you to look for all movies in the coming weeks featuring Robert De Niro, as shown in Figure 25-9.

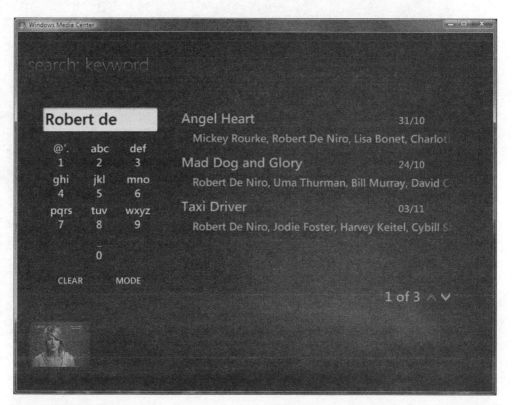

Figure 25-9 *Keyword searching is great for looking for actors or locations.*

Getting Online Media

Although Media Center is rich in multimedia functionality out of the box, plenty of software companies are looking for ways to exploit its easily extensible architecture to supply added value. Software companies can extend Media Center's capability in two ways:

- Using the Media Center Software Development Kit, specifically the new WinFX and Presentation Layer Application development capabilities
- Developing online services that you access through the Online Media menu option

Here we'll take you on a whistle-stop tour of some of the online services available out of the box (see Figure 25-10).

> **NOTE** If you are interested in learning more about writing your own Media Center plug-ins using the Media Center Software Development Kit, you can download everything you need from http://www.microsoft.com/downloads.

Figure 25-10 *Online Media, a menu option off the main menu in Media Center, is the primary interface for third-party applications on Media Center.*

Some of these services are free, but most involve at least a registration of some kind; all have premium services that involve a credit card payment to access the best content.

Sky offers a service whereby existing subscribers can access movies and TV shows through the Media Center (over the Internet) at no extra cost over and above an existing Sky contract.

The BBC News Player offers a free direct stream of news broadcasts from the BBC web site through the Media Center interface and allows you to select which news-related categories might be of interest to you.

Online media services are certainly a growth area, and it's certainly worth popping in from time to time to see whether a service that suits you has been added.

Setting Parental Controls

The last feature we'll look at in Media Center (and there is so, so much more to learn) is the parental controls feature. Accessed through the General Settings menu option, parental controls allow you to control which DVD ratings are allowed to be viewed on the system. As shown in Figure 25-11, you can set a maximum rating and can block unrated movies if you desire. You can set a four-digit PIN to stop your children from changing the threshold to a higher rating.

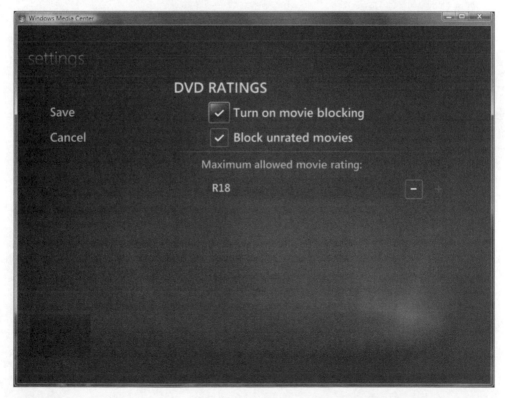

Figure 25-11 *Use parental controls to set an upper limit on DVD movie ratings.*

CHAPTER 26

Managing General Windows Vista Security

indows Vista's general level of security is light years ahead of Windows XP. Put another way, the five long years along the road to the gold version of Windows Vista gave Microsoft time to incorporate the best of the security feedback it received and to put into place mechanisms to protect users from threats and themselves.

In this chapter, we'll cover some of the more general parts of Windows Vista's many layers of security—those we haven't covered elsewhere in the book. These include User Account Control, Data Execution Prevention, workgroups and domains, and security templates.

User Account Control

User Account Control (UAC) is a new security feature that limits the authority of accounts users are running in, restricting them from entering protected areas or performing sensitive actions on the system. Briefly, users log in, whether they are power users, ordinary users, or administrators, and they are assigned a regular security token. However, when a user requests to perform an action that requires administrative privileges, the UAC displays a login prompt, and the user must enter credentials; at that time, Windows Vista assigns an administrative security token to them that allows them to carry out the protected function. You can see a sample of this acknowledgment prompt in Figure 26-1; note the Secure Desktop feature in effect, which grays out all areas of the screen except the acknowledgment prompt.

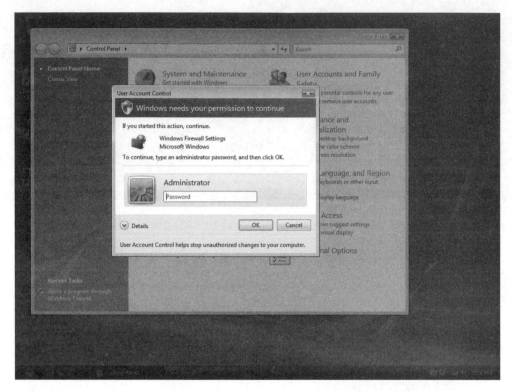

Figure 26-1 *A UAC acknowledgment prompt*

This really bothers some people, especially power users, who think they don't need to be protected from themselves. For the people who subscribe to that school of thought, it's relatively easy to turn off UAC entirely. Fire up the venerable msconfig.exe, and on the Tools tab, scroll down to Disable UAC, and click the Launch button at the bottom right. You'll need to reboot.

Personally, we want to like UAC. We really do. But after installing and beginning to live in Vista day in and day out since mid-April 2006, we've found that the current behavior of UAC is really, really annoying—to the point of driving-us-bonkers annoying. At first, it was unusable. Whenever we tried to perform a task that needed to elevate our security permissions, Windows would blank out the desktop, shade it in dark gray, restrict our access to it, and bring the elevation prompt to the forefront. It sounds pretty neat in theory, and it might even be useful—there's no getting around the elevation prompt with this Secure Desktop feature in place—but for some reason on a dual-core Pentium D at 3.2GHz with 2GB of RAM and, at the time, a nine-month old video card, the video refresh was so exceedingly slooooow that our monitors blanked out for about five seconds, displayed the blacked-out desktop, and then, once we completed the elevation dialog box, blanked again for five seconds before finally returning to normal. That was completely unacceptable.

In later builds, and after replacing an nVidia display adapter with a more modern ATI card with twice the memory, the performance of UAC improved and the intrusiveness decreased. Secure Desktop, in fact, become a lot less bothersome, because Microsoft enabled it so that programs requiring acknowledgment of a UAC prompt would sit minimized in the taskbar, with their buttons blinking, until you explicitly clicked them—only then would the Secure Desktop grab your focus and lock everything else out. However, it's still quite annoying when you're initially setting up a system off a bare metal hard drive, installing programs, updating drivers, tweaking system settings, and generally sticking your fingers into areas of the operating system that make Vista's security twitch. The bottom line, at least for us, is that we've found that the UAC process isn't necessarily so bad; it's the Secure Desktop feature, which kills your ability to do anything and everything when you switch your focus to a window, that has activated UAC.

There is a compromise here. There's a way to at least turn off that annoying Secure Desktop blanking feature. You might find that disabling this feature while you are setting up a system and then reenabling it later is a decent way to keep systems secure and stay true to the spirit of UAC while not driving you batty:

1. Click the Start button.

2. In the search area, type **gpedit.msc**, and press Enter. The Group Policy Object Editor opens, although before that you'll probably need to allow the program to run, so click Allow in the security box that opens.

3. In the left pane, expand Computer Configuration, Windows Settings, Security Settings, and Local Policies, and then click Security Options.

4. Scroll to the bottom, and double-click User Account Control: Switch to the Secure Desktop When Prompting for Elevation.

5. Select Disabled, and click OK.

6. Close the Group Policy Object Editor.

Using Workgroups and Domains

At some point in your use of Windows Vista, a question about participating in domains versus workgroups is sure to arise. First, a quick refresher of what each is: a *workgroup* is a decentralized collection of computers designed to facilitate resource sharing among a handful of computers. There is no common security database, and all user files and folders, as well as profile information, are stored locally on each computer. A *domain* is a group of network resources delineated by the network administrator with a centralized and shared security database. Domains allow for central login and easier management of their member clients and servers.

When you install Windows, by default your machine participates in a workgroup named, obviously enough, WORKGROUP. (Previous versions of Windows, namely Windows XP, joined default workgroups named MSHOME.) All machines that have an identical workgroup name setting are said to *participate* in that workgroup, and all members of a workgroup can see all other machines participating in that workgroup. You can create a workgroup yourself by simply specifying one machine as a member of that workgroup; you can name it anything you like. If you want your Vista machine to see other machines that already exist in your network, you probably will want to change the Vista machine's workgroup setting to MSHOME.

If your machine is located at an office, you may need to join the computer to an existing domain. Usually domains are based on server machines running Windows NT, Windows 2000, or Windows Server 2003, and your administrator will probably want your machine to be a member of that domain so it can be centrally managed and so it inherits consistent security policy configurations as specified by the administrator. To join the computer to a domain, you may need that administrator present, as discussed in the procedure a bit later in this section. If you performed an upgrade installation, your machine may already be joined to the domain, and you won't have to worry about this (if you had to press Ctrl+Alt+Delete to log in by default, this is probably the case).

Here's how to create or change a Vista machine's workgroup or domain participation settings:

1. From the Start menu, right-click Computer, and select Properties.

2. Find the section on the View Basic Information About Your Computer page named Computer Name, Domain, and Workgroup Settings. You can see the current settings there.

3. Click the Change Settings link. You may have to acknowledge a UAC prompt following the click.

4. Click the Change button. The Computer Name/Domain Changes dialog box appears, as shown in Figure 26-2.

Figure 26-2 *The Computer Name/Domain Changes dialog box*

5. Click the domain or workgroup option, whichever you'd like. Enter the names of the domain or workgroup, respectively, and click OK. You may be asked to enter administrative credentials if you are trying to add a computer to a domain and your current account doesn't have the appropriate permissions to add a member to an existing domain.

6. Click OK. You will have to reboot, no matter which security environment you chose.

Managing Data Execution Prevention

Data Execution Prevention (DEP) is a security feature in Windows XP, in Windows Server 2003, and now in Windows Vista that looks for malicious code trying to execute. If DEP's analysis of a process beginning execution makes DEP think the resulting code will cause some sort of unwanted activity, DEP intervenes and shuts the process down.

It sounds good in theory, but too often DEP shuts down legitimate programs—particularly third-party installers used by software developers that release their products for download off the Web. Equally too often, DEP fails to show any sort of warning or information prompt telling you it shut off a process, leaving you scratching your head, wondering why your machine is ignoring you. You might want to turn off DEP globally by issuing the following at an elevated command prompt (that is, a shell running with administrative credentials):

```
bcdedit.exe /set {current} nx AlwaysOff
```

As you might imagine, it's almost as simple to turn it on again should you want DEP's protection back on your side. The following command will do the trick:

```
bcdedit.exe /set {current} nx AlwaysOn
```

Understanding and Using Security Templates

Security templates list all the possible security attributes and settings for a given system and their associated configurations. By using the Security Templates snap-in, you can easily provision a standard collection of security settings across multiple systems using either remote registry editing or Group Policy. For administrators who have a large number of systems to manage and for those who provision quite a few systems on a regular basis, security templates can save a lot of time; they can assist with setting up a new machine or rolling out a new organizational security policy to many systems.

They're also helpful because you can define multiple templates, since few large organizations have a single security standard for all computers.

You can begin using security templates by loading the Security Templates snap-in:

1. Run MMC from the command line to load the MMC in author mode. Author mode allows you to construct new consoles from scratch and add snap-ins to them.

2. From the Console menu, select Add/Remove Snap-in. Then select Add. This opens a dialog box entitled Add Standalone Snap-in.

3. From the list, select Security Templates, click Add, and then click Close.

4. Click OK in the next box to confirm the addition of the snap-in.

You now have the Security Templates snap-in added to a console, as shown in Figure 26-3. From this snap-in, you can expand the Security Templates section in the console tree on the left and then see all the templates that have been configured.

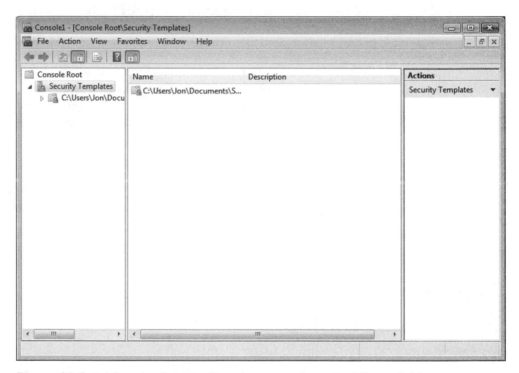

Figure 26-3 *Adding the Security Templates snap-in to the Microsoft Management Console*

Each security template has seven configurable areas, which you can display by double-clicking the label in the pane on the right inside the snap-in after selecting a template from the list in the pane on the left. Table 26-1 describes the areas.

Table 26-1 Template Policy Areas

Framework Area	Description
Account policies	This area applies security configuration to user accounts, including passwords, account lockouts, and Kerberos ticket policies. Password and account lockout policies apply to workstations and servers; Kerberos ticket policies apply only to domain controllers.
Local policies	This area allows you to set auditing and event logging policies, user rights assignments, and registry keys that directly affect system security. It also controls auditing of events, including application actions and security notifications. Note that settings in this area apply to all Windows 2000 or later systems, not to only a specific kind of system.
Restricted groups	This particularly useful area allows you to define policies regarding a user's membership into security groups that allow elevated privileges. It's simple to define a policy where domain users can never be members of the local Administrators group; other policies are equally easy.
System services	This area contains start-up options for services and access controls on them.
Registry	In this area you can configure access permissions on specific keys in the registry. In addition, you can audit the access and modification of registry entries.
File system	This area allows you to preconfigure access permissions on selected file system directories.
Event log	In this area, you can specify how the Application, Security, and System event logs fill and rotate and what their maximum size might be. You also can configure who has access to view the logs.

Each template is nothing more than an ASCII text file with an .inf extension that lists all the settings. Looking at the file is often a more useful and quicker way to determine applicable settings. For example, the following is a portion of a sample security template:

```
[Profile Description]
%SCEHiSecWSProfileDescription%
[version]
signature="$CHICAGO$"
revision=1
DriverVer=10/01/2002,5.2.3790.0
[System Access]
```

```
;----------------------------------------------------------------
;Account Policies - Password Policy
;----------------------------------------------------------------
MinimumPasswordAge = 2
MaximumPasswordAge = 42
MinimumPasswordLength = 8
PasswordComplexity = 1
PasswordHistorySize = 24
ClearTextPassword = 0
LSAAnonymousNameLookup = 0
EnableGuestAccount = 0
;----------------------------------------------------------------
;Account Policies - Lockout Policy
;----------------------------------------------------------------
LockoutBadCount = 5
ResetLockoutCount = 30
LockoutDuration = -1
;----------------------------------------------------------------
;Local Policies - Security Options
;----------------------------------------------------------------
;DC Only
;ForceLogoffWhenHourExpire = 1
;NewAdministatorName =
;NewGuestName =
;SecureSystemPartition
```

You might want to make your own customized policy modifications. Creating a custom security template affords you an easy way to package, deploy, and apply these modifications with a minimum of administrative headache.

To create your own security template, follow these steps:

1. In the Security Templates console, expand Security Templates in the tree pane on the left, and right-click the default directory location.

2. Then, select New Template from the context menu that appears.

3. Now you can make any policy modifications you want in any one of the policy areas supported by the tool: account policies, local policies, the event log, restricted groups, system services, the registry, and the file system. Your additions, deletions, and other changes are saved in the template immediately.

Where Security Is Covered Elsewhere

This chapter is a sort of "catchall" chapter, where more minor security topics are covered in a central location. But many of the improvements and new features in Windows Vista are security related, and we've given them the attention they deserve in other parts of this book. Here is a list of other chapters where we cover security-related features and processes:

- User Account Control (UAC) and Network Access Protection (NAP), covered in Chapter 7

- NTFS file and folder permissions, covered in Chapter 10

- BitLocker, the drive encryption system, covered in Chapter 11

- New security and hardening improvements in Windows Internet Explorer, covered in Chapter 17

- The Windows Firewall with Advanced Security, covered in Chapter 27

- Windows Defender, the new anti-malware solution, covered in Chapter 28

Implementing the Windows Firewall

A s you are probably aware, the Windows Firewall was introduced in Windows XP Service Pack 2 and was a great improvement to overall client security.

With Vista, the Windows Firewall is further improved, with better security features built into the standard product that cover many users' most common complaints. For example, Microsoft has fixed the age-old concern that the previous version protected computers only from unsolicited inbound connections and not from unsolicited outbound ones—now you can do both, although you'll have to dig into the advanced firewall to make this happen.

The interface of the firewall is now split into two functional interfaces; one is for the standard Windows Firewall for users who don't need to understand the complexity of what's possible, and the second interface is for the Windows Firewall with Advanced Security, which is a second product that is integrated with the Windows Firewall but capable of so much more. This chapter covers both of these firewalls, their optimum configuration, and the best way to secure your system using them.

Using the Standard-Issue Windows Firewall

By default the Windows Firewall is installed and enabled on all network connections. If you need to switch it off for a particular connection, you are required to explicitly deselect it.

To access the Windows Firewall configuration, click the Start button, open the Control Panel, select Security, and then click Windows Firewall.

From the screen shown in Figure 27-1, you can immediately see that the Windows Firewall is running (the green tick inside the shield icon) and how it's configured, that is, whether it informs you about program blocking and which network locations are protected.

> **TIP** You can modify standard Windows Firewall settings in only one place. The links on the task menu on the left side of Figure 27-1 all open the same Windows Firewall Settings dialog box; in each case, the links open the dialog box to a different tab.

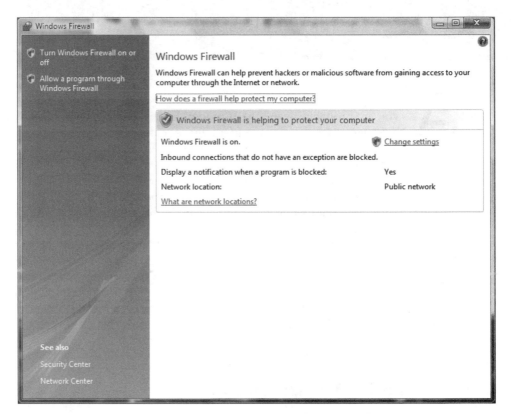

Figure 27-1 *The Windows Firewall is switched on by default for all network connections.*

> **NOTE** It is possible to run more than one firewall on your system, although in practice this is not commonly done since there may be conflicts that are hard to diagnose. The Windows Firewall is now good enough to offer the assurance that other vendors' firewalls once offered the Windows user; however, sometimes it's not always a good idea to use more than one firewall.

To configure the Windows Firewall, you need to click Change Settings to reveal the Windows Firewall Settings dialog box. Here you'll discover three tabs, General, Exceptions, and Advanced, which we'll cover in the following sections in turn.

General Settings

The General tab of the Windows Firewall Settings dialog box allows you to control the overall capability of the firewall functionality, determining whether security is enabled or disabled or is in a higher awareness state where it further blocks all incoming connections, with no exceptions from the exceptions list.

Figure 27-2 shows the default state where the Windows Firewall is enabled but all exceptions are permitted.

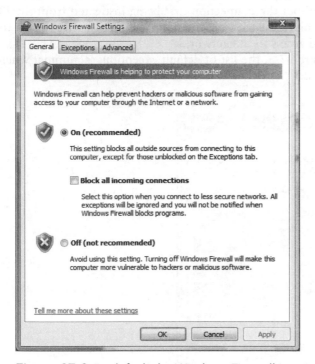

Figure 27-2 *By default the Windows Firewall is switched on with exceptions allowed.*

If you are connecting your PC to a public network and you are unsure of the security or protection offered on that network, such as in an airport wireless hotspot or a fixed Ethernet connection in a hotel room, you should temporarily block all incoming connections. In doing so, you'll find that some of your previously happy applications might not work; however, your system will be better protected from network-bound threats.

If you need to switch the firewall off for some reason, possibly to troubleshoot a networking or an application problem, you can select the Off radio button and then click Apply.

> **NOTE** To make sure you remain as secure and protected as possible, Vista will notify you when the firewall is switched off and will plant an icon in the system tray to keep reminding you when it's not switched back on again. Notice also that the once green and pleasant-looking banner at the top of the dialog box has turned red and that the once serene green shield is now red with a white *x* denoting danger.

Exceptions

By default, the Windows Firewall blocks all incoming connection requests to your computer. This probably sounds like the most secure way to operate, and it is; however, sometimes this barrier prevents certain functionality that you require from actually working. A good example is when a Media Center extender requests some multimedia from Vista without the connection first being instigated from the PC. In this case, you'll need to unblock the Media Center application or network port to give that application unfettered access to the network.

As you can see in Figure 27-3, the list of default exceptions is minimal when you first start configuring Vista.

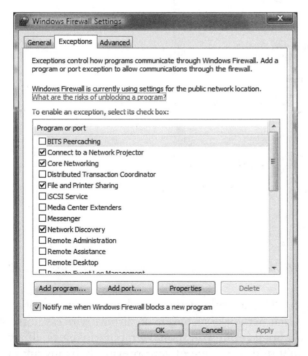

Figure 27-3 *Only a few firewall exceptions are enabled by default.*

> **NOTE** Two kinds of exceptions exist: application exceptions and port exceptions. Where possible, you should create application exceptions because they are more specific and harder to break. Port exceptions, on the other hand, open a hole in the firewall's defenses that remains permanent even when the application you wanted to use it for no longer requires the connection. If you open a port, try to remember to close it again when you no longer require it.

If an application requires you to set an exception, you can create the exception either for the application name (more secure) or for the networking port that application wants to use to access the network (less secure). The problem you'll find, however, is that many applications access the network using a random port, and an exception cannot be mapped in this way. If this is the case, you'll have no option but to use application exceptions.

If the application exception has already been defined, such as with Media Center extenders, it's a simple matter of selecting the checkbox and clicking Apply. If you need to create a new exception, click either Add Program or Add Port.

Clicking Add Program opens the Add a Program dialog box where you must highlight the application you want to permit, as shown in Figure 27-4.

Figure 27-4 *You select applications in the Programs list.*

> **NOTE** When you've highlighted a program you want to create an exception for, click Change Scope. The *scope* is the range of systems that can exploit this exception. By default, an exception is granted to all computers, including ones on the Internet. Other more secure options are My Network (Subnet) Only, where the exception applies only to systems with the same subnet mask as yours (more than likely on your own LAN), or a custom list where you specify the IP addresses and subnet mask of permitted systems (using IPv4 or IPv6 addresses).

To find a new application not in the list, click Browse, and locate the application on the file system.

When you have added the application, click OK, and then select the box next to the application name. Click Apply to process the exception.

If you need to add a port exception, click Add Port. You'll see the screen shown in Figure 27-5.

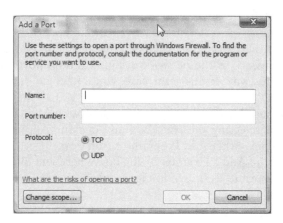

Figure 27-5 *Port exceptions require a name, port number, and protocol definition.*

You'll need to name the protocol or application you are creating the exception for, configure the port number (the application specification should tell you this), and inform Vista which of the two IP protocols are being used: TCP or UDP.

Many ports are already defined and reserved for specific applications and protocols, so for a full list of what has been adopted as the industry standard, take a look at http://www.iana.org/assignments/port-numbers.

Advanced Settings

Frankly, Advanced Settings is a bit of a misnomer here. If you click Advanced Settings, you'll see why. This is where you can be more granular in your approach to which network connections use the firewall and which don't. If you don't want a specific connection to use the firewall, simply deselect the checkbox, and click Apply. To reinstate the firewall on a connection, reselect the checkbox, and click Apply.

Using the Windows Firewall with Advanced Security

The Windows Firewall with Advanced Security is fully integrated with the standard Windows Firewall we've been covering so far. Nevertheless, this new addition to Vista is much more functionally rich and sophisticated than what you've seen so far. Any changes made in the Windows Firewall are reflected and upheld in the Windows Firewall with Advanced Security, and similarly, any changes made in the Windows Firewall with Advanced Security are carried across into the Windows Firewall, if there is an appropriate correlation. Make no mistake, though; they are different products and have different uses. The Windows Firewall with Advanced Security is not for the fainthearted, so continue only if you are sure you know what you are doing.

To start the Windows Firewall with Advanced Security, click the Start button, select Control Panel, click the System and Maintenance category, and then select the Administrative Tools category. When you see the Administrative Tools list, double-click Windows Firewall with Advanced Security. This will open the configuration interface shown in Figure 27-6.

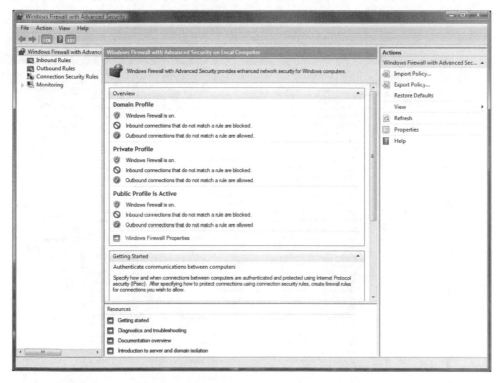

Figure 27-6 *Use Windows Firewall with Advanced Security for sophisticated security policies.*

The basic features of the standard Windows Firewall are extended to introduce more granular bidirectional control over security policies that can be enforced at the local and domain levels.

You can create policies pertaining to the control of users and computers akin to many enterprise-ready firewalls, and you can set the system to extensively audit firewall traffic and alert you about attacks or anomalies.

> **TIP** If you want to start automating Windows Firewall with Advanced Security settings from the command line—in a batch file, for example—you can use the `netsh firewall` command. For more information about this command, check the command-line help or search `http://www.microsoft.com`.

Inbound and Outbound Rules

Inbound rules define how the firewall handles inward-bound connections. Click the Inbound Rules node in the top left of the interface to see a list of rules, as applied to your system currently. These rules, by and large, mirror the exceptions list you saw when configuring the standard Windows Firewall. In the example highlighted in Figure 27-7, you'll see that the Media Center Extenders exception is not enabled here; however, in this case, you can exploit seven different rules to better configure the connection if they are required.

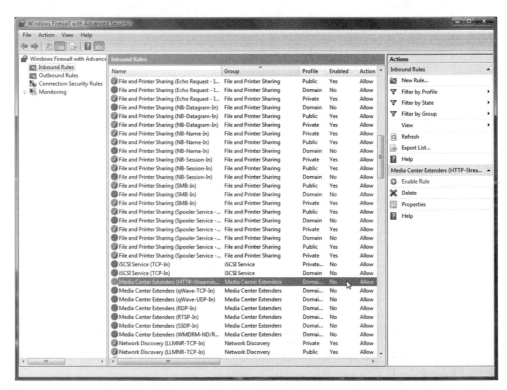

Figure 27-7 *Inbound rules tend to mirror the exceptions list used in the standard firewall.*

Outbound rules (listed immediately beneath the Inbound Rules node) are rules that apply to an application on your local computer trying to access the network, be it a local network or the Internet. This rule set is *not* mirrored in the standard Windows Firewall and is a new line of defense for Vista.

Double-clicking any rule, be it inbound or outbound, will show you the details of what that rule will do and how configurable it is, as shown in Figure 27-8.

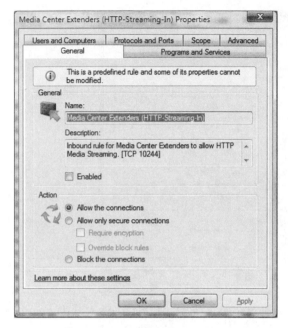

Figure 27-8 *Rules are configured to scope what's permitted or denied from a port or application.*

To create a new rule, be it inbound or outbound, right-click the appropriate node on the left side of the screen, and select New Rule.

This dialog box has six tabs to consider when creating a new rule.

Rules: The General Tab

Selecting Enabled will activate this rule. If you subsequently select Allow the Connections, all connections that apply to this rule, regardless of whether they are secured using IPSec, are permitted. Allow Only Secure Connections will block connections that meet the criteria unless they are also protected using IPSec. Choosing Require Encryption forces all connections to apply encryption using the Data Protection settings defined on the IPSec Settings tab. Override Block Rules, also known as *authenticated bypass*, allows you to override specific blocking rules if the connection is presented with appropriate credentials, based on a computer or group being specified on the Users and Computers tab.

Rules: The Programs and Services Tab

You can specify, using this tab, how the Windows Firewall with Advanced Security maps programs (specified by application name and path) or services to network services; then when it gets a match, the firewall takes the action on the General tab. Figure 27-9 shows an example of the service settings.

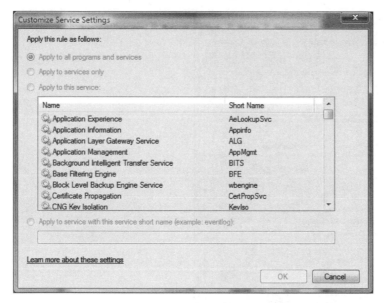

Figure 27-9 *Services that are exploited as a result of this rule's criteria being met*

Rules: The Users and Computers Tab

The Users and Computers tab contains two boxes, one for authorized computers and one for authorized users, as shown in Figure 27-10. Authorized computers and authorized users are essentially accounts that are members of a domain-based Active Directory database. These settings are not applicable in a Windows workgroup scenario.

Figure 27-10 *Add domain computers or user accounts that will be used to enforce rules upon.*

Rules: The Protocols and Ports Tab

Specifying a custom protocol by its protocol number is possible using any standard protocol definition described by the Internet Assigned Numbers Authority (IANA). A *local* port is a port on a computer where the firewall profile has been applied—in most home computer scenarios, this is the local machine.

A *remote* port is a port on a computer trying to communicate with the local computer (the one where the profile has been applied).

Figure 27-11 shows the Protocols and Ports tab.

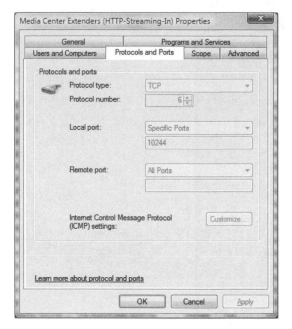

Figure 27-11 *Configure protocols and ports that are affected by the firewall rule.*

Internet Control Message Protocol (ICMP) settings allow you to determine how the firewall rule handles ICMP messages, breaking down the overarching set into constituent protocol numbers.

Rules: The Scope Tab

The *scope*, as with the standard Windows Firewall, defines the range of IP addresses to which the rule applies. In this way, you can limit the reach of the rule to specific IP addresses either locally or remote to your systems.

Rules: The Advanced Tab

The Advanced tab allows you to select which firewall profile the rule will be applied against, choosing from All Profiles or These Profiles, where These Profiles contains a check list of available profiles on your system.

You can select Customize next to Interface Types to change the way the rule is applied on each of your network interface types, such as for wireless, remote access, or a local area network.

Connection Security Rules

Connection security rules force a bilateral authentication between systems before a connection can be established. When you create a connection security rule, you have to complete the following procedure:

1. Right-click Connection Security Rules, and then select New Rule. This opens the New Connection Security Rule Wizard, as shown in Figure 27-12.

2. The next step is to select the rule type. *Isolation* rules are used to restrict connections. *Authentication exemption* rules negate the need for security between cited systems. *Server-to-server* rules specify the security rules to be used between two fixed systems on your network. A *tunnel* rule is used when the security is enforced over a virtual private network (VPN) or IPSec Layer Two Tunneling Protocol (L2TP) connection. You can define *custom* rules to perform any combination of these checks. When you're ready, click Next.

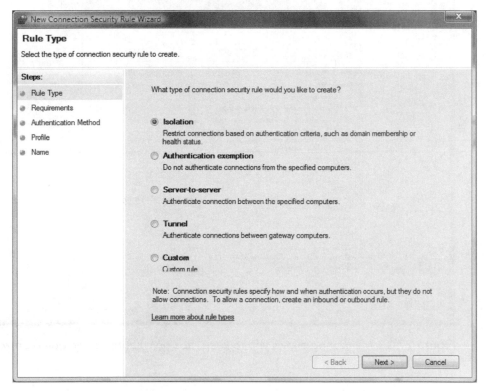

Figure 27-12 *Use the New Connection Security Rule Wizard to create a new rule.*

3. Then you must specify the requirements for when you want the rule exercised. You can opt to ask for authentication if possible, enforce authentication at all times (denying the connection when authentication is not possible), and enforce inbound authentication while being more slack on outgoing. When you're done, click Next.

4. The next screen shows the authentication method you will use. Select the one that best suits your environment and obviously what's possible with the technology you employ. For example, Kerberos 5 is not possible without a domain environment being present. When you're ready, click Next.

5. Finally, give the security rule and meaningful name, and then click Finish.

Monitoring

Monitoring is extremely useful if you want to see what has been hitting your firewall, what connection attempts have been thwarted, and what sort of activity, malignant or benign, you are experiencing over time. Figure 27-13 shows an example of what the Monitoring screen looks like.

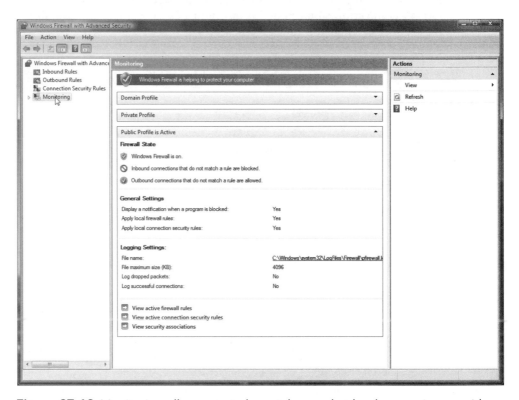

Figure 27-13 *Monitoring allows you to keep tabs on what has been going on with your connections.*

The three monitoring sections that are applicable to each of the three firewall profiles are Domain, Private, and Public.

The Domain profile is used when Vista is a member of a Windows server domain. The Private profile is used when Vista is not connected to a corporate domain; instead, it is connected to a private network, such as in your home. The Public profile is used when you are using your system on an untrusted network, such as in a wireless hotspot at an airport.

Configuring Profiles

Configuring the firewall profiles is easy and quite straightforward compared to the previously covered inbound, outbound, and security rule creation. Referring to the top-level Windows Firewall with Advanced Security screen shown in Figure 27-6, click Windows Firewall Properties. This opens the Windows Firewall with Advanced Security on Local Computer dialog box, as shown in Figure 27-14.

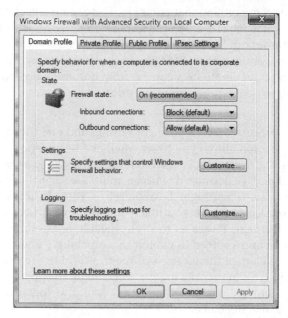

Figure 27-14 *Configure a profile to behave appropriately in each networked environment.*

The dialog box has four tabs, allowing you to configure each of the following profiles and settings:

- The Domain Profile tab is for configuring how the firewall behaves in a Windows Server–based domain environment.

- The Private Profile tab allows you to set a different method of operation for the firewall when it's connected outside the domain environment yet still on a network you trust, such as your home LAN.

- The Public Profile tab describes how the firewall reacts when you are connected to a public access network, such as in an airport or a hotel room.

- The IPSec Settings tab specifies how Vista reacts in a situation where IPSec is needed to communicate over the network to other systems.

You can set the firewall state in each case to Off, although by default it is set to On (recommended). Selecting Block (default), next to Inbound Connections, blocks all connection requests except for those specifically excluded, and selecting Block All Connections will ignore exceptions and block everything. The Allow setting allows everything to connect through the firewall.

> **TIP** Using the Allow setting in a profile still allows you to monitor what's going on through the firewall, but instead of proactively blocking connection requests, it will let them pass through, logging everything that comes in. This can be a useful security measure since you can watch what the bad guys are up to and obtain better evidence of what they are targeting. So-called honeypot systems attract hackers with what seems like an open system where in fact the hacker is monitored, getting more and more information about where he's coming from before finally raising the defenses again, just as the police break down his door.

Each profile also has two Customize buttons, one for settings and one for logging. Clicking the Settings Customize button allows you to set whether a notification will be displayed when the firewall successfully blocks an inbound connection, as well as defines whether a unicast response is permitted when a multicast or broadcast IP packet is received on the interface. This might be required if you are using your computer to pick up digital broadcasts where you might be obtaining a license as a result of hooking into the digital stream. This is set to Yes by default, but in some cases, this may be switched off if you will never need to exploit this capability. The Logging Customize button permits you to change the location of the firewall log file, increase its size from the default 4096KB, set whether the log file will contain dropped packets (of which there will be loads), and set whether the log file will also log successful connections (of which there will also be loads).

The IPSec Settings tab allows you to customize the method by which IPSec negotiates its security (clicking the Customize button), whereby you can select the different encryption and key exchange algorithms used in connections and define the authentication methods used between computers. These are extremely advanced settings and are applicable only if you are in a domain environment. A network security administrator would set these via a policy.

CHAPTER 28

Using Windows Defender

Spyware, malware, viruses, and annoyware (our term) are an increasingly prevalent problem these days. Traditionally, Microsoft has relied on the third-party vendor ecosystem to produce products that counteract these inconveniences and threats, but Microsoft has now determined that it's in its best interest to address the problems itself.

So emerges a product called Windows Defender, which we will explore in the pages to come.

What Is Spyware?

The parliament of Victoria, Australia, defines spyware as follows:

> *A general term for a class of software that monitors the actions of a computer user. This software falls into a number of categories: Software that may be installed legitimately to provide security or workplace monitoring, software with relatively benign purposes that may be associated with marketing data collection and software that is maliciously installed, either as a general violation of a user's privacy or to collect information to allow further attacks on their computer or online transactions (e.g. "keylogging" to gain passwords).*

That sounds like a typical government definition, yes? A few other various definitions get a bit more granular into what actions the nasty code tries to take. Note the following:

Adware: Subjects a user to unwanted advertising

Spyware: Monitors a user's online activities and reports to a central marketing source

Scumware: Adds advertising links to Web pages without the creator's consent and/ or without paying the creator or host

Browser hijackers: Changes browser preferences, like the default home page and preferred search engine, to ad-laden sites and prevents the user from reverting to previous settings

Generally, we can all agree that *malware*, the overarching term to describe all this nasty code, permanently opens certain security holes and vulnerabilities for future use; is typically very badly written, causing serious performance issues; and doesn't have a facility to uninstall it. Most of the time, malware also leaves a distributed footprint, which makes manual removal difficult to complete.

Introducing Windows Defender

Windows Defender detects and removes all the unwanted code described in the previous section. Windows Defender protects your computer against the source of aggravating symptoms such as deteriorating system responsiveness, pop-up ads, Internet settings modification by unauthorized software, and the lifting of your personal and confidential information. Windows Defender was developed around the core of an older product called GIANT AntiSpyware, which was originally manufactured by GIANT Company Software. Microsoft acquired GIANT on December 16, 2004. Although the original GIANT product supported older versions of Windows, support for the non-NT-based Windows versions was eliminated in beta versions of the newer product.

Windows Defender offers several benefits for you:

- Windows Defender scans for spyware, adware, and other malware on your computer, either on-demand or on a certain schedule you set.

- You can configure Windows Defender to automatically remove or quarantine malware it finds during its scans, taking the burden off you.

- Windows Defender actively protects against spyware and nefarious software by notifying you whether potentially harmful software tries to install itself and guides you into making good decisions about what to do next.

- The software updates itself automatically on a regular basis.

Getting Real-Time Protection

Real-time protection (RTP) monitors critical system areas that are changed when programs modify your Windows configuration. These modifications either are legitimate, occurring as a result of programs you want installed, or are a result of malware that has infiltrated your machine and is attempting to install itself. When RTP sees a change in these system areas, Windows Defender pops up on your screen, prompting you to choose whether to allow or block the change. If you recognize the program that is making the changes, you can allow the modification to take place; you also have the chance to block spyware from getting a foothold in your system.

RTP monitors the following areas of your system:

Auto Start: RTP looks at services or programs that try to start automatically when the system boots. Often malware tries to start at boot so it can breach your privacy without making itself obvious to you.

System configuration (settings): RTP monitors software that tries to read or change your system's settings, particularly in terms of the security configuration. Malware will sometimes try to adjust the security configuration of your machine to gain a stronger foothold into it.

Internet Explorer add-ons: RTP detects software trying to add itself to Internet Explorer. Typically, nefarious software disguises itself as a browser extension, tempting you to install it to improve your browser experience.

Internet Explorer configurations (settings): RTP detects browser security settings. Even the most basic forms of spyware will attempt to change these settings and install various unwanted pieces of code and processes on your system.

Internet Explorer downloads: RTP monitors ActiveX controls and other software that is designed to run within Internet Explorer itself. Spyware often uses Internet Explorer as a transmission vector into your system.

Services and drivers: RTP looks for unwanted code trying to register itself as a background service or hardware driver. Malware will often try to plant itself in the background, and since these areas typically run without a lot of operating system supervision, spyware will typically hide as a service or driver.

Application execution: RTP monitors programs that load, watching for additional activity that's unrelated to the core application. Sometimes, malware will bundle itself with a regular program that could be considered legitimate and then execute itself when the program on which it is piggybacking begins running.

Application registration: RTP looks for code that tries to schedule its own execution at certain times within the day. Some malware tries to hide its execution by telling Windows to run it late at night or very early in the morning, when you aren't around to witness its signs of life.

Windows add-ons: RTP tries to detect add-ons to Windows that could pose a danger to your system's stability or integrity.

Using Windows Defender

The user interface of Windows Defender is quite simple. To open it, type **Windows Defender** in the search area of the Start menu, and click the result. You'll see the basic interface shown in Figure 28-1.

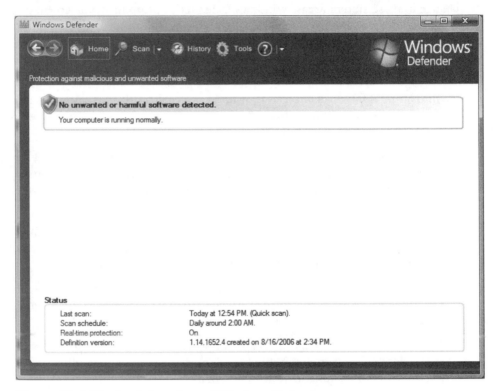

Figure 28-1 *The basic interface of Windows Defender*

To perform a scan manually, click the Scan button at the top of the window. If you simply click the button, Windows Defender will perform a quick scan over various "hotspots" in your system. Click the arrow beside Scan to choose a full system scan, which (as you might expect) will take longer, or a custom scan of drives, volumes, files, and folders that you select.

The History button shows you a list of the items Windows Defender has detected in the past and the actions you chose to take at the time, as shown in Figure 28-2. You can filter the list it displays by clicking either the Allowed Items link or the Quarantined Items link.

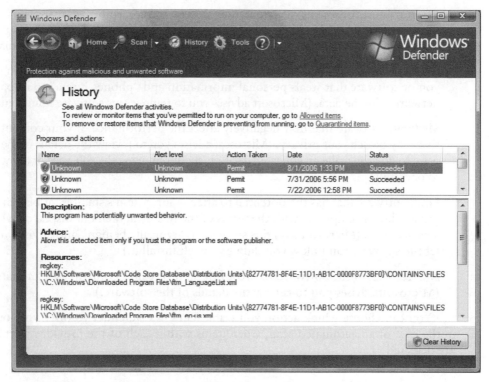

Figure 28-2 *The Windows Defender history list*

Configuring Options

Windows Defender includes a number of options that you can configure to make the program operate as you want. To access the options, click the Tools menu, and then choose the Options link.

First, in the Automatic Scanning section, which is shown in Figure 28-3, you can elect to have Windows Defender automatically scan your system for malware on a regular schedule. You can choose the frequency of the automated scan, the approximate time the scan will commence, and the depth of the scan (a quick scan or a full system scan). You can also have Windows Defender check for updated definitions before starting the scan and apply default actions to any suspicious malware items it finds during the automatic scan.

Next, in the Default Actions section, which is also shown in Figure 28-3, you can set what action Windows Defender takes when it encounters a suspicious process, service, or program. You can categorize the actions based on the level of the alert, which are delineated as follows:

Severe: Viruses or worms that are known to exist and are confirmed malware, which can pose a substantial risk to your system and other machines that are accessible to you on your network. (Microsoft advises you to remove this software immediately.)

High: Software that makes changes to your system without confirming them with you or software that steals personal information and "phones home" to its parent network with the data. (Microsoft advises you to remove this software immediately.)

Medium: Software that may negatively affect the performance of your computer or that may breach your privacy. (Microsoft advises you to review the details of the software so you can make an educated decision about removing the software or allowing it to operate.)

Low: Software that has the potential to affect your system's stability or breach your privacy but is complying with the terms of the license agreement displayed when it was installed. (Microsoft says this software is "typically benign" and advises you to let the software run unless you didn't yourself install it.)

Not Yet Classified: Software Microsoft hasn't, or can't, confirm as legitimate. (Microsoft advises you to review the details of the software.)

You can choose which action you want Windows Defender to offer you, or take in the case of an automated scan, when items within each of the previous alert levels are detected.

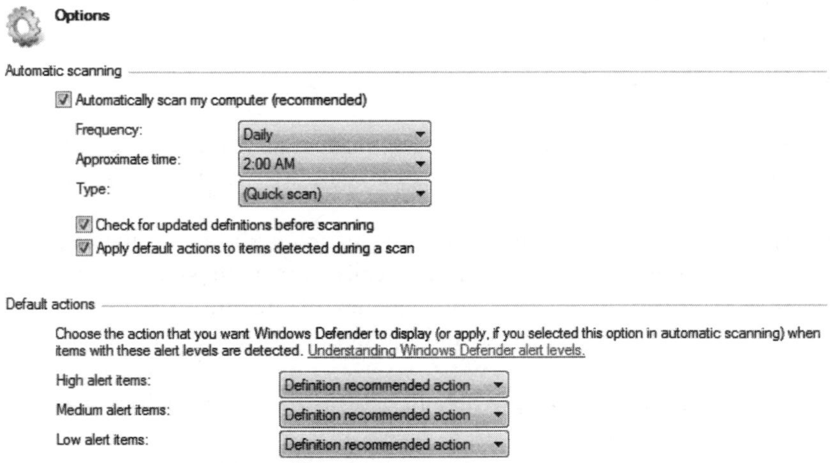

Figure 28-3 *Configuring Windows Defender options, part one*

| **NOTE** Figure 28-3 doesn't show the Severe, Low, and Not Yet Classified alert levels.

After this, you come across the real-time protection options, where you can choose how the RTP functionality of Windows Defender operates. Security agents run in the background and, as you know, monitor critical areas of the system. You can choose which areas of the system these agents monitor, including automatic start-up items, system configuration items, Internet Explorer add-ons, settings, downloads, service and driver installations, application execution or registration with the system, and Windows add-on software. You can also elect to have Windows Defender prompt you if it detects software that has not yet been classified or if it detects that software you've permitted to run makes changes to your system. You can also choose to hide the software's icon in the system tray unless an action requires your attention. Figure 28-4 shows this section.

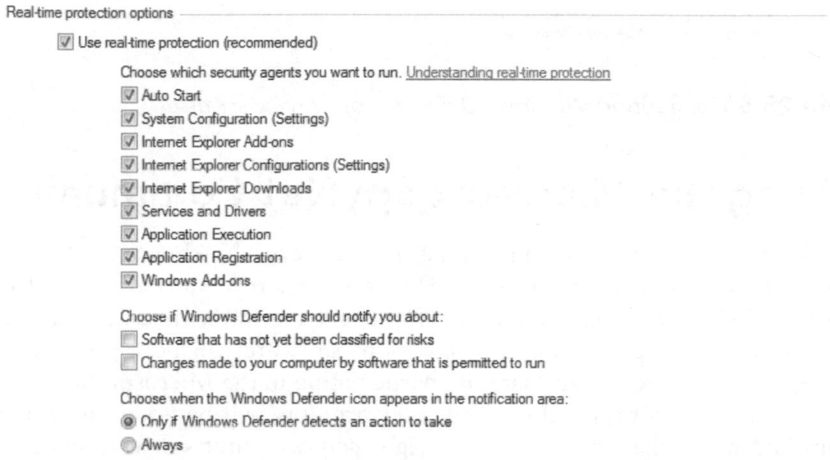

Real-time protection options
☑ Use real-time protection (recommended)

Choose which security agents you want to run. Understanding real-time protection
☑ Auto Start
☑ System Configuration (Settings)
☑ Internet Explorer Add-ons
☑ Internet Explorer Configurations (Settings)
☑ Internet Explorer Downloads
☑ Services and Drivers
☑ Application Execution
☑ Application Registration
☑ Windows Add-ons

Choose if Windows Defender should notify you about:
☐ Software that has not yet been classified for risks
☐ Changes made to your computer by software that is permitted to run

Choose when the Windows Defender icon appears in the notification area:
◉ Only if Windows Defender detects an action to take
○ Always

Figure 28-4 *Configuring Windows Defender options, part two*

Next, head to the Advanced Options section, as shown in Figure 28-5; you can choose to have Windows Defender scan archived files and folders (such as ZIP files) for malware, to use heuristics to try to detect potentially unwanted activity on your system, and to create a system restore point before taking actions on items it detects. You can also add certain locations that Windows Defender will ignore during its scans.

Finally, you arrive at the Administrator Options section, also shown in Figure 28-5; this is where administrators can enable or disable Windows Defender, or they can allow users without administrative rights to use Windows Defender as well.

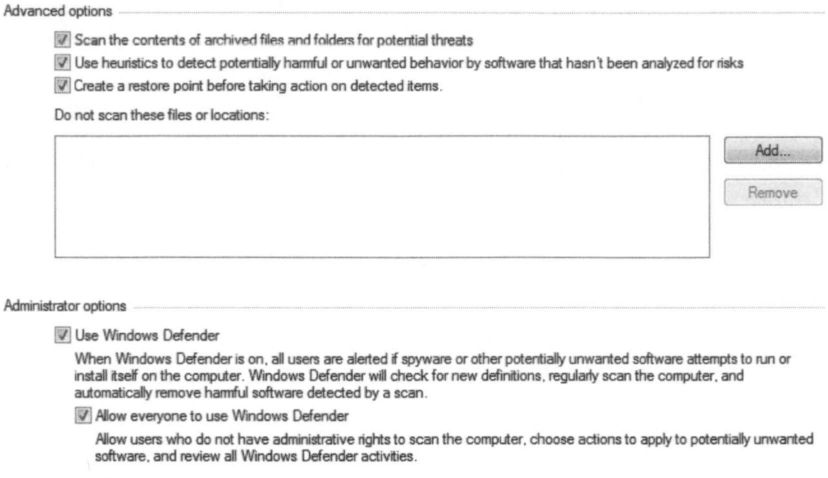

Advanced options

☑ Scan the contents of archived files and folders for potential threats
☑ Use heuristics to detect potentially harmful or unwanted behavior by software that hasn't been analyzed for risks
☑ Create a restore point before taking action on detected items.

Do not scan these files or locations:

[Add...]
[Remove]

Administrator options

☑ Use Windows Defender

When Windows Defender is on, all users are alerted if spyware or other potentially unwanted software attempts to run or install itself on the computer. Windows Defender will check for new definitions, regularly scan the computer, and automatically remove harmful software detected by a scan.

☑ Allow everyone to use Windows Defender

Allow users who do not have administrative rights to scan the computer, choose actions to apply to potentially unwanted software, and review all Windows Defender activities.

Figure 28-5 *Configuring Windows Defender options, part three*

Joining the Microsoft SpyNet Community

The Microsoft SpyNet community is a group of users who choose to share how they respond to Windows Defender alerts. The premise is this: since not all software that Windows Defender thinks is spyware is indeed malware, measuring an aggregate group response to certain identical pieces of software can be a good indicator of whether that software is legitimate. By participating in the Microsoft SpyNet community, your responses to Windows Defender prompts will be added to the aggregate ratings and help other users make the right choices about software installations on their machines. Users can see community ratings by viewing the bar graph of the proportion of users who have allowed items in question.

Microsoft also uses the SpyNet ratings to choose which software to officially evaluate and include in later Windows Defender definition updates. These definitions are like antivirus updates, in that they contain signatures unique to individual pieces of code that make detecting when such code is present on a system easy. In addition to identifying certain pieces of code that are unique to specific software, the definitions include code that is representative of different programmatic techniques that malware uses to attach itself to and infiltrate your system; in this way, even if Windows Defender doesn't recognize the specific malware it finds on your system, it can detect that it is likely software you'll want to block because of its behavior.

To join Microsoft SpyNet, from within Windows Defender, click the Tools menu, and then click the Microsoft SpyNet link. You'll see the screen in Figure 28-6 appear. Choose whether to join the community with a basic membership, which sends basic information about the software that Windows Defender detects and the actions you choose to take with it, or an advanced membership, which sends more details—including possibly some personal information—to help Microsoft reclassify software and update its definitions. Or you can officially decline membership in SpyNet by clicking the third option. You can also change your mind at any time.

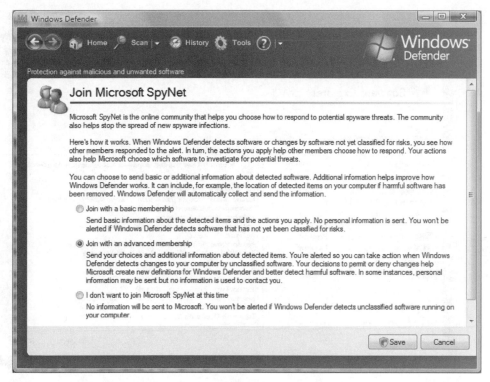

Figure 28-6 *Joining the Microsoft SpyNet community*

Using Software Explorer

Software Explorer gives you an in-depth view of running programs and processes on your computer. Although Task Manager will give you a simple listing of programs and the various properties of their sessions, Software Explorer will delve into the details of the programs and services themselves, revealing their publishers and origins and giving you easy access to enable or disable their automatic start-up.

To access Software Explorer, go to Tools, and then click Software Explorer from the menu that appears. You may have to acknowledge a User Account Control (UAC) prompt. After doing so, you'll see the interface shown in Figure 28-7.

Software Explorer sorts and displays programs in certain categories. The Category drop-down list is in the middle of the screen. You can choose from Startup Programs, Currently Running Programs, Network Connected Programs, and Winsock Service Providers.

Figure 28-7 *The Software Explorer interface*

In the Details pane, you can see relevant properties of the selected program, including the following:

Auto Start: Details whether the program loads automatically upon Windows booting on the system

Startup Type: Shows what part of Windows invokes the autostart functionality: via the registry, the Startup folder on the Start menu, or somewhere else

Ships with OS: Indicates whether the program comes with Windows Vista on the CD or DVD or whether it is distributed separately

Classification: Details whether the program has been vetted by Microsoft to make sure it doesn't sacrifice the privacy or integrity of your computer

SpyNet Voting: Indicates whether voting using the SpyNet community voting mechanism is permitted and, if so, what the current rating is

Digitally Signed By: Shows whether a piece of software has been signed, and, if so, who signed it

When viewing selected programs, the buttons at the bottom of the Software Explorer change to show the supported procedures for each selection. When viewing programs that load at start-up, you can click the Remove button to remove the program from your system, the Disable button to kill the start-up functionality of the program, or the Enable button to allow a previously disabled program to start. When viewing a currently running program, you can click the Task Manager button or click the End Process button to kill that process's session. Finally, when viewing a network-connected program, you can click the End Process button, and you can also click the Block Connection button to enable a packet filter that kills that process's access to the network.

CHAPTER 29

Best Practices: A Six-Step Guide to Better Security

Security is a large and complex topic, and it changes every time Windows is revised. In this chapter, we'll present six very effective steps you can take to increase security on your Windows Vista system.

Step 1: Strengthen Your Password Policy

It's arguable but completely believable that passwords are the weakest link in any security system. With more powerful computers working at faster speeds, what used to be a nearly impossible task—password cracking—has now become not quite trivial but indeed much simpler. So, it's always important that your users choose good passwords that will cause difficulty to automated cracker programs.

Of course, you can't teach old dogs new tricks, which is why you sometimes need to force your users, or yourself, into compliance. Here are several suggestions for a stringent policy that won't cause an uprising among your users:

Maximum password age: 90 days. This forces your users to change to a unique password every given interval. If you set this for too long of an interval, an attacker has an increased chance of obtaining a current password, but if you set it for too short of an interval, you'll waste your security budget answering complaints about why your users have to change their passwords again. It also increases the chance of passwords on sticky notes attached to monitors, and you know that isn't good.

Minimum password age: one day. Clever users may discover that, without this setting, they can circumvent the password-age requirement by changing their password as mandated by the policy and then immediately changing the password back to their preferred phrase. Using this option requires the user to keep the changed password for at least one day before changing it back.

Minimum password length: eight characters. It's easy to compute the probability that a three-letter password could be guessed in fewer permutations (and thus more rapidly) than a longer password. This is a surprisingly effective front against persistent password-cracking attempts.

Enforce password history: five passwords. Windows will store a list of a user's previous passwords in the registry. Setting this option prevents the person from alternating between two common passwords, thereby forcing them to be creative and not reuse old passwords that may have been cracked.

Account lockout: locks after five failed attempts; resets counter after ten minutes. Hackers can use software that attempts "brute-force" attacks on user accounts, using a list of common passwords and a dictionary to attempt to crack an account over and over again. The lockout feature disables an account after a given number of attempts with failed passwords. The feature also includes a counter that resets the number of attempts.

Lockout duration: 15 minutes. This option goes hand in hand with the previous configuration. The lockout duration feature resets accounts disabled by the account lockout feature. It's important to remember the fundamental economic concept that idle users equal lost money. In a small business, this isn't as much of an issue, because the administrator is usually available for five minutes to unlock a disabled account, but in organizations with thousands of sloppy typists, it can make for a large help-desk budget. Use this with caution.

You can find the password policy and account lockout policy by opening the Group Policy Object Editor. Click the Start menu, type **gpedit.msc**, acknowledge the UAC prompt, and then navigate through Computer Configuration, Windows Settings, Security Settings, and Account Policies. Figure 29-1 shows the screen.

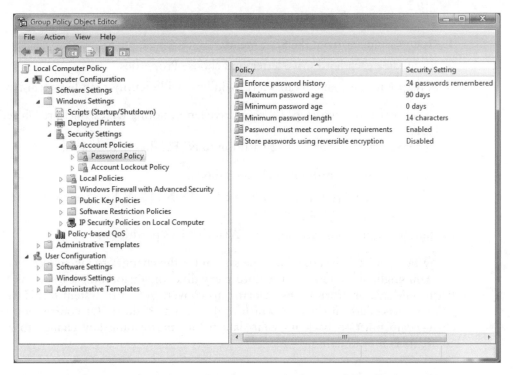

Figure 29-1 *Setting the password and account lockout policies for a machine*

Step 2: Use or Convert Drives to NTFS

Part of hardening your overall Windows Vista system is to ensure that your file system is adequately secured. Microsoft provides NT File System (NTFS) support in Windows Vista. NTFS allows for more robust security features and user permissions and also adds some basic fault tolerance with which the older FAT file system just cannot compete. Make sure all of your hard drives are formatted with NTFS unless you have systems that dual-boot to another, older operating system that doesn't support NTFS on the same disk.

To check your hard drive partitions, do the following:

1. Open Computer from the Start menu.
2. Right-click each hard drive letter, and choose Properties.
3. Navigate to the General tab. Here, Windows will identify the file system type.

Follow the previous steps for each drive letter, noting which ones are labeled FAT or FAT32.

To convert a FAT or FAT32 partition to NTFS, do the following:

1. Open a command prompt in elevated mode.
2. At the command prompt, enter **convert** *x*: **/FS:NTFS /V**. Replace *x* with one of the drive letters you noted previously.
3. Repeat the previous step for each FAT or FAT32 partition.

When you're finished, reboot the system for the changes to take effect.

You might also choose to use third-party disk conversion utilities, such as Norton PartitionMagic or Norton Disk Doctor, to convert your file system to NTFS. It's a painless procedure, no matter which tool you use to do it. Of course, you should always remember to back up your data before performing any change to a disk's configuration or function.

Step 3: Understand and Use File System Security

One of the most dreaded and tedious but most necessary tasks of system administration is setting file and folder-level permissions, which are significant in protecting data from unauthorized use on your network.

Windows Vista, among other Microsoft operating systems, supports two kinds of permissions: standard and special. *Standard* permissions are often sufficient for files and folders on a disk, whereas *special* permissions break standard permissions down into finer combinations and allow more control over who is allowed to do what functions to an object on a disk. Table 29-1 describes the standard permissions available in Windows Vista.

Table 29-1 Windows Vista Standard Permissions

Type	Description
Read (R)	Allows a user or group to read the file.
Write (W)	Allows a user or group to write to the contents of a file or folder and also create new files and folders.
Read and execute (RX)	Allows a user or group to read attributes of a file or folder, view its contents, and read files within a folder. Files inside folders with RX rights inherit the right onto themselves.
List folder contents (L)	Similar to RX, but files within a folder with L rights will not inherit RX rights. New files, however, automatically get RX permissions.
Modify (M)	Allows a user or group to read, write, execute, and delete files, programs, and folders.
Full control (F)	Similar to M but also allows a user or group to take ownership and change permissions. Users or groups can delete files and subfolders within a folder if F rights are applied to that folder.

You should understand the following key points about how permissions work:

- First, file permissions always take precedence over folder permissions. If a user can execute a program in a folder, he can do so even if he doesn't have RX permissions on the folder in which that program resides. Similarly, a user can read a file for which he explicitly has permission, even if that file is in a folder for which he has no permission, by simply knowing the location of that file. For example, you can hide a file listing employee Social Security numbers in a protected folder in Payroll to which user James Smith has no folder permissions. However, if you explicitly give James R rights on that file, then by knowing the full path to the file, he can open the file from a command line or from the Run command on the Start menu.

- Second, permissions are cumulative: they "add up" based on the overall permissions a user gets as a result of his total group memberships. Deny permissions *always* trump Allow permissions. This applies even if a user is added to a group that is denied access to a file or folder that the user was previously allowed to access through his other memberships.

Windows Vista offers 14 default special permissions, shown in Table 29-2. The table also shows how these default special permissions correlate to the standard permissions discussed earlier.

Table 29-2 Windows Vista Special Permissions

Special Permission	R	W	RX	L	M	F
Traverse Folder/Execute File			×	×	×	×
List Folder/Read Data	×		×	×	×	×
Read Attributes	×		×	×	×	×
Read Extended Attributes	×		×	×	×	×
Create Files/Write Data		×			×	×
Create Folders/Append Data		×			×	×
Write Attributes		×			×	×
Write Extended Attributes		×			×	×
Delete Subfolders and Files						×
Delete					×	×
Read Permissions	×		×	×	×	×
Change Permissions						×
Take Ownership						×

The default special permissions are further described in the following list:

Traverse Folder/Execute File: Traverse Folder indicates the ability to access a folder nested within a tree even if parent folders in that tree deny a user access to the contents of those folders. Execute File indicates the ability to run a program.

List Folder/Read Data: List Folder indicates the ability to see file and folder names within a folder, and Read Data indicates the ability to open and view a file.

Read Attributes: This indicates the ability to view basic attributes of an object (read-only, system, archive, and hidden).

Read Extended Attributes: This indicates the ability to view the extended attributes of an object—for example, summary, author, title, and so on, for a Microsoft Word document. These attributes will vary from program to program.

Create Files/Write Data: Create Files indicates the ability to create new objects within a folder; Write Data lets a user overwrite an existing file. This does *not* allow the user to add data to existing objects in the folder.

Create Folders/Append Data: Create Folders indicates the ability to nest folders. Append Data allows the user to add data to an existing file but not delete data within that file or delete the file itself.

Write Attributes: This allows a change to the basic attributes for a file.

Write Extended Attributes: This allows a change to the extended attributes of a file.

Delete Subfolders and Files: Delete Subfolders and Files allows a user to delete the contents of a folder regardless of whether any individual file or folder within the folder in question explicitly grants or denies the Delete permission to a user.

Delete: This allows you to delete a single file or folder but not other files or folders within that folder.

Read Permissions: This indicates the ability to view NTFS permissions on an object but not to change them.

Change Permissions: This indicates the ability to both view and change NTFS permissions on an object.

Take Ownership: This grants permission to take ownership of a file or folder, which inherently allows the ability to change permissions on an object. This is granted to administrator-level users by default.

To set NTFS permissions on a file or folder in Windows Vista, follow these steps:

1. Navigate to the file or folder on which you want to set permissions.
2. Right-click the file or folder, and select Properties.
3. Navigate to the Security tab.
4. In the top pane, add the users and groups for whom you want to set permissions. Then click each item, and in the bottom pane, grant or disallow the appropriate permissions, as shown in Figure 29-2.

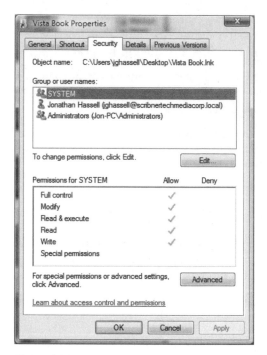

Figure 29-2 *Granting permissions on a folder to a user*

Step 4: Configure the Windows Firewall

It's simply a given that you should install a firewall. If you have a case of "the cheaps," you should use the included Windows Firewall to control access to services running on the machine. It's a simple process to configure the Windows Firewall, and by doing so you harden the exterior interfaces to the machine from public access. To examine and configure your firewall settings, follow these steps:

1. From the Control Panel, click Security.

2. Click Windows Firewall.

Windows Firewall includes the General, Exceptions, and Advanced tabs, which are accessible through the Change Settings link—you'll need to acknowledge a UAC prompt, as you might expect. On the General tab, you can turn the firewall on, choose whether to enable exceptions, or turn the firewall off. If you select Don't Allow Exceptions, the firewall will block all requests to connect to your computer, including requests from programs or services that are listed on the Exceptions tab, which we'll describe in the next paragraph. It will also block both the discovery of network devices and file and printer sharing. You can still, however, browse the network and view web pages as usual, as well as send and receive email or use IM programs.

On the Exceptions tab, you can add program and port exceptions to permit certain types of inbound traffic. You can set a scope for each exception. For example, to add a program, click Add Program, and then select the program you want to except from the list. You can also click the Change Scope button on the exceptions list to allow this program to be unblocked for a range of computers, a single host, or the entire network. Similarly, you can add a port by clicking the Add Port button, entering the name of the protocol and the port number you're allowing, specifying whether the protocol is TCP or UDP, and then clicking OK. You can change the scope of a port exception in the same way as a program exception by clicking the Change Scope button in the Add a Port dialog box.

On the Advanced tab, you can configure connection-specific rules that apply to any network card or virtual interface, the configuration for logging security-related events, the ICMP (ping) acceptance or rejection rules, and a reversion to Windows Vista's default firewall configuration if you've bungled your setup.

Configuring Profiles

In the Windows Firewall first seen in Windows XP Service Pack 2, Microsoft introduced the concept of *profiles*, which are like hardware profiles in that they represent the configuration of the Windows Firewall depending on its current environment and connectivity situation. The Windows Firewall allows for two profiles. The *standard* profile, which is used by default in workgroup environments (that is, XP machines that do not participate in a domain), simply rejects all incoming traffic; the *domain* profile, which is used by default on machines joined to a Windows domain, allows exceptions to be made for inbound and outbound traffic based on services and applications you have installed. The settings in the standard profile are typically more restrictive than the domain profile's settings because you wouldn't have the services and applications necessary to participate in a domain—this profile is great for traveling laptops that connect from hotel rooms, coffee shops, and other wide-open Internet access terminals.

You should ensure that you configure settings for both profiles as soon as possible unless you are not connected to a domain. That way, your security is established from the beginning. You can determine which profile the Windows Firewall is using by opening the command line and running the following command:

```
netsh firewall show currentprofile
```

Configuring Through Group Policy

If you're running Windows Vista in an Active Directory environment, you can configure the Windows Firewall through Group Policy, which is a great way to establish a consistent configuration across all of your systems. If you are deploying your first Windows Vista system, you'll need to run the Group Policy Object Editor from one Windows Vista machine to update the set of Group Policy objects available across your domain—once you do this, you can perform Group Policy configuration from any domain-participating workstation, no matter the operating system.

Step 5: Think About Patching and Update Policies

Chances are that if you are reading this chapter, you are responsible for the security of not only your own system but for others on your network as well. (If that is an unwarranted assumption, feel free to skip to step 6.) Thus, it's important to think about how you handle patches and updates. You probably already have a policy dictating how often hardware gets upgraded, but arguably software updates have much more of an impact on your IT resources. Get smart, and develop a plan today.

But how? What elements make up a good policy? Here are some questions to ask when developing the policy:

What applications are running on your network? Patching is a comprehensive subject, and it requires you to have an extensive inventory of what software is running anywhere on your networking, including operating systems, off-the-shelf third-party applications, software developed in-house, applications running over the Web or on an intranet, and so on. Each piece requires consideration.

Do different departments have different security or hardening requirements? You may have a cluster of client computers in an area handling sensitive information, or you may have a group of computers exposed to an environment with a completely different threat model and vulnerability risk. Larger organizations are more likely to need a compartmentalized approach to patching. How can you address increased security needs in one area while balancing time and resources in other areas? These questions require answers in a complete updating policy.

Do you have equipment, time, and expertise to test patches? If you are a one-person IT department in a small business with 75 to 100 computers, then you probably don't have a lot of available hours to fully test patches, in which case you probably need to simply bite the bullet and install patches as they come—this risk of killing your applications doesn't outweigh problems a virus or worm outbreak will cause. It's easy enough, in a smaller environment, to roll back patches that begin to cause difficulties.

Have you developed a system for evaluating the severity of patches? Will you take Microsoft's word for it? Do you have an environment that differs significantly from a regular environment so that risks are magnified or reduced? These are all issues to consider.

Do you have third-party software protecting against certain threats already? If you have a desktop firewall in place and fully updated antivirus software, perhaps you don't necessarily need to deploy every patch immediately as it becomes available. Perhaps you already have sufficient protection in place, which will buy you some time to evaluate the importance of applying an update.

Once you've determined the scope of your policy, here are some suggested elements to include:

How patches will be approved or declined, or whether they will go through such a process: Who is responsible for the final say on a patch's distribution? What sort of time frame will you allow a patch to be considered? Is there a default decision if no one has any comments on the matter? What group is ultimately responsible for obtaining a patch in a form appropriate for distribution? Or do you simply want to bypass the approval process and allow all patches to come down from the respective manufacturers?

The method for patch distribution: Will you use a Microsoft-provided solution such as Windows Server Update Services? Or do you already have an investment in management software, such as SMS or Altiris products? Are these methods sufficient to comply with the eventually final patch policy, or do you need to adjust your budget to obtain and deploy an additional solution? What sort of client software, if any, is required, and what is the method for deploying that end of the solution?

The frequency and window patches will be applied: What sort of "grace period" does the group with approval responsibility have to act on the patch? What are the ultimate bandwidth and processing requirements for patches, both on the client and server ends? Are there scheduled processes that could affect update distribution and possible reboots to finalize the update? Is this a once-a-month or once-weekly ordeal, or does it take place at some other interval?

How patch rollback will be handled: If you encounter a problematic patch, how will you address those ramifications? Do you schedule backups for target computers just before patches are applied? What sort of service time frame will you promise your end users in case their systems are affected by a misapplied patch? Who is responsible for doing a post-mortem on the patch to make sure such an instance can be avoided in the future?

The procedure for a patch correcting a problem of unusual severity: If you have a zero-day exploit that has massive ramifications for your computers, how do you handle its application? Do you bypass the regular procedures? Who pitches in to help? How do you handle service issues regarding this? Who needs to be informed, how will this happen, and what kind of notice do those stakeholders need?

When the patch policy itself will be reevaluated: It's smart to reconsider these policies on a regular basis—perhaps every six months for the initial period the policy is in effect and then less often after you have successfully implemented it.

Step 6: Audit Sensitive Events

You can modify auditing controls and properties through Group Policy objects (GPOs) in Windows Vista. You can view the policies by opening gpedit.msc as described earlier in this chapter. Navigate through Computer Configuration, Windows Settings, Security Settings, Local Policies, and Audit Policy, as shown in Figure 29-3.

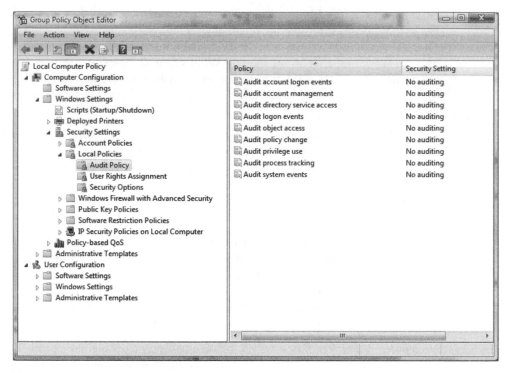

Figure 29-3 *Setting the audit policy for a machine*

The settings for each Group Policy object indicate on what type of events and on what type of result a log entry will be written. The options for auditing policies are outlined here:

- Audit Account Logon Events

- Audit Account Management

- Audit Directory Service Access

- Audit Logon Events

- Audit Object Access

- Audit Policy Change

- Audit Privilege Use

- Audit Process Tracking

- Audit System Events

You can configure individual objects to be audited by editing the system access control list (SACL) for any given object, which is much like assigning permissions except that it's indicating to Windows on what type of access an event log entry should be writing. You can access the SACL for an object by clicking the Advanced button on the Security tab in its Properties dialog box. On the Auditing tab, after acknowledging a UAC prompt if necessary, you can click Add to include new auditing events for an object, or you can click View and Edit to modify an existing auditing event. Figure 29-4 shows the SACL for an object.

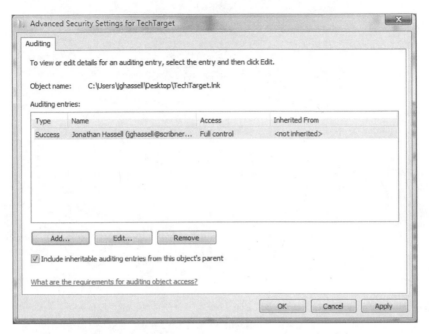

Figure 29-4 *The SACL for an object*

> **NOTE** Only NTFS files and folders can be audited. FAT partitions don't support auditing events because they don't contain the necessary permission information. Consider it another reason to ditch FAT and go with NTFS.

Recommended Items to Audit

You'll want to take particular note of the following items from your event logs:

- Login and logout events, which can indicate repeated logon failures and can point to a particular user account that's being used for an attack
- Account management, which indicates users who have tried to use or have used their granted user- and computer-administration power
- Startup and shutdown, which shows both the user who has tried to shut down a system and what services may not have started up properly upon the reboot
- Policy changes, which can indicate the users who are tampering with security settings
- Privilege use, which can show any attempts to change permissions to certain objects

CHAPTER 30

Maintaining the Windows Registry

The registry has become this mythical place where data crusts over and pops up in the most unexpected places. If you have ever misspelled your name when installing an application, you know exactly what we mean.

In this chapter, we'll demystify the registry, show you how it's structured and what its various parts are, show you how to use the Registry Editor application, and explain where to go for more advanced tools to manipulate the Windows registry.

Presenting a Brief Structural Overview

The registry consists of five predefined keys, which are listed here along with their abbreviations, as you will find them often referenced within technical documentation:

- HKEY_CLASSES_ROOT (HKCR)
- HKEY_CURRENT_USER (HKCU)
- HKEY_LOCAL_MACHINE (HKLM)
- HKEY_USERS (HKU)
- HKEY_CURRENT_CONFIG (HKCC)

These predefined keys contain a lot of subkeys (or just *keys*, as they're sometimes referred to), which are a lot like subfolders of parent folders. Keys contain values that describe some information or properties on the system. Every key on the system has a value, called a *default value*, whether or not it is explicitly defined. When there is a value other than an undefined default value, that value will have three parts to it—the name of the value, the data type, and the actual data that represents the value.

All of this is put together—the predefined key, its subkeys, and the associated values—into what's called a *hive*. The hive is stored as separate files on the disk, partly for data integrity and partly to make it easier to back up.

You can use several different data types as values. We've listed them here, in addition to the type names as referenced in the Registry Editor user interface:

REG_SZ (string value): This data type is a string that contains Unicode and ANSI characters and is automatically terminated by a "00" byte at the end of the string. This is one of the most frequently used types in the registry.

REG_MULTI_SZ (multi-string value): This data type is similar to REG_SZ but allows a group of strings to refer to a single value.

REG_EXPAND_SZ (expandable string value): This data type is also a zero-terminated string, but it is meant to contain environment variables such as %SystemRoot%.

REG_BINARY (binary value): This data type contains only 0s and 1s and stores data in binary format.

REG_DWORD (DWORD value): This data type is a 32-bit numerical value, but you can also use it as a Boolean to store 0s and 1s to indicate on/off, yes/no, and so on. This is informally called a *double word*.

REG_QWORD: Similar to the double word, this is a *quadruple word* and is supported only in 64-bit editions of Windows Vista.

REG_LINK: Like a hyperlink, the REG_LINK data type points to another hive, key, or subkey in the registry. Only applications accessing the registry through the registry's application programming interface (API) are permitted to establish REG_LINK data types.

REG_NONE: This data type is used when the presence of a value means something to an application but the actual data contained in the value is irrelevant.

Using the Registry Editor

You can access the Registry Editor, your main tool for interacting with the Windows registry graphically, by clicking the Start menu and typing **regedit** in the Search box. You may have to acknowledge a UAC prompt or log in using administrative credentials in order to access the registry.

Figure 30-1 shows the default Registry Editor window.

You can see the predefined keys and subkeys in the left pane of the window, much like a Windows Explorer view to which you've become accustomed. In the right pane, you can see the values—their names, the data types, and the data associated with the values. The status bar at the bottom of the window shows you the "path" to the current values you are seeing, in case (like in Figure 30-1) the scroll in the left pane has been activated because you're treading deep into a group of keys.

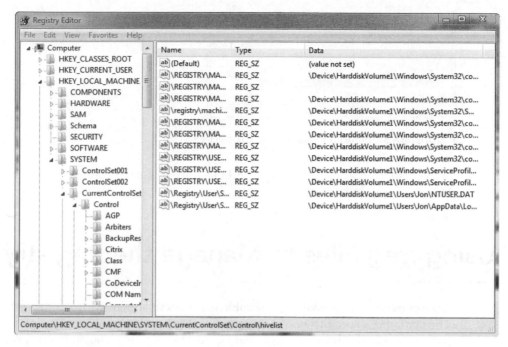

Figure 30-1 *The default Registry Editor window*

To find a particular item within the registry, your best bet is to activate the Find feature. Pressing Ctrl+F opens the Find screen, as shown in Figure 30-2, and you can also select Edit ➤ Find. Be sure to start at the top of the left pane when you're looking for something and aren't sure where it's located, because unlike in other applications, the Find feature in the Registry Editor does not flip back to the beginning of the registry when it reaches the end—it searches forward in the hives from your current location, and when it reaches the end, it stops.

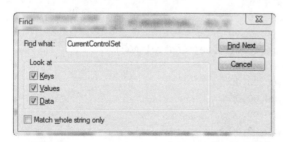

Figure 30-2 *Finding a key, value, or data using Find*

You can edit a value and its properties by simply double-clicking it once you have located it in the registry. You can edit the data in the value by replacing the text in the Value Data field in the dialog box. Figure 30-3 shows the Edit String dialog box.

Figure 30-3 *Editing a value and its properties*

To add new keys or value, on the Edit menu, expand the New submenu, and select the item you want to create.

Using .reg Files to Manage the Registry

You can export any primary key or subkey to a text file that, with an .reg extension, is formatted in a specific template that allows the Registry Editor application to subsequently read it back into the registry and make appropriate changes. Exporting keys to text files is a great way to back up certain sections of the registry before you make any changes, and it's also a great way to make identical registry changes on a large number of computers quickly and easily.

To export a key, select the key within the Registry Editor application, right-click it, and select Export. Choose a location and a name for the exported file, note the .reg extension that is automatically appended to the file, and then click OK.

If you right-click the newly created file outside the Registry Editor and select Edit, the file will open in Notepad. The following is an example of the HKEY_LOCAL_MACHINE\SYSTEM\CurrentControlSet\Control\AGP key exported to a text file:

```
Windows Registry Editor Version 5.00

[HKEY_LOCAL_MACHINE\SYSTEM\CurrentControlSet\Control\AGP]
"102B0520"=hex:80,00,00,00,00,00,00,00
"102B0521"=hex:80,00,00,00,00,00,00,00
"102B0525"=hex:80,00,00,00,00,00,00,00
"10DE0100"=hex:00,01,00,00,00,00,00,00
"53339102"=hex:00,01,00,00,00,00,00,00
"53338C10"=hex:00,01,00,00,00,00,00,00
"53338C12"=hex:00,01,00,00,00,00,00,00
```

You can see the header line, which identifies the version of the Registry Editor application that created the file. Don't change this if you intend to import the file back into a Windows Vista machine. The name of the key being exported is next, surrounded in square brackets. This should not be abbreviated in any way. Then, the value name is enclosed in quotation marks, the data type is after the equal sign, and the data is stored within that value after the colon. REG_SZ values don't have identifiers in an exported .reg file, and they must be enclosed in quotation marks. Other data types are indicated in the .reg file as such:

REG_DWORD: dword

REG_BINARY: hex

REG_EXPAND_SZ: hex(2)

REG_MULTI_SZ: hex(7)

REG_RESOURCE_LIST: hex(8)

REG_FULL_RESOURCE_DESCRIPTOR: hex(9)

REG_RESOURCE_REQUIREMENTS_LIST: hex(a)

REG_NONE: hex(0)

You can delete existing values with an .reg file as well. To do so, just use a hyphen as the data for any value. For example:

```
"102B0520"=-
```

To delete an entire key, insert a hyphen (like a subtraction sign) in front of the name of the key inside the first square bracket. For example:

```
[-HKEY_LOCAL_MACHINE\SYSTEM\CurrentControlSet\Control\AGP]
```

Finally, to import a changed .reg file back into the registry, just double-click it.

Understanding the Typical Registry Caveats

You've probably read articles or hot tech tips that implore you to back up your registry before making any changes. And they're exactly right—the registry is so central to Windows Vista's operation that any changes might have unintended consequences that could undermine the stability or integrity of your computer. Here are some ways to protect against that happening:

- Back up the section of the registry you're about to change. Use the Export function to make an .reg file backup of the keys in question, as discussed in the previous section. To restore the section, either double-click the .reg file in Windows Explorer or choose File ➤ Import with the Registry Editor application.

- If you are using System Restore, you automatically get system-state "snapshots" that you can use to roll back your system to a previous state in the event of a problem. If you set restore points manually, you'll get most of the protection you need. See Chapter 32 for more information about creating and using restore points.

Using Advanced Registry Tools

Unfortunately, Windows Vista's own registry tools are really simplistic—as you've seen here—and are not capable of any real-time monitoring, advanced recovery, or any other procedures you might need to undertake in times of trouble. May we recommend a free tool called Process Explorer, written by Mark Russinovich, who is now a Microsoft Fellow? Figure 30-4 shows the main Process Explorer window.

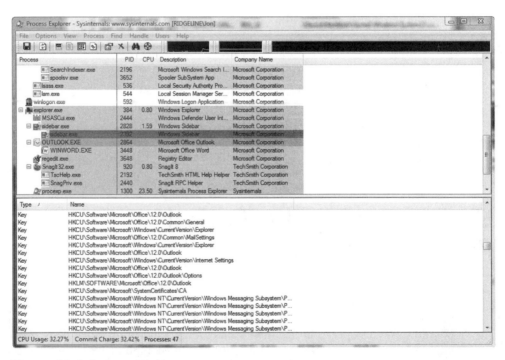

Figure 30-4 *Process Explorer*

Process Explorer has many great capabilities, but the one germane to this chapter is its ability to peer into a process and view the registry keys it is using. For example, in Figure 30-4, we selected Outlook.exe, and in the lower pane, we can see all the keys that Outlook is looking at, including keys in HKEY_LOCAL_MACHINE and HKEY_CURRENT_USER. This is great because you can see, in real time, exactly the keys and values at which a particular running process is looking.

You can download Process Explorer from the Microsoft web site at http://www. microsoft.com/technet/sysinternals/ProcessesAndThreads/ProcessExplorer.mspx.

CHAPTER 31

Troubleshooting

Sooner or later, something will go wrong with Windows Vista. What separates uberusers from general users is how you deal with such issues. In this chapter, we'll cover how to use Event Viewer and the Reliability and Performance Monitor tool; how to use advanced start-up options to diagnose the problem; how to view its effects across the whole machine; and how to get into a position to fix it.

Using Event Viewer

Windows Vista includes a revamped version of Event Viewer that takes advantage of the improvements offered in the latest version of the Microsoft Management Console (MMC). Take a look at the new interface in Figure 31-1.

Many logs are available for perusal, including Windows-specific logs and logs created by other applications and services installed on your machine. Windows-specific logs include the application log, security log, setup log, system log, and ForwardedEvents log:

Application log: This log contains events created by programs running on the operating system.

Security log: This log contains integrity-related events of interest to security professionals, including resource use, logon attempts, and privilege use.

Setup log: This log pertains to events recorded by applications and services during their respective setup processes.

System log: Windows system components such as driver failures, impending hardware problems, and the like, log their events here.

ForwardedEvents log: This log contains events collected by the current machines from other, remote computers by way of an event subscription.

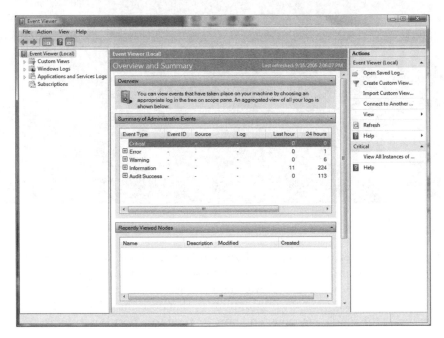

Figure 31-1 *The new Event Viewer interface*

Applications and services logs are a new type of log unique to Windows Vista and its brother operating system, Windows Server 2007. These logs record events that are limited in scope to a single application, rather than events that have systemwide implications. These logs include more simplistic events appropriate for the typical IT professional (admin and operational logs) but can also include programmer-specific information useful in debugging (analytic and debug logs).

Events have common properties that make them easy to identify, analyze, and troubleshoot within the Event Viewer application. All events share the following elements:

Source: This property refers to the application or service that initially logged the event. Sometimes the name of the software will be clear; otherwise, short names might be used, particularly by drivers written by third parties.

EventID: This is a number that partly identifies the nature of an event. Coupled with the source, event IDs can be searched in a product support database to get a full description, and typically possible resolutions, of an issue.

Level: This is a designation of the severity of an event. Errors represent issues that likely will cause data loss or some equally undesirable circumstance. Drivers and software applications detect conditions unfavorable to normal operation and issue warnings. Information events typically have no severity at all and simply refer to regular operating events, such as system start-up. Audit Success and Audit Failure events refer to respective successes and failures when auditing mode is enabled.

User: This is the user or security context under which the event was logged.

OpCode: This is a numeric code that refers to the "phase of operation" the software was in when the event was logged, such as initialization or shutdown.

Logged: This is the time stamp for that particular event.

Task Category: This represents activities or other subdivisions of event types, as specified by the software or application manufacturer.

Keywords: These are the applicable terms that are useful search and filtering terms, such as *security*, *failure*, or other commonly used filter terms.

Computer: This is the machine on which the event occurred.

We won't bore you with the basics of operating Event Viewer's most fundamental features, because you have probably already used them before; if not, they are easy to learn. Instead, we'll highlight a couple of features new to the Windows Vista edition of Event Viewer, namely, custom views and event subscriptions, and we'll show how to get the most out of them.

Using Custom Views in Event Viewer

Event Viewer in Windows Vista contains a key improvement over previous versions: the ability to create and, perhaps more importantly, save custom views. Although in previous incarnations of Event Viewer you could filter on certain attributes of events to come up with a certain picture of activities in your machine, you couldn't create multiple filters that continuously refresh, and you couldn't save these custom filters for use later—a frustrating problem since often creating the correct filter could take a lot of time.

The current version of Event Viewer solves these problems. In fact, Microsoft includes quite a few preconfigured custom views that ship with the default MMC view of Event Viewer; they're located in the console tree in the left pane of the window, under Applications and Services Logs. You can see various event views as they pertain to Internet Explorer, Media Center, system performance, and other queries.

You will probably still want to create a custom view. Don't fear—to do so, follow these steps:

1. From within Event Viewer, choose Create Custom View in the right pane. The Create Custom View dialog box appears, as shown in Figure 31-2.

2. Select the criteria by which to filter the view. Select a time frame in the Logged drop-down list, choose a severity level for the view, and filter by a particular log or a source application or service.

3. If you know specific event IDs you want to filter either by including them or by excluding them, enter them in the unlabeled box. Precede with a minus sign any event IDs you want to exclude.

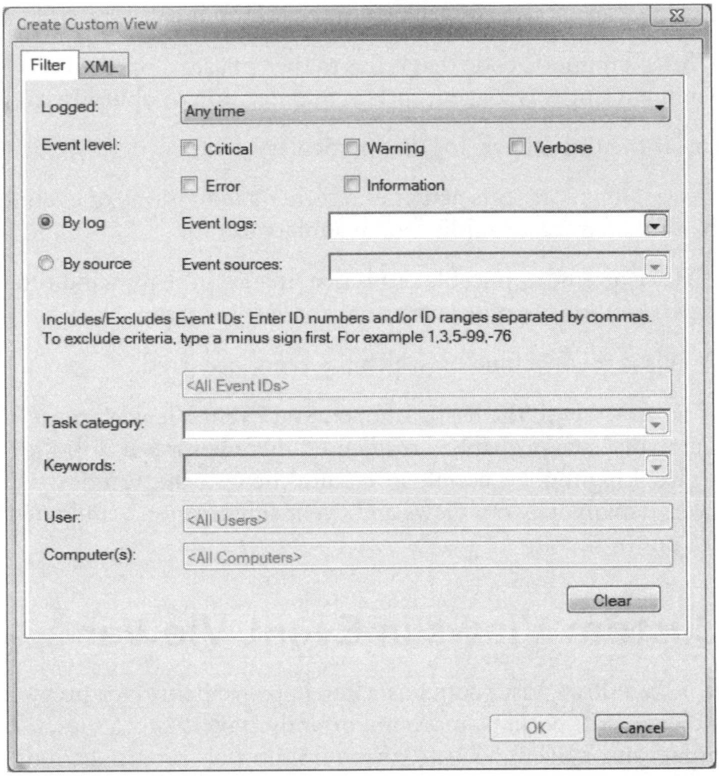

Figure 31-2 *Creating a custom view*

4. Select a particular category, keywords, or users and computers.

5. Click OK to create the view.

6. The Save Filter to Custom View dialog box appears. Enter a friendly name for the custom view, a description if you want (it is optional), and then select the folder in which to store the view within Event Viewer.

7. Check the All Users box to make the filter available to any user with rights to use Event Viewer; uncheck it to restrict the view's access just to you.

8. Click OK to finish.

Using Event Subscriptions

Event subscriptions—another new feature to Windows Vista's Event Viewer—allow a single computer to receive forwarded events matching a specific filter from multiple computers, like a log consolidation service. Using event subscriptions requires configuration on both ends, and you need to enable the Windows Remote Management (WinRM) and the Windows Event Collector (Wecsvc) services. Here's how to perform that initial setup on Windows Vista machines participating in a domain:

1. Log on to all applicable computers with an account with administrative privileges.

2. On the computers on which events should be forwarded, in the Start menu, find and select the Command Prompt application, right-click it, and select Run As Administrator.

3. Acknowledge the UAC prompt, if applicable.

4. At the command line, type **winrm quickconfig**.

5. Type **Y** to acknowledge the changes.

6. On the computers that should be receiving forwarded events, in the Start menu, find and select the Command Prompt application, right-click it, and select Run As Administrator.

7. Acknowledge the UAC prompt, if applicable.

8. At the command line, type **wecutil qc**.

9. Type **Y** to acknowledge the changes.

10. Add the computer account of each receiving computer to the local Administrators group on the individual source computers.

> **NOTE** Setting up forwarding and collecting in a workgroup environment is a bit more detailed and involves manually adding Windows Firewall exceptions, limiting subscriptions to pull mode, and adding users to groups on each machine depending on your filtering preferences. See the Event Viewer's Help for detailed information about each of these instances if you're using Windows Vista in a workgroup environment.

With that bit of configuration out of the way, you can now create a new subscription:

1. On the receiving computer, click Subscriptions in the left pane.

2. In the right pane, select Add Subscription. The Subscription Properties dialog box appears, as shown in Figure 31-3.

3. Enter a name and description for the subscription as appropriate.

4. In the Destination Log drop-down box, select the log in which to store collected events.

5. Click Add, and then identify computers from which to receive events. You can test each entry by clicking it and then clicking the Test button.

6. You can specify a filter under Events to Collect. Click the Select Events button. If you've already defined a filter in a custom view and want to apply that same filter to this subscription, select the Copy from Existing Custom View option. Otherwise, click Edit, and define your query (which was discussed in the previous subsection).

7. Click OK.

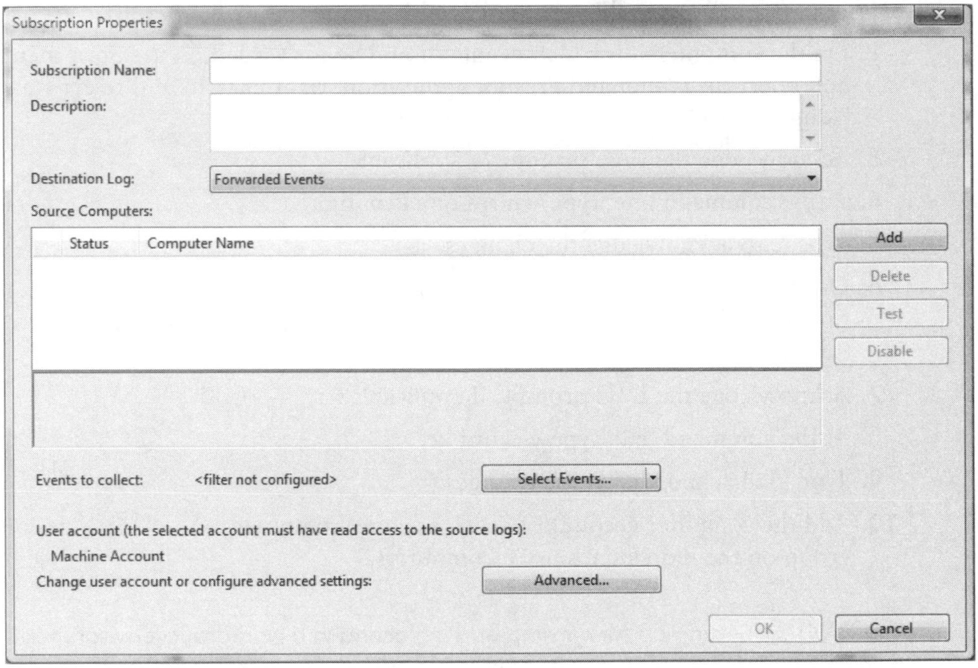

Figure 31-3 *The Subscription Properties dialog box*

Using the Reliability and Performance Monitor

The Reliability and Performance Monitor (known to power users of old as PerfMon.MSC) offers a unified view of your system's health and stability and is a great way to get a comprehensive overview of what is happening on your system and, in the event of trouble, who the likely culprits are and what havoc they are creating.

Key to this particular console is the System Stability Index, which is somewhat obscurely placed in the top-right corner of the console view. The System Stability Index, a statistic ranging from one to ten, is a measurement of aggregated failures over a specific period of time, weighted on the severity of specific failures and problems. Problems that affect the score of the index are listed as reliability events in the System Stability Report, the area in the lower part of the screen. These events are "given" to the Reliability and Performance Monitor by the RACAgent scheduled task, which is enabled by default on new installations of Windows Vista.

What factors into the calculation of the System Stability Index? The index weighs recent failures more heavily than past failures, so the index in practice increases as system reliability over time improves. The index ignores days when the system is hibernating, is in a lighter sleep mode, or is powered off. Also, if there are not enough events to confidently generate an index, a dotted line appears on the graph area of the window to show the general trend of reliability.

You can open the Reliability and Performance Monitor by clicking the Start menu and typing **Reliability and Performance Monitor** in the Search box. (You may need to acknowledge a UAC prompt to complete the task.) Take a look at the main screen of the Reliability and Performance Monitor, as shown in Figure 31-4. Note the index at the top right of the dialog box and the historical graph of the index values in the main part of the screen.

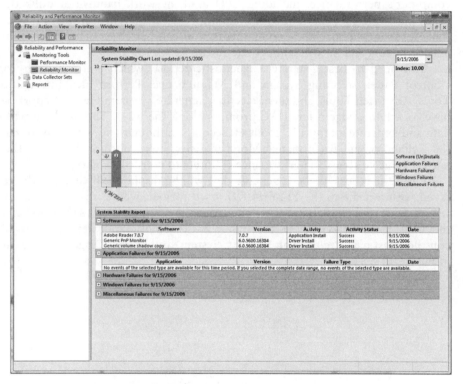

Figure 31-4 *The Reliability and Performance Monitor console view*

At the bottom of the window, reliability events appear—events that could affect the System Stability Index. These are cataloged under categories, including Software Installations and Uninstallations, Application Crashes, Hardware Problems, General Windows Vista Faults, and Miscellaneous Failures. You can click a specific date in the System Stability Index graph to see events corresponding to that date.

Perhaps the most useful way to use the information provided by the Reliability and Performance Monitor is to view it as a trend line—typically, consistent problems that affect system integrity start and repeat at fairly regular intervals. By using the graph to pinpoint the time where system stability is deteriorating, you stand a greater chance of identifying the problematic software or hardware and developing an appropriate plan of action to rectify it.

The System Diagnostics Report aggregates some of the information available in the Reliability and Performance Monitor console with other statistics relating to the computer's performance, including CPU load, network bandwidth utilization, and other hardware information. By combining reliability event information with usage statistics from the machine's components, you can better see what effect a problem may be having and how to compensate for it.

You need to first generate a diagnostic report, which you can do by opening Control Panel, selecting System and Maintenance, Performance Information and Tools, Advanced Tools, and then selecting Generate a System Health Report (you will have to acknowledge a few UAC prompts along the way). The machine will collect data and generate a report in about 60 seconds, although you will need to make sure the Reliability and Performance Monitor dialog box isn't already open—the utility needs exclusive access to performance counters to construct the report.

Once the report has been generated, it will be displayed. By default, the report is saved with a name in the *YYYYMMDD-nnnn* format, where *n* is the iteration of the report generated on that day. Since the reports are automatically saved, you can access them in archives accessible through the Reliability and Performance Monitor console—just navigate through Reports, System, and System Diagnostics, as indicated in Figure 31-5.

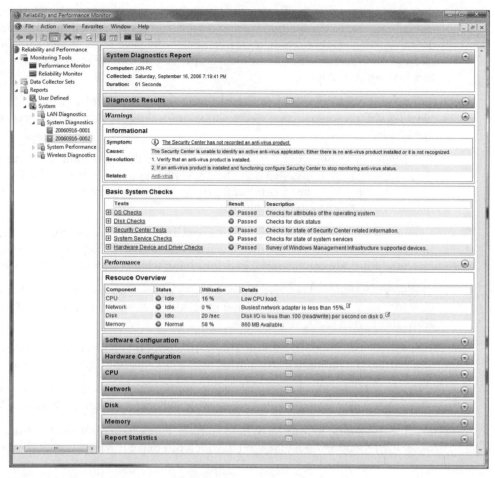

Figure 31-5 *The System Diagnostics Report view*

Setting Advanced Boot Options

You might be having a problem so severe that it is preventing the entire operating system from starting up correctly. In these instances, the Advanced Boot Options menu is available upon Windows Vista boot and can be accessed by hitting F8 before Windows starts. This menu of options allows you to choose an alternate start-up path that may assist in troubleshooting a problem:

Safe Mode: Safe mode has been around a while; it's a mode in which all but the most critical drivers are disabled. Most services are shut down as well. It's intended to create an environment that neuters potentially offensive services and software and allows you to remove them, edit their properties, or otherwise massage them into functioning correctly.

Safe Mode with Networking: This is the same as the Safe mode, but it enables the network drivers so you can get access to your local network and the Internet if applicable.

Safe Mode with Command Prompt: This is perhaps the most limited way to access the operating system installed on your disk—it completely bypasses the Windows GUI and simply launches a command prompt. This is a great way to remove files that are causing start-up problems.

Enable Boot Logging: This option logs every driver that loads during the start-up process to a file in the root of the system drive, called `ntbtlog.txt`. Examining the last line of this file can be useful in determining what is causing a halted boot.

Enable VGA Mode: This starts Windows with your existing video driver but with a very low resolution, color depth, and refresh rate. If you're having display problems, this option can save the day.

Last Known Good Configuration: This starts a boot that has the same configuration and settings, including registry entries, as the last successful start-up on record.

Debugging Mode: This enables debugging mode, which is useful only if you are doing application compatibility testing with a checked version of Windows Vista.

Disable Automatic Restart on System Failure: This will keep Windows from automatically rebooting on a blue screen, which can make it hard to catch the exact error message displayed.

Disable Driver Signature Enforcement: This removes the safety feature of the driver-signing requirements and allows you to use unsigned drivers.

> **TIP** You might also use the Startup Repair tool, an option on your original Windows Vista installation disc. Boot with the disc in your drive, and select the tool. It will run a series of automated diagnostics, looking for typical problems with your system, and then attempt to correct them automatically so that at the least you can get back into your machine. Unfortunately, it can't fix much, but it can be a time-saver when you are troubleshooting in a pinch.

CHAPTER 32

Recovering from Serious Issues

I t is bound to happen at some point to you or to someone you love—your computer will freeze, and when you try to reboot it, it will simply refuse to come up. Whether you were the guilty party in installing an unsigned driver or an ancient 16-bit application that never even worked on Windows XP, or if the problem came up at random through no actions of your own, you will need to have tools in your arsenal to return your PC back to life.

Fortunately, Windows Vista comes equipped with an entirely new facility, called the Windows Recovery Environment, in which you can boot into an otherwise unusable computer and perform many maintenance and repair tasks. And the old standby, System Restore, has been completely renovated to better assist you in recovering from a problematic application, driver, or patch installation.

Read on to discover what these tools can do for you in an emergency.

Using the Windows Recovery Environment

Based on the Windows Preinstallation Environment (WinPE), which is licensed to third parties and original equipment manufacturers (OEMs) to create their own self-installation routines, the Windows Recovery Environment (WinRE) is a special version of Windows that runs from a RAM disk that expands on the capabilities of the Recovery Console that was present in previous versions of Windows.

WinRE is loaded through a couple of different methods: it can start automatically (if you install WinRE on the hard disk as described later in this chapter) or manually through your original Windows Vista media or the on-disk recovery environment. If WinRE is installed on the disk, you can hit F8 during the boot sequence to activate it.

The beauty of WinRE is that it detects and repairs most problems completely automatically, without any sort of interaction with the user and without the user having to know exactly what the issue is that is preventing Windows Vista from being able to start or function correctly. According to Jim Allchin of Microsoft, an analysis of their support calls reflected that the top five issues that made Windows XP machines unbootable were as follows:

> *1) registry corruptions, 2) corrupt file systems (also known as* NTFS metadata corruptions), *3) missing OS loader, 4) inaccessible boot devices (often caused by installing a bad storage driver), and 5) system file corruptions (some part of the OS getting deleted). These problems could happen because of hardware memory corruptions, disk corruptions, other hardware issues, buggy device drivers, or a kernel software issue. Regardless of how the system got into that state, the idea was to create an environment that would use heuristics to essentially implement a differential diagnosis to identify the issue and then use the resources in the other parts of the system configuration, combined with backup data (such as system restore points) and a copy of key system image information, to put the system back into an operating state—without user intervention.*

WinRE detects when boots fail because the Windows loader sets a flag to show that the boot process has started each time Windows is booted. If the boot is successful, that flag is removed just before the logon screen is displayed to the user. However, if the boot fails, Windows never has an opportunity to clear the flag, and on a subsequent boot, the loader sees the existing flag and launches WinRE instead of Windows Vista.

Once WinRE is loaded into memory, the Startup Repair tool looks for the common problems mentioned previously. If Startup Repair can find the problem, it tries to fix it through automatically using restore points, reinstalling drivers from its cache, or rebuilding registry hives or the file system. It also looks for faulty hardware, such as problems on hard disk drives and memory, and reports that.

WinRE goes a long to way to detract from the notion that the best way to fix Windows problems is to flatten the disk and reinstall. Using WinRE and the Startup Repair tool, you can fix Windows problems easily.

Exploring Other Recovery Options in the WinRE Environment

Aside from the Startup Repair tool, you can access the following from within WinRE, as shown in Figure 32-1:

System Restore: This tool helps you use restore points to roll back changes to your system that caused problems. See "Using System Restore" later in this chapter for more information about System Restore and how to use it.

CompletePC Restore: If you use the CompletePC backup program, you can boot from WinRE and restore that backup image from here.

Windows Memory Diagnostic Tool: This memory test program runs a thorough battery of simulations and tests in your memory to check for common chip errors. You can select from basic, standard, or extended testing by pressing F1 once, and the process begins.

Command prompt: This opens a command prompt window so you can use commands, similar in nature to the old Recovery Console in Windows 2000 and Windows XP.

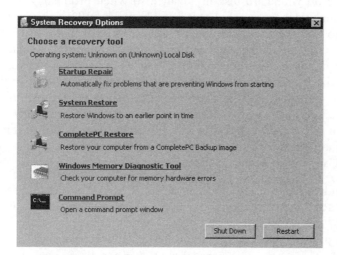

Figure 32-1 *The WinRE recovery options environment*

If you choose the Command Prompt option, you can use the following commands to accomplish some repair tasks without using the Startup Repair tool:

bootrec /scanos: Scans for operating system installations that you can use during booting

bootrec /rebuildbcd: Rebuilds the boot list

bcdedit: Edits the list of operating systems available for boot

bootrec /fixboot: Fixes the boot record of your volume

bootrec /fixmbr: Fixes the master boot record of the physical drive

diskpart: Lists all partitions on a disk

Accessing WinRE

Unfortunately, if you buy your system complete with an operating system installed from an OEM (Dell, HP, or even smaller companies fit into this category), the media included with your new PC will probably not provide the capability to boot to WinRE. However, most of these same OEMs will provide WinRE on a recovery partition that you can access through a start-up menu when you first power on the computer. If you don't purchase your PCs through an OEM and instead install full or upgrade copies of Vista onto your computers, you will not be able to access WinRE through the regular F8 start-up menu because you are *self-hosting*—in other words, you are hosting the instance of WinRE from within the installation of Vista that you are trying to recover. In this case, the best way to gain access to WinRE is to boot off the installation DVD you purchased.

If you have a standard Windows Vista disc that you bought off the shelf, though, you can install WinRE on your hard disk in advance so when problems occur, you don't have to rifle through your software collection and boot off DVDs to begin troubleshooting. You have to consider a few issues, though. First, you need to choose a partition on your disk that is not the same as the Windows operating system partition—this is a safeguard in case something corrupts your main partition and you can't boot into it. Second, the partition should be the first partition on the disk so that it doesn't interfere with any advanced volumes on the disk, such as dynamic volumes. Now, these are not requirements in that WinRE will install just fine on any visible drive to Windows. But to maximize your shot at being able to access WinRE on your hard drive in times of emergency, you should heed those warnings.

To install WinRE on your disk, follow these steps:

1. Download the Windows Automated Installation Kit (WAIK). You can find this at `http://www.microsoft.com/downloads/thankyou.aspx?familyId=c7d4bc6d-15f3-4284-9123-679830d629f2&displayLang=en`. Note that the file is quite large—about 830MB—so proceed with caution if you have a slow connection.

2. Click Start ➤ All Programs ➤ Windows AIK ➤ Windows PE Tools Command Prompt.

3. Create a directory for an image and a mount point by entering **mkdir c:\winre_image** followed by **mkdir c:\winre_mount**.

4. Copy the Windows PE image from the your original Windows Vista DVD using ImageX by issuing the following command:

   ```
   imagex.exe /export /boot e:\sources\boot.wim 2 c:\winre_image\winre.wim \
   "Windows Recovery Environment"
   ```

5. Mount the image using ImageX by entering the following command:

   ```
   imagex /mountrw c:\winre_image\winre.wim 1 c:\winre_mount
   ```

6. Create a file called `winpeshl.ini` that contains the following text:

   ```
   [LaunchApp]
   AppPath=x:\sources\recovery\recenv.exe
   ```

7. Copy this file to the `\Windows\System32` directory in your mounted WinRE directory using the following command:

   ```
   copy winpeshl.ini c:\winre_mount\Windows\System32
   ```

8. Unmount the image by using ImageX through the following command:

   ```
   imagex.exe /unmount /commit c:\winre_mount
   ```

9. Copy the `winre.wim` image you just created to the root of the recovery partition you chose at the beginning of this procedure.

10. Copy `boot.sdi` from your WAIK directory to the same partition. By default, you can find the source `boot.sdi` file in `C:\Program Files\Windows WAIK\Tools\PETools\x86\boot`.

11. Next, configure WinRE through a script provided in the WAIK. Run the following from an elevated command prompt (be sure to replace D: with whatever partition you chose as the WinRE target):

```
C:\Program Files\Windows WAIK\Recovery\SetAutoFailover.cmd
/target D: /wim /nohide
```

12. You're finished. Restart your computer, and press F8 during the boot process. You should see an Advanced menu, and on it should be the option Repair Your Computer, which will launch WinRE.

Using System Restore

System Restore (SR) is a Windows Vista service that solves errors and issues you're having in Vista by swapping out corrupted or misconfigured files and system elements with copies created in the background at various points in time. This makes SR useful for issues that are caused by file or registry changes or by problematic modifications in other system databases, such as COM and WMI. SR can change Windows system files, registry settings, programs, scripts, batch files, and other executable files. Your documents, email, photos, and other personal files, however, are not touched.

What happens under the hood when you invoke SR? The process first involves creating *restore points*, which are markers along the timeline of your system. Restore points are created once a day by default and also when Vista detects changes to your system, such as an application or driver installation. (You can also choose to create a manual restore point if you're not convinced the automatic restore points are being detected and set correctly.) When the restore point is created, SR makes a complete image of everything on your drive, including files, registry settings, scripts, and the like. This image is minimized so that only changes made after the restore point is created are actually stored, thus saving disk space; effectively, though, Vista is able to reconstruct the image so that it's as if an image were made of the entire disk. When the time comes to restore from a particular restore point, SR restores all registry settings from the image and then looks for files that have changed. SR then restores system files as necessary from that image. If for some reason the restore operation fails, SR sends error reports via the Windows Error Reporting facility upon the first reboot after the restore.

> **NOTE** You can find the list of files that Vista SR monitors inside this file: `C:\Windows\System32\filelist.xml`. On an XP installation, this file resides in `C:\Windows\System32\Restore\filelist.xml`.

You'll find SR useful in several scenarios:

- When you purchase and install an application, or install an older application on Windows Vista, that is incompatible with your current install. SR will roll back your system to its state before the application installation.

- When you install an updated driver, or try to get an old driver for an ancient piece of hardware to install on Vista, and it mucks everything up. This happens all too often, but Vista can save you a bare-metal reinstall by rolling back just the bad driver installation, leaving your good drivers intact.

- When you can't even boot into your system because of a failed configuration change, faulty application or driver installation, or just a family member being a nuisance and deleting your registry. (This has happened to one of us.) In Vista, you can now access SR and your library of restore points offline by booting into WinRE, as discussed earlier in this chapter. In XP, SR was available only if you could get into Safe Mode, which was sometimes unreachable if a serious error occurred.

You might be wondering about SR's suitability when it comes to recovering from malware infestations. System Restore is not designed to fix these types of maladies. During the Windows Vista development process, Microsoft provided antivirus software manufacturers with detailed information about programmatically scanning restore points and deleting them if those third-party applications detect a virus. The logic is as follows: presumably, the antivirus product that a user purchased is installed, in memory, and running when the user begins to perform a restore operation. Behind the scenes, the antivirus software monitors disk activities while SR is staging files for restoration, so if a virus is detected within the staged files, the operation is blocked, the restore never actually begins, and the user can't complete the restore.

Note the following issues about SR's capabilities, operation, and limitations:

Applications may break during the restore process: SR can't automatically detect this, so after an SR operation, you need to investigate for applications that the restore broke.

Drives with BitLocker enabled can still use SR without any difficulty: The volume shadow copy infrastructure, on which SR is based, is higher in the food chain than BitLocker. You just need to unlock the volume first, which you'll be prompted to do.

System Restore is incompatible when dual-booting Windows XP and Windows Vista on the same machine: When you boot into Windows Vista after using Windows XP, Vista detects that something wrote to the disk without tracking changes into the shadow copy, so it invalidates existing shadow copies that Windows XP created. The reverse is also true—XP invalidates restore points created by Vista. Installing the different versions of Windows into separate directories is not a workaround, since SR tracks changes across the entire disk, not just individual folders. So, don't depend on SR to save you if you dual-boot XP and Vista.

If you disable SR in Vista, you will lose all restore points: With the Windows XP version of System Restore, third-party software vendors and sometimes even Microsoft Knowledge Base articles recommended disabling System Restore when deleting a virus, spyware, or other malware. This guidance is incorrect when related to the Vista version of SR, because this version was designed and built with these scenarios in mind and can protect against restoring from points that are infected or otherwise compromised.

What's New in Windows Vista System Restore?

The functionality of System Restore in Windows Vista is the same as it was in Windows XP, when the feature was introduced, but the mechanics underneath the user interface have been completely redesigned. SR can recover your systems in more situations than the XP version of SR could, including a restore operation in offline mode in the new Windows Recovery Environment.

The approach of System Restore in Windows Vista is also different. Instead of using a filter driver that keeps track of the changes made to system files on the hard drive, which was not very efficient and sometimes slow, SR uses the Volume Shadow Copy Service (VSS), which allows SR to almost immediately return to "snapshots" of critical files at different points in time. SR, as a result, is faster and more efficient in Vista, making it easier to recover from errors. By using VSS, SR will store only a differential copy of changed blocks in relation to the files on your disk, reducing the amount of space needed by SR. Initially, SR is permitted to use a maximum of 15 percent of your disk; within that space, VSS automatically manages the shadow copies, deleting old restore points when space is needed. There isn't a maximum age for any particular restore point, because VSS runs at the disk level with a chunk of disk space allocated for tracking changes. Therefore, in theory, you could have just one restore point if you changed many, many files, or you could have something like 60 restore points under a more typical scenario.

Using System Restore

You can use the System Restore user interface to perform a restore operation or to manually set a restore point. To do either task, open the SR interface by typing the following directly into the Run line on the Start menu:

```
rstrui.exe
```

If you have the UAC enabled, you'll need to permit the SR user interface to open by acknowledging and either entering credentials or pressing Enter.

Performing a Restore Operation

When you first open the SR user interface, the Restore System Files and Settings screen appears, as shown in Figure 32-2. Vista will recommend a restore point it has created for you based on the last major change to your system; if you want to go with the operating system's recommendation, choose the Recommended Restore option, and click Next. If you want to choose a different restore point, choose the second option, and click Next.

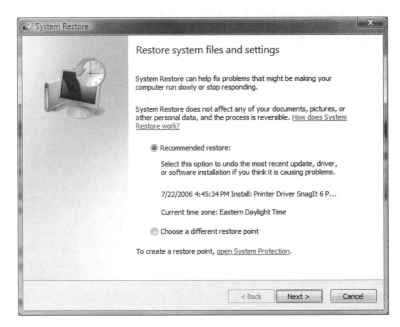

Figure 32-2 *Confirming a restore operation*

If you elected to choose your own restore point, you'll see the Choose a Restore Point screen, as shown in Figure 32-3. You can pick one of the most recent restore points from the list, or if you need to roll back to a state older than five days, click the appropriate checkbox at the bottom of the screen to expand the list. Select the restore point you want to use, and then click Next.

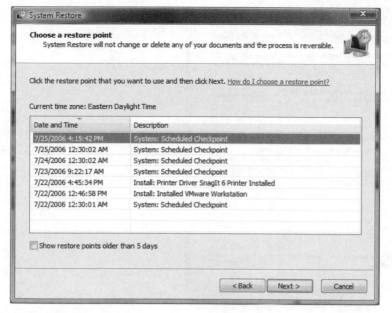

Figure 32-3 *Selecting a restore point manually*

If you accepted Vista's recommendation, or after you've manually selected the restore point you want to use, you'll see a screen asking you to confirm the restoration. Click Finish to begin the operation. SR will reboot your computer during the restore operation, and after the reboot, the rollback will be completed.

Creating a Restore Point Manually

Back on the Restore System Files and Settings screen, click the Open System Protection link at the bottom of the screen. You'll be transported to the System Properties window, and the System Protection tab will be selected for you, as shown in Figure 32-4.

Create a custom restore point by clicking the Create button. Vista will prompt you to name the restore point; give it a description that will make it easy to identify later, such as "Before customizing network interface 2." Vista will trundle for a bit, creating the restore point, and then let you know that the point was successfully created. You'll see on the System Protection tab that the Most Recent entry under the Available Volumes list will update itself to the current time.

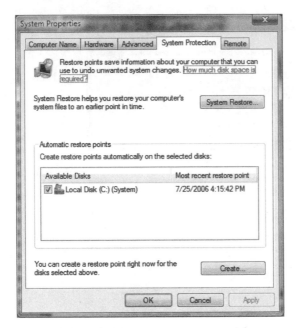

Figure 32-4 *The System Protection tab*

Being Aware of System Restore "Gotchas"

Beware the following scenarios when using SR in Windows Vista:

- User accounts created after a restore point was created will not be retained during a restore. Data in those users' folders, however, will not be touched.
- Computer names and domain memberships might be rolled back, and you might have to rename a computer or rejoin a domain after a restore operation. This could affect Group Policy application.
- You cannot create a new restore point in Safe Mode; you can only use existing restore points.

The Last Word

In this chapter, we discussed recovering from serious errors and configuration mistakes using an old friend, System Restore, and a new friend, the Windows Recovery Environment. You can use WinRE as a comprehensive resource for repairing problems that result in an unbootable system, because it's much more capable and flexible than the text-based Recovery Console included in Windows 2000 and Windows XP. And in Windows Vista, System Restore has been completely redesigned to reduce the performance penalties associated with monitoring changes and creating restore points, and it's easier than ever to roll back unwanted changes to your system, even if you cannot boot into Safe Mode.

Index

You Need the Companion eBook

Your purchase of this book entitles you to buy the companion PDF-version eBook for only $10. Take the weightless companion with you anywhere.

We believe this Apress title will prove so indispensable that you'll want to carry it with you everywhere, which is why we are offering the companion eBook (in PDF format) for $10 to customers who purchase this book now. Convenient and fully searchable, the PDF version of any content-rich, page-heavy Apress book makes a valuable addition to your programming library. You can easily find and copy code—or perform examples by quickly toggling between instructions and the application. Even simultaneously tackling a donut, diet soda, and complex code becomes simplified with hands-free eBooks!

Once you purchase your book, getting the $10 companion eBook is simple:

❶ Visit **www.apress.com/promo/tendollars/**.

❷ Complete a basic registration form to receive a randomly generated question about this title.

❸ Answer the question correctly in 60 seconds, and you will receive a promotional code to redeem for the $10.00 eBook.

2560 Ninth Street • Suite 219 • Berkeley, CA 94710

eBookshop

THE EXPERT'S VOICE™

Offer valid through 8/26/07.